Accounting and Finance
for Non-Specialists

A Companion Website accompanies *Accounting and Finance for Non-Specialists*, 4th edition by Peter Atrill and Eddie McLaney

Visit the *Accounting and Finance for Non-Specialists* Companion Website at www.booksites.net/atrillmclaney to find valuable teaching and learning material including:

For Students:
- Study material designed to help you improve your results
- Multiple Choice Questions relevant to a range of core study areas to help test your learning
- Additional Exercises, also tailored to core study areas such as business, engineering, tourism and computing
- Solutions to the Review questions found at the end of each chapter
- Links to relevant sites on the World Wide Web

For Lecturers:
- A secure, password protected site with teaching material
- Complete, downloadable Instructor's Manual
- PowerPoint slides for use with the book
- Downloadable Appendix on Recording Financial Transactions
- Extra cases with solutions

Also: This site has a syllabus manager, search functions, and email results functions.

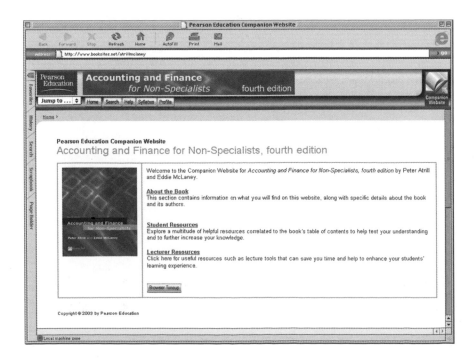

Fourth Edition

Accounting and Finance
for Non-Specialists

Peter Atrill & Eddie McLaney

 Prentice Hall
FINANCIAL TIMES

An imprint of **Pearson Education**

Harlow, England • London • New York • Boston • San Francisco • Toronto • Sydney • Singapore • Hong Kong
Tokyo • Seoul • Taipei • New Delhi • Cape Town • Madrid • Mexico City • Amsterdam • Munich • Paris • Milan

Pearson Education Limited
Edinburgh Gate
Harlow
Essex CM20 2JE
England

and Associated Companies throughout the world

Visit us on the World Wide Web at:
www.pearsoned.co.uk

First published in 1995 by Prentice Hall Europe
Second edition in 1997
Third edition published in 2001 by Pearson Education Limited
Fourth edition in 2004

© Prentice Hall Europe 1995, 1997
© Pearson Education Limited 2001, 2004

ISBN 0 273 67962 7

British Library Cataloguing-in-Publication Data
A catalogue record for this book is available from the British Library

10 9 8 7 6 5 4 3
08 07 06 05 04

Typeset by 35
Printed and bound in China
GCC/03

Contents

Preface

This text provides an introduction to accounting and finance. It is aimed primarily at students who are not majoring in accounting or finance but who are, nevertheless, studying introductory level accounting and finance as part of their course in business, economics, hospitality management, tourism, engineering or some other area. Students who are majoring in either accounting or finance should, however, find the book useful as an introduction to the main principles, which can serve as a foundation for further study. The text does not focus on the technical aspects, but rather examines the basic principles and underlying concepts, and the ways in which accounting statements and financial information can be used to improve the quality of decision making. To support this practical approach, there are, throughout the text, numerous illustrative extracts with commentary from company reports, survey data and other sources.

The text is written in an 'open-learning' style. This means that there are numerous integrated activities, worked examples and questions throughout the text to help you to understand the subject fully. You are expected to interact with the material and to check your progress continuously in a way not typically found in textbooks. Irrespective of whether you are using the book as part of a taught course or for personal study, we have found that this approach is more 'user-friendly' and makes it easier for you to learn.

We recognise that most of you will not have studied accounting or finance before, and we have therefore tried to write in a concise and accessible style, minimising the use of technical jargon. We have also tried to introduce topics gradually, explaining everything as we go. Where technical terminology is unavoidable we try to provide clear explanations. In addition, you will find all the key terms highlighted in the text, and then listed at the end of each chapter with a page reference to help you rapidly revise the main techniques and concepts. All these key terms are also listed alphabetically with a concise definition in the glossary towards the end of the book, so providing a convenient and single point of reference from which to revise.

A further important consideration in helping you to understand and absorb the topics covered is the design of the text itself. The page layout and colour scheme have been carefully considered to allow for the easy navigation and digestion of material. The layout features a large page format, an open design, and clear signposting of the various features and assessment material.

How to use this book

We have organised the chapters to reflect what we consider to be a logical sequence and, for this reason, we suggest that you work through the text in the order in which it is presented. We have tried to ensure that earlier chapters do not refer to concepts or terms that are not explained until a later chapter. If you work through the chapters in the 'wrong' order, you will probably encounter concepts and terms that were explained previously.

Irrespective of whether you are using the book as part of a lecture/tutorial-based course or as the basis for a more independent mode of study, we advocate following broadly the same approach.

Integrated assessment material

Interspersed throughout each chapter are numerous **Activities**. You are strongly advised to attempt all these questions. They are designed to simulate the sort of quick-fire questions that your lecturer might throw at you during a lecture or tutorial. Activities serve two purposes:

- to give you the opportunity to check that you have understood what has been covered so far;
- to encourage you to think about the topic just covered, either to see a link between that topic and others with which you are already familiar, or to link the topic just covered to the next.

The answer to each Activity is provided immediately after the question. This answer should be covered up until you have deduced your solution, which can then be compared with the one given.

Towards the middle/end of each chapter, except for Chapter 1, there is a **Self-assessment question**. This is more comprehensive and demanding than any of the activities, and is designed to give you an opportunity to check and apply your understanding of the core coverage of the chapter. The solution to each of these questions is provided at the end of the book. As with the activities, it is important that you attempt each question thoroughly before referring to the solution. If you have difficulty with a self-assessment question you should go over the chapter again.

End-of-chapter assessment material

At the end of each chapter there are four **Review questions**. These are short questions requiring a narrative answer or discussion within a tutorial group. They are intended to help you assess how well you can recall and critically evaluate the core terms and concepts covered in each chapter. Solutions to all of these questions can be found on the students' side of the Companion Website (see below).

At the end of each chapter, except for Chapter 1, there are five **Exercises**. These are mostly computational, and are designed to reinforce your knowledge and understanding. The exercises are graded according to their level of difficulty. The basic-level questions are fairly straightforward; the more advanced ones can be quite demanding, but are capable of being successfully completed if you have worked conscientiously through the chapter and have attempted the basic exercises. Solutions to two of the exercises in each chapter are provided at the end of the book and are identified by a coloured question number. Here, too, a thorough attempt should be made to answer each question before referring to the solution. Solutions to the other three exercises are available to lecturers on the Companion Website.

Acknowledgements

The authors wish to thank Vera Iordanova Atrill for her help in designing the graphs and diagrams, as well as for providing the PowerPoint slides.

We are grateful to the following for permission to reproduce copyright material:

Table Ch. 2, p. 40 from table on p. 39, *'Freehold land and buildings valuation'*, from *Spirax-Sarco Engineering plc Annual Report 2001*, Spirax-Sarco Engineering plc (2001); Exhibits 3.2 & 4.5 from tables on pp. 2 and 19, *Thorntons Plc Annual Report 2001*, Thorntons Plc, 2001; Exhibit 4.3, in part from table from *Great Britain Consumer Spend, April 2003*, Taylor Nelson Sofres plc, independent retail analysts, (2003); Exhibit 4.4 from table on p. 50 from *BP p.l.c. Annual Report and Accounts for the year ended 31 December 2002*, BP p.l.c., (2003); Exhibits 5.2 and 5.3 from tables on pp. 30 and 45 from *Fuller, Smith & Turner P.L.C., Report and Accounts 2002*, Fuller, Smith & Turner P.L.C., (2002); Exhibit 6.2 from table p. 53 *Key Performance Indicators*, from Marks & Spencer p.l.c. *Annual Report and Accounts 2002, Marks & Spencer p.l.c.*, Reproduced by kind permission of Marks & Spencer p.l.c.; Exhibit 8.4 adapted from table from *Cost System Design and Profitability Analysis in UK Manufacturing Companies, p. 55, Table 7.10*, CIMA Publishing, by C. Drury and M. Tayles, (2000), reprinted by permission of Elsevier Ltd.; Exhibit 9.1 from Figure 16 on p. 22 from *Financial Management and Working Capital Practices in UK SMEs*, Business Development Centre, Manchester Business School, (Chittenden, F., Poutziouris, P. and Michaelas, N., 1998), reprinted by kind permission of the authors; Exhibit 9.2 from Table 5.7, on p. 39 from *A survey of management accounting practices in UK manufacturing companies*, Association of Chartered Certified Accountants, (Drury, C., Braund, S., Osbourne, P., and Tayles, M., 1993), Copyright © 1993 The Association of Chartered Certified Accountants; Exhibit 10.2 adapted from *'The theory-practice gap in capital budgeting: evidence from the United Kingdom'*, in *Journal of Business Finance and Accounting, June/July 2000*, Blackwell Publishing, (Arnold, G.C., and Hatzopoulos, P., 2000), reproduced by kind permission of Blackwell Publishing Ltd.; Exhibit 11.1 based on information from *Debenhams plc Annual Report 2002*, Debenhams plc, (2002), *Rolls-Royce plc Annual Report 2001*, Rolls-Royce plc, (2002), *Somerfield plc Annual Report 2002*, Somerfield plc, (2002), *Stagecoach Group plc Annual Report 2002*, Stagecoach Group plc, (2002), and *Vodafone Group Plc Annual Report 2002*, Copyright © Vodafone Group Plc, 2002; Figure 12.3 from *Financial Statistics, February 2001*, Office for National Statistics, National Statistics website: *www.statistics.gov.uk*, © 2001 Crown Copyright, Crown copyright material is reproduced with the permission of the Controller of HMSO;

Figure 12.4 adapted from information kindly supplied by the Finance & Leasing Association, Copyright © 2001 Finance & Leasing Association; Figure 12.6 adapted from information published by the Factors & Discounters Association, Copyright © 2002 Factors & Discounters Association; Figure 12.9 adapted from information supplied by 3i Group plc, reprinted with the kind permission of 3i Group plc, Copyright © 2002 3i Group plc.

Exhibit 1.1 from Profit without honour from *The Financial Times Limited*, 29/30 June 2002, © John Kay.

We are grateful to the Financial Times Limited for permission to reprint the following material:

Exhibit 3.1 Running scared in the face of fraud allegations, © *Financial Times*, 29/30 June 2002; Exhibit 4.1 Monotub industries in a spin as founder get Titan for £1, © *Financial Times*, 23 January 2003; Exhibit 4.6 Laura Ashley to close 35 European stores, from FT.com, © *Financial Times*, 23 January 2003; Exhibit 4.7 Bulmer warns of a breach in covenants, © *Financial Times*, 25 January 2003; Exhibit 4.9 Jolly Fellow, © *Financial Times*, 9 October 2002; Figure 6.3 Dividend yield ratios, constructed from data appearing in the Financial Times, © *Financial Times*, 18 January 2003; Figure 6.4 Price/earnings ratios, constructed from data appearing in the Financial Times, © *Financial Times*, 18 January 2003; Exhibit 11.2 Brambles on the defensive over enormous failures, © *Financial Times*, 26 November 2002; Exhibit 12.1 Man launches £350m convertible bond, © *Financial Times*, 8 November 2002; Exhibit 12.3 Approval for Jarvis sale and leaseback, © *Financial Times*, 5 November 2002.

In some instances we have been unable to trace the owners of copyright material, and we would appreciate any information that would enable us to do so.

Chapter 1

Introduction to accounting and finance

Introduction

Welcome to the world of accounting and finance! In this opening chapter, we provide a broad outline of these subjects. We begin by considering the roles of accounting and finance and we shall see that both can be valuable tools for decision-making purposes. In subsequent chapters, we develop this decision-making theme by considering in some detail the kinds of financial reports and methods used to aid decision making.

For many of you, accounting and finance are not the main focus of your studies, and you may well be asking 'Why do I need to study these subjects?' So, after we have considered the key features of accounting and finance, we shall go on to discuss why some understanding of these subjects is likely to be relevant to you.

Objectives

Having completed this chapter, you should be able to:

- **explain the nature and roles of accounting and finance**
- **identify the main users of financial information and discuss their needs**
- **distinguish between financial and management accounting**
- **explain why an understanding of accounting and finance is likely to be relevant to your needs.**

What are accounting and finance?

Let us start our study of accounting and finance by trying to understand the purpose of each. **Accounting** is concerned with collecting, analysing and communicating economic information. This information is useful for those who need to make decisions and plans about businesses, and for those who need to control those businesses. For example, the managers of businesses may need accounting information to decide whether to:

- develop new products or services (such as a computer manufacturer developing a new range of computers);
- increase or decrease the price or quantity of existing products or services (such as a telecommunications business changing its mobile phone call and text charges);
- borrow money to help finance the business (such as a supermarket wishing to increase the number of stores it owns);
- increase or decrease the operating capacity of the business (such as a beef farming business reviewing the size of its herd);
- change the methods of purchasing, production or distribution (such as a clothes retailer switching from UK to overseas suppliers).

The information provided will help in identifying and assessing the financial consequences of such decisions.

Though managers working within a particular business are likely to be significant users of accounting information, they are by no means the only people who are likely to use accounting information about that particular business. There are those outside the business, which we shall identify later, who may need information to decide whether to:

- invest or disinvest in the ownership of the business;
- lend money to the business;
- offer credit facilities;
- enter into contracts for the purchase of products or services, and so on.

Accounting exists for a particular purpose, and that is to help people make better decisions. Sometimes the impression is given that the purpose of accounting is simply to prepare financial reports on a regular basis. While it is true that accountants undertake this kind of work, it does not represent an end in itself. The ultimate purpose of the accountant's work is to give people better information on which to base their decisions. This decision-making perspective of accounting fits in with the theme of this book and shapes the way in which we deal with each topic.

Finance, like accounting, exists to help decision makers. It is concerned with the ways in which funds for a business are raised and invested. This lies at the very heart of what a business is about. In essence, a business exists to raise funds from investors (owners and lenders) and then to use those funds to make investments (equipment, premises, stocks and so on) in an attempt to make the business, and its owners, wealthier. It is important that funds are raised in a way that is appropriate to the particular needs of the business and an understanding of finance should help in identifying:

- the main forms of finance available;
- the costs and benefits of each form of finance;
- the risks associated with each form of finance;
- the role of financial markets in supplying finance.

Once the funds are raised, they must be invested in a way that will provide the business with a worthwhile return. An understanding of finance should help in evaluating:

- the returns from an investment;
- the risks associated with an investment.

Businesses tend to raise and invest funds in large amounts for long periods of time. The quality of the investment decisions made can, therefore, have a profound impact on the fortunes of the business.

There is little point in trying to make a sharp distinction between accounting and finance. We have already seen that both are concerned with the financial aspects of decision making. There is considerable overlap between the two subjects and, in this book, we shall not emphasise the distinctions.

Accounting and user needs

For accounting to be useful, an accountant must be clear about *for whom* and *for what purpose* the information will be used. There may be various groups of people that are likely to have an interest in a particular organisation, in the sense of needing to make decisions about that organisation. (Although the points that will be made in this chapter and throughout this book may apply to a variety of organisations, such as nationalised industries, local authorities and charities, we are concentrating on private-sector businesses.)

The most important groups that use accounting information about private-sector businesses (user groups) are shown in Figure 1.1 on the next page.

Activity 1.1

Why do each of the user groups identified need financial information relating to a business?

Your answer may be as follows:

User group	Use
Customers	To assess the ability of the business to continue operations and to supply their needs.
Competitors	To assess the threat posed by the business to their market share and profitability. To provide a benchmark against which to assess their own efficiency and performance.
Employees (non-management)	To assess the ability of the business to continue to provide employment and to reward employees for their efforts.
Government	To assess how much tax the business should pay, whether the business complies with agreed pricing policies, and whether financial support is needed.

▶

Activity 1.1 continued

Community representatives	To assess the ability of the business to continue to provide employment for the community and to purchase community resources. To assess whether the business could help fund environmental improvements.
Investment analysts	To assess the likely risks and returns associated with the business in order to determine its investment potential, and to advise clients accordingly.
Suppliers	To assess the ability of the business to pay for the goods and services supplied.
Lenders	To assess the ability of the business to meet its obligations and to pay interest and to repay the amount borrowed.
Managers	To help make decisions and plans for the business, and to exercise control so that plans come to fruition.
Owners	To assess how effectively the managers are running the business, and to make judgements about likely levels of risk and return in the future.

You may have thought of other reasons why each group would find accounting information useful.

Figure 1.1 Main users of financial information relating to a business organisation

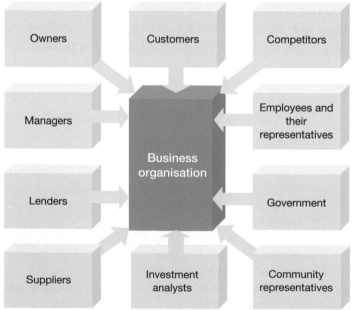

The figure shows that there are several user groups with an interest in the financial information relating to a business organisation. Most of them are outside the business but nevertheless have a stake in it. This is not meant to be an exhaustive list of potential users, but the user groups identified here are normally the most important.

Accounting as a service function

One way of viewing accounting is as a form of service. Accountants provide financial information to their 'clients', who are the various users identified in Figure 1.1. The quality of the service provided is determined by the extent to which the information needs of the various user groups have been met. It can be argued that, in order to meet the needs of users, financial information should possess certain key qualities, or characteristics. These are:

- **Relevance.** Accounting information must have the ability to influence decisions. Unless this characteristic is present, there is really not any point in producing the information. The information may be relevant to the prediction of future events (for example, in predicting how much profit is likely to be earned next year) or relevant in helping to confirm past events (for example, in establishing how much profit was made last year). The role of accounting in confirming past events is important because users often want to check on the accuracy of earlier predictions that they have made.
- **Reliability.** Accounting should be free from any significant error or bias. It should be capable of being relied on by users to represent what it is supposed to represent. Although both relevance and reliability are very important, the problem that we often face in accounting is that information that is highly relevant may not be very reliable, and vice versa. Activity 1.2 illustrates this point.

Activity 1.2

A manager is charged with selling a custom-built machine that the business no longer has use for. The business has recently received a bid for it. What information would be relevant to the manager when deciding whether to accept the bid? How reliable would that information be?

The manager would probably like to know the current market value of the machine to enable him to decide whether to accept the bid. The current market value would be highly relevant to the final decision, but it may not be very reliable because the machine is unique and there is likely to be little information concerning market values.

Where a choice has to be made between providing information that has either more relevance *or* more reliability, the maximisation of relevance would normally be the guiding rule.

- **Comparability.** This quality will enable users to identify changes in the business over time (for example, the trend in sales over the past five years) and also to evaluate the performance of the business in relation to other businesses. Comparability is achieved by treating items that are basically the same in the same manner for measurement and presentation purposes, and by making clear the policies that have been adopted in measuring and presenting the information.

→ ■ **Understandability.** Financial reports should be expressed as clearly as possible, and should be capable of being understood by those at whom the information is aimed. However, this does not mean that accounting reports should be understandable to those who have not studied accounting. The complexity of financial events and transactions cannot normally be that easily reported. It is best that we regard accounting reports in the same way as we regard a piece of modern art (an interesting thought!). To understand both, we really have to do a bit of homework. Generally speaking, accounting reports assume that the user not only has a reasonable knowledge of business and accounting but is also prepared to spend some time in studying the reports.

The threshold of materiality

The qualities, or characteristics, that have just been described will help us to decide whether financial information is potentially useful. If a particular piece of information has these qualities, then it may be useful. However, in order to make a final decision, we also have to consider whether the information is material, or significant. This means that we should ask whether its omission or misrepresentation in the financial reports would really alter the decisions that users make. Thus, in addition to possessing the characteristics mentioned above, financial information must achieve
→ a threshold of **materiality**. If the information is not regarded as material, it should not be included within the reports as it will merely clutter them up and, perhaps, interfere with the user's ability to interpret the financial results. The type of information and amounts involved will normally determine whether it is material.

Costs and benefits of accounting information

Having read the previous sections you may feel that, when considering a piece of financial information, providing the four main qualities identified are present and it is material it should be included in the financial reports. Unfortunately, there is one more hurdle to jump. Something may still exclude a piece of financial information from the financial reports even when it is considered to be useful. Consider Activity 1.3 below.

Activity 1.3

Suppose an item of information is capable of being provided. It is relevant to a particular decision, it is also reliable, comparable, understandable and material.

Can you think of a good reason why, in practice, you might choose not to provide the information?

The reason that you may decide not to provide, or discover, the information is that you judge the cost of doing so to be greater than the potential benefit of having the information. It is a question of balancing cost against the potential benefit.

As an example of the cost/benefit relationship, suppose that you wish to buy a particular hi-fi system, which you have seen in a local shop for sale at £200. You believe that other local shops may have the same system on offer for as little as £190. The only ways in which you can find out the prices at other shops are either to telephone them or visit them. Telephone calls cost money and involve some of your time. Visiting the shops may not involve the outlay of money, but more of your time will be involved. Is it worth the cost of finding out the price of the system at various shops? The answer is, of course, that if the cost of discovering the price is less than the potential benefit, it is worth having that information. Supplying accounting information to users is similar.

The provision of accounting information costs money. If no accounting information were produced, no accounting staff would need to be employed. Salaries of accounting staff are normally only a part of the cost of producing accounting information. To be worth having, the potential benefits from the information need to outweigh the cost of producing it. A real problem with making decisions about the relative cost and benefits of having accounting information is that both of these are normally very difficult, if not impossible, to identify with accuracy.

Going back to the hi-fi system, identifying the cost of finding the various selling prices before you decide whether to pay the £200 or to try to find one at £190 is problematical. It will probably involve considerations of the following factors:

- How many shops will you phone or visit?
- What will be the cost of each phone call?
- How long will it take you to make all of the phone calls or to visit all of the shops?
- What value do you place on your time?

The economic benefit of having the information on the price of hi-fi systems is probably even harder to assess, the following probably being relevant:

- What is the cheapest price that you might be quoted for the system?
- How likely is it that you will be quoted prices cheaper than £200?

As we can see, a decision on whether it is economically advantageous to discover other shops' prices for the hi-fi system is very difficult. It is possible to apply some 'science' to the decision, but a lot of subjective judgement is likely to be involved. It is normally exactly the same with decisions on producing accounting information in a business context.

No one would seriously advocate that the typical business should produce no accounting information. At the same time, no one would advocate that every item of information that could be seen as possessing one or more of the key characteristics (relevance, reliability, comparability and understandability and which is material) should be produced, irrespective of the cost of producing it (see Figure 1.2).

Accounting as an information system

We have already seen that accounting can be seen as the provision of a service to 'clients'. Another way of viewing accounting is as part of the total information system within a business. Users, both inside and outside the business, have to make

Figure 1.2 **The characteristics that influence the usefulness of accounting information**

Materiality   *Cost/Benefit*

Comparability

Characteristics
that make
financial
information
useful

Relevance   Reliability

Understandability

Necessary for   *Limitation to the*
including   *application of*
information in the   *the qualitative*
financial statements   *characteristics*

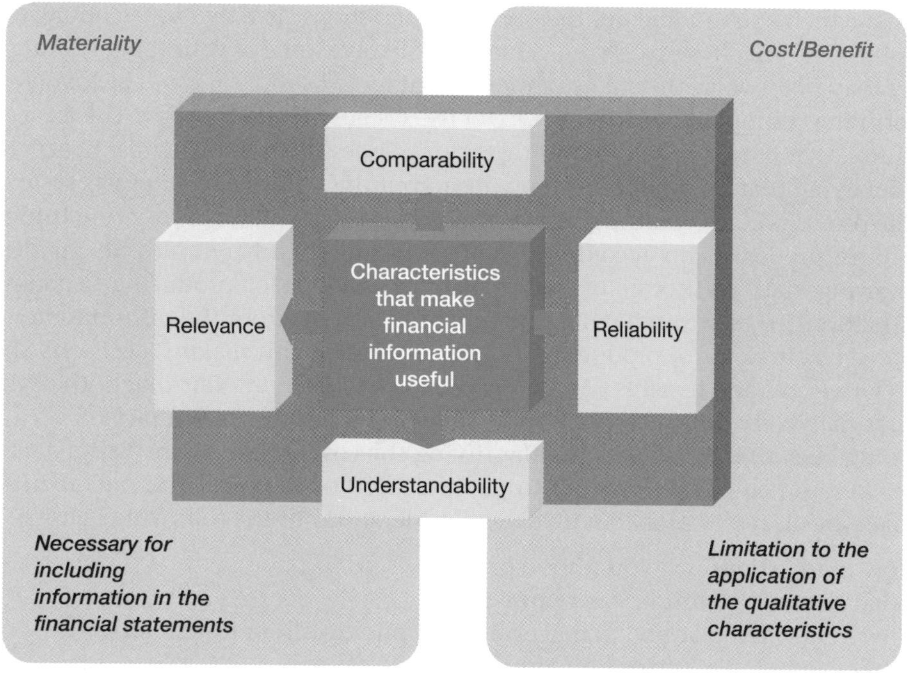

The figure shows that there are four main qualitative characteristics that influence the useful-ness of accounting information. In addition, accounting information should be material and the benefits of providing the information should outweigh the costs.

decisions concerning the allocation of scarce economic resources. To ensure that these resources are allocated in an efficient and effective manner, users require economic information on which to base decisions. It is the role of the accounting system to provide that information, and this will involve both information gathering and communication.

The **accounting information system** is depicted in Figure 1.3. It has certain features that are common to all information systems within a business. These are:

- identifying and capturing relevant information (in this case financial information);
- recording the collected information in a systematic manner;
- analysing and interpreting the collected information;
- reporting the information in a manner that suits the needs of users.

Given the decision-making emphasis of the book, we shall be concerned primarily with the final two elements of the process – the analysis and reporting of financial information. We are concerned with the way in which information is used by, and is useful to, decision makers, rather than the way in which it is collected and recorded.

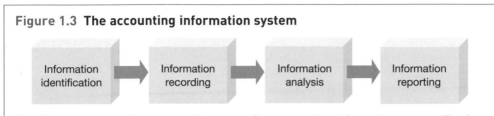

Figure 1.3 The accounting information system

| Information identification | | Information recording | | Information analysis | | Information reporting |

The figure shows the four sequential stages of an accounting information system. The first two stages are concerned with preparation, whereas the last two stages are concerned with using the information collected.

Planning and control

We saw earlier that managers are important users of financial information. They need financial information to help them to plan and control the activities of the business. Planning and control can be seen as a sequence of logical steps that we shall now briefly describe; however, this topic will be considered in more depth in Chapter 9.

It is vital that businesses plan their future. Each business must have a clear view of where it is going and how it is going to get there. The first step in the planning process is to identify the objectives of the business. Objectives tend to be framed in broad terms and, once established, they are likely to remain in force for a long period, say, ten years. To achieve the objectives that have been identified, a number of possible options (strategies) may be available. Each option must be considered carefully to see how closely it fits with the objectives that have been set, and to see whether the resources to pursue the options are available. Following this examination, the most appropriate option can be identified and used as the basis for preparing long-term plans. These long-term plans set out how the business will work towards the achievement of its objectives over a period of, say, five years. Within the framework of the long-term plans, a business will then usually prepare short-term plans (budgets) covering a period of one year. Their role is to convert the long-term plans into actionable blueprints for the immediate future.

However well planned the activities of the business may be, they will come to nothing unless steps are taken to achieve them. The process of ensuring that planned events actually occur is known as *control*. To exercise control, there must be a timely flow of information available to managers to help them compare actual performance with earlier planned performance. Where there are divergences between actual and planned performance, appropriate action must be taken. The planning, decision-making and control process is depicted in Figure 1.4.

Figure 1.4 sets out the key steps in the planning and control process. The starting point is to identify the business objectives: from there, it is possible to formulate plans. Once these plans have been established, they can form the basis for controlling the activities of the business.

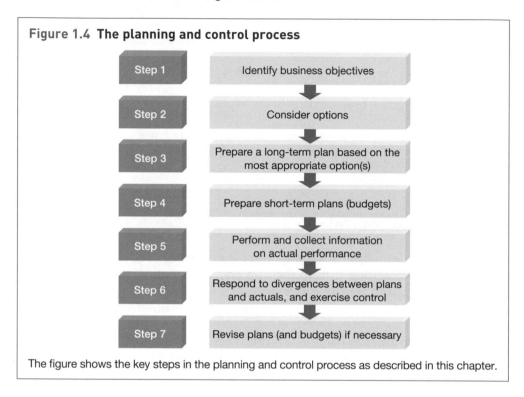

Figure 1.4 The planning and control process

The figure shows the key steps in the planning and control process as described in this chapter.

Accounting and finance has a vital role to play in each step of the planning and control process that has just been outlined.

- *Step 1* of the process involves identifying the objectives of the business. As we shall see later, a key objective of private-sector businesses is to increase the wealth of their owners. It is important, therefore, that we have suitable financial indicators, such as profit, that can be used to help set the objectives.
- *Step 2* involves considering the various options available to achieve the objectives of the business. Financial information should help to quantify the likely costs and benefits associated with each option in financial terms. As a result, we should see more clearly whether an option is worth pursuing.
- *Step 3* involves the preparation of long-term plans, based on the most appropriate option available. Financial information should lie at the heart of these plans. It is important to set out the financing and investment requirements for the business and the expected levels of sales and expenses over the planning period. By doing so, the managers will have clear, quantifiable targets to be achieved.
- *Step 4* involves the development of short-term plans. The role of financial information here is basically the same as in the third step.
- *Step 5* in the process involves collecting information on actual performance. As many aspects of planning will normally be expressed in financial terms, information regarding actual performance, which is required to exercise control, should

also be couched in financial terms. This will make it easier for managers to compare differences between planned and actual performance, and to assess the extent to which plans have been achieved.

- *Step 6* involves responding to divergences from planned performance. Where things have not gone according to plan, the size of the differences between planned and actual performance, expressed in financial terms, can help managers to set their priorities.
- *Step 7* is to revise the plans or budgets, if necessary. This will involve going through the main steps of the process once again and so will require the financial information already identified.

Business objectives

In the previous section, we mentioned that businesses seek to enhance the wealth of their owners. Throughout this book we shall assume that this is the main objective of a business. This may come as a surprise, as there are other objectives that a business may pursue that are related to the needs of others associated with the business. For example, a business may seek to provide good working conditions for its employees, or it may seek to conserve the environment for the local community. While a business may pursue these objectives, it is normally set up with a view to increasing the wealth of its owners, and in practice the behaviour of businesses over time appears to be consistent with this objective.

Does this mean that the needs of other groups associated with the business (employees, customers, suppliers, the community and so on) are not really important? The answer to this question is almost certainly 'No' if the business wishes to survive and prosper over the longer term. Satisfying the needs of other groups will normally be consistent with the need to increase the wealth of the owners over the longer term. A dissatisfied workforce, for example, may result in low productivity, strikes and so forth, which will in turn have an adverse effect on the wealth of the owners. Similarly, a business that upsets the local community by polluting the environment may attract bad publicity, resulting in a loss of customers and heavy fines.

Exhibit 1.1 Short-term gains, long-term problems

In recent years, many businesses have been criticised for failing to consider the long-term implications of their policies on the wealth of the owners. John Kay argues that some businesses have achieved growth in short-term increases in wealth by sacrificing their longer-term prosperity. He points out that:

> . . . The business of Marks and Spencer, the retailer, was unparalleled in reputation but mature. To achieve earnings growth consistent with a glamour rating the company squeezed suppliers, gave less value for money, spent less on stores. In 1998, it achieved the highest (profit) margin in sales in the history of the business. It had also compromised its position to the point where sales and profits plummeted.

▶

Exhibit 3.2 continued

> Banks and insurance companies have taken staff out of branches and retrained those that remain as sales people. The pharmaceuticals industry has taken advantage of mergers to consolidate its research and development facilities. Energy companies have cut back on exploration.
>
> We know that these actions increased corporate earnings. We do not know what effect they have on the long-run strength of the business – and this is the key point – do the companies themselves know? Some rationalisations will genuinely lead to more productive businesses. Other companies will suffer the fate of Marks and Spencer.

Source: 'Profit without honour': John Kay, *Financial Times* Weekend, 29/30 June 2002

In the case of large businesses, the owners are often divorced from day-to-day control of the business, and professional managers are employed to act on their behalf. This means that the wealth objectives of the owners should become the managers' objectives. However, there is always a risk that these managers will pursue their own interests, such as increasing their pay and 'perks' (for example, expensive cars and lavish offices) at the expense of the owners' interests. This can be a problem for the owners, which may be dealt with at least in part by monitoring carefully the actions of managers through the use of regular financial reports. Thus accounting has an important role to play in helping the owners to assess whether the wealth enhancement objective is being pursued.

Has accounting become too interesting?

In recent years, accounting has become front-page news in the US and in the UK and has become a major talking point among those connected with the world of business. Unfortunately, the attention that accounting has attracted has been for all the wrong reasons. We have seen that investors rely on financial reports to help to keep an eye on both their investment and the managers. However, what if the managers provide misleading financial reports to investors? Recent revelations suggest that the managers of some large companies have been doing just this.

Two of the most notorious cases have been that of Enron, an energy-trading business based in Texas, which is accused of entering into complicated financial arrangements in order to obscure losses and to inflate profits, and Worldcom, a major long-distance telephone operator in the US, which is accused of re-classifying $3.9 billion of expenses in order to inflate the profit figure that the business reported to its owners (shareholders) and to others. In the wake of these scandals, there was much closer scrutiny by investment analysts and investors of the financial reports that businesses produce and this has led to further businesses, in both the US and the UK, being accused of using dubious accounting practices to bolster profits.

Various reasons have been put forward to explain this spate of scandals. Some may have been caused by the pressures on managers to meet unrealistic expectations of investors for continually rising profits. Some may have been caused by the greed of unscrupulous executives whose pay is linked to financial performance. However, they may all reflect a particular economic environment.

> **Exhibit 1.2 The thoughts of Warren Buffett**
>
> Warren Buffett is one of the world's shrewdest and most successful investors. He believes that the accounting scandals mentioned above were perpetrated during the 'new economy boom' of the late 1990s when confidence was high and exaggerated predictions were being made concerning the future. He states that during that period:
>
> > You had an erosion of accounting standards. You had an erosion, to some extent, of executive behaviour. But during a period when everybody 'believes', people who are inclined to take advantage of other people can get away with a lot.
>
> He believes that the worst is now over and that the 'dirty laundry' created during this heady period is being washed away and that the washing machine is now in the 'rinse cycle'. However, he points out that:
>
> > It's only in the rinse cycle that you find out how dirty the laundry has been.
>
> Source: *The Times*, Business Section, 26 September 2002, p. 25

Whatever the causes, the result of these accounting scandals has been to undermine the credibility of financial statements and to introduce much stricter regulations concerning the quality of financial information. We shall return to this issue in later chapters when we consider the financial statements.

Financial and management accounting

Accounting is usually seen as having two distinct strands:

- **Management accounting**, which seeks to meet the needs of a business's managers.
- **Financial accounting**, which seeks to meet the accounting needs of all of the other users identified in Figure 1.1.

The differences between the two types of accounting reflect the different user groups that they address. Briefly, the major differences are as follows:

- *Nature of the reports produced.* Financial accounting reports tend to be general-purpose reports. That is, they contain financial information that will be useful for a broad range of users and decisions rather than being specifically designed for the needs of a particular group or set of decisions. Management accounting reports, on the other hand, are often specific-purpose reports. That is, they are designed with either a particular decision in mind or for a particular manager.
- *Level of detail.* Financial accounting reports provide users with a broad overview of the position and performance of the business for a period. As a result, information is aggregated and detail is often lost. Management accounting reports, however, often provide managers with considerable detail to help them with a particular operational decision.
- *Regulations.* Financial reporting, for many businesses, is subject to accounting regulations that exist to try to ensure that reports are produced following a

standardised format. Because management accounting reports are for internal use only, there is no regulation from external sources concerning their form and content; they can be designed to meet the needs of particular managers.

- *Reporting interval.* For most businesses, financial accounting reports are produced on an annual basis. However, large companies may produce semi-annual reports, and a few produce quarterly reports. Management accounting reports may be produced as frequently as required by managers. In many businesses, managers are provided with certain reports on a daily, weekly or monthly basis, which allows them to check progress frequently.

- *Time horizon.* Financial accounting reports reflect the performance and position of the business to date. In essence, they are backward looking. Management accounting reports, on the other hand, often provide information concerning future performance as well as past performance. It is an over-simplification, however, to suggest that financial accounting reports never incorporate expectations concerning the future. Occasionally, businesses will release forecast information to other users in order to raise capital or to fight off unwanted takeover bids.

- *Range and quality of information.* Financial accounting reports concentrate on information that can be quantified in monetary terms. Management accounting also produces such reports, but will, in addition, produce reports that contain information of a non-financial nature, such as measures of physical quantities of stocks and output. Financial accounting places greater emphasis on the use of objective, verifiable evidence when preparing reports. Management accounting reports may use information that is less objective and verifiable in order to provide managers with the information that they require.

We can see from the above that management accounting is less constrained than financial accounting. It may draw from a variety of sources, and use information that has varying degrees of reliability. The only real test to be applied when assessing the value of the information produced for managers is whether or not it improves the quality of decisions made.

Activity 1.4

Are the information needs of managers and those of other users so very different? Is there any overlap between the information needs of managers and the needs of other users?

The distinction between management and financial accounting suggests that there are differences between the information needs of managers and those of other users. While differences undoubtedly exist, there is also a good deal of overlap between the needs of managers and the needs of other users. For example, managers will at times be interested in receiving an historic overview of business operations of the sort provided to other users. Equally, the other users would be interested in receiving information relating to the future, such as the forecast level of profits, and non-financial information such as the state of the order book, and product innovations.

The distinction between the two areas reflects, to some extent, the differences in access to financial information. Managers have much more control over the form and content of information they receive. Other users have to rely on what managers are prepared to provide or what the financial reporting regulations state must be provided. Although the scope of financial accounting reports has increased over time, fears surrounding loss of competitive advantage and of user ignorance concerning the reliability of forecast data have led businesses to resist providing other users with the detailed and wide-ranging information that is available to managers.

Broadly, Chapters 2 to 6 of this book deal with areas that are usually considered to be in the area of financial accounting, and the following three chapters are concerned with management accounting. The final three chapters are concerned with finance – that is, the raising and investing of funds.

Why do I need to know anything about accounting and finance?

At this point you may be asking yourself 'Why do I need to study accounting and finance? I don't intend to become an accountant!' Well, from the explanation of what accounting and finance is about, which was given earlier in the chapter, it should be clear that the accounting/finance function within an organisation is a central part of its management information system. On the basis of information provided by the system, managers make decisions concerning the allocation of resources. These decisions may concern whether to continue with certain business operations, whether to invest in particular projects, whether to sell particular products and so on. Such decisions can have a profound effect on all those connected with the organisation. It is important, therefore, that *all* those who intend to work in organisations should have a fairly clear idea of certain important aspects of accounting and finance. These aspects include:

- how financial reports should be read and interpreted;
- how financial plans are made;
- how investment decisions are made;
- how businesses are financed.

Many, perhaps most, students have a career goal of being a manager within an organisation – perhaps a personnel manager, marketing manager or IT manager. If you are one of these students, an understanding of accounting and finance is very important. When you become a manager, even a junior one, it is almost certain that you will have to use financial reports to help you to carry out your management tasks. It is equally certain that it is largely on the basis of financial information and reports that your performance as a manager will be judged.

As a manager, it is likely that you will be expected to help in forward planning for the organisation. This will often involve the preparation of projected financial statements and setting of financial targets.

If you do not understand what the financial statements really mean and the extent to which the financial information is reliable, you will find yourself at a distinct disadvantage to others who know their way round the system. As a manager, you will also be expected to help decide how the limited resources available to the business should be allocated between competing options. This will require an ability to evaluate the costs and benefits of the different options available. Once again, an understanding of accounting and finance is important to carrying out this management task.

This is not to say that you cannot be an effective and successful personnel, marketing or computing manager unless you are a qualified accountant as well. It does mean, however, that you need to acquire a bit of 'street wisdom' in accounting and finance in order to succeed. This accounting and finance book is aimed at giving you just that.

Exhibit 1.3

The search for profit is a major objective of most businesses and progress in this search is reported by the accounting information system. If managers find that the reported profits are inadequate, this can be an important driver for change within a business. This change can, in turn, have a profound effect on the working lives of those within the business and also those outside the business.

The search for profit

Many clothes retailers have been concerned with profit levels in recent years. This has led them to make radical changes to the ways in which they operate. Low inflation and competition in the high street have forced the retailers to keep costs under strict control in order to meet their profit objectives. This has been done in various ways including:

- moving production to cheaper countries and closing inflexible manufacturing off-shoots;
- using fewer manufacturers and working more closely with manufacturers in the design of clothes. This has enabled the retailers to add details, such as embroidery or unusual design features, and to command a higher price for relatively little cost;
- improving communication to suppliers of materials and to manufacturers so that design and sourcing decisions can be made faster and more accurately. This has meant that the time to make garments has been reduced from as much as nine months to just a few weeks;
- predicting more accurately what customers want in order to avoid being left with stocks of unwanted items.

The effect of implementing these changes has been to reduce costs, and thereby improve profits, and to have more flexibility in the cost structure so that the clothes retailers are more able to weather a downturn.

Source: Adapted from 'Margin of success for clothing retailers', *The Times*, p. 30, 20 November 2002

Summary

The main points of this chapter may be summarised as follows:

- *What are accounting and finance?*
  - ❑ Accounting provides financial information for a range of users to help them make better judgements and decisions concerning a business.
  - ❑ Finance also helps users to make better decisions and is concerned with the financing and investing activities of the business.

- *Accounting and user needs*:
  - ❑ for accounting to be useful, there must be a clear understanding of *for whom* and *for what purpose* the information will be used;
  - ❑ accounting can be viewed as a form of service as it involves providing financial information required by the various users;
  - ❑ to provide a useful service, accounting must possess certain qualities, or characteristics. These are relevance, reliability, comparability and understandability. In addition, accounting information must be material;
  - ❑ providing a service to users can be costly and financial information should be produced only if the cost of providing the information is less than the benefits gained.

- *Accounting information*:
  - ❑ accounting is part of the total information system within a business. It shares the features that are common to all information systems within a business, which are the identification, recording, analysis and reporting of information;
  - ❑ managers are among the most important users of financial information, and they use financial information in planning and controlling business activities;
  - ❑ planning involves having a clear view of where the business is going and how it is going to get there. Controlling involves comparing planned performance with actual performance and taking corrective action where necessary.

- *Accounting and business objectives*:
  - ❑ a business may pursue a variety of objectives but the main objective for virtually all businesses is to enhance the wealth of its owners. This does not mean, however, that the needs of other groups connected with the business, such as employees, should be ignored.

- *Management and financial accounting*:
  - ❑ accounting has two main strands – management accounting and financial accounting;
  - ❑ management accounting seeks to meet the needs of the business's managers and financial accounting seeks to meet the needs of the other user groups;
  - ❑ these two strands differ in terms of the types of reports produced, the level of reporting detail, the time horizon, the degree of standardisation and the range and quality of information provided.

- *Why study accounting?*
  - ❏ Everyone connected with business should be a little 'streetwise' about accounting and finance. Financial information and decisions exert an enormous influence over the ways in which a business operates.

→ **Key terms**

accounting *p 1*
finance *p 2*
relevance *p 5*
reliability *p 5*
comparability *p 5*

understandability *p 6*
materiality *p 6*
accounting information system *p 8*
management accounting *p 13*
financial accounting *p 13*

Further reading

If you would like to explore in more depth topics covered in this book, we recommend the following:

Atrill, P. and McLaney, E. *Accounting: an introduction*, 2nd edn, Prentice Hall, 2002.

Elliott, B. and Elliott, J. *Financial accounting and reporting*, 6th edn, Prentice Hall, 2002.

Horngren, C., Bhimani, A., Foster, G. and Datar, S. *Management and cost accounting*, 2nd edn, Prentice Hall, 2002.

McLaney, E. *Business finance: theory and practice*, 6th edn, Prentice Hall, 2003.

? **Review questions**

Answers to these questions can be found on the students' side of the Companion Website.

1.1 What is the purpose of producing accounting information?

1.2 Identify the main users of accounting information for a university. Do these users, or the way in which they use accounting information, differ very much from the users of accounting information for private-sector businesses?

1.3 Management accounting has been described as 'the eyes and ears of management'. What do you think this expression means?

1.4 Financial accounting statements tend to reflect past events. In view of this, how can they be of any assistance to a user in making a decision when decisions, by their very nature, can only be made about future actions?

Chapter 2

Measuring and reporting financial position

Introduction

We saw in the previous chapter that accounting has two distinct strands – financial accounting and management accounting. This chapter, and the following four chapters, will examine the three major financial statements that form the core of financial accounting. We begin our examination by providing an overview of these statements and we shall see how each contributes towards an assessment of the overall financial position and performance of a business. Following this overview, we begin a more detailed examination by turning our attention towards one of these financial statements – the balance sheet. We shall see how it is prepared, and we shall examine the principles underpinning this statement. We shall also consider its value for decision-making purposes.

Objectives

When you have completed this chapter, you should be able to:

- **explain the nature and purpose of the three major financial statements**
- **prepare a simple balance sheet and interpret the information that it contains**
- **discuss the accounting conventions underpinning the balance sheet**
- **discuss the limitations of the balance sheet in portraying the financial position of a business.**

The major financial statements – an overview

The major financial statements are designed to provide a picture of the overall financial position and performance of the business. In order to provide this overall picture, the accounting system will normally produce three major financial reports on a regular recurring basis. These are concerned with answering the following questions:

■ What cash movements (that is, cash in and cash out) took place over a particular period?

■ How much wealth (that is, profit) was generated by the business over a particular period?

■ What is the accumulated wealth of the business at the end of a particular period?

These three questions are addressed by the three financial statements, with each statement dealing with a particular question. These financial statements are:

→ ■ the **cash flow statement**;

→ ■ the **profit and loss account**;

→ ■ the **balance sheet**.

Taken together, they provide an overall picture of the financial health of the business.

Perhaps the best way to introduce these financial statements is to look at an example of a very simple business. From this we shall be able to see the sort of information that each of the statements can usefully provide. It is, however, worth pointing out that, whilst a simple business is our starting point, the principles that we consider are also applied to more complex businesses. Thus, we shall encounter these principles in later chapters.

Example 2.1

Paul was unemployed and unable to find a job. He therefore decided to embark on a business venture. Christmas was approaching, and so he decided to buy gift wrapping paper from a local supplier and to sell it on the corner of his local high street. He felt that the price of wrapping paper in the high street shops was excessive, and that this provided him with a useful business opportunity.

He began the venture with £40 in cash. On the first day of trading, he purchased wrapping paper for £40 and sold three-quarters of his stock for £45 cash.

What cash movements took place during the first day of trading?

On the first day of trading, a *cash flow statement* showing the cash movements for the day can be prepared as follows:

Cash flow statement for day 1

	£
Opening balance (cash introduced)	40
Add Cash from sales of wrapping paper	45
	85
Less Cash paid to purchase wrapping paper	40
Closing balance of cash	45

How much wealth (that is, profit) was generated by the business during the first day of trading?

A *profit and loss account* can be prepared to show the wealth (profit) generated on the first day. The wealth generated will represent the difference between the sales made and the cost of the goods (that is, wrapping paper) sold:

Profit and loss account for day 1

	£
Sales	45
Less Cost of goods sold ($^3/_4$ of £40)	30
Profit	15

Note that it is only the *cost* of the wrapping paper sold that is matched against the sales in order to find the profit, and not the whole of the cost of wrapping paper acquired. Any unsold stock (in this case $^1/_4$ of £40 = £10) will be charged against the future sales of it.

What is the accumulated wealth at the end of the first day?

To establish the accumulated wealth at the end of the first day, we can draw up a *balance sheet*. This will list the resources held at the end of that day:

Balance sheet at the end of day 1

	£
Cash (closing balance)	45
Stock of goods for resale ($^1/_4$ of £40)	10
Total business wealth	55

We can see from the above financial statements that each provides part of a picture that sets out the financial performance and position of the business. We begin by showing the cash movements. Cash is a vital resource that is necessary for any business to function effectively. Cash is required to meet debts that may become due and to acquire other resources (such as stock). Cash has been described as the 'life blood' of a business, and movements in cash are usually given close scrutiny by users of financial statements.

However, it is clear that reporting cash movements alone would not be enough to portray the financial health of the business. The changes in cash over time do not give an insight into the profit generated. The profit and loss account provides us with information concerning this aspect of performance. For day 1, for example, we saw that the cash balance increased by £5, but the profit generated, as shown in the profit and loss account, was £15. The cash balance did not increase by the amount of the profit made because part of the wealth generated (£10) was held in the form of stocks.

To gain an insight to the total wealth of the business, a balance sheet is drawn up at the end of the day. Cash is only one form in which wealth can be held. In the case of this business, wealth is also held in the form of a stock of goods for resale. Hence, when drawing up the balance sheet, both forms of wealth held will be listed. In the case of a large business, there may be many other forms in which wealth will be held, such as land and buildings, equipment, motor vehicles, and so on.

Let us now continue with our example.

Example 2.1 (continued)

On the second day of trading, Paul purchased more wrapping paper for £20 cash. He managed to sell all of the new stock and all of the earlier stock, for a total of £48.

The cash flow statement on day 2 will be as follows:

Cash flow statement for day 2

	£
Opening balance (from the end of day 1)	45
Add Cash from sales of wrapping paper	48
	93
Less Cash paid to purchase wrapping paper	20
Closing balance	73

The profit and loss account for day 2 will be as follows:

Profit and loss account for day 2

	£
Sales	48
Less Cost of goods sold (£20 + £10)	30
Profit	18

The balance sheet at the end of day 2 will be:

Balance sheet at the end of day 2

	£
Cash (closing balance)	73
Stock of goods for resale	–
Total business wealth	73

We can see that the total business wealth increased to £73 by the end of day 2. This represents an increase of £18 (that is, £73 – £55) over the previous day – which, of course, is the amount of profit made during day 2 as shown on the profit and loss account.

Activity 2.1

On the third day of his business venture, Paul purchased more stock for £46 cash. However, it was raining hard for much of the day and sales were slow. After Paul had sold half of his total stock for £32, he decided to stop trading until the following day.

Have a go at drawing up the three financial statements for day 3 of Paul's business venture.

Activity 2.1 continued

Cash flow statement for day 3

	£
Opening balance (from the end of day 2)	73
Add Cash from sales of wrapping paper	32
	105
Less Cash paid to purchase wrapping paper	46
Closing balance	59

Profit and loss account for day 3

	£
Sales	32
Less Cost of goods sold ($\frac{1}{2}$ of £46)	23
Profit	9

Balance sheet at the end of day 3

	£
Cash (closing balance)	59
Stock of goods for resale ($\frac{1}{2}$ of £46)	23
Total business wealth	82

Note that the total business wealth had increased by £9 (that is, the amount of the day's profit) even though the cash balance had declined. This is because the business is holding more of its wealth in the form of stock rather than cash, compared with the end of day 2.

We can see that the profit and loss account and cash flow statement are both concerned with measuring flows (of wealth and cash respectively) during a particular period (for example, a particular day, a particular month or a particular year). The balance sheet, however, is concerned with the financial position at a particular moment in time.

Figure 2.1 illustrates this point. The profit and loss account, cash flow statement and balance sheet, when taken together, are often referred to as the 'final accounts' of the business.

For external users, these statements are normally backward looking because they are based on information concerning past events and transactions. This can be useful in providing feedback on past performance, and in identifying trends that provide clues to future performance. However, the statements can also be prepared using projected data to help assess likely future profits, cash flows and so on. The financial statements are normally prepared on a projected basis for internal decision-making purposes only. Managers are usually reluctant to publish these projected statements for external users, as they may reveal valuable information to competitors.

Now that we have an overview of the financial statements, we shall consider each statement in more detail. In Chapter 3 we shall look at the profit and loss account, and in Chapter 5 we shall go into more detail on the cash flow statement.

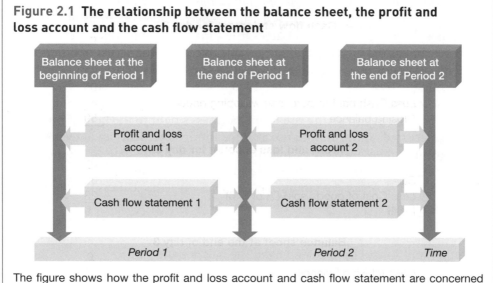

Figure 2.1 The relationship between the balance sheet, the profit and loss account and the cash flow statement

The figure shows how the profit and loss account and cash flow statement are concerned with measuring flows of wealth over time. The balance sheet, however, is concerned with measuring the stock of wealth at a particular moment in time.

The balance sheet

The purpose of the balance sheet is simply to set out the financial position of a business at a particular moment in time. (The balance sheet is sometimes referred to as the *position statement*, because it seeks to provide the user with a picture of financial position.) We saw above that the balance sheet will reveal the forms in which the wealth of the business is held and how much wealth is held in each form. We can, however, be more specific about the nature of the balance sheet by saying that it sets out the **assets** of the business on the one hand, and the **claims** against the business on the other. Before looking at the balance sheet in more detail, we need to be clear about what these terms mean.

Assets

An asset, for accounting purposes, is essentially a resource held by the business that has certain characteristics. The major characteristics of an asset are:

■ *A probable future benefit exists*. This simply means that the item is expected to have some future monetary value. This value can arise through its use within the business or through its hire or sale. Thus, an obsolete piece of equipment that could be sold for scrap would still be considered an asset, whereas an obsolete piece of equipment that could not be sold for scrap would not be regarded as an asset.

■ *The business has an exclusive right to control the benefit.* Unless the business has exclusive rights over the resource it cannot be regarded as an asset. Thus, for a business offering holidays on barges, the canal system may be a very valuable resource, but as the business will not be able to control the access of others to the system, it cannot be regarded as an asset of the business. (However, the barges owned by the business would be regarded as assets.)

■ *The benefit must arise from some past transaction or event.* This means that the transaction (or other event) giving rise to the business's right to the benefit must have already occurred, and will not arise at some future date. Thus an agreement by a business to purchase a piece of machinery at some future date would not mean the item is currently an asset of the business.

■ *The asset must be capable of measurement in monetary terms.* Unless the item can be measured in monetary terms, with a reasonable degree of reliability, it will not be regarded as an asset for inclusion on the balance sheet. Thus, the loyalty of customers may be extremely valuable to the business but is usually impossible to quantify and so will be excluded from the balance sheet.

We can see that these conditions will strictly limit the kind of items that may be referred to as 'assets' in the balance sheet. Certainly not all resources exploited by a business will be assets of the business for accounting purposes. Once an asset has been acquired by a business, it will continue to be considered an asset until the benefits are exhausted or the business disposes of it in some way.

Activity 2.2

Indicate which of the following items could appear as an asset on the balance sheet of a business. Explain your reasoning in each case.

1 £1,000 owing to the business by a customer who is unable to pay.
2 The purchase of a patent from an inventor that gives the business the right to produce a new product. Production of the new product is expected to increase profits over the period during which the patent is held.
3 The business hiring a new marketing director who is confidently expected to increase profits by over 30 per cent over the next three years.
4 The purchase of a machine that will save the business £10,000 each year. It is currently being used by the business but it has been acquired on credit and is not yet paid for.

Your answer to the above problems should be along the following lines:

1 Under normal circumstances a business would expect a customer to pay the amount owed. Such an amount is therefore typically shown as an asset under the heading 'debtors'. However, in this particular case the debtor is unable to pay. Hence the item is incapable of providing future benefits, and the £1,000 owing would not be regarded as an asset. Debts that are not paid are referred to as 'bad debts'.
2 The purchase of the patent would meet all of the conditions set out above and would therefore be regarded as an asset.

▶

Activity 2.2 continued

> 3 The hiring of a new marketing director would not be considered as the acquisition of an asset. One argument against its classification as an asset is that the business does not have exclusive rights of control over the director. (Nevertheless, it may have an exclusive right to the services that the director provides.) Perhaps a stronger argument is that the value of the director cannot be measured in monetary terms with any degree of reliability.
>
> 4 The machine would be considered an asset even though it is not yet paid for. Once the business has agreed to purchase the machine, and has accepted it, the machine is legally owned by the business even though payment is still outstanding. (The amount outstanding would be shown as a claim, as we shall see below.)

The sorts of items that often appear as assets in the balance sheet of a business include:

- freehold premises;
- machinery and equipment;
- fixtures and fittings;
- patents and trademarks;
- debtors;
- investments.

Activity 2.3

Can you think of three additional items that might appear as assets in the balance sheet of a business?

You may be able to think of a number of other items. Some that you may have identified are:

- motor vehicles
- stock of goods
- computer equipment
- cash at bank.

Note that an asset does not have to be a physical item – it may also be a non-physical right to certain benefits. Assets that have a physical substance and can be touched are referred to as **tangible assets**. Assets that have no physical substance but which, nevertheless, provide expected future benefits (such as patents) are referred to as **intangible assets**.

Claims

A claim is an obligation on the part of the business to provide cash, or some other form of benefit, to an outside party. A claim will normally arise as a result of the outside party providing funds in the form of assets for use by the business. There are essentially two types of claim against a business:

- **Capital**. This represents the claim of the owner(s) against the business. This claim is sometimes referred to as the *owner's equity*. Some find it hard to understand how the owner can have a claim against the business, particularly when we consider the example of a sole-proprietor-type business where the owner *is*, in effect, the business. However, for accounting purposes, a clear distinction is made between the business (whatever its size) and the owner(s). The business is viewed as being quite separate from the owner and this is equally true for a sole proprietor like Paul, the wrapping-paper seller, in Example 2.1 or a large company like Marks and Spencer plc. It is seen as a separate entity with its own separate existence and when financial statements are prepared, they are prepared for the business rather than for the owner(s). This means that the balance sheet should reflect the financial position of the business as a separate entity. Viewed from this perspective, any funds contributed by the owner will be seen as coming from outside the business and will appear as a claim against the business in its balance sheet.
- **Liabilities**. Liabilities represent the claims of individuals and organisations, apart from the owner, that have arisen from past transactions or events such as supplying goods or lending money to the business.

Once a claim has been incurred by a business, it will remain as an obligation until it is settled.

Now that the meaning of the terms *assets* and *claims* has been established, we can go on and discuss the relationship between the two. This relationship is quite simple and straightforward. If a business wishes to acquire assets, it will have to raise the necessary funds from somewhere. It may raise the funds from the owner(s) or from other outside parties or from both. To illustrate the relationship let us take the example of a business, as set out in Example 2.2.

Example 2.2

Jerry and Co. deposits £20,000 in a bank account on 1 March in order to commence business. Let us assume that the cash is supplied by the owner (£6,000) and by a lender (£14,000) and paid into the business bank account. The raising of the funds in this way will give rise to a claim on the business by both the owner (capital) and the lender (liability). If a balance sheet of Jerry and Co. is prepared following the above transactions, the assets and claims of the business will appear as follows:

Jerry and Co.
Balance sheet as at 1 March

Assets	£	Claims	£
Cash at bank	20,000	Capital	6,000
		Liability – loan	14,000
	20,000		20,000

We can see from the balance sheet that has been prepared that the total claims are the same as the total assets. Thus:

Assets = Capital + Liabilities

This equation – which is often referred to as the *balance sheet equation* – will always hold true. Whatever changes that may occur to the assets of the business or the claims against the business, there will be compensating changes elsewhere that will ensure that the balance sheet always 'balances'. By way of illustration, consider the following transactions for Jerry and Co:

2 March   Purchased a motor van for £5,000, paying by cheque.
3 March   Purchased stock in trade (that is, goods to be sold) on one month's credit for £3,000.
4 March   Repaid £2,000 of the loan from the lender.
6 March   Owner introduced another £4,000 into the business bank account.

A balance sheet may be drawn up after each day in which transactions have taken place. In this way, the effect can be seen of each transaction on the assets and claims of the business. The balance sheet as at 2 March will be as follows:

Jerry and Co.
Balance sheet as at 2 March

Assets	£	Claims	£
Cash at bank (20,000 – 5,000)	15,000	Capital	6,000
Motor van	5,000	Liabilities – loan	14,000
	20,000		20,000

As can be seen, the effect of purchasing a motor van is to decrease the balance at the bank by £5,000 and to introduce a new asset – a motor van – to the balance sheet. The total assets remain unchanged. It is only the 'mix' of assets that will change. The claims against the business will remain the same because there has been no change in the way in which the business has been funded.

The balance sheet as at 3 March, following the purchase of stock, will be as follows:

Jerry and Co.
Balance sheet as at 3 March

Assets	£	Claims	£
Cash at bank	15,000	Capital	6,000
Motor van	5,000	Liabilities – loan	14,000
Stock	3,000	Liabilities – trade creditor	3,000
	23,000		23,000

The effect of purchasing stock has been to introduce another new asset (stock) to the balance sheet. In addition, the fact that the goods have not yet been paid for means that the claims against the business will be increased by the £3,000 owed to the supplier, who is referred to as a *trade creditor* on the balance sheet.

Activity 2.4

Try drawing up a balance sheet for Jerry and Co. as at 4 March.

The balance sheet as at 4 March, following the repayment of part of the loan, will be as follows:

Jerry and Co.
Balance sheet as at 4 March

Assets	£	Claims	£
Cash at bank (15,000 – 2,000)	13,000	Capital	6,000
Motor van	5,000	Liabilities – loan (14,000 – 2,000)	12,000
Stock	3,000	Liabilities – trade creditor	3,000
	21,000		21,000

The repayment of £2,000 of the loan will result in a decrease in the balance at the bank of £2,000 and a decrease in the loan claim against the business by the same amount.

Activity 2.5

Try drawing up a balance sheet as at 6 March for Jerry and Co.

The balance sheet as at 6 March, following the introduction of more funds, will be as follows:

Jerry and Co.
Balance sheet as at 6 March

Assets	£	Claims	£
Cash at bank (13,000 + 4,000)	17,000	Capital (6,000 + 4,000)	10,000
Motor van	5,000	Liabilities – loan	12,000
Stock	3,000	Liabilities – trade creditor	3,000
	25,000		25,000

The introduction of more funds by the owner will result in an increase in the capital of £4,000 and an increase in the cash at bank by the same amount.

This example illustrates the point that the balance sheet equation (assets equals capital plus liabilities) will always hold true. This is because it reflects the fact that, if a business wishes to acquire assets, it must raise funds equal to the cost of those assets. The funds raised must be provided by the owners (capital), or by others (liabilities) or by both the owners and others. Hence the total cost of assets acquired should always equal the total capital plus liabilities.

It is worth pointing out that a business would not draw up a balance sheet after each day of transactions as shown in the example above. Such an approach is likely to be impractical, given even a relatively small number of transactions each day.

A balance sheet for the business is usually prepared at the end of a defined reporting period. Determining the length of the reporting interval will involve weighing up the costs of producing the information against the perceived benefits of the information for decision-making purposes. In practice, the reporting interval will vary between businesses, and could be monthly, quarterly, half-yearly or annually. For external reporting purposes, an annual reporting cycle is the norm (although certain businesses, typically larger ones, report more frequently than this). However, for internal reporting purposes to managers, many businesses produce monthly financial statements.

The effect of trading operations on the balance sheet

In the example we considered earlier, we dealt with the effect on the balance sheet of a number of different types of transactions that a business might undertake. These transactions covered the purchase of assets for cash and on credit, the repayment of a loan, and the injection of capital. However, one form of transaction, trading, has not yet been considered. To deal with the effect of trading transactions on the balance sheet, let us return to our earlier example.

Example 2.2 (continued)

The balance sheet that we drew up for Jerry and Co. as at 6 March was as follows:

Jerry and Co.
Balance sheet as at 6 March

Assets	£	Claims	£
Cash at bank	17,000	Capital	10,000
Motor van	5,000	Liabilities – loan	12,000
Stock	3,000	Liabilities – trade creditor	3,000
	25,000		25,000

Let us assume that, on 7 March, the business managed to sell all of the stock for £5,000 and received a cheque immediately from the customer for this amount. The balance sheet on 7 March, after this transaction has taken place, will be as follows:

Jerry and Co.
Balance sheet as at 7 March

Assets	£	Claims	£
Cash at bank (17,000 + 5,000)	22,000	Capital [10,000 + (5,000 – 3,000)]	12,000
Motor van	5,000	Liabilities – loan	12,000
Stock (3,000 – 3,000)	–	Liabilities – trade creditor	3,000
	27,000		27,000

We can see that the stock (£3,000) has now disappeared from the balance sheet, but the cash at bank has increased by the selling price of the stock (£5,000). The net effect has therefore been to increase assets by £2,000 (that is £5,000 – £3,000). This increase represents the net increase in wealth (the profit) that has arisen from trading. Also note that the capital of the business has increased by £2,000, in line with the increase in assets. This increase in capital reflects the fact that increases in wealth as a result of trading or other operations will be to the benefit of the owners and will increase their stake in the business.

Activity 2.6

What would have been the effect on the balance sheet if the stock had been sold on 7 March for £1,000 rather than £5,000?

The balance sheet on 7 March would be as follows:

Jerry and Co.
Balance sheet as at 7 March

Assets	£	Claims	£
Cash at bank (17,000 + 1,000)	18,000	Capital [10,000 + (1,000 – 3,000)]	8,000
Motor van	5,000	Liabilities – loan	12,000
Stock (3,000 – 3,000)	–	Liabilities – trade creditor	3,000
	23,000		23,000

As we can see, the stock (£3,000) will disappear from the balance sheet, but the cash at bank will rise by only £1,000. This will mean a net reduction in assets of £2,000. This reduction represents a loss arising from trading and will be reflected in a reduction in the capital of the owner.

Thus we can see that any decrease in wealth (loss) arising from trading or other transactions will lead to a reduction in the owner's stake in the business. If the business wished to maintain the level of assets as at 6 March, it would be necessary to obtain further funds from the owner or from lenders, or both.

What we have just seen means that the balance sheet equation can be extended as follows:

$$\text{Assets} = \text{Capital} + (-)\ \text{Profit (Loss)} + \text{Liabilities}$$

The profit for the period may be shown separately in the balance sheet as an addition to capital. Any funds introduced or withdrawn by the owner for living expenses or other reasons are also shown separately. By doing this, we provide more comprehensive information for users of the financial statements. If we assume that the above business sold the stock for £5,000, as in the earlier example, and further assume that the owner withdrew £1,500 for his or her own use, the capital of the owner would appear as follows on the balance sheet:

		£
	Capital	
	Opening balance	10,000
	Add Profit	2,000
		12,000
	Less Drawings	1,500
	Closing balance	10,500

If the drawings were in cash, the balance of cash would decrease by £1,500 in the balance sheet.

Note that, like all balance sheet items, the amount of capital is cumulative. This means that any profit made that is not taken out as drawings by the owner(s) remains in the business. These retained profits have the effect of expanding the business.

The classification of assets

To help users of financial information to locate items of interest easily on the balance sheet, it is customary to group assets and claims into categories. Assets are normally categorised as being either fixed or current. The distinction between these two categories is as follows:

→ ■ **Fixed assets** are defined primarily according to the purpose for which they are held. Fixed assets are held with the intention of being retained and used to generate wealth rather than being held for resale (although they may be sold by the business when there is no further use for the asset). They can be seen as the tools of the business. Fixed assets are normally held by the business on a continuing basis, typically for more than one year.

Activity 2.7

Can you think of two examples of assets that may be classified as fixed assets within a particular business?

Examples of assets that are often defined as being fixed are:

■ freehold premises
■ plant and machinery
■ motor vehicles
■ patents.

This is not an exhaustive list. You may have thought of others.

■ **Current assets** are assets that are not held on a continuing basis. They include cash itself and other assets that are expected to be turned into cash at some future point in time. Current assets are normally held as part of the day-to-day trading activities of the business. The most common current assets are stock, trade debtors (that is, customers who owe money for goods or services supplied on credit), and cash itself. The current assets mentioned are interrelated, and circulate within a business as shown in Figure 2.2. We can see that cash can be used to purchase stock, which is then sold as credit. When the trade debtors pay, the business receives an injection of cash, and so on.

Figure 2.2 The circulating nature of current assets

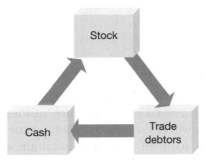

The figure shows how stock may be sold on credit to customers. When the customers pay, the trade debtors will be converted into cash, which can then be used to purchase more stock, and so the cycle begins again.

It is important to appreciate that the classification of an asset may vary (that is, between fixed and current) according to the nature of the business being carried out. This is because the *purpose* for which a particular type of business holds a certain asset may vary. For example, a motor vehicle manufacturer will normally hold a stock of the motor vehicles produced for resale, and would therefore classify them as part of the current assets. On the other hand, a business that uses motor vehicles for transportation purposes would classify them as fixed assets.

Activity 2.8

The assets of Kunalun and Co., a large metalworking business, are shown below:

■ Cash at bank
■ Fixtures and fittings
■ Office equipment
■ Motor vehicles
■ Freehold factory premises
■ Plant and machinery

▶

Activity 2.8 continued

- Computer equipment
- Stock of work-in-progress (that is, partly completed goods).

Which of the above do you think should be defined as fixed assets, and which should be defined as current assets?

Your answer to the above activity should be as follows:

Fixed assets	*Current assets*
Fixtures and fittings	Cash at bank
Office equipment	Stock of work-in-progress
Motor vehicles	
Freehold factory premises	
Plant and machinery	
Computer equipment	

In some cases an item referred to as 'goodwill' may appear as a fixed asset on the balance sheet. When a business takes over another business, the amount that is paid for the business taken over will often exceed the total value of the individual accounting assets that have been acquired. This additional amount represents a payment for *goodwill*, which arises from acquiring intangible benefits such as the quality of products produced, the skill of the workforce, the relationship with customers, and so on. 'Qualitative' items such as these are normally excluded from the balance sheet as they are difficult to measure. However, when they have been acquired by a business at an agreed price, the amount paid provides an objective basis for measurement. Hence, goodwill can be regarded as an accounting asset and included on the balance sheet. It is regarded as a fixed asset as it is not held primarily for resale and will be held on a continuing basis.

The classification of claims

As we have already seen, claims are normally classified into capital (owner's claim) and liabilities (claims of outsiders). Liabilities are further classified into two groups:

- **Long-term liabilities** represent those amounts due to outside parties that are not liable for repayment within the next 12 months after the balance sheet date.
- **Current liabilities** represent amounts due for repayment to outside parties within 12 months of the balance sheet date.

Unlike assets, the purpose for which the liabilities are held is not an issue. It is only the period for which a liability is outstanding that is important. Thus a long-term liability will turn into a current liability when the settlement date comes within 12 months of the balance sheet date.

Activity 2.9

Can you think of examples of a long-term liability and a current liability?

Two examples of a long-term liability would be a long-term mortgage (that is, a loan secured on property) or a long-term loan. Two examples of a current liability would be trade creditors (that is, amounts owing to suppliers for goods supplied on credit) and a bank overdraft (a form of bank borrowing that is repayable on demand).

Balance sheet formats

Now that we have looked at the classification of assets and liabilities, it is possible to consider the format of the balance sheet. Although there is an almost infinite number of ways in which the same balance sheet information could be presented, there are in practice two basic formats. The first of these follows the style we adopted with Jerry and Co. earlier. A more comprehensive example of this style is shown in Example 2.3.

Example 2.3

Brie Manufacturing
Balance sheet as at 31 December 2003

	£	£		£
Fixed assets			*Capital*	
Freehold premises		45,000	Opening balance	50,000
Plant and machinery		30,000	*Add* Profit	14,000
Motor vans		19,000		64,000
		94,000	*Less* Drawings	4,000
				60,000
			Long-term liabilities	
			Loan	50,000
Current assets			*Current liabilities*	
Stock-in-trade	23,000		Trade creditors	37,000
Trade debtors	18,000			
Cash at bank	12,000			
		53,000		
		147,000		147,000

Within each category of asset (fixed and current), shown in Example 2.3, the items are listed in reverse order of liquidity (nearness to cash). Thus, the assets that are furthest from cash are listed first and the assets that are closest to cash are listed last. In the case of fixed assets, freehold premises are listed first as these assets are usually the most difficult to turn into cash and motor vans are listed last as there is usually a ready market for them. In the case of current assets, we have already seen that stock is converted to debtors and then debtors are converted to cash. Hence, under the heading of current assets, stock is listed first, followed by debtors and finally cash itself.

This ordering of assets is a standard practice, which is followed irrespective of the format used. Note also that the current assets are listed individually in the first column, and a subtotal of current assets (£53,000) is carried out to the second column to be added to the subtotal of fixed assets (£94,000). This convention is designed to make the balance sheet easier to read.

An obvious change to the format illustrated in Example 2.3 is to show claims on the left and assets on the right. Some people prefer this approach because the claims can be seen as the source of finance for the business, and the assets show how that finance has been deployed. It could be seen as more logical to show sources first and uses second.

The format shown above is sometimes referred to as the *horizontal layout*. However, in recent years, a more common form of layout for the balance sheet is the *narrative* or *vertical* form of layout. This format is really based on a rearrangement of the balance sheet equation. With the horizontal format above, the balance sheet equation is set out as in Figure 2.3. The vertical format merely rearranges this equation as shown in Figure 2.4.

Figure 2.3 The equation for the horizontal layout

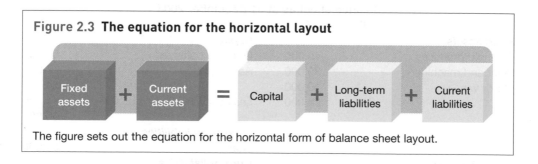

The figure sets out the equation for the horizontal form of balance sheet layout.

Figure 2.4 The equation for the vertical layout

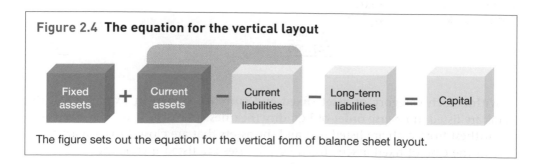

The figure sets out the equation for the vertical form of balance sheet layout.

The vertical layout not only rearranges the equation but, as the name suggests, presents the information vertically rather than horizontally. Thus, the balance sheet starts with fixed assets and works downwards towards capital at the end. The balance sheet of Brie Manufacturing that was arranged in horizontal format in Example 2.3 can be rearranged in vertical format as shown in Example 2.4.

Example 2.4

Brie Manufacturing
Balance sheet as at 31 December 2003

	£	£
Fixed assets		
Freehold premises		45,000
Plant and machinery		30,000
Motor vans		19,000
		94,000
Current assets		
Stock-in-trade	23,000	
Trade debtors	18,000	
Cash at bank	12,000	
	53,000	
Less **Current liabilities**		
Trade creditors	37,000	
		16,000
Total assets *less* current liabilities		110,000
Less **Long-term liabilities**		
Loan		50,000
Net assets		60,000
Capital		
Opening balance		50,000
Add Profit		14,000
		64,000
Less Drawings		4,000
		60,000

Some people find the vertical format of Example 2.4 easier to read than the horizontal format as it usefully highlights the relationship between current assets and current liabilities. The figure derived from deducting current liabilities from the current assets is sometimes referred to as *net current assets* or *working capital*. We can see that for Brie Manufacturing this figure is £16,000, indicating that the short-term, liquid assets more than cover the short-term claims against the business.

? Self-assessment question 2.1

The following information relates to Simonson Engineering as at 30 September 2003:

	£
Plant and machinery	25,000
Trade creditors	18,000
Bank overdraft	26,000
Stock-in-trade	45,000
Freehold premises	72,000
Long-term loans	51,000
Trade debtors	48,000
Capital at 1 October 2002	117,500
Cash in hand	1,500
Motor vehicles	15,000
Fixtures and fittings	9,000
Profit for the year to 30 September 2003	18,000
Drawings for the year to 30 September 2003	15,000

Required:
Prepare a balance sheet in the vertical format.

The balance sheet as a position at a point in time

As we have already seen, the balance sheet is a statement of the financial position of the business at *a specified point in time*. The balance sheet has been compared to a photograph. A photograph 'freezes' a particular moment in time and will represent the situation only at that moment in time. Hence, events may be quite different immediately before and immediately after the photograph was taken. Similarly, the balance sheet represents a 'snapshot' of the business at a particular moment in time. When examining a balance sheet, therefore, it is important to establish the date at which it has been drawn up. This information should be prominently displayed in the balance sheet heading, as shown above. The more recent the balance sheet date, the better when we are trying to assess the current financial position.

A business will normally prepare a balance sheet as at the close of business on the last day of its accounting year. In the UK, businesses are free to choose their accounting year. When making a decision on which year end date to choose, commercial convenience can often be a deciding factor. Thus, a business operating in the retail trade may choose to have a year end date early in the calendar year (for example 31 January) because trade tends to be slack during that period and more staff time is available to help with the tasks involved in the preparation of the annual accounting statements (such as checking the amount of stock held). Since trade is slack, it is also a time when the amount of stock held by the business is likely to be untypically low as compared with other times of the year. Thus the balance sheet, though showing a fair view of what it purports to show, may not show a picture of what is more typically the position of the business over the year.

Accounting conventions and the balance sheet

Accounting is based on a number of rules or conventions that have evolved over time. They have evolved in order to deal with practical problems experienced by preparers and users, rather than to reflect some theoretical ideal. In preparing the balance sheets earlier, we have adhered to various **accounting conventions**, although they have not been explicitly mentioned. We shall now identify and discuss the major conventions that we have applied.

Business entity convention

For accounting purposes, the business and its owner(s) are treated as being quite separate and distinct. This is why owners are treated as being claimants against their own business in respect of their investment in the business. The **business entity convention** must be distinguished from the legal position that may exist between businesses and their owners. For sole proprietorships and partnerships, the law does not make any distinction between the business and its owner(s). For limited companies, on the other hand, there is a clear legal distinction between the business and its owners. (As we shall see in Chapter 4, the limited company is regarded as having a separate legal existence.) For accounting purposes these legal distinctions are irrelevant, and the business entity convention applies to all businesses.

Money measurement convention

Accounting normally deals with only those items that are capable of being expressed in monetary terms. Money has the advantage that it is a useful common denominator with which to express the wide variety of resources held by a business. However, not all such resources are capable of being measured in monetary terms and so will be excluded from a balance sheet. The **money measurement convention**, therefore, limits the scope of accounting reports.

Activity 2.10

Can you think of resources held by a business that are not normally included on the balance sheet because they cannot be quantified in monetary terms?

In answering this activity you may have thought of the following:

- the quality of the workforce
- the reputation of the business's products
- the location of the business
- the relationship with customers
- the ability of the managers.

Accounting is a developing subject, and the boundaries of financial measurement can change. In recent years, attempts have been made to measure particular resources of a business that have been excluded previously from the balance sheet. For example, we have seen attempts to measure the 'human assets' of the business. It is often claimed that employees are the most valuable 'assets' of a business. By measuring these assets and putting the amount on the balance sheet, it is sometimes argued that we have a more complete picture of the financial position. For similar reasons, we have also seen attempts by certain large businesses to measure the value of brand names that they have developed through promotional and advertising activities. However, many doubt whether the value of human 'assets' and internally generated brands can be established with any degree of reliability. Thus, there are mixed views as to whether extending the boundaries of financial measurement will succeed in making the balance sheet a more useful representation of the financial position of a business.

Exhibit 2.1 Putting human assets on the balance sheet

It may be surprising to learn that, although human 'assets' are not shown on the balance sheet of a business as a general rule, there are exceptions to this rule. The most common exception arises with professional football clubs. Although football clubs cannot own players, they can own the rights to the players' services. Where these rights are acquired by compensating other clubs for releasing the players from their contracts, the amounts paid provide a reliable basis for measurement. This means that the rights to services can be regarded as an asset of the club for accounting purposes.

Manchester United Football Club has acquired several key players in this way and reports the cost of acquiring those players' rights to services in its balance sheet. The balance sheet for 2002 shows the cost of registering its current squad of players as £108 million. The item of players' registrations is shown as an intangible asset in the balance sheet as it is the rights to services not the players that are the assets. The figure of £108 million includes the cost of bought-in players such as Rio Ferdinand but not 'home-grown' players such as David Beckham.

Source: Manchester United Annual Report 2002

Another approach to overcoming some of the limitations of money measurement is to publish a narrative financial statement. Rather than trying to 'quantify the unquantifiable', a narrative financial statement, which describes and explains key issues, could be published to help users assess financial health. Thus, in order to give a more complete picture of financial position, a narrative statement might incorporate a discussion of such matters as investment policy, financial structure and liquidity, as well as valuable resources that have not been quantified. Many large businesses now produce such a statement, which is referred to as a 'financial review'.

Historic cost convention

Assets are shown on the balance sheet at a value that is based on their **historic cost** (that is, acquisition cost). This method of measuring asset value has been adopted by accountants in preference to methods based on some form of current value. Many commentators find this particular convention difficult to support, as outdated historical costs are unlikely to help in the assessment of current financial position. It is often argued that recording assets at their current value would provide a more realistic view of financial position and would be relevant for a wide range of decisions. However, a system of measurement based on current values can present a number of problems.

Activity 2.11

Can you think of reasons why current value accounting may pose problems for both preparers and users of financial statements?

The term 'current value' can be defined in a number of ways. For example, it can be defined broadly as either the current replacement cost or the current realisable value (selling price) of an item. These two types of valuation may result in quite different figures being produced to represent the current value of an item. (Think, for example, of second-hand car values: there is often quite a difference between buying and selling prices.) In addition, the broad terms 'replacement cost' and 'realisable value' can be defined in different ways. We must therefore be clear about what kind of current value accounting we wish to use. There are also practical problems associated with attempts to implement any system of current value accounting. For example, current values, however defined, are often difficult to establish with any real degree of objectivity. This may mean that the figures produced are heavily dependent on the opinion of managers. Unless the current value figures are capable of some form of independent verification, there is a danger that the financial statements will lose their credibility among users.

By reporting assets at their historic cost, it is argued that more reliable information is produced. Reporting in this way reduces the need for subjective opinion, as the amount paid for a particular asset is usually a matter of demonstrable fact. However, information based on past costs may not always be relevant to the needs of users.

Later in the chapter, we shall consider the valuation of assets in the balance sheet in more detail. We shall see that the historic cost convention is not always rigidly adhered to, and that departures from this convention often occur.

Going concern convention

The **going concern convention** holds that the business will continue operations for the foreseeable future. In other words, there is no intention, or need, to sell off the assets of the business. Such a sale may arise where the business is in financial difficulties and it needs to pay the creditors. This convention is important because the market (sale) value of fixed assets is often low in relation to the values at which they appear in the balance sheet, and an expectation of having to sell off the assets would mean that anticipated losses on sale should be fully recorded. However, where there is no expectation of a need to sell off the assets, the value of fixed assets can continue to be shown at their recorded values (that is, based on historic cost). This convention therefore provides support for the historic cost convention under normal circumstances.

Dual aspect convention

Each transaction has two aspects, both of which will affect the balance sheet. Thus the purchase of a motor car for cash results in an increase in one asset (motor car) and a decrease in another (cash). The repayment of a loan results in the decrease in a liability (loan) and the decrease in an asset (cash/bank).

Activity 2.12

What are the two aspects of each of the following transactions?

- Purchase £1,000 stock on credit.
- Owner withdraws £2,000 in cash.
- Repayment of a loan of £3,000.

Your answer should be as follows:

- Stock increases by £1,000, creditors increase by £1,000.
- Capital reduces by £2,000, cash reduces by £2,000.
- Loan reduces by £3,000, cash reduces by £3,000.

➡   Recording the **dual aspect** of each transaction ensures that the balance sheet will continue to balance.

Prudence convention

➡ The **prudence convention** holds that financial statements should err on the side of caution. The convention represents an attempt to deal with the uncertainty surrounding many events reported in the financial statements, and evolved to counteract the excessive optimism of some managers and owners, which resulted in an overstatement of financial position. This convention requires the recording of all losses in full, and applies to both actual losses and to expected losses. For example, if certain goods purchased for resale proved to be unpopular with customers and, as a result, the goods are to be sold below their original cost, the prudence convention requires that the expected loss from the future sales should be recognised immediately rather than when the goods are eventually sold. Profits, on the other hand, are not recognised until they are realised (that is, when the goods are actually sold). When the prudence convention conflicts with another convention, it is prudence that will normally prevail.

Activity 2.13

Can you think of a situation where certain users might find a prudent view of the financial position of a business will work to their disadvantage?

Applying the prudence convention can result in an understatement of financial position as unrealised profits are not recognised but expected losses are recognised in full. This may result in owners selling their stake in the business at a price that is lower than they would have received if a more balanced approach to valuation were employed.

The degree of bias towards understatement may be difficult to judge. It is likely to vary according to the views of the individual carrying out the valuation.

Stable monetary unit convention

The **stable monetary unit convention** holds that money, which is the unit of measurement in accounting, will not change in value over time. However, in the UK and throughout much of the world, inflation has been a persistent problem over the years. This has meant that the value of money has declined in relation to other assets. In past years, high rates of inflation have resulted in balance sheets, which are drawn up on an historic cost basis, reflecting figures for assets that were much lower than if current cost values were employed. The money value of freehold land and buildings, in particular, increased rapidly during much of the past 30 to 40 years, at least partly as a result of a reduction in the value of each £1. Where land and buildings were held for some time by a business, there was often a significant difference between their original cost and their current market value. This led to the criticism that balance sheet values were seriously understated, and, as a result, some businesses broke away from the use of historic cost as the basis for valuing this particular asset. Instead, freehold land is periodically revalued in order to provide a more realistic statement of financial position. Although this represents a departure from accounting convention, it is a practice that has become increasingly common.

Activity 2.14

Refer to the vertical format balance sheet of Brie Manufacturing shown earlier. What would be the effect of revaluing the freehold land to a figure of £110,000 on the balance sheet?

The effect on the balance sheet would be to increase the freehold land to £110,000 and the gain on revaluation (that is, £110,000 – £45,000 = £65,000) would be added to the capital of the owner, as it is the owner who will benefit from the gain. The revised balance sheet would therefore be as follows:

Activity 2.14 continued

Brie Manufacturing
Balance sheet as at 31 December 2003

	£	£
Fixed assets		
Freehold premises		110,000
Plant and machinery		30,000
Motor vans		19,000
		159,000
Current assets		
Stock-in-trade	23,000	
Trade debtors	18,000	
Cash at bank	12,000	
	53,000	
Less Current liabilities		
Trade creditors	37,000	
		16,000
Total assets less current liabilities		175,000
Less Long-term liabilities		
Loan		50,000
Net assets		125,000
Capital		
Opening balance		50,000
Add: Revaluation gain		65,000
Profit		14,000
		129,000
Less Drawings		4,000
		125,000

In practice, the revaluation of land and buildings often has a significant effect on the size of the balance sheet figures for tangible fixed assets. In past years in the UK, this effect has usually been beneficial, as property has risen in value throughout much of the past four decades. However, during the early 1990s we witnessed a fall in property values, and we also witnessed some reluctance among those businesses that revalued their land and buildings upwards in earlier years to make downward revaluations in recessionary years. A common reason cited was that the fall in value was considered to be only temporary.

Objectivity convention

➡ The **objectivity convention** seeks to reduce personal bias in financial statements. As far as possible, financial statements should be based on objective verifiable evidence rather than on matters of opinion.

Activity 2.15

Which of the above conventions does the objectivity convention support and which does it conflict with?

The objectivity convention provides further support (along with the going concern convention) for the use of historic cost as a basis of valuation. It can conflict, however, with the prudence convention, which requires the use of judgement in determining values.

The basis of valuation of assets on the balance sheet

It was mentioned earlier that, when preparing the balance sheet, the historic cost convention is normally applied for the reporting of assets. However, this point requires further elaboration as, in practice, it is not simply a matter of recording each asset on the balance sheet at its original cost. We shall now consider the valuation procedures used for both current assets and fixed assets.

Current assets

Where the net realisable value (that is, selling price less any selling costs) of current assets falls below the cost of the assets, the former will be used as the basis of valuation instead of the latter. This reflects the influence of the prudence convention on the balance sheet. Current assets are assets that are to be turned into cash (if they are not already in this form) in the normal course of events and usually in the near future and so any loss arising from a fall in value below their original cost is shown on the balance sheet.

Exhibit 2.2 Reporting the valuation basis of current assets

The published financial statements of large businesses will normally show the basis upon which the current assets of the business are valued. For example, International Power plc, a power-generating business, stated in its 2001 financial statements:

Current asset investments
Current asset investments are stated at the lower of cost and market value.

Stocks
Operating stocks of fuel and stores are valued at the lower of cost and net realisable value. They are included as current assets.

In some cases, the way in which the cost of stocks has been derived (usually when the goods are manufactured by the business rather than bought in) will be stated and, in a few cases, the basis for deriving net realisable value is stated. For example, the published financial statements of Thorntons, the chocolate makers, include the following statement:

Net realisable value is the estimated value which would be realised after deducting all costs of completion, marketing and selling.

Source: International Power plc, Annual Report 2001; Thorntons plc, Annual Report 2001

Fixed assets

Many fixed assets, such as plant and machinery, motor vehicles, computer equipment and buildings, have a limited useful life. Ultimately, these assets will be used up as a result of wear and tear, obsolescence, and so on. The amount of a particular asset that has been used up over time, as a result of being used since the business first acquired it, is referred to as *depreciation*. Depreciation is an expense of running the business and the amount involved each year appears in the profit and loss account. The total depreciation relating to a fixed asset will normally be deducted from the cost of the asset on the balance sheet. This procedure is not really a contravention of the historic cost convention. It is simply recognition of the fact that a proportion of the fixed asset has been consumed in the process of generating benefits for the business. (The concept of depreciation is considered in more detail in the next chapter.)

There are, however, examples where the historic cost convention is contravened. We saw earlier that some assets *appreciate* in value over time. Freehold property was mentioned as an example of an asset that has appreciated in value a great deal in past years. As a result of this appreciation, it has become widespread practice to revalue freehold property by using current market values rather than historic cost. This practice not only contravenes the historic cost convention, it also contravenes the objectivity convention. This is because an opinion of what is the current market value is substituted for a cost figure (which is usually a matter of verifiable fact).

Exhibit 2.3 Dealing with market valuations

In practice, the reporting of market values for land and buildings is done in various ways. One approach is to stick with the historic cost figures in the balance sheet and then to show the market values as a note to the balance sheet. The published balance sheet for 2002 for Oxford Instruments plc, a business specialising in advanced instrument technology, records the historic cost (less depreciation) of its property as £21,756,000 on the balance sheet. However, the business states, as a note to the financial statements, that the directors believe that the open market value of the freehold land and buildings exceeds the balance sheet figure stated by £6.0 million. By reporting market values in this way, the historic cost convention has not been breached. However, where the historic cost figures are substituted for market value figures in the balance sheet, as discussed above, the convention is breached. In such cases it is usual to report the historic cost figures as a note to the balance sheet.

In some cases, a mixture of cost and valuation figures may be used on the balance sheet. The published balance sheet for 2001 of Spirax-Sarco-Engineering plc records freehold land and buildings in this way. A breakdown of the figures, and the relevant valuation dates, are as follows:

Exhibit 2.3 continued

	£000
Freehold land and buildings	
Valuation	
1976	63
1986	6,819
1991	2,421
Cost	39,107
	48,410

The business states as a note to the financial statements that the historic cost (less depreciation) of freehold land and buildings for 2001 was £37,607(000). Thus, it seems that the revaluations in 1976, 1986 and 1991 led to valuation figures for freehold land and buildings that exceeded their historic cost.

We can see that there are exceptions to the rule that assets are recorded at their historic cost. Moreover, the list of exceptions appears to be growing. In recent years, the balance sheets of many businesses have increasingly reflected a mixture of valuation approaches. This trend is a matter of concern for the accountancy profession, as users are likely to find a variety of valuation methods confusing when trying to assess financial position.

Interpreting the balance sheet

We have seen that the conventional balance sheet has a number of limitations. This has led some users of financial information to conclude that the balance sheet has little to offer in the way of useful information. However, this is not necessarily the case. The balance sheet can provide useful insights into the financing and investing activities of a business. We shall consider this in detail in Chapter 6 when we deal with the analysis and interpretation of the financial statements.

Summary

The main points of the chapter may be summarised as follows:

■ *The major financial statements*:
  ❑ there are three major financial statements – the cash flow statement, the profit and loss account and the balance sheet;
  ❑ the cash flow statement shows the cash movements over a particular period;
  ❑ the profit and loss account shows the wealth (profit) generated over a particular period;
  ❑ the balance sheet shows the accumulated wealth at a particular point in time.

- *The balance sheet*:
  - ❏ sets out the assets of the business, on the one hand, and the claims against those assets, on the other;
  - ❏ assets are resources of the business that have certain characteristics, such as the ability to provide future benefits;
  - ❏ claims are obligations on the part of the business to provide cash, or some other benefit, to outside parties;
  - ❏ claims are of two types – capital and liabilities;
  - ❏ capital represents the owner's claim and liabilities represent the claims of others, apart from the owner.

- *Classification of assets and liabilities*:
  - ❏ assets are normally categorised as being fixed or current;
  - ❏ fixed assets are held for use within the business on a continuing basis;
  - ❏ current assets are assets that are not held on a continuing basis and include cash and items that are expected to be converted into cash;
  - ❏ long-term liabilities represent those amounts not due for repayment within 12 months;
  - ❏ current liabilities represent amounts due for repayment within 12 months.

- *Balance sheet formats*:
  - ❏ the horizontal format sets out the assets on one side of the balance sheet and the capital and liabilities on the other side;
  - ❏ the vertical format begins with the assets at the top of the balance sheet and deducts the liabilities. The resulting figure represents the net assets of the business. The capital of the business is shown at the bottom of the balance sheet.

- *Accounting conventions*:
  - ❏ accounting conventions have evolved to deal with practical problems experienced by preparers;
  - ❏ the main conventions relating to the balance sheet include business entity, money measurement, historic cost, going concern, dual aspect, prudence, stable monetary unit and objectivity.

- *Asset valuation*:
  - ❏ current assets are shown at the lower of cost or net realisable value;
  - ❏ fixed assets are normally shown at historic cost less any amounts written off for depreciation. However, there are cases where the current market values are used rather than cost.

→ **Key terms**

cash flow statement *p 20*	current liabilities *p 34*
profit and loss account *p 20*	accounting conventions *p 39*
balance sheet *p 20*	business entity convention *p 39*
assets *p 24*	money measurement
claims *p 24*	convention *p 39*
tangible assets *p 26*	historic cost convention *p 41*
intangible assets *p 26*	going concern convention *p 41*
capital *p 27*	dual aspect convention *p 42*
liabilities *p 27*	prudence convention *p 42*
fixed assets *p 32*	stable monetary unit
current assets *p 33*	convention *p 43*
long-term liabilities *p 34*	objectivity convention *p 44*

? **Review questions**

Answers to these questions can be found on the students' side of the Companion Website.

2.1 An accountant prepared a balance sheet for a business using the horizontal layout. In the balance sheet, the capital of the owner was shown next to the liabilities. This confused the owner, who argued: 'My capital is my major asset and so should be shown as an asset on the balance sheet.' How would you explain this misunderstanding to the owner?

2.2 'The balance sheet shows how much a business is worth.' Do you agree with this statement? Discuss.

2.3 What is meant by the balance sheet equation? How does the form of this equation differ between the horizontal and vertical balance sheet format?

2.4 In recent years there have been attempts to place a value on the 'human assets' of a business in order to derive a figure that can be included on the balance sheet. Do you think humans should be treated as assets? Would 'human assets' meet the conventional definition of an asset for inclusion on the balance sheet?

? **Exercises**

Exercise 2.5 is more advanced than 2.1–2.4. Those questions with a coloured number have answers at the back of the book.

2.1 While on holiday in Bridlington, Helen had her credit cards and purse stolen from a beach while she was swimming. She was left with only £40, which she had stored in her hotel room, but she had three days of her holiday remaining. She was determined to continue her holiday, and decided to make some money to do so. She decided to sell orange juice to holidaymakers using the local beach. On day 1 she purchased 80 cartons of orange juice at £0.50 each for cash and sold 70 of these at £0.80 each. On the following day she purchased 60 cartons for cash at £0.50 each and sold 65 at £0.80 each. On the third and final day she purchased another 60 cartons for cash at £0.50 each. However, it rained and, as a result, business was poor. She managed to sell 20 at £0.80 each but sold off the rest of her stock at £0.40 each.

Required:
Prepare a profit and loss account and cash flow statement for each day's trading, and prepare a balance sheet at the end of each day's trading.

2.2 On 1 March Joe Conday started a new business. During March he carried out the following transactions:

March 1 Deposited £20,000 in a bank account.
     2 Purchased fixtures and fittings for £6,000 cash, and stock £8,000 on credit.
     3 Borrowed £5,000 from a relative for a two-year period and deposited it in the bank.
     4 Purchased a motor car for £7,000 cash and withdrew £200 for own use.
     5 Another motor car costing £9,000 was purchased. The motor car purchased on 4 March was given in part exchange at a value of £6,500. The balance of purchase price for the new car was paid in cash.
     6 Conday won £2,000 in a lottery and paid the amount into the business bank account. He also repaid £1,000 of the loan.

Required:
(a) Draw up a balance sheet for the business at the end of each day using the horizontal format.
(b) Show how the balance sheet you have prepared as at 6 March would be presented in the vertical format. (Present the balance sheet in good form.)

2.3 The following is a list of assets and claims of a manufacturing business at a particular point in time:

	£
Bank overdraft	22,000
Freehold land and buildings	245,000
Stock of raw materials	18,000
Trade creditors	23,000
Plant and machinery	127,000
Loan from Industrial Finance Corporation	100,000
Stock of finished goods	28,000
Delivery vans	54,000
Trade debtors	34,000

Required:
Write out a balance sheet in the standard vertical format incorporating these figures.
Hint: There is a missing item that needs to be deduced and inserted.

2.4 The following is a list of the assets and claims of Crafty Engineering at 30 June last year:

	£000
Creditors	86
Motor vehicles	38
Loan from bank	260
Machinery and tools	207
Bank overdraft	116
Stock-in-trade	153
Freehold premises	320
Debtors	185

(Note that one figure is missing and needs to be deduced.)

Required:
(a) Prepare the balance sheet of the business as at 30 June last year from the above information using the vertical format.
(b) Discuss the significant features revealed by this financial statement.

2.5 The balance sheet of a business at the start of the week is as follows:

Assets	£	Claims	£
Freehold premises	145,000	Capital	203,000
Furniture and fittings	63,000	Bank overdraft	43,000
Stock-in-trade	28,000	Trade creditors	23,000
Trade debtors	33,000		
	£269,000		£269,000

During the week the following transactions took place:

■ Sold stock for £11,000 cash. This stock had cost £8,000.
■ Sold stock for £23,000 on credit. This stock had cost £17,000.
■ Received cash from trade debtors totalling £18,000.
■ The owners of the business introduced £100,000 of their own money, which was placed in the business bank account.
■ The owners brought a motor van, valued at £10,000, into the business.
■ Bought stock-in-trade on credit for £14,000.
■ Paid trade creditors £13,000.

Required:
Show the balance sheet at the end of the week after all of these transactions have been reflected.

Chapter 3

Measuring and reporting financial performance

Introduction

In this chapter, we shall continue our examination of the major financial statements by looking at the profit and loss account. This statement was briefly considered in Chapter 2 and we shall now examine it in some detail. We shall see how this statement is prepared and how it links with the balance sheet. We shall also consider some of the key measurement problems to be faced when preparing this statement.

Objectives

Having completed this chapter, you should be able to:

- discuss the nature and purpose of the profit and loss account
- prepare a profit and loss account from relevant financial information
- discuss the main measurement issues that must be considered when preparing the profit and loss account
- explain the main accounting conventions underpinning the profit and loss account.

The profit and loss account (income statement)

In the previous chapter, we examined the nature and purpose of the balance sheet. We saw that this statement was concerned with setting out the financial position of a business at a particular moment in time. However, it is not usually enough for users to have information relating only to the amount of wealth held by a business at one moment in time. Businesses exist for the primary purpose of generating wealth, or profit, and it is the profit generated *during a period* that is the main concern of many users of financial statements. Although the amount of profit generated is of particular interest to the owners of a business, other groups such as managers, employees and suppliers will also have an interest in the profit-making ability of the business. The purpose of the profit and loss (P and L) account – or income statement, as it is sometimes called – is to measure and report how much **profit** (wealth) the business has generated over a period. As with the balance sheet that we examined in Chapter 2, the profit and loss account is prepared following the same principles, irrespective of whether the business is a sole proprietorship or a limited company.

The measurement of profit requires that the total revenues of the business, generated during a particular period, be identified. **Revenue** is simply a measure of the inflow of assets (such as cash, or amounts owed to a business by debtors) or the reduction in liabilities that arise as a result of trading operations. Different forms of business enterprise will generate different forms of revenue. Some examples of the different forms that revenue can take are as follows:

- sales of goods (for example, of a manufacturer);
- fees for services (for example, of a solicitor);
- subscriptions (for example, of a club);
- interest received (for example, of an investment fund).

The total expenses relating to each accounting period must also be identified. An **expense** represents the outflow of assets (or increase in liabilities) that is incurred as a result of generating revenues, or attempting to generate them. The nature of the business will again determine the type of expenses that will be incurred. Examples of some of the more common types of expenses are:

- the cost of buying goods that are subsequently sold – known as *cost of sales* or *cost of goods sold*;
- salaries and wages;
- rent and rates;
- motor vehicle running expenses;
- insurances;
- printing and stationery;
- heat and light;
- telephone and postage, and so on.

The profit and loss account for a particular period simply shows the total revenue generated during that period and deducts from this the total expenses incurred in generating that revenue. The difference between the total revenue and total expenses will represent either profit (if revenues exceed expenses) or loss (if expenses exceed revenues). Thus, we have:

Profit (loss) for the period = Total revenue for the period
less **Total expenses incurred**
in generating the revenue

Relationship between the profit and loss account and the balance sheet

The profit and loss account and the balance sheet should not be viewed in any way as substitutes for one another. Rather they should be seen as performing different functions. The balance sheet is, as stated earlier, a statement of the financial position of a business at a single moment in time – a 'snapshot' of the stock of wealth held by the business. The profit and loss account, on the other hand, is concerned with the *flow* of wealth over a period of time. The two statements are closely related. The profit and loss account can be viewed as linking the balance sheet at the beginning of the period with the balance sheet at the end. Thus, at the commencement of business, a balance sheet will be produced to reveal the opening financial position. After an appropriate period, a profit and loss account will be prepared to show the wealth generated over the period. A balance sheet will also be prepared to reveal the new financial position at the end of the period covered by the profit and loss account. This balance sheet will incorporate the changes in wealth that have occurred since the previous balance sheet was drawn up.

We saw in the previous chapter (p. 31) that the effect on the balance sheet of making a profit (loss) means that the equation can be extended as follows:

$$\text{Assets} = \text{Capital} + (-) \text{ Profit (Loss)} + \text{Liabilities}$$

The amount of profit or loss for the period affects the balance sheet as an adjustment to capital.

The above equation can be extended to:

$$\text{Assets} = \text{Capital} + (\text{Revenues} - \text{Expenses}) + \text{Liabilities}$$

In theory, it would be possible to calculate profit and loss for the period by making all adjustments for revenues and expenses through the capital account. However, this would be rather cumbersome. A better solution is to have an 'appendix' to capital in the form of a profit and loss account. By deducting expenses from the revenues for the period, the profit and loss account derives the profit (loss) for adjustment in the capital item in the balance sheet. This figure represents the net effect of operations for the period. Providing this 'appendix' means that a detailed and more informative view of performance is presented to users.

The format of the profit and loss account

The format of the profit and loss account will vary according to the type of business to which it relates. To illustrate a profit and loss account, let us consider the case of a retail business (that is, a business that purchases goods in their completed state and resells them). This type of business usually has straightforward operations, and as a result the profit and loss account is relatively easy to understand.

Example 3.1 sets out a typical format for the profit and loss account of a retail business.

Example 3.1

Hi-Price Stores
Trading and profit and loss account for the year ended 31 October 2003

	£	£
Sales		232,000
Less Cost of sales		154,000
Gross profit		78,000
Add Interest received from investments		2,000
		80,000
Less Salaries and wages	24,500	
Rent and rates	14,200	
Heat and light	7,500	
Telephone and postage	1,200	
Insurance	1,000	
Motor vehicle running expenses	3,400	
Loan interest	1,100	
Depreciation – fixtures and fittings	1,000	
Depreciation – motor van	600	
		54,500
Net profit		25,500

The first part of the statement is concerned with calculating the **gross profit** for the period. The trading revenue, which arises from selling the goods, is the first item that appears. Deducted from this item is the trading expense, which is the cost of acquiring the goods sold during the period. The difference between the trading revenue and trading expense is referred to as gross profit. This represents the profit from simply buying and selling goods without taking into account any other expenses or revenues associated with the business. This first part of the statement, which is concerned with the calculation of gross profit, is referred to as the *trading account* or *trading section*. The remainder of the statement is referred to as the *profit and loss account* or *P and L section*. Hence the heading of **trading and profit and loss account**, shown above. (It is often the case, however, that the term *profit and loss account* is used to describe the whole of this statement.)

Having calculated the gross profit, any additional sources of revenues of the business are then added to this figure. In the above example, interest from investments represents an additional source of revenue. From this subtotal of gross profit and additional revenues, the other expenses (overheads) that have to be incurred in order to operate the business (salaries and wages, rent and rates and so on) are deducted. The final figure derived is the **net profit** for the period. This net profit figure represents the wealth generated during the period that is attributable to the owner(s) of the business and which will be added to their capital in the balance sheet. As can be seen, net profit is a residual – that is, the amount left over after deducting all expenses incurred in generating the sales for the period.

The profit and loss account – some further aspects

Having set out the main principles involved in preparing a profit and loss account, we need to consider some further points.

Cost of sales

➡ The **cost of sales** figure for a period can be identified in different ways. In some businesses, the cost of sales is identified at the time a sale has been made. Sales are closely matched with the cost of those sales and so identifying the cost of sales figure for inclusion in the profit and loss account is not a problem. Many large retailers (for example, supermarkets) have point-of-sale (checkout) devices that not only record each sale but also simultaneously pick up the cost of the particular sale. Other businesses that sell a relatively small number of high-value items (for example, an engineering business that produces custom-made equipment) also tend to match sales with the cost of the goods sold at the time of the sale. However, some businesses (for example, small retailers) do not usually find it practical to match each sale to a particular cost of sale figure as the accounting period progresses. They find it easier to identify the cost of sales figure at the end of the accounting period.

To understand how this is done, it is important to recognise that the cost of sales figure represents the cost of goods that were *sold* during the period rather than the cost of goods that were *purchased* during the period. Part of the goods purchased during a particular period may remain in stock and not be sold until a later period. To derive the cost of sales for a period, it is necessary to know the amount of opening stocks and closing stocks for the period and the cost of goods purchased during the period. Example 3.2 below illustrates how the cost of sales is derived.

Example 3.2

Hi-Price Stores, which we considered in Example 3.1 above, began the year ended 31 October 2003 with unsold stock of £40,000 and during that year purchased stock at a cost of £189,000. At the end of the year, unsold stock of £75,000 was still held by the business.

The opening stock at the beginning of the year *plus* the goods purchased during the year will represent the total goods available for resale. Thus:

	£
Opening stock	40,000
Plus Goods purchased	189,000
Goods available for resale	229,000

The closing stock will represent that portion of the total goods available for resale that remains unsold at the end of the period. Thus, the cost of goods actually sold during the period must be the total goods available for resale *less* the stocks remaining at the end of the period.

That is:

	£
Goods available for resale	229,000
Less Closing stock	75,000
Cost of goods sold (or cost of sales)	154,000

These calculations are sometimes shown on the face of the trading account as in Example 3.3.

Example 3.3

	£	£
Sales		232,000
Less Cost of sales		
Opening stock	40,000	
Plus Goods purchased	189,000	
	229,000	
Less Closing stock	75,000	154,000
Gross profit		78,000

The trading account above is simply an expanded version of the earlier trading account for Hi-Price Stores shown in Example 3.1. We have simply included the additional information concerning stock balances and purchases for the year provided in Example 3.2.

Classification of expenses

The classifications for the revenue and expense items, as with the classifications of various assets and claims in the balance sheet, are often a matter of judgement by those who design the accounting system. In the profit and loss account in Example 3.1, the insurance expense could have been included with telephone and postage under a single heading – say, general expenses. Such decisions are normally based on how useful a particular classification will be to users. However, for businesses that trade as limited companies, there are statutory rules that dictate the classification of various items appearing in the accounts for external reporting purposes. These rules will be discussed in Chapter 4.

Activity 3.1

The following information relates to the activities of H & S Retailers for the year ended 30 April 2003:

	£
Motor vehicle running expenses	1,200
Rent received from subletting	2,000
Closing stock	3,000
Rent and rates payable	5,000
Motor vans	6,300
Annual depreciation – motor vans	1,500
Heat and light	900
Telephone and postage	450
Sales	97,400
Goods purchased	68,350
Insurance	750
Loan interest payable	620
Balance at bank	4,780
Salaries and wages	10,400
Opening stock	4,000

Prepare a trading and profit and loss account for the year ended 30 April 2003. (*Hint*: Not all items shown above should appear on this statement.)

Your answer to this activity should be as follows:

H & S Retailers
Trading and profit and loss account for the year ended 30 April 2003

	£	£
Sales		97,400
Less Cost of sales		
Opening stock	4,000	
Plus Purchases	68,350	
	72,350	
Less Closing stock	3,000	69,350
Gross profit		28,050
Rent received		2,000
		30,050
Less Salaries and wages	10,400	
Rent and rates	5,000	
Heat and light	900	
Telephone and postage	450	
Insurance	750	
Motor vehicle running expenses	1,200	
Loan interest	620	
Depreciation – motor van	1,500	
		20,820
Net profit		9,230

In the case of the balance sheet, we saw that the information could be presented in either a horizontal format or a vertical format. This is also true of the trading and profit and loss account. Where a horizontal format is used, expenses are listed on the left-hand side and revenues on the right-hand side, the difference being either net profit or net loss. The vertical format has been used above as it is easier to understand and is now almost always used.

The reporting period

We have seen already that for reporting to those outside the business, a financial reporting cycle of one year is the norm, though some large businesses will produce a half-yearly, or interim, financial statement to provide more frequent feedback on progress. For those who manage a business, however, it is important to have much more frequent feedback on performance. Thus it is quite common for profit and loss accounts to be prepared on a quarterly or monthly basis in order to show the progress made during the year.

Profit measurement and the recognition of revenue

A key issue in the measurement of profit concerns the point at which revenue is recognised. It is possible to recognise revenue at different points in the production/selling cycle, and the particular point chosen could have a significant effect on the total revenues reported for the period.

Activity 3.2

A manufacturing business sells goods on credit (that is, the customer is allowed to pay some time after the goods have been received). Below are four points in the production/selling cycle at which revenue might be recognised by the business:

1 when the goods are produced
2 when an order is received from a customer
3 when the goods are delivered to, and accepted by, the customer
4 when the cash is received from the customer.

A significant amount of time may elapse between these different points. At what point do you think the business should recognise revenue?

Although you may have come to a different conclusion, the point at which we normally recognise revenue is 3 above. The reasons for this are explained below.

The *realisation convention* in accounting is designed to solve the revenue recognition problem (or at least to provide some consistency). This convention states that revenue should be recognised only when it has been realised. Normally, realisation is considered to have occurred when:

- the activities necessary to generate the revenue (for example, delivery of goods, carrying out of repairs, and so on) are substantially complete;
- the amount of revenue generated can be objectively determined;
- there is reasonable certainty that the amounts owing from the activities will be received.

Activity 3.3

Look back at the various points in the production/selling cycle at which revenue might be recognised as set out in the previous activity. At which of these points do you think the criteria for realisation will be fulfilled for the manufacturing business?

The criteria will probably be fulfilled when the goods are passed to the customers and are accepted by them. As we mentioned earlier, this is the normal point of recognition when goods are sold on credit. It is also the point at which there is a legally enforceable contract between the parties.

→ The **realisation convention** in accounting means that a sale on credit is usually recognised *before* the cash is received. Thus, the total sales figure shown in the profit and loss account may include sales transactions for which the cash has yet to be received. The total sales figure in the profit and loss account will therefore be different from the total cash received from sales.

Not all businesses will wait to recognise revenue until *all* of the work necessary to generate the revenue is complete. A construction business, for example, that is engaged in a long-term project such as building a dam will not usually wait until the contract is complete before doing so. Were it to wait, this could mean that no revenue would be recognised by the business until several years after the work first commenced. Instead, the business will normally recognise a proportion of the total value of the contract when an agreed stage of the contract has been completed. This approach to revenue recognition is really a more practical interpretation of the realisation convention, rather than a deviation from it.

Exhibit 3.1 **Recognising revenue**

Applying the principles of revenue recognition that we discussed above may seem fairly straightforward. However, this is not always the case, particularly for businesses operating within new sectors of the economy. Such businesses often have different views about the point at which revenue should be recognised. The telecommunications industry provides a useful illustration of this point. This industry includes businesses that lease network capacity to other, similar businesses so that those businesses can improve their network coverage. In practice, the sale of such capacity can be recognised as revenue either in the period in which the network lease agreement is made or in the period over which the lease agreement extends, which can be as long as 20 years. This difference in approach to revenue recognition can, of course, have a profound impact on both reported revenues and profit for a period.

Source: 'Running scared in the face of fraud allegations', *Financial Times* Weekend, 29/30 June 2002, p. 16

Profit measurement and the recognition of expenses

Having decided on the point at which revenue is recognised, we must now turn to the issue of the recognition of expenses. The **matching convention** in accounting is designed to provide guidance concerning the recognition of expenses. This convention states that expenses should be matched to the revenues that they helped to generate. In other words, expenses must be taken into account in the same profit and loss account in which the associated sale is recognised. Applying this convention may mean that a particular expense reported in the profit and loss account for a period may not be the same figure as the cash paid in respect of that item during the period. The expense reported may be either more or less than the cash paid during the period. Let us consider two examples that illustrate this point.

When the expense for the period is more than the cash paid during the period

Example 3.4

Domestic Ltd retails household electrical appliances. It pays its sales staff a commission of 2 per cent of sales generated, and total sales for the year amounted to £300,000. This will mean that the commission to be paid in respect of the sales for the period will be £6,000. However, by the end of the period, the sales commission paid to staff was £5,000. If the business reported only the amount paid, it would mean that the profit and loss account would not reflect the full expense for the year. This would contravene the *matching convention* because not all of the expenses associated with the revenues of the period would have been matched in the profit and loss account. This will be remedied as follows:

- Sales commission expense in the profit and loss account will include the amount paid *plus* the amount outstanding (that is, £6,000 = £5,000 + £1,000).
- The amount outstanding (£1,000) represents an outstanding liability at the balance sheet date and will be included under the heading 'accruals' or **accrued expenses** in the balance sheet. As this item will have to be paid within 12 months of the balance sheet date, it will be treated as a current liability.
- The cash will be reduced to reflect the commission paid (£5,000) during the period.

  These points are illustrated in Figure 3.1.

In principle, all expenses should be matched to the period in which the sales to which they relate are reported. However, it is sometimes difficult to match closely certain expenses to sales in the same precise way that we have matched sales commission to sales. It is unlikely, for example, that electricity charges incurred can be linked directly to particular sales in this way. As a result, the electricity charges incurred by, say, a retailer would be matched to the *period* to which they relate. Example 3.5 illustrates this.

Figure 3.1 Accounting for sales commission

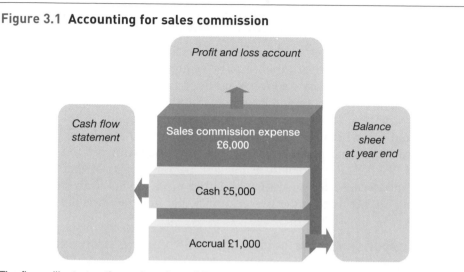

The figure illustrates the main points of Example 3.3. We can see that the sales commission expense of £6,000 (which appears in the profit and loss account) is made up of a cash element £5,000 and an accrued element £1,000. The cash element appears in the cash flow statement and the accruals element will appear as a year end liability in the balance sheet.

Example 3.5

Domestic Ltd has reached the end of its accounting year and has only been charged electricity for the first three quarters of the year (amounting to £1,900). This is simply because the electricity company has yet to send out bills for the quarter that ends on the same date as Domestic Ltd's year end. In this situation, an estimate should be made of the electricity expense outstanding (that is, the bill for the last three months of the year is estimated). This figure (let us say the estimate is £500) is dealt with as follows:

- Electricity expense in the profit and loss account will include the amount paid, plus the amount of the estimate (that is, £1,900 + £500 = £2,400) in order to cover the whole year.
- The amount of the estimate (£500) represents an outstanding liability at the balance sheet date, and will be included under the heading 'accruals' or 'accrued expenses' in the balance sheet. As this item will have to be paid within 12 months of the balance sheet date, it will be treated as a current liability.
- The cash will be reduced to reflect the electricity paid (£1,900) during the period.

The above treatment will have the desired effect of increasing the electricity expense to the 'correct' figure for the year in the profit and loss account, presuming that the estimate is reasonably accurate. It will also have the effect of showing that, at the end of the accounting year, Domestic Ltd owed the amount of the last quarter's electricity bill. Dealing with the outstanding amount in this way reflects the dual aspect of the item, and will ensure that the balance sheet equation is maintained.

Activity 3.4

Let us say the estimate for outstanding electricity was correct. How will the payment of the electricity bill be dealt with?

When the electricity bill is eventually paid, it will be dealt with as follows:

■ Reduce cash by the amount of the bill.
■ Reduce the amount of the accrued expense as shown on the balance sheet.

If there is a slight error in the estimate, a small adjustment (either negative or positive depending on the direction of the error) can be made to the following year's expense. Dealing with the estimation error in this way is not strictly correct, but the amount is likely to be insignificant.

Activity 3.5

Can you think of other expenses, apart from electricity charges, that cannot be linked directly to sales and for which matching will therefore be done on a time basis?

You may have thought of the following examples:

■ rent and rates
■ insurance
■ interest payments
■ licences.

This is not an exhaustive list. You may have thought of others.

When the amount paid during the year is more than the full expense for the period

It is not unusual for a business to be in a situation where it has paid more during the year than the full expense for that year. Example 3.6 below illustrates how we deal with this.

Example 3.6

Images Ltd, an advertising agency, pays rent for its premises quarterly in advance (on 1 January, 1 April, 1 July and 1 October) and, on the last day of the accounting year (31 December), it pays the next quarter's rent (£4,000) to the following 31 March, which is a day earlier than required. This would mean that a total of five quarters' rent was paid during the year. If Images Ltd reports the cash paid in the profit and loss account, this would be more than the full expense for the year. This treatment would also contravene the matching convention because a higher figure than the expenses associated with the revenues of the year would appear in the profit and loss account.

The problem is overcome by dealing with the rental payment as follows:

- Show the rent for four quarters as the appropriate expense in the profit and loss account (that is, $4 \times £4,000 = £16,000$).
- Reduce the cash to reflect the full amount of the rent paid during the year (that is, $5 \times £4,000 = £20,000$).
- Show the quarter's rent paid in advance (£4,000) as a **prepaid expense** on the asset side of the balance sheet. (The prepaid expense will appear as a current asset in the balance sheet, under the heading 'prepayments'.)

In the next accounting period, this prepayment will cease to be an asset and will become an expense in the profit and loss account of that period. This is because the rent prepaid relates to that period and will be 'used up' during that period.

In practice, the treatment of accruals and prepayments will be subject to the **materiality convention** of accounting. This convention states that, where the amounts involved are immaterial, we should consider only what is expedient. This may mean that an item will be treated as an expense in the period in which it is paid, rather than being strictly matched to the revenues to which it relates. For example, a business may find that, at the end of an accounting period, there is a bill of £5 owing for stationery used during the year. The time and effort involved in recording this

Figure 3.2 Accounting for rent payable

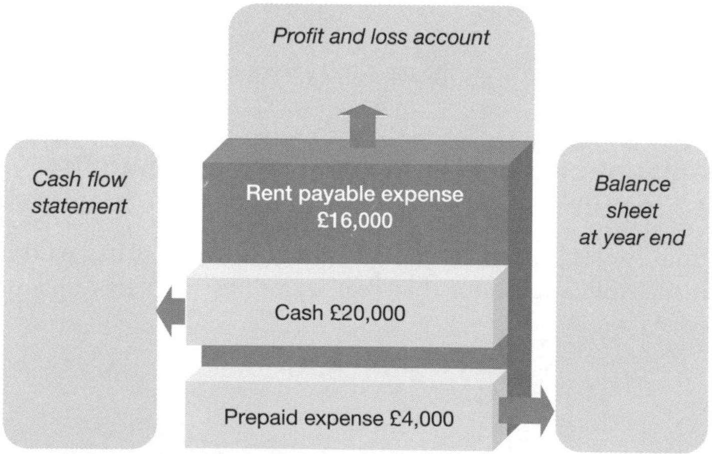

The figure illustrates the main points of Example 3.6. We can see that the rent expense of £16,000 (which appears in the profit and loss account) is made up of four quarters' rent at £4,000 per quarter. This is the amount that relates to the period and is 'used up' during the period. The cash paid of £20,000 (which appears in the cash flow statement) is made up of the cash paid during the period, which is five quarters at £4,000 per quarter. Finally, the prepayment of £4,000 (which appears on the balance sheet) represents the payment made on 31 March and relates to the next financial year.

as an accrual would have little effect on the measurement of profit or financial position for a business of any size, and so it would be ignored when preparing the profit and loss account for the period. The bill would, presumably, be paid in the following period and therefore be treated as an expense of that period.

Profit and cash

The foregoing sections on revenues and expenses reveal that revenues do not usually represent cash received, and expenses are not the same as cash paid. As a result, the net profit figure (that is, total revenue minus total expenses) will not normally represent the net cash generated during a period. It is therefore important to distinguish between profit and liquidity. Profit is a measure of achievement, or productive effort, rather than a measure of cash generated. Although making a profit will increase wealth, we have already seen in the previous chapter that cash is only one form in which that wealth may be held.

Profit measurement and the calculation of depreciation

The expense of **depreciation**, which appeared in the profit and loss account above, requires further explanation. Fixed assets (with the exception of freehold land) do not have a perpetual existence. They are eventually used up in the process of generating revenues for the business. In essence, depreciation is an attempt to measure that portion of the cost of a fixed asset that has been used up in generating the revenues recognised during a particular period. The depreciation charge is considered to be an expense of the period to which it relates.

To calculate a depreciation charge for a period, four factors have to be considered:

- the cost of the asset;
- the useful life of the asset;
- the residual value of the asset;
- the depreciation method.

The cost of the asset

This will include all costs incurred by the business to bring the asset to its required location and to make it ready for use. Thus, in addition to the costs of acquiring the asset, any delivery costs, installation costs (for example, setting up a new machine) and legal costs incurred in the transfer of legal title (for example, in the case of freehold property) will be included as part of the total cost of the asset. Similarly, any costs incurred in improving or altering an asset in order to make it suitable for its intended use within the business will also be included as part of the total cost.

Activity 3.6

Andrew Wu (Engineering) Ltd purchased a new motorcar for its marketing director. The invoice received from the motorcar supplier revealed the following:

	£	£
New BMW 325i		26,350
Delivery charge	80	
Alloy wheels	660	
Sun roof	200	
Petrol	30	
Number plates	130	
Road fund licence	160	1,260
		27,610
Part exchange – Reliant Robin		1,000
Amount outstanding		26,610

What is the total cost of the new car that will be treated as part of the business's fixed assets?

The cost of the new car will be as follows:

	£	£
New BMW 325i		26,350
Delivery charge	80	
Alloy wheels	660	
Sun roof	200	
Number plates	130	1,070
		27,420

These costs include delivery costs and number plates as they are a necessary and integral part of the asset. Improvements (alloy wheels and sun roof) are also regarded as part of the total cost of the motorcar. The petrol costs and road fund licence, however, represent a cost of operating the asset rather than a part of the total cost of acquiring the asset and making it ready for use: hence these amounts will be charged as an expense in the period incurred (although part of the cost of the licence may be regarded as a prepaid expense in the period incurred).

The part-exchange figure shown is part payment of the total amount outstanding, and is not relevant to a consideration of the total cost.

The useful life of the asset

An asset has both a *physical life* and an *economic life*. The physical life of an asset will be exhausted through the effects of wear and tear and/or the passage of time. It is possible, however, for the physical life to be extended considerably through careful maintenance, improvements, and so on. The economic life of an asset is decided by the effects of technological progress and by changes in demand. After a while, the benefits of using the asset may be less than the costs involved. This may be because the asset is unable to compete with newer assets, or because it is no longer relevant to the needs of the business. The economic life of an asset may be much shorter than its physical life. For example, a computer may have a physical life of eight years and an economic life of three years.

It is the economic life of an asset that will determine the expected useful life for the purpose of calculating depreciation. Forecasting the economic life of an asset, however, may be extremely difficult in practice. Both the rate at which technology progresses and shifts in consumer tastes can be swift and unpredictable.

Residual value (disposal value)

When a business disposes of a fixed asset that may still be of value to others, some payment may be received. This payment will represent the **residual value**, or *disposal* *value*, of the asset. To calculate the total amount to be depreciated with regard to an asset, the residual value must be deducted from the cost of the asset. The likely amount to be received on disposal is, once again, often difficult to predict.

Depreciation method

Once the amount to be depreciated (that is, the cost of the asset less the residual value) has been estimated, the business must select a method of allocating this depreciable amount over the useful life of the fixed asset. Although there are various ways in which the total depreciation may be allocated and, from this, a depreciation charge for a period derived, there are really only two methods that are commonly used in practice.

The first of these is known as the **straight-line method**. This method simply allocates the amount to be depreciated evenly over the useful life of the asset. In other words, an equal amount of depreciation will be charged for each year the asset is held.

Example 3.7

To illustrate this method, consider the following information:

Cost of machine	£40,000
Estimated residual value at the end of its useful life	£1,024
Estimated useful life	4 years

To calculate the depreciation charge for each year, the total amount to be depreciated must be calculated. This will be the total cost *less* the estimated residual value: that is, £40,000 − £1,024 = £38,976. Having done this, the annual depreciation charge can be derived by dividing the amount to be depreciated by the estimated useful life of the asset of four years. The calculation is therefore:

$$\frac{£38,976}{4} = £9,744$$

Thus, the annual depreciation charge that appears in the profit and loss account in relation to this asset will be £9,744 for each of the four years of the asset's life.

The amount of depreciation relating to the asset will be accumulated for as long as the asset continues to be owned by the business. This accumulated depreciation figure will increase each year as a result of the annual depreciation amount charged to the profit and loss account. This accumulated amount will be deducted from the cost of the asset on the balance sheet.

Thus, for example, at the end of the second year the accumulated depreciation will be £9,744 × 2 = £19,488, and the asset details will appear on the balance sheet as follows:

	£	£
Machine at cost	40,000	
Less Accumulated depreciation	19,488	
		20,512

The balance of £20,512 shown above is referred to as the *written-down value* or *net book value* of the asset. It represents that portion of the cost of the asset that has still to be written off (that is, treated as an expense). It must be emphasised that this figure does *not* represent the current market value, which may be quite different.

The straight-line method derives its name from the fact that the written-down value of the asset at the end of each year, when graphed against time, will result in a straight line, as shown in Figure 3.3.

The second approach to calculating depreciation for a period is referred to as the **reducing-balance method**. This method applies a fixed percentage rate of depreciation to the written-down value of an asset each year. The effect of this will be high annual depreciation charges in the early years and lower charges in the later years. To illustrate this method, let us take the same information used in Example 3.7. It

Figure 3.3 Graph of written-down value against time using the straight-line method

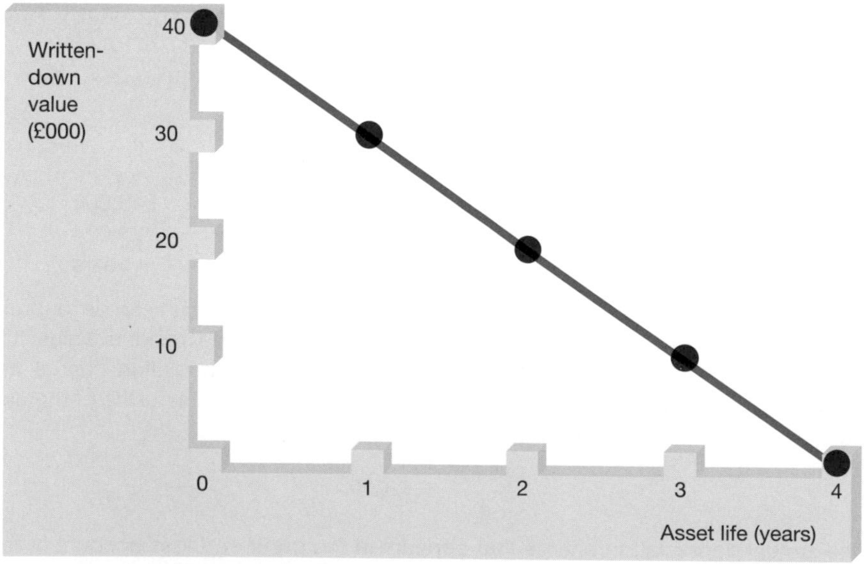

The figure shows that the written-down value of the asset declines by a constant amount each year. This is because the straight-line method provides a constant depreciation charge each year. The result, when plotted on a graph, is a straight line.

can be shown that using a fixed percentage of 60 per cent of the written-down value to determine the annual depreciation charge will have the effect of reducing the written-down value to £1,024 after four years.

The calculations will be as follows:

	£
Cost of machine	40,000
Year 1 Depreciation charge (60%* of cost)	(24,000)
Written-down value (WDV)	16,000
Year 2 Depreciation charge (60% WDV)	(9,600)
Written-down value	6,400
Year 3 Depreciation charge (60% WDV)	(3,840)
Written-down value	2,560
Year 4 Depreciation charge (60% WDV)	(1,536)
Residual value	1,024

* Deriving the fixed percentage to be applied requires the use of the following formula:

$$P = (1 - \sqrt[n]{R/C}) \times 100\%$$

where: P = the depreciation percentage;
  n = the useful life of the asset (in years);
  R = the residual value of the asset;
  C = the cost of the asset.

The fixed percentage rate will, however, be given in all examples used in this text.

We can see that the pattern of depreciation is quite different for the two methods. If we plot the written-down value of the asset, which has been derived using the reducing-balance method, against time, the result will be as shown in Figure 3.4.

Activity 3.7

Assume that the machine used in the example above was owned by a business that made a profit *before* depreciation of £20,000 for each of the four years in which the asset was held.

  Calculate the net profit for the business for each year under each depreciation method, and comment on your findings.

Your answer should be as follows:

Straight-line method

	(a) Profit before depreciation £	(b) Depreciation £	(a–b) Net profit £
Year 1	20,000	9,744	10,256
Year 2	20,000	9,744	10,256
Year 3	20,000	9,744	10,256
Year 4	20,000	9,744	10,256

Activity 3.7 continued

Reducing-balance method

	(a) Profit before depreciation £	(b) Depreciation £	(a–b) Net profit/ (loss) £
Year 1	20,000	24,000	(4,000)
Year 2	20,000	9,600	10,400
Year 3	20,000	3,840	16,160
Year 4	20,000	1,536	18,464

The above calculations reveal that the straight-line method of depreciation results in a constant net profit figure over the four-year period. This is because both the profit before depreciation and the depreciation charge are constant over the period. The reducing-balance method, however, results in a changing profit figure over time. In the first year a net loss is reported, and thereafter a rising net profit is reported.

Figure 3.4 Graph of written-down value against time using the reducing-balance method

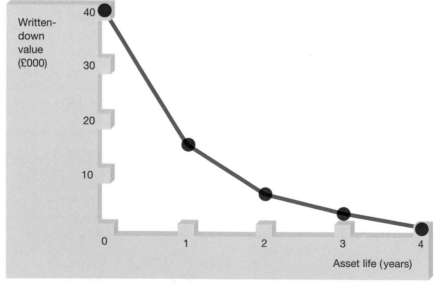

The figure shows that, under the reducing-balance method, the written-down value of an asset falls by a larger amount in the earlier years than in the later years. This is because the depreciation charge is based on a fixed-rate percentage of the written-down value.

Although the *pattern* of net profit over the period will be quite different, depending on the depreciation method used, the *total* net profit for the period will remain the same. This is because both methods of depreciating will allocate the same amount of total depreciation (£38,976) over the four-year period. It is only the amount allocated *between years* that will differ.

In practice, the use of different depreciation methods may not have such a dramatic effect on profits as suggested in the activity above. Where a business replaces some of its assets each year, the total depreciation charge calculated under the reducing balance method will reflect a range of charges (from high through to low), as assets will be at different points in the replacement cycle. This could mean that the total depreciation charge may not be significantly different from the total depreciation charge that would be derived under the straight-line method.

Selecting a depreciation method

How does a business choose which depreciation method to use for a particular asset? The most appropriate method should be the one that best matches the depreciation expense to the revenues that it helped generate. The business may therefore decide to undertake an examination of the pattern of benefits associated with each asset. Where the benefits are likely to remain fairly constant over time (buildings, for example), the straight-line method may be considered appropriate. Where assets lose their efficiency over time and the benefits decline as a result (for example, certain types of machinery), the reducing-balance method may be considered more appropriate. Where the pattern of economic benefits is uncertain, the straight-line method is usually chosen.

The accountancy profession has developed an accounting standard to deal with the problem of depreciation. As we shall see in Chapter 4, the purpose of accounting standards is to narrow the areas of difference in accounting between businesses by producing rules on best accounting practice. The standard for handling depreciation endorses the view that the depreciation method chosen should reflect the pattern of economic benefits flowing from the asset. The standard also requires that businesses disclose a fair amount of detail concerning depreciation charges in their financial statements. Thus, information such as the methods of depreciation used, the total depreciation for the period, the accumulated amount of depreciation at the beginning and end of the financial period and either the depreciation rates applied or the useful lives of the assets must be disclosed.

Exhibit 3.2

Thorntons plc, the manufacturer and retailer of confectionery, uses both the straight-line method and the reducing-balance method to depreciate its fixed assets. The financial statements for the year ended 30 June 2001 show the type of depreciation method used for certain classes of fixed assets and the period over which they are depreciated as follows:

▶

Exhibit 3.2 continued

In equal annual instalments	
Factory freehold premises	50 years
Short leasehold land and buildings	Period of the lease
Retail fixtures and fittings	5 years
Retail equipment	4 to 5 years
Retail shop improvements	10 years
Other equipment and vehicles	3 to 7 years
Manufacturing plant and machinery	12 to 15 years
In reducing annual instalments	
Motor cars	$33^1/_3$ % per year

Source: Thorntons plc, Annual Report 2001

We can see wide variations in the expected useful lives of the fixed assets held. We can see also that the vast majority of the fixed assets are depreciated using the straight-line method. It seems that the straight-line method is generally much more popular than the reducing-balance method.

In the case of certain intangible fixed assets such as research and development expenditure, determining the correct period over which the benefits extend may be extremely difficult. In practice, there are different approaches to dealing with this problem. Some businesses adopt a prudent view and write off such assets immediately, whereas others may write off the assets over time.

Depreciation and the replacement of fixed assets

There seems to be a misunderstanding in the minds of some people that the purpose of depreciation is to provide the funds for the replacement of an asset when it reaches the end of its useful life. However, this is *not* the purpose of depreciation as conventionally defined. It was mentioned earlier that depreciation represents an attempt to allocate the cost (less any residual value) of an asset over its expected useful life. The resulting depreciation charge in each period represents an expense, which is then used in the calculation of net profit for the period. Calculating the depreciation charge for a period is therefore necessary for the proper measurement of financial performance, and must be done whether or not the business intends to replace the asset in the future.

If there is an intention to replace the asset, the depreciation charge in the profit and loss account will not ensure that liquid funds are set aside by the business specifically for this purpose. Although the effect of a depreciation charge is to reduce net profit, and therefore to reduce the amount available for distribution to owners, the amounts retained within the business as a result may be invested in ways that are unrelated to the replacement of the specific asset.

Figure 3.5 Calculating an annual depreciation charge

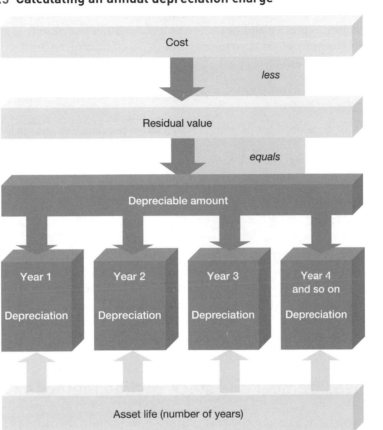

The figure shows how an annual depreciation charge is derived. The cost of an asset less the residual value will represent the amount to be depreciated. This amount is depreciated over the useful life (four years in this particular case) of the asset using an appropriate depreciation method.

Activity 3.8

Suppose that a business sets aside liquid funds, equivalent to the depreciation charge each year, with the intention of using these to replace the asset at the end of its useful life.

Will this ensure that there will be sufficient funds available for this purpose?

No. Even if funds are set aside each year that are equal to the depreciation charge for the year, the total amount accumulated at the end of the asset's useful life may be insufficient for replacement purposes. This may be because inflation or technological advances have resulted in an increase in the replacement cost.

Depreciation and judgement

When reading the above sections on depreciation it may have struck you that accounting is not as precise and objective as is sometimes suggested. There are areas where subjective judgement is required, and depreciation provides a good illustration of this.

Activity 3.9

What kind of judgements must be made to calculate a depreciation charge for a period?

In answering this activity, you may have thought of the following:

■ the expected residual or disposal value of the asset
■ the expected useful life of the asset
■ the choice of depreciation method.

Making different judgements on these matters would result in a different pattern of depreciation charges over the life of the asset, and therefore in a different pattern of reported profits. However, underestimations or overestimations that are made in relation to the above will be adjusted for in the final year of an asset's life, and so the total depreciation charge (and total profit) over the asset's life will not be affected by estimation errors.

Profit measurement and stock costing methods

The way in which we measure the cost of stock is important, because the cost of the stock sold during a period will affect the calculation of net profit, and the remaining stock held at the end of the period will affect the portrayal of the financial position. In the last chapter, we saw that historic cost is the basis for valuing assets, and so it is tempting to think that determining the cost of stocks held is not a difficult issue. However, in a period of *changing prices*, the costing of stock can be a problem.

A business must determine the cost of the stock sold during the period and the cost of the stock remaining at the end of the period. To do this, both of these costs are calculated as if it had been physically handled in a particular assumed manner. The assumption made has nothing to do with how the stock is *actually* handled; it is concerned only with which assumption is likely to lead to the most useful accounting information.

Two common assumptions used are:

■ **first in, first out (FIFO)**: that is, the earliest stocks held are the first to be sold;
■ **last in, first out (LIFO)**: that is, the latest stocks held are the first to be sold.

Another approach to deriving the cost of stocks is to assume that stocks entering the business lose their separate identity, and any issues of stock reflect the average cost of the stocks that are held. This is the **weighted average cost (AVCO)** method, where the weights used in deriving the average cost figures are the quantities of each batch of stock purchased. Example 3.8 below provides a simple illustration of the way in which each method is applied.

Example 3.8

A business commenced on 1 May to supply oil to factories. During this month, the following transactions took place:

	Tonnes	Cost per tonne
May 2 Purchased	10,000	£10
10 Purchased	20,000	£13
18 Sold	10,000	

Using the FIFO approach, it is the first 10,000 tonnes that are assumed to be sold first. The remainder, which are the later purchases, will comprise the closing stock. Thus we have:

Cost of sales (10,000 @ £10 per tonne)	£100,000
Closing stock (20,000 @ £13 per tonne)	£260,000

Using the LIFO approach, the later purchases are assumed to be the first to be sold and so the earlier purchases, plus any later purchases that remain unsold, will comprise the closing stock. Thus we have:

Cost of sales (10,000 @ £13 per tonne)	£130,000
Closing stock (10,000 @ £13 per tonne +10,000 @ £10 per tonne)	£230,000

Using the AVCO approach, the weighted average of the stock purchased during the period will be determined as follows:

Average cost = $[(10{,}000 \times £10) + (20{,}000 \times £13)]/(10{,}000 + 20{,}000) = £12$ per tonne

This cost per tonne will then be used to derive both the cost of goods sold and the cost of the remaining stocks. Thus we have:

Cost of sales (10,000 @ £12 per tonne)	£120,000
Closing stock (20,000 @ £12 per tonne)	£240,000

Activity 3.10

What would be the effect on the business of adopting each stock costing method in terms of:

(a) the size of the reported profit for the period, and
(b) the assets shown on the balance sheet at the end of the period?

Can you explain the effect of each method on reported profit and financial position?

Activity 3.10 continued

The FIFO method gives the lowest cost of sales figure, which when deducted from sales will give the highest gross profit figure. This method gives the lowest cost of sales figure because it reflects the cost of the earlier (and cheaper) stocks. This method will also give the highest stock figure in the balance sheet at the end of the period. This is because it is the later (and more expensive) stocks that are reflected in this figure.

The last in, first out approach gives the highest cost of sales figure and so will give the lowest gross profit figure. This approach gives the highest cost of sales figure because it reflects the cost of the later (and more expensive) stocks. This approach will also give the lowest stock figure in the balance sheet at the end of the period. This is because it is the earlier (and cheaper) stocks that are reflected in this figure. The weighted average cost will provide a cost of sales figure and closing stock figure that fall between the two extremes.

Where stock prices are rising, the FIFO method will give the highest gross profit and LIFO will give the lowest gross profit, with the AVCO method providing a figure between these two extremes. During a period of falling prices, the position of FIFO and LIFO is reversed.

It is important to recognise that the different stock valuation methods will only have an effect on the reported profit *between years*. The figure derived for closing stock will be carried forward and matched with sales in a later period. Thus, if the cheaper purchases of stocks are matched to sales in the current period, it will mean that the dearer purchases will be matched to sales in a later period. Over the life of the business, therefore, the total profit will be the same whichever valuation method is used.

The accountancy profession has produced an accounting standard to deal with the issue of stock valuation. The standard identifies a number of methods of arriving at the cost of stocks that are acceptable. Although FIFO and AVCO are regarded as acceptable, the LIFO approach is not. The LIFO approach is also unacceptable to the Inland Revenue for taxation purposes. As a result, LIFO is rarely used in the United Kingdom, although it is in widespread use in the United States.

Stock valuation and accounting conventions

We saw in the previous chapter that the closing stock figure will appear as part of the current assets of the business, and that the convention of prudence requires that current assets be valued at the lower of cost and net realisable value. (The net realisable value of stocks is the estimated selling price less any further costs that may be necessary to complete the goods and any costs involved in selling and distributing the goods.) This rule may mean that the valuation method applied to stocks will switch each year and differ from one type of stock to the next depending on whether cost or net realisable value is the lower. In practice, however, the cost of the stocks held is usually below the current net realisable value – particularly during a period of rising prices. It is, therefore, the cost figure that will normally appear in the balance sheet.

Activity 3.11

Can you think of any circumstances where the net realisable value will be lower than the cost of stocks held, even during a period of generally rising prices?

The net realisable value may be lower where:

- goods have deteriorated or have become obsolete
- there has been a fall in the market price of the goods
- the goods are being used as a 'loss leader'
- bad purchasing decisions have been made.

The accounting standard mentioned earlier supports the lower of cost and net realisable value rule and states that, when comparing the cost with the net realisable value, each item of stock should be compared separately. If this is not practical, categories of similar stock should be grouped together.

Stock valuation and depreciation provide two examples where the **consistency convention** must be applied. This convention holds that when a particular method of accounting is selected to deal with a transaction, this method should be applied consistently over time. Thus it would not be acceptable to switch from, say, FIFO to AVCO between periods (unless there are exceptional circumstances that make this appropriate). The purpose of this convention is to try to ensure that users are able to make valid comparisons between periods.

Activity 3.12

Stock valuation provides a further example where subjective judgement is required to derive the figures for inclusion in the financial statements. For a retail business, what are the main areas where judgement is required?

The main areas are:

- the choice of cost method (FIFO, LIFO, AVCO);
- deriving the net realisable value figure for stocks held.

Profit measurement and the problem of bad debts

Most businesses sell goods on credit. When credit sales are made, the revenue is usually recognised as soon as the goods are passed to, and accepted by, the customer. Recording the dual aspect of a credit sale will involve:

- increasing the sales; and
- increasing debtors

by the amount of the credit sale.

With this type of sale, there is always the risk that the customer will not pay the amount due, however reliable the customer appeared to be at the time of the sale. Where it becomes reasonably certain that the customer will not eventually pay, the debt is considered to be 'bad', and this must be taken into account when preparing the financial statements.

Activity 3.13

What would be the effect of not taking into account the fact that a debt is bad, when preparing the financial statements, on the portrayal of financial performance and position?

The effect would be to overstate the assets (debtors) on the balance sheet and to over-state profit in the profit and loss account, as the sale (which has been recognised) will not result in any future benefits arising.

To provide a more realistic picture of financial performance and position, the **bad debt** must be 'written off'. This will involve:

- reducing the debtors; and
- increasing expenses (by creating an expense known as 'bad debts written off') by the amount of the bad debt. The matching convention requires that the bad debt is written off in the same period as that in which the sale that gave rise to the debt is recognised.

Note that, when a debt is bad, the accounting response is not simply to cancel the original sale. If we did this, the profit and loss account would not be so informative. Reporting the bad debts as an expense can be extremely useful in the evaluation of management performance.

Activity 3.14

Bad debts represent further areas where judgement is required in deriving expenses figures for a particular period. What will be the effect of different judgements concern-ing the amount of bad debts on the profit for a particular period and on the total profit reported over the life of the business?

Judgement is often required in order to derive a figure for bad debts incurred during a period. There may be situations where views will differ concerning whether or not a debt is irrecoverable. The decision concerning whether or not to write off a bad debt will have an effect on the expenses for the period, and hence on the reported profit. However, over the life of the business, the total reported profit will not be affected as incorrect judge-ments in one period will be adjusted for in a later period.

Activity 3.14 continued

Suppose, for example, that a debt of £100 was written off in a period, and that, in a later period, the amount owing was actually received. The increase in expenses of £100 in the period in which the bad debt was written off would be compensated for by an increase in revenues of £100 when the amount outstanding was finally received (bad debt recoverable). If, on the other hand, the amount owing of £100 was never written off in the first place, the profit for the two periods would not be affected by the bad debt adjustment, and would therefore be different, but the total profit for the two periods would be the same.

Let us now try to bring together some of the points that we have raised in this chapter through a self-assessment question.

? Self-assessment question 3.1

TT and Co is a new business that started trading on 1 January 2003. The following is a summary of transactions that occurred during the first year of trading:

1 The owners introduced £50,000 of capital, which was paid into a bank account opened in the name of the business.

2 Premises were rented from 1 January 2003 at an annual rental of £20,000. During the year, rent of £25,000 was paid to the owner of the premises.

3 Rates on the premises were paid during the year as follows:

For the period 1 January 2003 to 31 March 2003   £500
For the period 1 April 2003 to 31 March 2004   £1,200

4 A delivery van was bought on 1 January 2003 for £12,000. This is expected to be used in the business for four years and then to be sold for £2,000.

5 Wages totalling £33,500 were paid during the year. At the end of the year, the business owed £630 of wages for the last week of the year.

6 Electricity bills for the first three quarters of the year were paid totalling £1,650. After 31 December 2003, but before the accounts had been finalised for the year, the bill for the last quarter arrived showing a charge of £620.

7 Stock-in-trade totalling £143,000 was bought on credit.

8 Stock-in-trade totalling £12,000 was bought for cash.

9 Sales on credit totalled £152,000 (cost £74,000).

10 Cash sales totalled £35,000 (cost £16,000).

11 Receipts from trade debtors totalled £132,000.

12 Payments to trade creditors totalled £121,000.

13 Van running expenses paid totalled £9,400.

At the end of the year it was clear that a trade debtor who owed £400 would not be able to pay any part of the debt. The business uses the straight-line method for depreciating fixed assets.

Required:
Prepare a balance sheet as at 31 December 2003 and a profit and loss account for the year to that date. (Use the outline financial statements produced below to help you.)

TT and Co
Balance sheet as at 31 December 2003

	£	£	£
Fixed assets			
Motor van			
Current assets			
Stock-in-trade			
Trade debtors			
Prepaid expenses			
Cash	___		
Less Current liabilities			
Trade creditors			
Accrued expenses	___	___	___
Capital			___
Original			
Add Profit			___
			___

Profit and loss account for the year ended 31 December 2003

	£	£
Sales		
Less Cost of sales		___
Gross profit		
Less Rent		
Rates		
Wages		
Electricity		
Bad debts		
Van expenses		
Van depreciation		___
Net profit for the year		___

Interpreting the profit and loss account

When a profit and loss account is presented to users it is sometimes the case that the only item that will concern them will be the final net profit figure, or *bottom line* as it is sometimes called. Although the net profit figure is a primary measure of performance, and its importance is difficult to overstate, the profit and loss account contains other information that should also be of interest. In order to evaluate business performance effectively, it is important to find out how the final net profit figure was derived. Thus the level of sales, the nature and amount of expenses incurred, and the profit in relation to sales are important factors in understanding the performance of the business over a period. The analysis and interpretation of financial statements is considered in detail in Chapter 6.

Summary

The main points of this chapter may be summarised as follows:

- *The profit and loss (P and L) account*:
  - ❏ measures and reports how much profit (loss) has been generated over a period;
  - ❏ profit (loss) for the period is the difference between the total revenues and total expenses for the period;
  - ❏ links the balance sheets at the beginning and end of a financial period;
  - ❏ the profit and loss account of a retail business will first calculate gross profit, then add any additional revenues and then deduct any overheads for the period. The final figure derived is the net profit (loss) for the period;
  - ❏ gross profit represents the difference between the sales for the period and the cost of sales.

- *Expenses and revenues*:
  - ❏ cost of sales may be identified by either matching the cost of each sale to the particular sale or by adjusting the goods purchased during the period to take account of opening and closing stocks;
  - ❏ the classification of expenses is often a matter of judgement, although there are statutory rules for businesses that trade as limited companies;
  - ❏ the realisation convention states that revenue is recognised when it has been realised;
  - ❏ the matching convention states that expenses should be matched to the revenues that they help generate;
  - ❏ a particular expense reported in the profit and loss account may not be the same as the cash paid. This will result in some adjustment for accruals or prepayments;
  - ❏ the materiality convention states that where the amounts are immaterial, we should consider only what is expedient.

- *Depreciation of fixed assets*:
  - ❏ depreciation requires a consideration of the cost, useful life and residual value of an asset. It also requires a consideration of the method of depreciation;
  - ❏ the straight-line method of depreciation allocates the amount to be depreciated evenly over the useful life of the asset;

- ❏ the reducing-balance method applies a fixed percentage rate of depreciation to the written-down value of an asset each year;
- ❏ the depreciation method chosen should reflect the pattern of benefits associated with the asset;
- ❏ depreciation is an attempt to allocate the cost (less residual value) of an asset over its useful life. It does not provide funds for replacement of the asset.

■ *Stock costing methods*:
- ❏ the way in which we derive the cost of stocks is important in the calculation of profit and the presentation of financial position;
- ❏ the first in, first out (FIFO) method assumes that the earliest stocks held are the first to be sold;
- ❏ the last in, first out (LIFO) method assumes that the latest stocks are the first to be sold;
- ❏ the weighted average cost (AVCO) method applies an average cost to all stocks sold;
- ❏ when prices are rising, FIFO gives the lowest cost of sales and highest closing stock figure and LIFO gives the highest cost of sales figure and the lowest closing stock figure. AVCO gives a figure for cost of sales and closing stock that lies between FIFO and LIFO;
- ❏ when prices are falling, the positions of FIFO and LIFO are reversed;
- ❏ stocks are shown at the lower of cost and net realisable value;
- ❏ when a particular method of accounting, such as a stock costing method, is selected, it should be applied consistently over time.

■ *Bad debts*:
- ❏ where it is reasonably certain that a credit customer will not pay, the debt is regarded as 'bad' and written off.

→ **Key terms**

profit   *p 53*
revenue   *p 53*
expense   *p 53*
gross profit   *p 55*
trading and profit and loss
   account   *p 55*
net profit   *p 55*
cost of sales   *p 56*
realisation convention   *p 60*
matching convention   *p 61*
accrued expenses   *p 61*

prepaid expense   *p 64*
materiality convention   *p 64*
depreciation   *p 65*
residual value   *p 67*
straight-line method   *p 67*
reducing-balance method   *p 68*
first in, first out (FIFO)   *p 74*
last in, first out (LIFO)   *p 74*
weighted average cost (AVCO)   *p 75*
consistency convention   *p 77*
bad debt   *p 78*

? Review questions

Answers to these questions can be found on the students' side of the Companion Website.

3.1 'Although the profit and loss account is a record of past achievement, the calculations required for certain expenses involve estimates of the future.' What is meant by this statement? Can you think of examples where estimates of the future are used?

3.2 'Depreciation is a process of allocation and not valuation.' What do you think is meant by this statement?

3.3 What is the convention of consistency? Does this convention help users in making a more valid comparison *between* businesses?

3.4 'An asset is similar to an expense.' Do you agree?

? Exercises

Exercises 3.4 and 3.5 are more advanced than 3.1–3.3. Those with a coloured number have answers at the back of the book.

3.1 You have heard the following statements made. Comment critically on them.

(a) 'Capital only increases or decreases as a result of the owners putting more cash into the business or taking some out.'
(b) 'An accrued expense is one that relates to next year.'
(c) 'Unless we depreciate this asset we shall be unable to provide for its replacement.'
(d) 'There is no point in depreciating the factory building. It is appreciating in value each year.'

3.2 Singh Enterprises has an accounting year to 31 December. On 1 January 2000 the business purchased a machine for £10,000. The machine had an expected useful life of four years and an estimated residual value of £2,000. On 1 January 2001 the business purchased another machine for £15,000. This machine had an expected useful life of five years and an estimated residual value of £2,500. On 31 December 2002 the business sold the first machine purchased for £3,000.

Required:
Show the relevant profit and loss account extracts and balance sheet extracts for the years 2000, 2001 and 2002.

3.3 The owner of a business is confused, and comes to you for help. The financial statements for his business, prepared by an accountant, for the last accounting period revealed an increase in profit of £50,000. However, during the accounting period the bank balance declined by £30,000. What reasons might explain this apparent discrepancy?

3.4   Spratley Ltd is a builders' merchant. On 1 September the business had 20 tonnes of sand in stock at a cost of £18 per tonne and at a total cost of £360. During the first week in September, the business purchased the following amounts of sand:

September	Tonnes	Cost per tonne
		£
2	48	20
4	15	24
6	10	25

On 7 September the business sold 60 tonnes of sand to a local builder.

Required:
Calculate the cost of goods sold and the closing stock figures from the above information using the following stock costing methods:

(a)   first in, first out
(b)   last in, first out
(c)   weighted average cost.

3.5   The following is the balance sheet of TT and Co at the end of its first year of trading (from Self-assessment question 3.1):

TT and Co
Balance sheet as at 31 December 2003

	£	£	£
Fixed assets			
Motor van: Cost			12,000
Depreciation			2,500
			9,500
Current assets			
Stock-in-trade	65,000		
Trade debtors	19,600		
Prepaid expenses*	5,300		
Cash	750		
		90,650	
Less **Current liabilities**			
Trade creditors	22,000		
Accrued expenses**	1,250		
		23,250	
			67,400
			£76,900
Capital			
Original			50,000
Add Profit			26,900
			£76,900

* The prepaid expenses consisted of rates (£300) and rent (£5,000).
** The accrued expenses consisted of wages (£630) and electricity (£620).

During 2004, the following transactions took place:

1   The owners withdrew capital in the form of cash of £20,000.
2   Premises continued to be rented at an annual rental of £20,000. During the year, rent of £15,000 was paid to the owner of the premises.
3   Rates on the premises were paid during the year as follows: for the period 1 April 2004 to 31 March 2005 £1,300.
4   A second delivery van was bought on 1 January 2004 for £13,000. This is expected to be used in the business for four years and then to be sold for £3,000.
5   Wages totalling £36,700 were paid during the year. At the end of the year, the business owed £860 of wages for the last week of the year.
6   Electricity bills for the first three quarters of the year and £620 for the last quarter of the previous year were paid totalling £1,820. After 31 December 2004, but before the accounts had been finalised for the year, the bill for the last quarter arrived showing a charge of £690.
7   Stock-in-trade totalling £67,000 was bought on credit.
8   Stock-in-trade totalling £8,000 was bought for cash.
9   Sales on credit totalled £179,000 (cost £89,000).
10 Cash sales totalled £54,000 (cost £25,000).
11 Receipts from trade debtors totalled £178,000.
12 Payments to trade creditors totalled £71,000.
13 Van running expenses paid totalled £16,200.

The business uses the straight-line method for depreciating fixed assets.

Required:
Prepare a balance sheet as at 31 December 2004 and a profit and loss account for the year to that date.

Chapter 4

Accounting for limited companies

Introduction

In the UK, most businesses, except the very smallest, trade in the form of limited companies. In this chapter we shall examine the nature of limited companies and see how they differ in practical terms from sole proprietorships. We shall consider the ways that finance is provided by the owners as well as the rules governing the way in which companies must account to their owners and to other interested parties. We shall also see how the financial statements that we covered in the previous two chapters are prepared for this type of business enterprise.

Objectives

Having completed this chapter, you should be able to:

- discuss the nature of the limited company
- describe the main features of the owners' claim in a limited company
- outline the statutory and non-statutory rules that surround accounting for limited companies
- explain how the profit and loss account and balance sheet of a limited company differ in detail from that of a sole proprietorship business.

The nature of limited companies

Let us begin our examination of limited companies by discussing their legal nature. A **limited company** has been described as an artificial person that has been created by law. This means that a company has many of the rights and obligations that 'real' people have. For example, it can sue or be sued by others and it can enter into contracts in its own name. This contrasts sharply with other types of business, such as a sole proprietor business, where it is the owner(s) rather than the business that must sue, enter into contracts and so on, because the business has no separate legal identity.

With the rare exceptions of those that are created by Act of Parliament or by Royal Charter, all UK companies are created as a result of the Registrar of Companies, a government official, entering the name of the new company on the Registry of Companies, having ensured that the necessary formalities have been met. These formalities are the very simple matters of filling in a few forms and paying a modest registration fee. Thus, in the UK, companies can be formed very easily and cheaply (for about £100).

Normally, companies are owned by at least two people. The owners are usually known as *members* or *shareholders*. The ownership of a company is normally divided into a number, frequently a large number, of **shares**, each of equal size. Each owner, or shareholder, owns one or more shares in the company. As a limited company has its own legal identity, it is regarded as being quite separate from those who own and manage it. This fact leads to two important features of the limited company: perpetual life and limited liability.

Perpetual life

A company is normally granted a perpetual existence and so will continue even where an owner of shares in the company dies. The shares of the deceased person will simply pass to the beneficiary of his or her estate. The granting of perpetual existence means that the life of a company is quite separate from the lives of those individuals who own or manage it. It is not, therefore, affected by changes in ownership that arise when individuals buy and sell shares in the company.

Though a company may be granted a perpetual existence when it is first formed, it is possible for either the shareholders or the courts to bring this existence to an end. When this is done, the assets of the company are sold off to meet outstanding liabilities. Any surplus arising from the sale can then be used to pay the shareholders. Shareholders may agree to end the life of a company where it has achieved the purpose for which it was formed or where the shareholders feel the company has no real future. The courts may bring the life of a company to an end where creditors have applied to the courts for this to be done because they have not been paid amounts owing.

Where shareholders agree to end the life of a company, it is referred to as a 'voluntary liquidation'. The demise of one company by this method is described in Exhibit 4.1 below, which is an extract from an article on the *Financial Times* website.

Exhibit 4.1 Monotub Industries in a spin as founder gets Titan for £1　**FT**

Monotub Industries, maker of the Titan washing machine, yesterday passed into corporate history with very little ceremony and with only a whimper of protest from minority shareholders.

At an extraordinary meeting held in a basement room of the group's West End headquarters, shareholders voted to put the company into voluntary liquidation and sell its assets and intellectual property to founder Martin Myerscough for £1. (The shares in the company were at one time worth 650p each.)

Exhibit 4.1 continued

> The only significant opposition came from Giuliano Gnagnatti who, along with other shareholders, has seen his investment shrink faster than a wool twin-set on a boil wash.
>
> The not-so-proud owner of 100,000 Monotub shares, Mr Gnagnatti, the managing director of an online retailer, . . . described the sale of Monotub as a 'free gift' to Mr Myerscough. This assessment was denied by Ian Green, the chairman of Monotub, who said the closest the beleaguered company had come to a sale was an offer for £60,000 that gave no guarantees against liabilities, which are thought to amount to £750,000.
>
> The quiet passing of the washing machine, eventually dubbed the Titanic, was in strong contrast to its performance in many kitchens.
>
> Originally touted as the 'great white goods hope' of the washing machine industry with its larger capacity and removable drum, the Titan ran into problems when it kept stopping during the spin cycle, causing it to emit a loud bang and leap into the air.
>
> Summing up the demise of the Titan, Mr Green said: 'Clearly the machine had some revolutionary aspects, but you can't get away from the fact that the machine was faulty and should not have been launched with those defects.'
>
> The usually vocal Mr Myerscough, who has promised to pump £250,000 into the company and give Monotub shareholders £4 for every machine sold, refused to comment on his plans for the Titan or reveal who his backers were. But . . . he did say that he intended to 'take the Titan forward'.
>
> *Source*: 'Monotub Industries in a spin as founder gets Titan for £1', Lisa Urquhart, *Financial Times*, 23 January 2003, FT.com

Limited liability

Since the company is a legal person in its own right, it must take responsibility for its own debts and losses. This means that once the shareholders have paid what they have agreed to pay for the shares, their obligation to the company, and to the company's creditors, is satisfied. Thus shareholders can limit their losses to that which they have paid, or agreed to pay, for their shares. This is of great practical importance to potential shareholders, since they know that what they can lose, as part owners of the business, is limited.

Contrast this with the position of sole proprietors or partners (that is the owners or part owners of unincorporated businesses). Here, there is not the opportunity that shareholders have to 'ring fence' the assets that they choose not to put into the business. If a sole proprietary business finds itself in a position where liabilities exceed the business assets, the law gives unsatisfied creditors the right to demand payment out of what the sole proprietor may have regarded as 'non-business' assets. Thus the sole proprietor could lose everything – house, car, the lot. This is because the law sees Jill, the sole proprietor, as being the same as Jill the private individual. The shareholder, by contrast, can lose only the amount invested in that company. Legally, the business operating as a limited company, in which Jack owns shares, is not the same as Jack himself. This is true even where Jack and his close associates own all of the shares in the company.

Exhibit 4.2 Carlton and Granada 1 – Nationwide Football League 0

A recent example of shareholders taking advantage of limited liability status is that of two television companies, Carlton and Granada, which each owned 50 per cent of ITV Digital (formerly ON Digital). ITV Digital collapsed because it was unable to meet its liabilities. Before its collapse, the company had signed a contract to pay the Nationwide Football League more than £89 million on both 1 August 2002 and 1 August 2003 for the rights to broadcast football matches over three seasons. However, the company was unable to meet this commitment and the shareholders could not be held liable for the amounts owing. This case is unusual insofar that the Nationwide Football League tried to sue Carlton and Granada because it believed that the two companies had guaranteed the contract between ITV Digital and the Nationwide Football League (this, of course, is a separate issue to their limited liability status as shareholders). However, the courts did not uphold the Nationwide Football League's case.

Activity 4.1

We have just said that the fact that shareholders can limit their losses to that which they have paid, or have agreed to pay, for their shares is of great practical importance to potential shareholders.

Can you think of any practical benefit to a private-sector economy, in general, of this ability of shareholders to limit losses?

Business is a risky venture – in some cases a very risky one. People with money to invest will tend to be more content to do so where they know the limit of their liability. This means that more businesses will tend to be formed and that existing ones will find it easier to raise additional finance from existing and/or additional part owners. This is good for the private-sector economy, since businesses will tend to form and expand more readily. Thus, the wants of society are more likely to be met where limited liability exists.

Though **limited liability** has this advantage to the providers of capital (the shareholders), it is not necessarily to the advantage of all others who have a stake in the business. Limited liability is attractive to shareholders because they can, in effect, walk away from the unpaid debts of the company, if the contribution of the shareholders has not been sufficient to meet those debts. This is likely to make any individual, or another business, that is considering advancing credit, wary of dealing with the limited company. This can be a real problem for smaller, less established companies. For example, suppliers may insist on cash payment before delivery. Alternatively, a supplier may require a personal guarantee from a major shareholder that the debt will be paid before allowing a company trade credit. In the latter case, the supplier will circumvent the company's limited liability status by establishing the personal liability of an individual. Larger, more established companies, on the other hand, tend to have built up the confidence of suppliers.

Legal safeguards

It is mainly to warn individuals and other businesses contemplating dealing with a limited company that the liability of the owners (shareholders) of that company is limited that this fact must be indicated in the name of the company. As we shall see later in this chapter, there are other safeguards for those dealing with a limited company, in that the extent to which shareholders may withdraw their investment from the company is restricted.

Another important safeguard for those dealing with a limited company is that all limited companies must produce annual financial statements (profit and loss account, balance sheet and cash flow statement), and in effect make these available to the public. Later in this chapter we shall consider the financial statements of limited companies in some detail.

Management of companies – the role of directors

A limited company may have a separate legal identity, but it is not a human being capable of making decisions and plans about the business and exercising control over it. Human beings must undertake these management tasks. The most senior level of management of a company is the board of directors.

The shareholders elect **directors** (by law there must be at least one director) to manage the company on a day-to-day basis, on behalf of those shareholders. In a small company, the board may be the only level of management, and may consist of all the shareholders. In larger companies the board may consist of ten or so directors, out of many thousands of shareholders. The directors need not even be shareholders. Below the board of directors could be several layers of management comprising thousands of people.

Whatever the size of the company, the directors are responsible to the shareholders, and to some extent to the world at large, for the conduct of the company. The directors' term of office is limited, and they must stand for election at the end of that term if they wish to continue in office.

Public and private companies

When a company is registered with the Registrar of Companies, it must be registered as either a public or a private company. The main practical difference between these is that a **public company** can offer its shares for sale to the general public, but a **private company** is restricted from doing so. A public limited company must signal its status to all interested parties by having the words 'public limited company' or the abbreviation 'plc' in its name. For a private limited company, the word 'limited' or 'Ltd' must appear as part of its name.

Private limited companies tend to be smaller businesses where the ownership is divided between relatively few shareholders, who are usually fairly close to one another – for example a family company. Numerically, there are vastly more private limited companies in the UK than there are public ones, but since the public ones tend to be individually larger, they probably represent a much more important group economically. Many private limited companies are no more than the vehicle through which businesses that are little more than sole proprietorships operate.

Exhibit 4.3

In certain industrial sectors, such as banking and insurance, public companies account for all or nearly all of their particular market. Even the food retailing sector, which has a huge number of small stores, is dominated by a handful of large supermarkets. The total sales and grocery market share of two leading supermarkets are set out below in order to illustrate their economic impact:

	Sales* £ million	Grocery market share** (by volume)
Tesco plc	25,654	26.7%
Sainsbury plc	18,206	16.8%

* Taken from 2002 annual reports.
** Market share for 2000 Taylor, Nelson Sofre Independent retail analysts.

Source: Market share reproduced from *Great Britain Consumer Spend April 2003,* Taylor Nelson Sofres plc, independent retail analysts

We can see that these two leading supermarkets account for just over 40 per cent of the grocery market.

As far as accounting requirements are concerned, there is no distinction between private and public companies.

Capital (owners' claim) of limited companies

The owner's claim of a sole proprietorship is normally captured in one figure on the balance sheet, usually labelled 'capital'. In the case of a limited company, this is usually a little more complicated, though in essence the same broad principles apply. With a company, the owners' claim is divided between shares – that is, the original investment – on the one hand, and **reserves** – that is, profits and gains subsequently made – on the other. There is also the possibility that there will be shares of more than one type and reserves of more than one type. Thus, within the basic divisions of share capital and reserves there may well be further subdivisions. This probably seems quite complicated, but we shall shortly consider the reasons for these subdivisions and all should become clearer.

The basic division

When a company is first formed, those who take steps to form it, usually known as the 'promoters' of the company, will decide how much needs to be raised by the potential shareholders to set up the company with the necessary assets to operate.

Example 4.1

Let us imagine that several people get together and decide to form a company on 31 March 2002 to carry out a new venture. They estimate that the company will need £50,000 in order to buy the necessary assets to operate the business. They raise the cash between themselves, which they use to buy shares in the company with a **nominal or par value** of £1 each.

At this point, the balance sheet of the company would be:

Balance sheet as at 31 March 2002

	£
Net assets (all in cash)	50,000
Capital and reserves	
Share capital	
50,000 shares of £1 each	50,000

The company now buys the necessary fixed assets and stock-in-trade and starts to trade. During the first year, the company makes a profit of £10,000. This, by definition, means that the owners' claim expands by £10,000. During the year, the shareholders (owners) make no drawings of their capital, and so at the end of the year the summarised balance sheet looks like this:

Balance sheet as at 31 March 2003

	£
Net assets (various assets less liabilities)	60,000
Capital and reserves	
Share capital	
50,000 shares of £1 each	50,000
Reserves (revenue reserve)	10,000
	60,000

The profit is shown in a *reserve*, known as a **revenue reserve**, because it arises from generating revenues (making sales). Note that we do not simply add the profit to the share capital. We must keep the two amounts separate (to satisfy company law). The reason for this is that there is a legal restriction on the maximum drawings of capital (or **dividends**) that the owners can make. This is normally defined by the amount of revenue reserves, so it is helpful to show these separately. We shall look at why there is this restriction, and how it works, a little later.

Share capital

Shares represent the basic units of ownership of a business. All companies issue **ordinary shares**, which are often referred to collectively as the **equity** of the company. The nominal value of the shares is at the discretion of the people who start up the company. For example, if the initial capital is to be £50,000, this could be divided into two shares of £25,000 each, five million shares of one penny each or any other combination that gives a total of £50,000. Each share must have equal value.

Activity 4.2

The initial capital requirement for a new company is £50,000 and there are to be two equal shareholders. Would you advise them to issue two shares of £25,000? Why?

Such large-denomination shares tend to be unwieldy. Suppose that one of the shareholders wanted to sell his or her shares. S/he would have to find one buyer. If there were shares of smaller denomination, it would be possible to sell part of the shareholding to various potential buyers. Furthermore, it would be possible to sell just part of the holding and to retain part.

In practice, £1 tends to be the maximum nominal value for shares and 25 pence and 50 pence are probably the most common nominal values.

Some companies also issue other classes of shares, **preference shares** being the most common. Preference shares guarantee that *if a dividend is paid*, the preference shareholders will be entitled to the first part of it up to a maximum value. This maximum is normally defined as a fixed percentage of the nominal value of the preference shares. If, for example, a company issues 10,000 preference shares of £1 each with a dividend rate of 6 per cent, this means that the preference shareholders are entitled to receive the first £600 (that is, 6 per cent of £10,000) of any dividend that is paid by the company for a year. The excess over £600 goes to the ordinary shareholders. Normally, any undistributed profits and gains accrue to the ordinary shareholders.

The ordinary shareholders are the primary risk-takers as they are entitled to share in the profits of the company only after other claims have been satisfied. However, there are no upper limits on the amount that they may receive. The potential rewards available to ordinary shareholders reflect the risks that they are prepared to take. As ordinary shareholders take most of the risks, power resides in their hands. Normally, only the ordinary shareholders are able to vote on issues that affect the company, such as who should be the directors.

Exhibit 4.4

The following table shows a breakdown of the range of holdings of ordinary shares of BP plc, an energy business that is the UK's largest company.

Register of members holding BP ordinary shares as at 31 December 2001

Range of holdings (No. of shares per shareholder)	Number of shareholders	Percentage of total shareholders	Percentage of total share capital
1–100	43,735	12.16	0.01
101–200	14,078	3.92	0.01
201–1,000	140,184	38.98	0.31
1,001–10,000	144,405	40.15	1.98
10,001–100,000	14,857	4.13	1.37
100,001–1,000,000	1,485	0.41	2.40
Over 1,000,000	903	0.25	93.92
	359,647	100.00	100.00

Source: Reproduced from BP p.l.c., Annual Report and Accounts for the year ended 31 December 2002

Note that, although the company has a large number of shareholders, only 903 shareholders, representing one quarter of one per cent of the total number of shareholders, own 93.92 per cent of the shares. However, one of these is JPMorgan Chase Bank, which holds 29.17% of the total share capital, but holds this as the approved depositary, holding shares on behalf of BP's underlying American Depositary Shares, which are in turn held by over 530,000 beneficial owners. The remaining 902 shareholders, each owning more than one million shares, are likely to be financial institutions such as insurance companies, pension funds and investment companies, which in turn represent a large number of underlying investors. In fact no one shareholder owns more than 3% of the share capital of BP p.l.c..

It is open to the company to issue shares of various classes, perhaps with some having unusual and exotic conditions, but in practice it is rare to find other than straightforward ordinary and preference shares. Though a company may have different classes of shares whose holders have different rights, within each class, all shares must be treated equally. The rights of the various classes of shareholders, as well as other matters relating to a particular company, are contained in that company's set of rules, known as the *articles and memorandum of association*. A copy of these rules must be lodged with the Registrar of Companies, who makes this available for inspection by the general public.

Reserves

In Example 4.1 we came across one type of reserve that a company may have – the revenue reserve. You may recall that this reserve represents the retained trading profits of the business at the end of the financial year. These ploughed-back profits create most of the typical company's reserves and represent overwhelmingly the largest source of new finance for UK companies.

Activity 4.3

Are revenue reserves amounts of cash?

The answer is no. We saw in Chapter 2 that profits are not the same as cash and so there is no reason why retained profits (or reserves) should represent a pool of cash. Retained profits form part of the capital of the owners. This means that it is a claim on the assets of the business and these assets are likely to include various items apart from cash. Other types of reserves that we shall consider later are also part of the capital of the business and so cannot be regarded as cash.

Reserves are classified as either revenue reserves or capital reserves. As we have already seen, revenue reserves arise from trading profit. They also arise from gains made on the disposal of fixed assets.

Capital reserves arise for two main reasons: issuing shares at a price that is above their nominal value (for example, issuing shares with a nominal value of £1 shares for £1.50), and revaluing (upwards) fixed assets. Where a company issues shares at a price above their nominal value, UK law requires that the excess of the issue price over the nominal value be shown separately.

Activity 4.4

Can you think why shares might be issued at above their nominal value?

Hint: This would not usually happen when a company is first formed and the initial shares are being issued.

Once a company has traded and has been successful, the shares would normally be worth more than the nominal value at which they were issued. If additional shares are to be issued to new shareholders to raise finance for further expansion, unless they are issued at a value higher than the nominal value, the new shareholders will be gaining at the expense of the original ones.

This point leads us on to Example 4.2.

Example 4.2

Let us assume that a company has one million ordinary shares in issue with a nominal value of £1 each and that, based on future prospects, the net assets of the company are worth £1.5 million. The company now wishes to raise an additional £0.6 million of cash for expansion and has decided to raise it by issuing new ordinary shares.

If the shares are issued for £1 each (that is 600,000 shares), the total number of shares will be:

$$1.0m + 0.6m = 1.6 \text{ million}$$

and their total value will be the value of the existing net assets plus the new injection of cash:

$$£1.5m + £0.6m = £2.1 \text{ million}$$

This means that the value of each share in the company after the new issue will be:

$$£2.1m/1.6m = £1.3125$$

The current value of each share is:

$$£1.5m/1.0m = £1.50$$

So the original shareholders will lose:

$$£1.50 - £1.3125 = £0.1875 \text{ a share}$$

and the new shareholders will gain:

$$£1.3125 - £1.0 = £0.3125 \text{ a share.}$$

The new shareholders will, no doubt, be delighted with this outcome; the original ones will not. To make things fair between the two groups of shareholders, the new shares should be issued at £1.50 each.

For the company to raise the £0.6 million required, 400,000 shares will have to be issued at £1.50 per share. The £1 nominal value of each share will be included with share capital in the balance sheet (that is, 400,000 shares at £1 = £0.4 million). The £0.50 premium for each share will be shown as a capital reserve, known as the **share premium** account (that is, 400,000 at £0.50 = £0.2 million).

It is not clear why UK company law insists on the distinction between nominal share values and the premium. Certainly other countries (for example, the United States), with a very similar set of laws governing the corporate sector, do not see the necessity to distinguish between share capital and share premium. Instead, the total value at which shares are issued is shown as one comprehensive figure on the company balance sheet.

Exhibit 4.5

Thorntons plc, the manufacturer and retailer of confectionery, had the following capital and reserves as at 30 June 2001:

Capital and reserves	£000
Share capital (10p ordinary shares)	6,656
Share premium	12,399
Revaluation reserve	505
Profit and loss account	29,667
	49,227

Note the importance of retained profit, which accounts for approximately 60 per cent of the total shareholders' investment in the company.

Source: Thorntons plc, Annual Report 2001

Bonus shares

It is always open to the company to take reserves of any kind (capital or revenue) and turn them into share capital. This will involve transferring the desired amount from the reserves to the share capital account and then distributing an appropriate number of new shares to existing shareholders in proportion to their existing share-holdings. New shares, arising from such a conversion, are known as **bonus shares**. Issues of bonus shares are quite frequently encountered in practice. Example 4.3 illustrates the effect of a bonus issue.

Example 4.3

The summary balance sheet of a company is as follows:

Balance sheet as at 31 March 2003

	£
Net assets (various assets less liabilities)	128,000
Capital and reserves	
Share capital	
50,000 shares of £1 each	50,000
Reserves	78,000
	128,000

The company decides that it will issue, to existing shareholders, one new share for every share owned by each shareholder. The balance sheet immediately following this will appear as follows:

Balance sheet as at 31 March 2003

	£
Net assets (various assets less liabilities)	128,000
Capital and reserves	
Share capital	
100,000 shares of £1 each (50,000 + 50,000)	100,000
Reserves (78,000 − 50,000)	28,000
	128,000

We can see that the reserves have decreased by £50,000 and the share capital has increased by the same amount. Share certificates for the 50,000 £1 ordinary shares that have been created from reserves will be issued to existing shareholders to complete the transaction.

Activity 4.5

A shareholder of the company in Example 4.3 owned 100 shares in the company before the bonus issue. How will things change for this shareholder as a result of the bonus issue as regards the number of shares owned and as regards the value of the shareholding?

The answer should be that the number of shares will double, from 100 to 200. Now the shareholder owns one five-hundredth of the company (200/100,000). However, before the bonus issue, the shareholder also owned one five-hundredth of the company (100/50,000). The company's assets and liabilities have not changed as a result of the bonus issue, so logically one five-hundredth of the value of the company should be identical to what it was before. Thus, each share is now worth half as much as before the bonus issue.

We can see that a bonus issue simply takes one part of the owners' claim (part of a reserve) and puts it into another part of the owners' claim (share capital). This transfer has no effect on the assets and liabilities of the company and has no effect on the wealth of the shareholders. This raises the question, of course, as to why a company should bother.

Activity 4.6

Can you think of any reasons why a company might want to make a bonus issue?

We think that there are two main reasons:

■ *Share price.* The share price of a company may be very high and, as a result, may become more difficult to trade. By increasing the number of shares in issue, the value of each share will be reduced, which may have the effect of making the shares more marketable.
■ *Lender confidence.* Where reserves arising from operating profits and/or realised gains on the sale of fixed assets are used to make the bonus issue, it has the effect of taking part of that portion of the owners' claim that could be drawn by the shareholders, as drawings (or dividends), and locking it up. The amount transferred becomes part of the permanent capital base of the business. (We shall see later in this chapter that there are severe restrictions on the ability of shareholders to withdraw their capital.) This move may help to increase confidence among lenders. A bonus issue will reduce the risk of the shareholders' investment in the company being depleted through dividend distributions, thereby leaving lenders in an exposed position.

It seems that many shareholders like bonus issues because they feel it makes them better off. However, we have seen that this is not, in fact, the case.

Rights issues

Rights issues are made when established companies seeking finance for expansion, or to solve a liquidity problem (cash shortage), issue additional shares to existing shareholders for cash. The new shares would be offered to existing shareholders, in proportion to their existing holding. This is a very common form of issuing shares because company law gives existing shareholders the first right of refusal on new shares issued for cash. Thus, existing shareholders are each given the 'right' to buy some new shares. Only where the existing shareholders agree to waive their right would the shares be offered to the wider investing public.

The company (which is owned by the existing shareholders) would typically prefer that existing shareholders buy the shares, irrespective of the legal position. This is because:

- the ownership (and, therefore, control) of the company remains in the same hands; and
- the costs of making the issue (advertising, complying with various company law requirements) tend to be less if the shares are to be offered to existing shareholders.

To encourage existing shareholders to take up their 'rights' to buy some new shares, those shares are virtually always offered at a price below the current market price of the existing ones.

Activity 4.7

In Example 4.2, the point was made that issuing new shares at below their current worth would advantage new shareholders but disadvantage the existing ones.

In view of this, does it matter that rights issues are almost always made at below the current value of the shares?

The answer is that it does not matter, *in these particular circumstances*. This is because, with a rights issue, the existing shareholders and the new shareholders are exactly the same people. Moreover, the new shares will be held in the same proportion by the shareholders as they hold the existing shares. Thus, a particular shareholder will be gaining on the new shares exactly as much as he or she is losing on the existing ones; in the end, no one is better or worse off as a result of the rights issue being made at a discount.

It should be clear that a rights issue is a totally different thing from a bonus issue. Rights issues result in an asset (cash) being transferred from shareholders to the company. Bonus issues involve no transfer of assets in either direction.

Rights issues are often announced in order to raise further funds for expansion, as explained earlier. However Exhibit 4.6, which is an article appearing on the *Financial Times* website, shows that this is not always the case.

Exhibit 4.6 **Laura Ashley to close 35 European stores**

Laura Ashley has taken the unusual step of launching a rights issue, not to fund expansion but to assist it in the closure of 35 of its lossmaking European stores, including all its remaining shops in Germany.

The UK clothing and home furnishing retailer, which earlier this month warned that full-year results would be below market expectations, is hoping to raise £9m ($14.6m) through the issue priced at about 8p a share.

It will go some way to pay for the estimated £7.7m cost of closing the stores, which have dragged down results at the group that is known for its floral offerings, both in clothing and furniture.

In its Christmas trading statement Laura Ashley blamed the fall in profits, that knocked almost 20 per cent off its already battered shares, on the heavy discounting in its European stores.

KC Ng, chief executive, said the rights issue and closures would place the company on a 'firmer footing' for further development.

Laura Ashley said that it remained committed to its remaining 18 European stores, despite the closure of 35 stores. The group is looking for franchise partners to keep the profitable stores going . . .

Source: 'Laura Ashley to close 35 European stores', Lisa Urquhart, *Financial Times*, 23 January 2003, FT.com

---

Transferring share ownership – the role of the Stock Exchange

The point has already been made that shares in a company may be transferred from one owner to another. The desire of some shareholders to sell their shares, coupled with the desire of others to buy those shares, has led to the existence of a formal market in which shares can be bought and sold. The London Stock Exchange, and similar organisations around the world, provide a market place in which shares in public companies may be bought and sold. Share prices are determined by the laws of supply and demand, which are, in turn, determined by investors' perceptions of the future economic prospects of the companies concerned.

Activity 4.8

If, as has been pointed out earlier, the change in ownership of shares does not directly affect the particular company, why do many public companies actively seek to have their shares traded in a recognised market?

The main reason is that investors are generally very reluctant to pledge their money unless they can see some way in which they can turn their investment back into cash. In theory, the shares of a particular company may be very valuable, as a result of the company having a very bright economic future, but unless this value is capable of being realised in cash, the benefit to the shareholders is dubious. After all, we cannot spend shares; we generally need cash.

This means that potential shareholders are much more likely to be prepared to buy new shares from the company (thus providing the company with new finance) where they can see a way of liquidating their investment (turning it into cash), as and when they wish. The Stock Exchanges provide the means of liquidation.

Though the buying and selling of 'second-hand' shares does not provide the company with cash, the fact that the buying and selling facility exists will make it easier for the company to raise new share capital when it needs to do so.

Long-term loans

At this point, it might be worth briefly considering another important source of long-term finance used by companies. Many companies borrow money on a long-term basis, perhaps on a ten-year contract. Lenders may be banks or other professional providers of loan finance. However, companies often raise loan finance in such a way that small investors, including private individuals, are able to lend small amounts. This is particularly the case with the larger, Stock Exchange listed, companies. They do this by making a *loan stock* or **debenture** issue, which, though large in total, can be taken up in small slices by individual investors, both private individuals and investing institutions, such as pension funds and insurance companies. In some cases, these slices of loans can be bought and sold through the Stock Exchange. This means that investors do not have to wait for the full term of the loan to obtain repayment, but can sell their slice of the loan to another would-be lender at intermediate points in the term of the loan. The fact that loan capital can be divided into small slices and perhaps traded on the Stock Exchange can lead to a confusion that loan stock are shares by another name. However this is not the case. It is the shareholders who own the company and who therefore share in its losses and profits. Loan stockholders lend money to the company under a legally binding contract, which normally specifies the rate of interest, the interest payment dates and the date of repayment of the loan itself. Usually long-term loans are secured on assets of the company.

Lenders often place restrictions, or covenants, on the borrowing company's freedom of action as a condition of granting a loan. The covenants typically restrict the level of risk to which the borrowing company, and the asset on which the loan has been secured, is exposed. To breach these covenants is regarded as a serious matter. The following exhibit appeared in the *Financial Times* and describes the problems of one company at risk of breaching its loan covenants.

Exhibit 4.7 Bulmer warns of breach in covenants **FT**

HP Bulmer, the cider maker crippled by over-ambitious expansion plans, yesterday admitted for the first time that the new management might have to put up a 'for sale' sign.

The company, which leads the UK cider market with its Strongbow brand, also warned that deteriorating trading conditions might lead to a breach of its banking covenants in April. But Miles Templeman, chief executive, said he was fully aware of the reality of the situation when he took up the post at the beginning of this month. His appointment followed the loss of the former chief executive and finance director as the company's problems unfolded. 'It may have got a little worse,' said Mr Templeman. 'But I still believe this is a good business and it is better for us to turn it round and build the value back in ourselves.'

In a statement on its working capital requirements, the company said that October and November had been difficult months for sales of its cider to pub-goers in the UK. At the same time the decision to quit the international businesses and to stop product innovation was proving more expensive than previously estimated.

In addition, margins in the take-home trade were still being squeezed, and the loss of a third-party contract for packing at the company's Belgian plant had cost £800,000. As a result, the company, which only in November announced that it had agreed new financing arrangements with its banks

▶

Exhibit 4.7 continued

until November this year, was at risk of breaching its covenants. Mr Templeman said the board would be examining all options, including initiating talks with potential buyers if necessary. It would also consider selling the Beer Seller, the company's wholesale business that specialises in supplies to independent pubs and restaurants, or a rights issue.

Regarded as an expert on brands, Mr Templeman wants to focus on the UK cider business, particularly Strongbow. Bulmer has about two-thirds of the UK market, and also owns Woodpecker and Scrumpy Jack.

Source: 'Bulmer warns of breach in covenants', David Blackwell, *Financial Times*, 25 January 2003

Long-term financing of companies can be depicted as in Figure 4.1.

Figure 4.1 Sources of long-term finance for the typical company

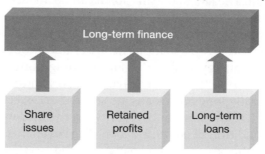

Companies derive their long-term financing needs from three main sources: new share issues, retained profits, and long-term borrowing. For the typical company, the sum of the first two (known as *equity finance*) exceeds the third. Retained profit is usually greater than either of the other two, in terms of the amount of finance raised in most years.

It is important to the prosperity and stability of the company that it strikes a suitable balance between finance provided by the shareholders (equity) and by lenders. This topic will be explored in Chapter 6. Equity and loan capital are, of course, not the only forms of finance available to a company. In Chapter 12, we consider other sources of finance available to businesses, including companies.

Restriction of the right of shareholders to make drawings of capital

Limited companies are required by law to distinguish between that part of their capital (shareholders' claim) that may be withdrawn by the shareholders and that part which may not. The withdrawable part is that which has arisen from trading profits and from realised profits on the disposal of fixed assets (to the extent that tax payments, on these profits and gains, as well as previous drawings have not extinguished this part of the capital). This withdrawable element of the capital is *revenue reserves*. The non-withdrawable part normally consists of that which has arisen from funds injected by shareholders buying shares in the company and that which came from upward revaluations of company assets which still remain in the company: that is, *share capital* and *capital reserves*.

Activity 4.9

Can you think of the reason why limited companies are required to distinguish different parts of their capital, whereas sole proprietorship businesses are not required to do so?

The reason for this situation is the limited liability that company shareholders enjoy, but which owners of unincorporated businesses do not. If a sole proprietor withdraws all of the owner's claim, or even an amount in excess of this, the position of the creditors of the business is not weakened since they can legally enforce their claims against the sole proprietor as an individual. With a limited company, the business and the owners are legally separate and so a legal right to enforce claims against individuals does not exist. To protect the company's creditors, however, the law insists that the shareholders cannot legally withdraw a specific part of the capital of a company.

The law does not specify how large the non-withdrawable part of a particular company's capital should be, but simply requires that anyone dealing with the company should be able to tell from looking at the company's balance sheet how large it is. In the light of this, a particular prospective lender, or supplier of goods or services on credit, can make a commercial judgement as to whether to deal with the company or not. However, the larger it is, the easier the company is likely to find it to persuade potential lenders to lend and suppliers to supply goods and services on credit. Let us consider Example 4.4.

Example 4.4

The summary balance sheet of a company is as follows:

Balance sheet

	£
Net assets (fixed and current assets less short-term liabilities)	43,000
Capital and reserves	
Share capital	
20,000 shares of £1 each	20,000
Reserves (revenue)	23,000
	43,000

A bank has been asked to make a £25,000 long-term loan to the company. If the loan were to be made, the balance sheet that would appear immediately following would be as shown below:

Balance sheet (after the loan)

	£
Net assets (fixed and current assets less short-term liabilities (43,000 + 25,000))	68,000
Less Long-term liability	25,000
	43,000
Capital and reserves	
Share capital	
20,000 shares of £1 each	20,000
Reserves (revenue)	23,000
	43,000

As things stand, there are net assets to a total balance sheet value of £68,000 to meet the bank's claim of £25,000. It would be perfectly legal, however, for the company to pay a dividend (withdraw capital) of £23,000. The balance sheet would then appear as follows:

Balance sheet (after the loan and dividend)

	£
Net assets (fixed and current assets less short-term liabilities (68,000 – 23,000))	45,000
Less Long-term liability	25,000
	20,000
Capital and reserves	
Share capital	
20,000 shares of £1 each	20,000
Reserves (revenue (23,000 – 23,000))	–
	20,000

This leaves the bank in a very much weaker position, in that there are now net assets (that is, total assets less short-term liabilities) with a balance sheet value of £45,000 to meet a claim of £25,000. Note that the difference between the amount of the bank loan and the net assets always equals the capital and reserves total. Thus, the capital and reserves represent a 'margin of safety' for creditors. The larger the amount of the owners' claim that is withdrawable by the shareholders, the smaller is the potential margin of safety for creditors.

Perhaps it is worth pointing out, as a practical footnote to Example 4.4, that most potential long-term lenders would seek to have their loan secured against a particular asset of the company, particularly an asset such as freehold property. This would give them the right to seize the asset concerned, sell it and satisfy their claim should the company default.

Activity 4.10

Would you expect a company to pay all of its revenue reserves as a dividend? What factors might be involved with a dividend decision?

It would be very rare for a company to pay all of its revenue reserves as a dividend; a legal right to do so does not necessarily make it a good idea. We have already seen that most companies regard ploughed-back profits as a major source of new finance and paying dividends will reduce this source of finance.

The factors that influence the dividend decision are likely to include:

■ the availability of cash to pay a dividend: it would not be illegal to borrow in order to pay a dividend, but it would be unusual and, possibly, imprudent;
■ the needs of the business for finance for new investments;
■ the expectations of shareholders concerning the amount of dividends to be paid.

You may have thought of others.

The law is quite specific that it is illegal, under normal circumstances, for shareholders to withdraw that part of their claim that is represented by shares and capital reserves. This means that potential creditors of the company know the maximum amount of the shareholders' claim that can be drawn by the shareholders. Figure 4.2 shows the important division between that part of the shareholders' claim that can be withdrawn as a dividend and that part which cannot.

Figure 4.2 Availability for dividends of various parts of the shareholders' claim

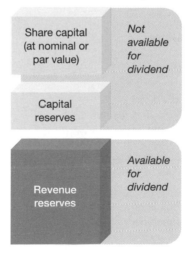

Total equity finance of limited companies consists of share capital, capital reserves and revenue reserves. Only the revenue reserves (which arise from realised profits and gains) can be used to fund a dividend. In other words, the maximum legal dividend is the amount of the revenue reserves.

The profit and loss account and balance sheet of limited companies

The financial statements of a limited company are, in essence, the same as those of a sole proprietor. There are, however, some differences of detail, and we shall see what these are by examining a profit and loss account and balance sheet of a limited company. Let us take a look at Example 4.5 below.

Example 4.5

Da Silva plc
Profit and loss account for the year ended 31 December 2003

	£m	£m
Sales		840
Less Cost of sales		520
Gross profit		320
Less Operating expenses		
Wages and salaries	98	
Heat and light	18	
Rent and rates	24	
Motor vehicle expenses	20	
Insurance	4	
Printing and stationery	12	
Depreciation	45	
Audit fee	4	
		225
Operating profit		95
Less Interest payable		10
Profit before tax		85
Less Tax on profit		24
Profit after tax		61
Less Proposed dividend	25	
Transfer to general reserve	20	45
Unappropriated profit carried forward		16

Balance sheet as at 31 December 2003

	£m	£m
Fixed assets		
Land and buildings		132
Plant and machinery		171
		303
Current assets		
Stock	65	
Debtors	112	
Cash	36	
	213	

	£m	£m
Less Creditors: amounts falling due within 12 months		
Creditors	74	
Corporation tax	12	
Proposed dividend	25	
	111	
Net current assets (working capital)		102
Total assets less current liabilities		405
Less Creditors: amounts falling due in more than 12 months		
10% debentures		100
Net assets		305
Share capital		
Ordinary shares of £0.50 each		200
Reserves		
Share premium account	30	
General reserve	50	
Profit and loss account	25	
		105
		305

We can see that the financial statements are very similar to those that we have already considered in respect of sole proprietors; the differences are fairly small. However, let us now go through and pick up these differences.

The profit and loss account

There are a number of features in the profit and loss account that need consideration.

Profit

We can see that, following the calculation of gross profit, four further measures of profit are shown.

- The first of these is **operating profit**. This represents the profit achieved for the year before any financing expenses are taken into account. By excluding the financing expenses from the calculation of profit, a better idea of the operating performance for the year may be achieved.
- The second measure of profit is the net profit for the year (profit before tax). Interest charges are deducted from the operating profit to derive this figure. This measure is already familiar to us, and in the case of a sole proprietor business, the profit and loss account would end here.

■ The third measure of profit is the net profit after tax. As the company is a separate legal entity, it is liable to pay tax (known as corporation tax) on the profits generated. (This contrasts with the sole proprietor business where it is the owner rather than the business that is liable for the tax on profits.) This measure of profit represents the amount that is available for the shareholders.

■ The final measure of profit is the unappropriated, or retained, profit for the year. We can see that most of the net profit after tax is appropriated, or allocated, to pay a dividend and to transfer to a general reserve (see below). Once these appropriations have been made we are left with the fourth measure of profit, which represents the unallocated profits. It is probably worth pointing out that the last part of the profit and loss account dealing with appropriations for taxation, dividends and transfers to reserves is known as the 'appropriation account'.

Audit fee

As we shall see later in this chapter, companies of any real size are required to have their financial statements audited by an independent firm of auditors, for which a fee is charged. Though it is also open to sole proprietors to have their financial statements audited, very few do so. This is therefore an expense that will normally be present in the profit and loss account of a company but not that of a sole proprietor.

Dividend

This represents the drawings of capital by the shareholders of the company. The fact that the dividend is described as being 'proposed' means that the cash had not yet been paid at 31 December 2003 (the year end). Sometimes shareholders receive a dividend before the end of the year. Companies may pay their shareholders an 'interim' dividend, part way through the year, and a 'final' dividend shortly after the year end.

Transfer to general reserve

After dividends have been deducted from the net profit after tax figure, the remaining profit is normally reinvested ('ploughed back') into the operations of the company. For this company, the amount reinvested is £36 million (that is, £61 million – £25 million). This amount could all have been unallocated and simply gone to increase the unappropriated profit figure. We can see, however, an amount (£20 million for this company) has been transferred to a separate general reserve, which is quite common in practice.

It is not entirely clear why directors decide to make transfers to general reserves, since the funds concerned remain part of the revenue reserves, and are, therefore, still available for dividend. The most plausible explanation seems to be that directors feel that taking funds out of the profit and loss account and placing them in a 'reserve' indicates an intention to retain the funds permanently in the company and not to use them to pay a dividend. Of course, the unappropriated profit is also a reserve, but that fact is not indicated in its title.

The balance sheet

The main points for consideration in the balance sheet are:

- *Terminology*. Two terms used in the balance sheet are 'Creditors: amounts falling due within 12 months' and 'Creditors: amounts falling due in more than 12 months'. These terms refer to current liabilities and long-term liabilities, respectively. The law requires that these terms be used in balance sheets reported to external users.
- *Corporation tax*. The amount that appears as part of the short-term liabilities represents 50 per cent of the tax on the profit for the year 2003. It is, therefore, 50 per cent of the charge that appears in the profit and loss account; the other 50 per cent will already have been paid. The unpaid 50 per cent will be paid shortly after the balance sheet date. These payment dates are set down by law.
- *Dividend*. The dividend proposed in the profit and loss account also appears under short-term liabilities, also to be paid early in the new accounting year.
- *Share capital and reserves*. We have already discussed this area earlier in the chapter. The general reserve balance must have stood at £30 million before the year end as it was increased to its final level of £50 million by the transfer of £20 million of the year 2003 profit. Similarly, the profit and loss account balance must have been £9 million, just before the year end. As was mentioned above, the general reserve and the profit and loss account balance are identical in all respects; they both arise from retained profits, and are both available for dividend.

Directors' duty to account – the role of law

Both logic and the law require that the directors account for their stewardship of the company. To do this, the directors must prepare annual financial statements for the shareholders and for others. To ensure the reliability of these statements, the directors must maintain adequate accounting records and systems of control. These responsibilities may be set out in the annual report of the company which contains the financial statements, for the benefit of shareholders.

Exhibit 4.8

Below is an extract from the 2002 annual report of Marks and Spencer plc, which sets out what the directors regard as their responsibilities concerning the annual financial statements.

Directors' responsibilities for preparing the financial statements

The directors are obliged under company law to prepare financial statements for each financial year and to present them annually to the Company's members in Annual General Meeting.

The financial statements, of which the form and content is prescribed by the Companies Act 1985 and applicable accounting standards, must give a true and fair view of the state of affairs of the Company and the Group at the end of the financial year, and of the profit for that period.

▶

Exhibit 4.8 continued

> The directors are also responsible for the adoption of suitable accounting policies and their consistent use in the financial statements, supported where necessary by reasonable and prudent judgements.
>
> The directors confirm that the above requirements have been complied with in the financial statements.
>
> In addition, the directors are responsible for maintaining adequate accounting records and sufficient internal controls to safeguard the assets of the Group and to prevent and detect fraud or any other irregularities, as described more fully on the Corporate Governance page.
>
> *Source*: Annual Report 2002, Marks and Spencer plc

When preparing the financial statements, the law sets down various rules, which are embodied in the Companies Acts 1985 and 1989. These rules go quite a long way in prescribing in detail the form and content of the financial statements that the directors must publish. The law also lays down to whom the financial statements should be sent. A copy of each year's financial statement must be sent to all of the company's shareholders and debenture holders and a copy must also be lodged with the Registrar of Companies, which will be made available for inspection by the public. These statements will also normally be laid before the shareholders at an Annual General Meeting of the company.

The directors of a company may find the Annual General Meeting (AGM) of the shareholders an uncomfortable experience if the financial statements convey bad news. Exhibit 4.9, which appeared in the *Financial Times*, briefly recounts some of the more entertaining aspects of the 2002 AGM for Marconi plc, a large telecommunications company that recorded staggering losses of £5,664 million in 2002. The company once enjoyed better times under the late Lord Weinstock, one of the UK's most able post-war managers.

Exhibit 4.9 Jolly fellow

Marconi's AGM was a predictably lively affair, with hundreds of shareholders turning up at London's Methodist Central Hall to moan about their ever-decreasing investment.

Derek Bonham, who took over as interim chairman in September bravely to sort out the mess left by others, explained that he would step down as soon as a suitable replacement was found. 'Jolly good!' shouted a heckler, loudly. Bonham shot back: 'And I will be pleased too, sir.'

But at least one shareholder, from Alderney, was looking to the future. He urged the company to return to profitability by teaming with the UK government to open a chain of casinos in the Channel Islands.

He then attempted to lead the gathered masses in three cheers for the late Lord Weinstock – but ended up in chastising them for clapping rather than cheering.

Source: 'Jolly fellow', *Financial Times*, 9 October 2002

The role of accounting standards

Accounting standards (sometimes called *financial reporting standards*) are rules and guidelines, established by the UK accounting profession, which should be followed by those who prepare the financial statements of companies. They do not strictly have the same status as company law. Accounting standards do, however, define what is meant by a true and fair view, in various contexts and circumstances. Since company law requires that accounting statements show a true and fair view, this gives accounting standards an important role in preparing company financial statements.

When UK accounting standards were first introduced in the 1970s, the committee responsible for developing them saw the role of accounting standards as being to 'narrow the difference and variety of accounting practice by publishing authoritative statements on best accounting practice which will, whenever possible, be definitive'. This continues to reflect the role of accounting standards.

International accounting standards

In recent years, we have seen a trend towards the internationalisation of business and it seems likely that this will continue. This phenomenon has led to a need for the international harmonisation of accounting rules. It can no longer be assumed that the potential users of the financial statements of a large company, whose head office is in the UK, are familiar with UK accounting standards. Whichever user group we care to think of – employees, suppliers, customers, shareholders – some members of that group are quite likely to be residents of another country.

These facts have led to the need for international accounting standards and the creation of the International Accounting Standards Board (IASB). The IASB has issued a number of standards and its influence is growing. IASB standards have recently been endorsed by the EU and, from 2005 onwards, all EU listed companies must prepare their financial statements in accordance with these standards. Furthermore, the UK government has issued a consultation paper proposing that IASB standards replace UK accounting standards.

The role of the Financial Services Authority in company accounting

Those companies that are listed on the London Stock Exchange must adhere to further rules in order to have their shares traded there. These additional rules are imposed by the Financial Services Authority (FSA) in its role as the UK listing authority. The rules include the following disclosures:

- summarised interim (half-year) financial statements in addition to the statutorily required annual financial statements;
- a geographical analysis of turnover;
- details of holdings of more than 20 per cent of the shares of other companies.

Figure 4.3 illustrates the sources of accounting rules with which larger UK companies must comply.

Figure 4.3 Sources of accounting regulations for a UK limited company listed on the London Stock Exchange

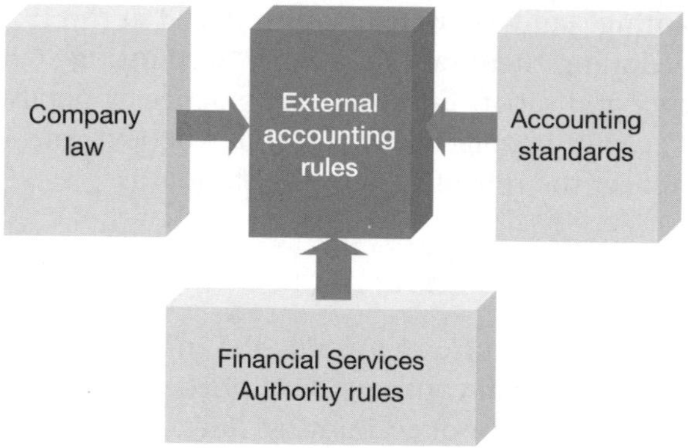

Company law provides the basic framework of company accounting regulation. This is augmented by accounting standards, which have virtually the force of law. The FSA imposes additional rules for companies listed on the London Stock Exchange.

Auditors

Shareholders, in all but the smallest companies, are required to elect a qualified and independent person or, more usually, a firm, to act as **auditors**. The main duty of auditors is to make a report as to whether, in their opinion, the financial statements do that which they are supposed to do, namely, show a true and fair view and comply with statutory and accounting standard requirements. To put themselves in a position where they can conscientiously make such a report, the auditors must scrutinise the annual financial statements, prepared by the directors, and the evidence on which those statements are based. The auditors' opinion must be included with the financial statements that are sent to shareholders, debenture holders and the Registrar of Companies.

The relationship between the shareholders, the directors and the auditors is illustrated in Figure 4.4. This shows that the shareholders elect the directors to act on their behalf in the day-to-day running of the company. The directors are required to 'account' to the shareholders on the performance, position and cash flows of

---

Figure 4.4 The relationship between the shareholders, the directors and the auditors

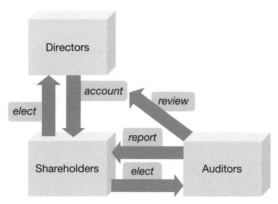

The directors are appointed by the shareholders to manage the company on the shareholders' behalf. The directors are required to report each year to the shareholders, principally by means of financial statements, on the company's performance and position. To lend greater credibility to the financial statements, the shareholders also appoint auditors to investigate the statements and to express an opinion on their reliability.

---

the company, on an annual basis. The shareholders also elect auditors whose role it is to give the shareholders an opinion as to whether they can regard the financial statements prepared by the directors as reliable.

Exhibit 4.10 provides an extract from the auditors' report for J.D. Wetherspoon plc, which owns and operates pubs throughout the UK.

Exhibit 4.10

The following extract from the auditors' report appeared with the annual financial statements of J.D. Wetherspoon plc for the year ended 28 July 2002. The extract describes the audit process that was carried out and sets out the opinion that was formed as a result.

Independent auditors' report to the members of J.D. Wetherspoon plc (extract)

Basis of audit opinion
We conducted our audit in accordance with auditing standards issued by the Auditing Practices Board. An audit includes examination, on a test basis, of evidence relevant to the amounts and disclosures in the financial statements. It also includes an assessment of the significant estimates and judgements made by the directors in the preparation of the financial statements, and of whether the accounting policies are appropriate to the company's circumstances, consistently applied and adequately disclosed.

We planned and performed our audit so as to obtain all the information and explanations which we considered necessary in order to provide us with sufficient evidence to give reasonable assurance that the financial statements are free from material misstatement, whether caused by fraud or other irregularity or error. In forming our opinion, we also evaluated the overall adequacy of the presentation of information in the financial statements.

▶

Exhibit 4.10 continued

Opinion

In our opinion the financial statements give a true and fair view of the state of the company's affairs at 28 July 2002 and of its profit and cash flows for the year then ended and have been properly prepared in accordance with the Companies Act 1985.

PricewaterhouseCoopers
Chartered Accountants and Registered Auditors
London
6 September 2002

Source: Annual Report 2002, J.D. Wetherspoon plc

We can see that the company has been given a 'clean bill of health' by the auditors. Where the auditors qualify their report, it is usually regarded as a serious matter.

Accounting rules and the quality of financial statements

Despite the proliferation of accounting rules and the independent checks that are imposed, there are concerns about the quality of company financial statements. There is evidence that the directors of some companies have employed particular accounting policies or structured particular transactions in such a way that portrays a picture of financial health that is in line with what they would like users to see rather than what is a true and fair view of financial position and performance. This practice is referred to as **creative accounting** and it poses a major problem for accounting rule-makers and for society generally.

Activity 4.11

Why might the directors of a company engage in creative accounting?

There are many reasons and these include:

■ to get around restrictions (for example, to report sufficient profit to pay a dividend)
■ to avoid government action (for example, the taxation of excessive profits)
■ to hide poor management decisions
■ to achieve sales or profit targets, thereby ensuring that performance bonuses are paid to the directors
■ to attract new share capital or loan capital by showing a healthy financial position
■ to satisfy the demands of major investors concerning levels of return.

The ways in which unscrupulous directors can manipulate the financial statements are many and varied. Exhibit 4.11 below, which is an extract from an article that appeared in *The Times*, identifies some of the more popular methods.

Exhibit 4.11 Dirty laundry: how companies fudge the numbers

Hollow swaps: telecoms companies sell useless fibre optic capacity to each other in order to generate revenues on their income statements. Example: Global Crossing.

Channel stuffing: a company floods the market with more products than its distributors can sell, artificially boosting its sales. SSL, the condom maker, shifted £60 million in excess stock on to trade customers. Also known as 'trade loading'.

Round tripping: also known as 'in-and-out trading'. Used to notorious effect by Enron. Two or more traders buy and sell energy among themselves for the same price and at the same time. Inflates trading volumes and makes participants appear to be doing more business than they really are.

Pre-dispatching: goods such as carpets are marked as 'sold' as soon as an order is placed . . . This inflates sales and profits.

Off-balance sheet activities: companies use special purpose entities and other devices such as leasing . . . to push assets and liabilities off their balance sheets . . .

Source: 'Dirty laundry: How companies fudge the numbers', *The Times* Business, 22 September 2002

Recently, there has been a wave of creative accounting scandals in both the US and the UK, although US companies have been the bigger 'sinners'. This fact may reflect the differences in approach to accounting standards between the two countries. UK accounting standards tend to focus on principles and try to show how detailed rules are based on these principles. It has been argued that this helps to encourage a willingness to comply with the spirit of a standard as well as with its detailed rules. US accounting standards, on the other hand, are based more on legalistic rules. Recent events have shown that ways of presenting accounting information may be devised that may go against the spirit of a particular standard but nevertheless keep within its rules.

It seems that accounting scandals are becoming more rare and that the quality of financial statements is improving. It is to be hoped that trust among investors and others will soon be restored. However, such scandals may re-emerge in the future. The recent wave of scandals coincided with a period of strong economic growth in both the US and the UK. It has been argued that during good economic times, investors and auditors become less vigilant and so the opportunity to manipulate the figures becomes easier. Thus, we must not become too complacent. Things may change again when we next experience a period of strong growth.

? Self-assessment question 4.1

This question requires you to correct some figures on a set of company financial statements. It should prove useful practice for the material that you covered in Chapters 2 and 3, as well as helping you to become familiar with the financial statements of a company.

Presented below is a draft set of simplified financial statements for Pear Limited for the year ended 30 September 2003.

▶

Self-assessment question 4.1 continued

Pear Limited
Profit and loss account for the year ended 30 September 2003

	£000	£000
Turnover		1,456
Cost of sales		768
Gross profit		688
Less Expenses		
Salaries	220	
Depreciation	249	
Other operating costs	131	600
Operating profit		88
Interest payable		15
Profit before taxation		73
Taxation at 30%		22
Profit after taxation		51

Balance sheet as at 30 September 2003

	£000	£000
Fixed assets		
Cost	1,570	
Depreciation	(690)	
		880
Current assets		
Stocks	207	
Debtors	182	
Cash at bank	21	
	410	
Less **Creditors: amounts due within one year**		
Trade creditors	88	
Other creditors	20	
Taxation	22	
Bank overdraft	105	
	235	
Net current assets		175
Less **Creditors: amounts due after more than one year**		
10% debenture – repayable 2008		(300)
		755
Capital and reserves		
Share capital		300
Share premium account		300
Retained profit at beginning of year	104	
Profit for year	51	155
		755

The following additional information is available:

1 Depreciation has not been charged on office equipment with a written-down value of £100,000. This class of assets is depreciated at 12 per cent per annum using the reducing-balance method.

Self-assessment question 4.1 continued

2 A new machine was purchased, on credit, for £30,000 and delivered on 29 September but has not been included in the financial statements.

3 An invoice for a sale on credit to the value of £18,000 for September has been omitted from the financial statements. (The cost of sales is stated correctly.)

4 A dividend has been proposed of £25,000.

5 The interest payable on the debenture for the second half year has not been included in the financial statements.

6 An invoice for electricity to the value of £2,000 for the quarter ended 30 September 2003 arrived on 4 October and has not been included in the financial statements.

7 The charge for taxation will have to be amended to take account of the above information. Make the simplifying assumptions that (i) the tax charge is based strictly on the profit before taxation and (ii) it is payable shortly after the end of the year.

Required:
Prepare a revised set of financial statements for the year ended 30 September 2003 incorporating the additional information in points 1–7 above.

Summary

The main points of this chapter may be summarised as follows:

- *The main features of a limited company*:
  - it is an artificial person that has been created by law;
  - it has a separate life to its owners and is granted a perpetual existence;
  - it must take responsibility for its own debts and losses but its owners are granted limited liability;
  - it is governed by a board of directors, which is elected by the shareholders;
  - a public company can offer its shares for sale to the public; a private company cannot.

- *Financing a limited company*:
  - the share capital of a company can be of two main types – ordinary shares and preference shares;
  - ordinary shares are the main risk-takers and are given voting rights; they form the backbone of the company;
  - preference shares are given a right to a fixed dividend before ordinary shareholders receive a dividend;
  - reserves are profits and gains made by the company and form part of the ordinary shareholders' claim;
  - loan capital provides another major source of finance.

- *Share issues*:
  - bonus shares are issued to existing shareholders when part of the reserves of the company are converted into share capital;

- ❏ rights shares give existing shareholders the right to buy new shares in proportion to their existing holding;
- ❏ the shares of public companies may be bought and sold on a recognised Stock Exchange.

- ■ *Reserves*:
  - ❏ reserves are of two types – revenue reserves and capital reserves;
  - ❏ revenue reserves arise from trading profits and from realised profits on the sale of fixed assets;
  - ❏ capital reserves arise from the issue of shares above their nominal value or from the upward revaluation of fixed assets;
  - ❏ revenue reserves can be withdrawn as dividends by the shareholders whereas capital reserves cannot.

- ■ *Financial statements of limited companies*:
  - ❏ the financial statements of limited companies are based on the same principles as those of sole proprietorship businesses. However, there are some differences in detail;
  - ❏ the profit and loss account has four measures of profit displayed: operating profit, net profit for the year (profit before tax), net profit after tax and unappropriated profit;
  - ❏ the profit and loss account also shows audit fees, transfers to reserves, corporation tax on profits for the year and dividends for the year;
  - ❏ the balance sheet refers to current liabilities as creditors: amounts falling due within 12 months and refers to long-term liabilities as creditors: amounts falling due in more than 12 months;
  - ❏ any unpaid tax and dividends will appear in the balance sheet as creditors: amounts falling due within 12 months;
  - ❏ the share capital plus the reserves will be shown as the owners' claim.

- ■ *Rules surrounding limited companies*:
  - ❏ the directors are legally obliged to keep proper accounting records and to prepare the financial statements;
  - ❏ the law requires that the financial statements show a true and fair view and prescribe much of the form and content of the financial statements;
  - ❏ accounting standards have been developed by the UK accounting profession to define what is meant by a true and fair view in various contexts;
  - ❏ companies that are listed on the London Stock Exchange are subject to additional rules to those imposed by the law and accounting standards;
  - ❏ auditors are appointed to provide an independent opinion as to whether the financial statements show a true and fair view;
  - ❏ despite the accounting rules that are in place, there have been recent examples of creative accounting by directors of companies.

→ **Key terms**

? **Review questions**

Answers to these questions can be found on the students' side of the Companion Website.

4.1 How does the liability of a limited company differ from the liability of a real person, in respect of amounts owed to others?

4.2 Some people are about to form a company, as a vehicle through which to run a new business. What are the advantages to them of forming a private limited company rather than a public one?

4.3 What is a reserve? Distinguish between a revenue reserve and a capital reserve.

4.4 What is a preference share? Compare the main features of a preference share with those of
(a) an ordinary share, and
(b) a debenture.

? **Exercises**

Exercises 4.4 and 4.5 are more advanced than 4.1–4.3. Those with a coloured number have an answer at the back of the book.

4.1 Briefly explain each of the following expressions, which you have seen in the financial statements of a limited company:

(a) reserve
(b) nominal value of shares
(c) rights issue.

4.2 Briefly explain each of the following expressions, which you have seen in the financial statements of a limited company:

(a) dividend

(b) debenture

(c) share premium account.

4.3 (a) Describe briefly the role played by each of the following in the publication of financial statements for public limited companies:

(i) the Companies Act 1985

(ii) the Accounting Standards Board

(iii) the Financial Services Authority.

(b) Comment on the differences between the published financial statements of a company and its internal management accounts.

4.4 Comment on the following quotation:

Limited companies can set a limit on the amount of debts that they will meet. They tend to have reserves of cash, as well as share capital, and they can use these reserves to pay dividends to the shareholders. Many companies have preference as well as ordinary shares. The preference shares give a guaranteed dividend. The shares of many companies can be bought and sold on the Stock Exchange; a shareholder selling shares can represent a useful source of new capital to the company. The auditors are appointed by the directors to check the books and prepare the annual financial statements. Accounting standards are produced by the government and set out the basic framework for the annual financial statements of companies. The basic requirement of company financial statements is that they should provide 'a correct and accurate view' of the company's affairs.

4.5 Rose Limited operates a small chain of retail shops, which sell high-quality teas and coffees. Approximately half of sales are on credit. Abbreviated and unaudited financial statements are given below:

Rose Limited
Profit and loss account for the year ended 31 March 2003

	£000	£000
Sales		12,080
Less Cost of sales		6,282
Gross profit		5,798
Less Labour costs	2,658	
Depreciation	625	
Other operating costs	1,003	
		4,286
Net profit before interest		1,512
Less Interest payable		66
Net profit before tax		1,446
Less Tax payable		434
Net profit after tax		1,012
Less Dividend payable		300
Retained profit for year		712
Retained profit brought forward		756
Retained profit carried forward		1,468

Balance sheet as at 31 March 2003

	£000	£000
Fixed assets		2,728
Current assets:		
Stocks	1,583	
Debtors	996	
Cash	26	
	2,605	
Less Creditors: amounts due within one year		
Trade creditors	1,118	
Other creditors	417	
Tax	434	
Dividends	300	
Overdraft	296	
	2,565	
Net current assets		40
Less Creditors: amounts due after more than one year		
Secured loan (repayable 2008)		300
		2,468
Share capital		
(50p shares fully paid)		750
Share premium		250
Retained profit		1,468
		2,468

Since the unaudited financial statements for Rose Limited were prepared, the following information has become available:

1 An additional £74,000 of depreciation should have been charged on fixtures and fittings.
2 Invoices for credit sales on 31 March 2003 amounting to £34,000 have not been included; cost of sales is not affected.
3 Stocks, which had been purchased for £2,000, have been damaged and are unsaleable.
4 Fixtures and fittings to the value of £16,000 were delivered just before 31 March 2003, but these assets were not included in the financial statements and the purchase invoice had not been processed.
5 Wages for Saturday-only staff, amounting to £1,000, have not been paid for the final Saturday of the year.
6 Tax is payable at 30 per cent of net profit before tax. Make the simplifying assumption that tax is payable shortly after the end of the year.

Required:
Prepare a balance sheet and profit and loss account for Rose Limited for the year ended 31 March 2003, incorporating the information in points 1–6 above.

Chapter 5

Measuring and reporting cash flows

Introduction

This chapter is devoted to the third major financial statement that we identified in Chapter 2 – the cash flow statement. This statement reveals the movements of cash over a period and the effect of these movements on the cash position of the business. It is an important financial statement because cash is important to the survival of a business. Without cash, no business can operate.

In this chapter, we shall see how the cash flow statement is prepared and how the information that it contains may be interpreted. We shall also see why the deficiencies of the profit and loss account in revealing cash flows over time make a separate cash flow statement necessary.

The cash flow statement is being considered after the chapter on limited companies because the format of the statement requires an understanding of this type of business. Limited companies are required to provide a cash flow statement, as well as the more traditional profit and loss account and balance sheet, for shareholders and other interested parties.

Objectives

When you have completed this chapter, you should be able to:

- **discuss the crucial importance of cash to a business**
- **explain the nature of the cash flow statement and discuss how it can be helpful in identifying cash flow problems**
- **prepare a cash flow statement**
- **interpret a cash flow statement.**

The cash flow statement

The cash flow statement is a fairly recent addition to the set of financial statements sent to shareholders and to others. There used to be no need for companies to produce more than a profit and loss account and balance sheet. The prevailing view seemed to have been that any financial information required would be contained within these two statements. This view may have been based partly on the assumption that if a business were profitable, it would also have plenty of cash. Though in the very long run this is likely to be true, it is not necessarily true in the short to medium term.

We have already seen in Chapter 3 that the profit and loss account sets out the revenues and expenses, rather than the cash receipts and cash payments, for the period. Thus, profit (loss), which represents the difference between the revenues and expenses for the period, may have little or no relation to the cash generated for the period. To illustrate this point, let us take the example of a business making a sale (a revenue). This will lead to an increase in wealth and will be shown in the profit and loss account. However, if the sale is made on credit, no cash changes hands – not at the time of sale at least. Instead, the increase in wealth is reflected in another asset – an increase in trade debtors. Furthermore, if an item of stock is the subject of the sale, wealth is lost to the business through the reduction in the stock. This means an expense is incurred in making the sale, which will be shown in the profit and loss account. Once again, however, no cash has changed hands at the time of sale. For such reasons, the profit and the cash generated for a period will rarely go hand in hand.

The following activity helps to underline how profit and cash for a period may be affected differently by particular transactions or events.

Activity 5.1

The following is a list of business/accounting events. In each case, state the effect (increase, decrease or no effect) on both cash and profit:

	Effect	
	on profit	on cash
1 Repayment of a loan	_____	_____
2 Making a sale on credit	_____	_____
3 Buying a fixed asset for cash	_____	_____
4 Receiving cash from a trade debtor	_____	_____
5 Depreciating a fixed asset	_____	_____
6 Buying some stock for cash	_____	_____
7 Making a share issue for cash	_____	_____

You should have come up with the following:

	Effect	
	on profit	on cash
1 Repayment of a loan	none	decrease
2 Making a sale on credit	increase	none
3 Buying a fixed asset for cash	none	decrease
4 Receiving cash from a trade debtor	none	increase
5 Depreciating a fixed asset	decrease	none
6 Buying some stock for cash	none	decrease
7 Making a share issue for cash	none	increase

Activity 5.1 continued

The reasons for these answers are as follows:

1 Repaying the loan requires that cash be paid to the creditors. Thus two figures in the balance sheet will be affected, but not the profit and loss account.
2 Making a sale on credit will increase the sales figure and probably profit or loss (unless the sale was made for a price that precisely equalled the expenses involved). No cash will change hands, however, at this point.
3 Buying a fixed asset for cash obviously reduces the cash balance of the business, but its profit figure is not affected.
4 Receiving cash from a debtor increases the cash balance and reduces the debtor's balance. Both of these figures are on the balance sheet. The profit and loss account is unaffected.
5 Depreciating a fixed asset means that an expense is recognised. This causes the value of the asset, as it is recorded on the balance sheet, to fall by an amount equal to the amount of the expense. No cash is paid or received.
6 Buying some stock for cash means that the value of the stock will increase and the cash balance will decrease by a similar amount. Profit is not affected.
7 Making a share issue for cash increases the owners' claim and increases the cash balance; profit is unaffected.

It is clear from the above that if we are to gain an insight to cash movements over time, the profit and loss account is not the answer. Instead we need a separate financial statement. This fact has become widely recognised in recent years and in 1991 a financial reporting standard, FRS 1, emerged that requires all but the smallest companies to produce and publish a cash flow statement.

Why is cash so important?

It is worth asking why is cash so important? After all, cash is just an asset that a business needs to help it to function. In that sense, it is no different from stock or fixed assets.

The reason for the importance of cash is that people and organisations will not normally accept other than cash in settlement of their claims against the business. If a business wants to employ people it must pay them in cash. If it wants to buy a new fixed asset to exploit a business opportunity, the seller of the asset will normally insist on being paid in cash, probably after a short period of credit. When businesses fail, it is their inability to find the cash to pay the amounts owed that really pushes them under.

These factors lead to cash being the pre-eminent business asset. It is the one that is watched most carefully when trying to assess the ability of businesses to survive and/or to take advantage of commercial opportunities as they arise. The following exhibit emphasises this point.

Exhibit 5.1 Ericsson rings the changes

Ericsson, the telecoms equipment maker, set a target to achieve a positive cash flow of nearly $1.3bn for the final quarter of 2001. This was done to ensure that the overall cash flow for the year was positive. Investors were watching the cash flow position of Ericsson very closely at this time. They were concerned that if cash flows remained negative, the business would be forced to raise new funds from an issue of shares. It was feared that this would dilute the return to existing shareholders and lead to a fall in the value of the shares.

  The determination of the business to avoid this situation was reflected in the fact that the annual bonuses of 3,000 managers were based on reaching a positive cash flow for the year. In order to achieve a positive cash flow for the year, the business cut one-fifth of its workforce, sold a property in central London for $167 million, and sold (but then leased back) software-testing equipment to improve cash flows by a further $750 million.

Source: Adapted from 'Ericsson nears cash flow target with equipment sale', *Financial Times*, 31 December 2001, FT.com

The main features of the cash flow statement

The cash flow statement is, in essence, a summary of the cash receipts and payments over the period concerned. All payments of a particular type, for example cash payments to acquire additional fixed assets, are added together to give just one figure that appears in the statement. The net total of the statement is the net increase or decrease of the cash of the business over the period. The statement is basically an analysis of the business's cash movements for the period.

The cash flow statement is now accepted, along with the profit and loss account and balance sheet, as a primary financial statement. The relationship between the three statements is shown in Figure 5.1. The balance sheet reflects the combination of assets (including cash) and claims (including the owners' capital) of the business *at a particular point in time*. Both the cash flow statement and the profit and loss account explain the *changes over a period* to two of the items in the balance sheet, namely cash and owners' claim respectively. In practice, this period is typically the business's accounting year.

The standard layout of the cash flow statement is summarised in Figure 5.2. Explanations of the terms used in the figure are as follows:

- **Net cash flow from operating activities.** This is the net inflow or outflow from trading operations. It is equal to the sum of cash receipts from trade debtors (and cash sales where relevant) less the sums paid to buy stock, to pay rent, to pay wages and so on. Note that it is the amounts of cash received and paid that feature in the cash flow statement, not the revenue and expense. It is, of course, the profit and loss account that deals with the revenues and expenses.
- **Returns on investments and servicing of finance.** This category deals with payments made to suppliers of fixed return finance to reward them for the use of their money. Fixed return finance includes preference shares and interest-bearing loans, and the rewards are preference dividends and interest respectively. Similarly, this part of the statement deals with cash that the business receives as interest and

Figure 5.1 The relationship between the balance sheet, the profit and loss account and the cash flow statement

The balance sheet shows the position, at a particular point in time, of the business's assets and claims. The profit and loss account explains how, over a period between two balance sheets, the owners' claim figure in the first balance sheet has altered as a result of trading operations to become the figure in the second balance sheet. The cash flow statement also looks at changes over the accounting period, but this statement explains the alteration in the cash balances shown in the two consecutive balance sheets.

Figure 5.2 Standard layout of the cash flow statement

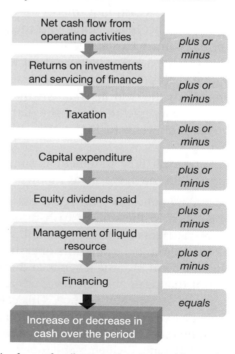

The figure sets out, in the form of a diagram, the standard layout for the cash flow statement as required by FRS1, *Cash Flow Statements*.

dividends from investments (in loans and shares) that it has made. The object of distinguishing between payments and receipts arising from financing and investment outside the business and money deriving from normal operating activities is to enable the reader of the statement to separate the cash flow arising from these different types of activity.

Note that dividends paid by a business to its ordinary shareholders are dealt with later in the statement. Note also that the word 'servicing' in this context refers to rewarding suppliers of finance for the use of their money. If they are not rewarded, they will not normally allow their money to be used.

- **Taxation.** This is fairly obvious, but we should be clear that the amounts shown here are payments and receipts of tax made during the period covered by the statement. Companies normally pay tax on their profits in four equal instalments. Two of these are during the year concerned, and the other two are during the following year. Thus by the end of each accounting year, one half of the tax will have been paid and the remainder will be a current liability at the end of the year, to be paid off during the following year. During any particular year, therefore, the tax payment would normally equal 50 per cent of the previous year's tax charge and 50 per cent of that of the current year.

- **Capital expenditure.** This part of the statement is concerned with cash payments made to acquire additional fixed assets and with cash receipts from the disposal of fixed assets. These fixed assets could be loans made by the business or shares in another business bought by the business, as well as the more usual fixed assets such as buildings, machinery and so on.

- **Equity dividends paid.** This is cash dividends paid to the business's own ordinary shareholders (equity holders) during the period covered by the statement. Businesses frequently declare a dividend that is shown in one year's profit and loss account but which is not paid until the following year, being treated as a short-term liability until it is paid. This means that the dividend 'for the year' is often not paid until the following year.

- **Management of liquid resources.** This part of the statement deals with cash receipts and payments arising from the acquisition and disposal of readily disposable investments. These are investments that the business did not or does not intend to hold for any other reason than to find a profitable resting place for what will probably be a short-term cash surplus. Readily disposable investments of this type will typically be investments in shares of businesses listed on the Stock Exchange, and government bonds (short-term loans to the government).

- **Financing.** This part of the statement is concerned with the long-term financing of the business. So we are considering borrowings (other than very short term) and finance from share issues. This category is concerned with repayment/redemption of finance as well as with the raising of it.

- **Increase or decrease in cash over the period.** The total of the statement must, of course, be the net increase or decrease in cash over the period covered by the statement. 'Cash' here means notes and coins in hand and deposits in banks and similar institutions that are accessible to the business within 24 hours' notice, without incurring a penalty for premature withdrawal.

Example 5.1 sets out a cash flow statement according to the requirements of FRS 1. The headings printed in bold type are specifically required, and are the primary categories into which cash payments and receipts for the period must be analysed. Note that in Example 5.1 there is a subtotal in the statement after 'capital expenditure'. This is to highlight the extent to which the cash flows of the period, arising from the 'normal' activities of the business (operations, servicing loans, tax and capital investment), cover the dividend on ordinary shares paid during the period.

Similarly there is a subtotal after the ordinary share dividend paid. The reason for drawing this subtotal is to highlight the extent to which the business has relied on additional external finance to support its trading and other normally recurring operations. It is claimed that, before the requirement for businesses to produce the cash flow statement, some businesses were able to obscure the fact that they were only able to continue their operations as a result of a series of borrowings and/or share issues. It is no longer possible to obscure such actions.

The effect on a business's cash balance of its various activities is shown in Figure 5.3. The activities that affect cash are analysed in the same way as is required by FRS 1. As explained below, the arrows in the figure show the *normal* direction of cash flow for the typical healthy, profitable business in a typical year.

Figure 5.3 Diagrammatic representation of the cash flow statement

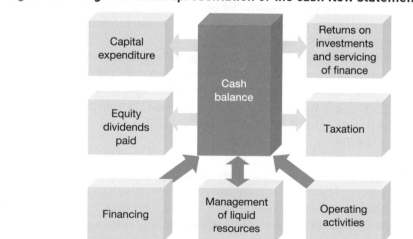

Various activities of the business each have their own effect on its cash balance, either positive (increasing the cash balance) or negative (reducing it). The increase or decrease in the cash balance over a period will be the sum of these individual effects, taking account of the direction (cash in or cash out) of each activity's effect on cash.

Note that the direction of the arrow shows the *normal* direction of the cash flow in respect of each activity. In certain circumstances each of these arrows could be reversed in direction; for example, in some circumstances the business might be eligible to claim a repayment of tax instead of having to pay it. Only with 'management of liquid resources' will there not be a 'normal' direction of the cash flow.

Normally 'operating activities' provide positive cash flow: that is, they help to increase the business's cash resources. In fact, for UK businesses, cash generated from day-to-day trading, even after deducting tax, interest and dividends, is overwhelmingly the most important source of new finance for most businesses in most time periods.

Example 5.1

Propulsion plc
Cash flow statement for the year ended 31 December 2003

	£m	£m
Net cash inflows from operating activities		55
Returns on investments and servicing of finance		
Interest received	1	
Interest paid	(2)	
Net cash outflow from returns on investment and servicing of finance		(1)
Taxation		
Corporation tax paid	(4)	
Net cash outflow for taxation		(4)
Capital expenditure		
Payments to acquire intangible fixed assets	(6)	
Payments to acquire tangible fixed assets	(23)	
Receipts from sales of tangible fixed assets	4	
Net cash outflow for capital expenditure		(25)
		25
Equity dividends		
Dividend on ordinary shares	(10)	
Net cash outflow for equity dividends		(10)
		15
Management of liquid resources		
Disposal of treasury bills	3	
Net cash inflow from management of liquid resources		3
Financing		
Repayments of debenture stock	(6)	
Net cash outflow for financing		(6)
Increase in cash		12

Activity 5.2

Last year's cash flow statement for Angus plc showed a negative cash flow from operating activities. What could be the reason for this, and should the business's management be alarmed by it? (*Hint*: We think that there are two broad possible reasons for a negative cash flow.)

Activity 5.2 continued

The two reasons are:

- The business is unprofitable. This leads to more cash being paid out to employees, suppliers of goods and services and so on, than is received from debtors in respect of sales. This would be particularly alarming, because a major expense for most businesses is depreciation of fixed assets. Since depreciation does not lead to a cash flow, it is not considered in 'net cash inflows' from operating activities. Interest paid on any money borrowed by the business would not be included here either, because it is taken into account under 'servicing of finance'. Thus, a negative operating cash flow might well indicate a very much larger trading loss – in other words, a significant loss of the business's wealth.
- The other reason might be less alarming. A business that is expanding its activities (level of sales) would tend to spend quite a lot of cash, relative to the amount of cash coming in from sales. This is because it will probably be expanding its assets (fixed and current) to accommodate the increased demand. In the first instance, it would not necessarily benefit, in cash flow terms, from all of the additional sales. For example, a business may well have to have stock-in-trade in place before additional sales can be made. Even when the additional sales are made, the sales would normally be made on credit, with the cash inflow lagging behind the sale. This would be particularly likely to be true of a new business, which would be expanding stocks and other assets from zero. Expansion typically causes cash flow strains for the reasons just explained. This can be a particular problem because the business's increased profitability might encourage a feeling of optimism, which could lead to lack of concern for the cash flow problem.

To continue with our consideration of the 'normal' direction of cash flows, generally a business would pay out more to service its loan finance than it receives from financial investments (loans made and shares owned) that it has made itself.

Companies pay tax on profits, so the cash flow would be from the company to the Inland Revenue, where the company is profitable, or there would not be a cash flow where the company is making a loss. Where a company makes a trading loss following a period of having paid tax on profits, it would be entitled to set the current loss against past profits and obtain a refund of past tax paid as a result. Thus there might be a positive cash flow from taxation.

Investing activities can give rise to positive cash flows when a business sells some fixed assets. Because most types of fixed asset wear out, and because businesses tend to seek to expand their asset base, the normal direction of cash in this area is out of the business: that is, negative.

Financing can go in either direction, depending on the financing strategy at the time. Since businesses seek to expand, there is a general tendency for this area to lead to cash coming into the business rather than leaving it.

Reporting the cash flow statement

Let us take a look at a real-life example of a cash flow statement. Below is the (slightly modified) cash flow statement for Fuller's for the 52 weeks ended 30 March 2002.

This company operates hotels, pubs and bars and also produces beer (including 'London Pride', its key brand).

Exhibit 5.2 **A taste of Fuller's**

Cash flow statement for the 52 weeks ended 30 March 2002

	£000	£000
Net cash inflows from operating activities		24,642
Returns on investments and servicing of finance		
Preference dividend paid	(120)	
Interest received	501	
Interest paid	(2,234)	
Net cash outflow on returns on investments and servicing of finance		(1,853)
Taxation		
Corporation tax paid	(4,942)	
Net cash outflow for taxation		(4,942)
Capital expenditure		
Payments to acquire tangible fixed assets	(26,980)	
Payments to acquire fixed asset investments	(328)	
Receipts from sales of tangible fixed assets	3,684	
Net cash outflow for capital expenditure		(23,624)
Equity dividends		
Dividend on ordinary shares	(3,631)	
Net cash outflow for equity dividends		(3,631)
Total net cash outflow before the use of liquid resources and financing		(9,408)
Management of liquid resources		
Net cash inflow from management of liquid resources		11,391
Financing		
Issue of equity shares	719	
Repurchase of equity shares	(498)	
Net cash inflow for financing		221
Movement in cash in the year		2,204

We shall consider the interpretation of the cash flow statement a little later. However, one striking feature of the above statement is the amount of capital expenditure that has been undertaken. The managing director of the company made the point in his review of operations that:

> . . . investment for the future has been the keyword. This year has seen the opening of three new hotels, almost doubling our room stock. We have not made this investment at the expense of retail business and we continue to expand both the successful managed (pub) estate and the tenanted estate. The unprecedented investment in plant and machinery has also paid dividends and given us the capacity to meet the ever-increasing demand for Fuller's beers.

Source: Fuller, Smith & Turner P.L.C., Annual Report and Accounts 2002, by kind permission

Deducing net cash inflows from operating activities

The first category of cash flow that appears in the cash flow statement, and the one that is typically the most important for most businesses, is the cash flow from operations. There are two methods that can be used to derive the figure for inclusion in the statement: the direct method and the indirect method.

The direct method

→ The **direct method** involves an analysis of the cash records of the business for the period, picking out all payments and receipts relating to operating activities. These are summarised to give the net figure for inclusion in the cash flow statement. This could be a time-consuming and laborious activity, though a computer could do it. Not many businesses adopt this approach.

The indirect method

→ The **indirect method** is the more popular method. It relies on the fact that, broadly, sales give rise to cash inflows, and expenses give rise to outflows. Broadly, therefore, the net profit figure will be closely linked to the net cash inflow from operating activities. Since businesses have to produce a profit and loss account in any case, information from it can be used as a starting point to deduce the cash inflow from operating activities.

Of course, within a particular accounting period, net profit will not normally equal the net cash inflow from operating activities. We saw in Chapter 3 that, when sales are made on credit, the cash receipt occurs some time after the sale. This means that sales made towards the end of an accounting year will be included in that year's profit and loss account, but most of the cash from those sales will flow into the business, and should be included in the cash flow statement, in the following year. Fortunately it is easy to deduce the cash received from sales if we have the relevant profit and loss account, as we shall see in Activity 5.3.

Activity 5.3

How can we deduce the cash inflow from sales using the profit and loss account and balance sheet for the business?

The balance sheet will tell us how much was owed in respect of credit sales at the beginning and end of the year (trade debtors). The profit and loss account tells us the sales figure. If we adjust the sales figure by the increase or decrease in trade debtors over the year, we deduce the cash from sales for the year.

Example 5.2

The sales figure for a business for the year is £34 million. The trade debtors were £4 million at the beginning of the year, but had increased to £5 million by the end of the year.

Basically, the debtors figure is affected by sales and cash receipts. It is increased when a sale is made and decreased when cash is received from a debtor. If, over the year, the sales and the cash receipts had been equal, the beginning-of-year and end-of-year debtors figures would have been equal. Since the debtors figure increased, it must mean that less cash was received than sales were made. Thus the cash receipts from sales must be £33 million (34 − (5 − 4)).

Put slightly differently, we can say that as a result of sales, assets of £34 million flowed into the business during the year. If £1 million of this went to increasing the asset of trade debtors, this leaves only £33 million that went to increase cash.

The same general point is true in respect of nearly all of the other items that are taken into account in deducing the operating profit figure. The exception is depreciation. This is not necessarily associated with any movement in cash during the accounting period.

All of this means that if we take the operating profit (that is, the profit before interest and tax) for the year, add back the depreciation charged in arriving at that profit, and adjust this total by movements in stock, debtors and creditors, we have the effect on cash.

Example 5.3

The relevant information from the financial statements of Dido plc for last year is as follows:

	£m
Net operating profit	122
Depreciation charged in arriving at net operating profit	34
At the beginning of the year	
Stock	15
Debtors	24
Creditors	18
At the end of the year	
Stock	17
Debtors	21
Creditors	19

The cash flow from operating activities is derived as follows:

		£m
Net operating profit		122
Add Depreciation		34
Net inflow of working capital from operations		156
Less Increase in stock (17 − 15)		2
		154
Add Decrease in debtors (21 − 24)	3	
Increase in creditors (19 − 18)	1	4
Net cash inflow from operating activities		158

Thus the net increase in working capital, as a result of trading, was £156 million. Of this, £2 million went into increased stocks. More cash was received from debtors than sales were made, and less cash was paid to creditors than purchases of goods and services on credit. Both of these had a favourable effect on cash, which increased by £158 million.

The indirect method of deducing the net cash flow from operating activities is summarised in Figure 5.4.

Figure 5.4 The indirect method of deducing the net cash flow from the operating activities

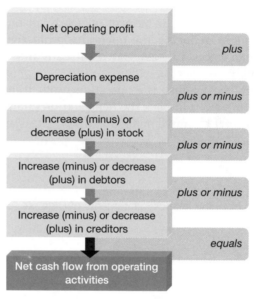

The figure sets out the indirect method of determining the depreciation charge to the net profit for the period and then adjusting for increases or decreases in stock, debtors and creditors.

Activity 5.4

The relevant information from the financial statements of Pluto plc for last year is as follows:

	£m
Net operating profit	165
Depreciation charged in arriving at net operating profit	41
At the beginning of the year:	
Stock	22
Debtors	18
Creditors	15
At the end of the year	
Stock	23
Debtors	21
Creditors	17

Activity 5.4 continued

What figure should appear in the cash flow statement for 'net cash inflow from operating activities'?

Net cash inflow from operating activities:

	£m	£m
Net operating profit		165
Add Depreciation		41
Net inflow of working capital from operations		206
Less Increase in stock (23 – 22)	1	
Increase in debtors (21 – 18)	3	4
		202
Add Increase in creditors (17 – 15)		2
Net cash inflow from operating activities		204

Exhibit 5.3 shows how the net cash flow from operating activities for Fuller's is calculated for the 52 weeks ended 30 March 2002 (see also Exhibit 5.2 above).

Exhibit 5.3 Fuller's figures

	£000
Operating profit	15,426
Depreciation	8,287
Loss on disposal of fixed assets	78
Impairment of fixed assets*	1,350
Net inflow of working capital from operations	25,141
Increase/decrease in working capital	
Stocks	191
Debtors	(941)
Creditors	251
Net cash inflow from operating activities	24,642

* The term 'impairment of fixed assets' represents a writing down of fixed assets and is similar to depreciation.

Source. Reproduced from Fuller, Smith & Turner P.L.C., Annual Report and Accounts 2002, by kind permission

We can see from the above that the net increase in working capital from operations is much higher than the operating profit for the period, reflecting the size of depreciation and other non-cash items appearing in the profit and loss account.

We can now go on to take a look at the preparation of a complete cash flow statement – see Example 5.4.

Example 5.4

Torbryan plc's profit and loss account for the year ended 31 December 2003 and the balance sheets as at 31 December 2002 and 2003 are as follows:

Profit and loss account for the year ended 31 December 2003

	£m	£m
Turnover		576
Less Cost of sales		307
Gross profit		269
Less Distribution costs	65	
Administrative expenses	26	91
		178
Other operating income		21
Operating profit		199
Interest receivable and similar income		17
		216
Less Interest payable and similar charges		23
Profit on ordinary activities before taxation		193
Less Tax on profit or loss on ordinary activities		46
Profit on ordinary activities after taxation		147
Retained profit brought forward from last year		26
		173
Less Proposed dividend on ordinary shares		50
Retained profit carried forward		123

Balance sheets as at 31 December 2002 and 2003

	2002	*2003*
	£m	*£m*
Fixed assets		
Land and buildings	241	241
Plant and machinery	309	325
	550	566
Current assets		
Stocks	44	41
Trade debtors	121	139
	165	180
Less **Creditors: amounts falling due within one year**		
Bank overdraft	28	6
Trade creditors	55	54
Corporation tax	16	23
Dividend proposed	40	50
	139	133
Net current assets	26	47
Total assets less current liabilities	576	613
Less **Creditors: amounts falling due after more than one year**		
Debenture loans	400	250
	176	363

	2002 £m	2003 £m
Capital and reserves		
Called-up ordinary share capital	150	200
Share premium account	–	40
Profit and loss account	26	123
	176	363

During 2003, the company spent £95 million on additional plant and machinery. There were no other fixed-asset acquisitions or disposals. The cash flow statement would be as follows:

Torbryan plc
Cash flow statement for the year ended 31 December 2003

	£m	£m
Net cash inflows from operating activities		262
(see Note 1 below)		
Returns on investments and servicing of finance		
Interest received	17	
Interest paid	(23)	
Net cash outflow from returns on investment and servicing of finance		(6)
Taxation		
Corporation tax paid (Note 2)	(39)	
Net cash outflow for taxation		(39)
Capital expenditure		
Payments to acquire tangible fixed assets	(95)	
Net cash outflow for capital expenditure		(95)
		122
Equity dividends paid		
Dividends paid (Note 3)	(40)	
Net cash outflow for dividends		(40)
		82
Management of liquid resources		–
Financing		
Repayments of debenture stock (Note 4)	(150)	
Issue of ordinary shares (Note 5)	90	
Net cash outflow for financing		(60)
Net increase in cash		22

To see how this relates to the cash of the business at the beginning and end of the year it is useful to provide a reconciliation as follows:

Analysis of cash during the year ended 31 December 2003

	£m
Balance at 1 January 2003	(28)
Net cash inflow	22
Balance at 31 December 2003	(6)

Notes

1   Calculation of net cash inflow from operating activities

	£m	£m
Operating profit (from the profit and loss account)		199
Add Depreciation of plant and machinery[a]		79
		278
Less Increase in debtors (139 – 121)	18	
Decrease in creditors (55 – 54)	1	19
		259
Add Decrease in stocks (44 – 41)		3
		262

[a] Since there were no disposals, the depreciation charges must be the difference between the start and end of the year's fixed asset values, adjusted by the cost of any additions.

	£m
Book value, at 1 January 2003	309
Add Additions	95
	404
Less Depreciation (balancing figure)	79
Book value, at 31 December 2003	325

2   Taxation

Tax is paid by companies 50 per cent during their accounting year and the other 50 per cent in the following year. Thus the 2003 payment would have been half the tax on the 2002 profit (that is, the figure that would have appeared in the current liabilities at the end of 2002), plus half of the 2003 tax charge (that is, $16 + (\frac{1}{2} \times 46) = 39$).

Probably the easiest way to deduce the amount paid during the year to 31 December 2003 is by following this approach:

	£m
Tax owed at start of the year (from the balance sheet as at 31 December 2002)	16
Add Tax charge for the year (from the profit and loss account)	46
	62
Less Tax owed at the end of the year (from the balance sheet as at 31 December 2003)	23
Tax paid during the year	39

This follows the logic that if we start with what the business owed at the beginning of the year, add on the increase in what was owed as a result of the current year's tax and then deduct what was owed at the end, the resulting figure must be what was paid during the year. A similar approach can be taken with equity dividend payments, if the situation is at all complicated.

3   Dividends

Since all of the dividend for 2003 was unpaid at the end of 2003, it seems that the business pays just one final dividend each year, some time after the year end. Thus it is the 2002 dividend that will actually have led to a cash outflow in 2003.

4   Debentures

It has been assumed that the debentures were redeemed for their balance sheet value. This is not, however, always the case.

5   Shares

The share issue raised £90 million, of which £50 million went into the share capital total on the balance sheet and £40 million into share premium.

What does the cash flow statement tell us?

The cash flow statement tells us how the business has generated cash during the period and where that cash has gone. Since cash is properly regarded as the life-blood of just about any business, this is potentially very useful information.

Tracking the sources and uses of cash over several years could show financing trends that a reader of the statements could use to help to make predictions about likely future behaviour of the company.

Looking specifically at the cash flow statement for Torbryan plc, in Example 5.4, we can see the following:

- Net cash flow from operations was strong, much larger than the profit figure. This would be expected because depreciation is deducted in arriving at profit. There was a general tendency for working capital to absorb some cash. This would not be surprising had there been an expansion of activity (sales output) over the year. From the information supplied, we do not know whether there was an expansion or not. (We have only one year's profit and loss account.)
- There were net outflows of cash in servicing of finance, payment of tax and increasing fixed assets.
- There seems to be a healthy figure of net cash flow after equity dividends.
- There was a fairly major outflow of cash to redeem some debt finance, partly off-set by the proceeds of a share issue.
- The net effect was a rather healthier-looking cash position in 2003 than was the case in 2002.

? Self-assessment question 5.1

Touchstone plc's profit and loss accounts for the years ended 31 December 2002 and 2003 and the balance sheets as at 31 December 2002 and 2003 are as follows:

Profit and loss accounts for the years ended 2002 and 2003

	2002 £m	2003 £m
Turnover	173	207
Less Cost of sales	96	101
Gross profit	77	106
Less Distribution costs	18	22
Administrative expenses	25	26
	34	58
Other operating income	3	4
Operating profit	37	62
Interest receivable and similar income	1	2
	38	64
Less Interest payable and similar charges	2	4
Profit on ordinary activities before taxation	36	60

▶

Self-assessment question 5.1 continued

	2002 £m	2003 £m
Less Tax on profit on ordinary activities	8	16
Profit on ordinary activities after taxation	28	44
Retained profit brought forward from last year	16	30
	44	74
Less Dividend (proposed and paid) on ordinary shares	14	18
Retained profit carried forward	30	56

Balance sheets as at 31 December 2002 and 2003

	2002 £m	2003 £m
Fixed assets		
Tangible assets:		
Land and buildings	94	110
Plant and machinery	53	62
	147	172
Current assets		
Stocks	25	24
Treasury bills (short-term investments)	–	15
Debtors	16	26
Cash at bank and in hand	4	4
	45	69
Less **Creditors: amounts falling due within one year**		
Trade creditors	26	23
Corporation tax	4	8
Dividend proposed	12	14
	42	45
Net current assets	3	24
Total assets less current liabilities	150	196
Less **Creditors: amounts falling due after more than one year**		
Debenture loans (10%)	20	40
	130	156
Capital and reserves		
Called-up ordinary share capital	100	100
Profit and loss account	30	56
	130	156

Included in 'cost of sales', 'distribution costs' and 'administration expenses', depreciation was as follows:

	2002 £m	2003 £m
Land and buildings	5	6
Plant and machinery	6	10

There were no fixed asset disposals in either year.

In both years an interim dividend was paid in the year in whose profit and loss account it was shown and a final dividend just after the end of the year concerned.

Required:
Prepare a cash flow statement for the business for 2003.

Summary

- *The need for a cash flow statement*:
  - ❑ cash is important because no business can operate without it;
  - ❑ the cash flow statement is specifically designed to reveal movements in cash over a period;
  - ❑ cash movements cannot be readily detected from the profit and loss account, which focuses on revenues and expenses rather than on cash receipts and cash payments;
  - ❑ profit (loss) and cash generated for the period are rarely equal;
  - ❑ the cash flow statement is a primary financial statement, along with the profit and loss account and the balance sheet.

- *Preparing the cash flow statement*:
  - ❑ the layout of the statement contains seven categories of cash movement: net cash flow from operating activities, returns on investments and servicing of finance, taxation, capital expenditure, equity dividends paid, management of liquid resources and financing;
  - ❑ the total of the cash movements under these seven categories will provide the net increase or decrease in cash for the period;
  - ❑ a reconciliation can be undertaken to check that the opening cash balance plus the net increase (decrease) in cash for the period equals the closing cash balance.

- *Calculating the net cash flows from operating activities*:
  - ❑ the net cash flows from operating activities can be derived from either the direct method or the indirect method;
  - ❑ the direct method is based on an analysis of the cash records for the period, whereas the indirect method uses information contained within the profit and loss account and balance sheets of the business;
  - ❑ the indirect method takes the net operating profit for the period, adds back any depreciation charge and then adjusts for changes in stocks, debtors and creditors during the period.

- *Interpreting the cash flow statement*:
  - ❑ the cash flow statement shows the main sources and uses of cash;
  - ❑ tracking the cash movements over several periods may reveal financing and investing patterns and may help predict future management action.

→ **Key terms**

net cash flow from operating
  activities   *p 125*
returns on investments and servicing
  of finance   *p 125*
taxation   *p 127*
capital expenditure   *p 127*

equity dividends paid   *p 127*
management of liquid
  resources   *p 127*
financing   *p 127*
direct method   *p 132*
indirect method   *p 132*

? Review questions

Answers to these questions can be found on the students' side of the Companion Website.

5.1 The typical business outside the service sector has about 50 per cent more of its resources tied up in stock than in cash, yet there is no call for a 'stock flow statement' to be prepared. Why is cash regarded as more important than stock?

5.2 What is the difference between the direct and indirect methods of deducing cash flow from operating activities?

5.3 Taking each of the categories of the cash flow statement in turn, in which direction would you normally expect the cash flow to be?
(a) cash flow from operations;
(b) cash flow from returns on investment and servicing of finance;
(c) cash flow from taxation;
(d) cash flow from capital expenditure;
(e) cash flow from equity dividends;
(f) cash flow from management of liquid resources;
(g) cash flow from financing.

5.4 What causes the net profit for the year not to equal the net cash inflow?

? Exercises

Exercises 5.3–5.5 are more advanced than 5.1 and 5.2. Those with coloured numbers have answers at the back of the book.

5.1 How will each of the following events ultimately affect the amount of cash?
(a) an increase in the level of stock-in-trade;
(b) a rights issue of ordinary shares;
(c) a bonus issue of ordinary shares;
(d) writing off the value of some stock-in-trade;
(e) the disposal of a large number of the business's shares by a major shareholder;
(f) depreciating a fixed asset.

5.2 The following information has been taken from the financial statements of Juno plc for last year and the year before last:

	Year before last £m	Last year £m
Net operating profit	156	187
Depreciation charged in arriving at net operating profit	47	55
Stock held at the end of:	27	31
Debtors at the end of:	24	23
Creditors at the end of:	15	17

Required:
What is the cash flow from operations figure for Juno plc for last year?

5.3   Torrent plc's profit and loss account for the year ended 31 December 2003 and the balance sheets as at 31 December 2002 and 2003 are as follows:

Profit and loss account

	£m	£m
Turnover		623
Less Cost of sales		353
Gross profit		270
Less Distribution costs	71	
Administrative expenses	30	101
		169
Other operating income		13
Operating profit		182
Interest receivable and similar income		14
		196
Less Interest payable and similar charges		26
Profit on ordinary activities before taxation		170
Less Tax on profit on ordinary activities		36
Profit on ordinary activities after taxation		134
Retained profit brought forward from last year		123
		257
Less Proposed dividend on ordinary shares		60
Retained profit carried forward		197

Balance sheets as at 31 December 2002 and 2003

	2002 £m	2003 £m
Fixed assets		
Land and buildings	310	310
Plant and machinery	325	314
	635	624
Current assets		
Stocks	41	35
Trade debtors	139	145
	180	180
Creditors: amounts falling due within one year		
Bank overdraft	6	29
Trade creditors	54	41
Corporation tax	23	18
Dividend proposed	50	60
	133	148
Net current assets	47	32
Total assets less current liabilities	682	656
Less Creditors: amounts falling due after more than one year		
Debenture loans	250	150
	432	506

	2002 £m	2003 £m
Capital and reserves		
Called-up ordinary share capital	200	300
Share premium account	40	–
Revaluation reserve	69	9
Profit and loss account	123	197
	432	506

During 2003, the business spent £67 million on additional plant and machinery. There were no other fixed asset acquisitions or disposals.

There was no share issue for cash during the year.

Required:

Prepare the cash flow statement for Torrent plc for the year ended 31 December 2003.

5.4 Chen plc's profit and loss accounts for the years ended 31 December 2002 and 2003 and the balance sheets as at 31 December 2002 and 2003 are as follows:

Profit and loss account

	2002 £m	2003 £m
Turnover	207	153
Cost of sales	(101)	(76)
Gross profit	106	77
Distribution costs	(22)	(20)
Administrative expenses	(26)	(28)
	58	29
Other operating income	4	–
Operating profit	62	29
Interest receivable and similar income	2	–
	64	29
Interest payable and similar charges	(4)	(4)
Profit on ordinary activities before taxation	60	25
Tax on profit or loss on ordinary activities	(16)	(6)
Profit on ordinary activities after taxation	44	19
Retained profit brought forward from last year	30	56
	74	75
Dividends on ordinary shares (paid and proposed)	(18)	(18)
Retained profit carried forward	56	57

Balance sheets as at 31 December 2002 and 2003

	2002 £m	2003 £m
Fixed assets		
Land and buildings	110	130
Plant and machinery	62	56
	172	186
Current assets		
Stocks	24	25
Debtors	26	25
Cash at bank and in hand	19	–
	69	50

	2002 £m	2003 £m
Less *Creditors: amounts falling due within one year*		
Bank overdraft	–	2
Trade creditors	23	20
Corporation tax	8	3
Dividend proposed	14	14
	45	39
Net current assets	24	11
Total assets less current liabilities	196	197
Less *Creditors: amounts falling due after more than one year*		
Debenture loans (10%)	40	40
	156	157
Capital and reserves		
Called-up ordinary share capital	100	100
Profit and loss account	56	57
	156	157

Included in 'cost of sales', 'distribution costs' and 'administration expenses', depreciation was as follows:

	2002 £m	2003 £m
Land and buildings	6	10
Plant and machinery	10	12

There were no fixed asset disposals in either year. In both years an interim dividend was paid in the year in whose profit and loss account it was shown and a final dividend was paid just after the end of the year concerned.

Required:
Prepare a cash flow statement for the business for 2003.

5.5 The following are the financial statements for Nailsea plc for the years ended 30 June 2003 and 2004:

Profit and loss accounts for years ended 30 June

	2003 £m	2003 £m	2004 £m	2004 £m
Sales		1,230		2,280
Less Operating costs	722		1,618	
Depreciation	270	992	320	1,938
Operating profit		238		342
Less Interest		–		27
Profit before tax		238		315
Less Tax		110		140
Profit after tax		128		175
Less Dividend		80		85
Retained profit for year		48		90

Balance sheets as at 30 June

	2003		2004	
	£m	£m	£m	£m
Fixed assets (see below)		2,310		2,640
Current assets				
Stock	275		450	
Debtors	100		250	
Bank	–		83	
	375		783	
Less Creditors: falling due within one year				
Bank overdraft	32		–	
Creditors	130		190	
Taxation	55		70	
Dividend	80		85	
	297		345	
Net current assets		78		438
		2,388		3,078
Less Creditors: falling due after more than one year				
9% debentures (repayable 2009)		–		300
		2,388		2,778
Share capital and reserves				
Share capital (fully paid £1 shares)		1,400		1,600
Share premium account		200		300
Retained profits		788		878
		2,388		2,778

Schedule of fixed assets

	Land & buildings £m	Plant & machinery £m	Total £m
Cost			
At 1 July 2003	1,500	1,350	2,850
Additions	400	250	650
At 30 June 2004	1,900	1,600	3,500
Depreciation			
At 1 July 2003	–	540	540
Charge for year at 20%	–	320	320
At 30 June 2004	–	860	860
Net book value at 30 June 2004	1,900	740	2,640

Required:

Prepare a cash flow statement for Nailsea plc for the year ended 30 June 2004.

Chapter 6

Analysing and interpreting financial statements

Introduction

In this chapter we shall consider the analysis and interpretation of the financial statements that we met in Chapters 2 and 3. We shall see how financial ratios can help in developing a financial profile of a business. We shall also consider problems that are encountered when applying this technique.

Objectives

When you have completed this chapter you should be able to:

- identify the major categories of ratios that can be used for analysis purposes
- calculate important ratios for determining the financial performance and position of a business, and explain the significance of the ratios calculated
- explain the importance of gearing to a business and its owners
- discuss the limitations of ratios as a tool of financial analysis.

Financial ratios

Financial ratios provide a quick and relatively simple means of examining the financial health of a business. A ratio simply relates one figure appearing in the financial statements to some other figure appearing in the financial statements (for example, net profit in relation to capital employed) or, perhaps, some resource of the business (for example, net profit per employee, sales per square metre of counter space, and so on).

Ratios can be very helpful when comparing the financial health of different businesses. Differences may exist between businesses in the scale of operations, and so a direct comparison of, say, the profits generated by each business may be misleading. By expressing profit in relation to some other measure (for example, sales), the problem of scale is eliminated. A business with a profit of, say, £10,000 and sales of £100,000 can be compared with a much larger business with a profit of, say, £80,000 and sales of £1,000,000 by the use of a simple ratio. The net profit to sales ratio for the smaller business is 10 per cent ([10,000/100,000] × 100%) and the same ratio for the larger business is 8 per cent ([80,000/1,000,000] × 100%). These ratios can be directly compared whereas comparison of the absolute profit figures would be less meaningful. The need to eliminate differences in scale through the use of ratios can also apply when comparing the performance of the same business over time.

By calculating a relatively small number of ratios, it is often possible to build up a reasonably good picture of the position and performance of a business. Thus, it is not surprising that ratios are widely used by those who have an interest in businesses and business performance. Although ratios are not difficult to calculate, they can be difficult to interpret and so it is important to appreciate that ratios are really only the starting point for further analysis.

Ratios help to highlight the financial strengths and weaknesses of a business, but they cannot, by themselves, explain why certain strengths or weaknesses exist, or why certain changes have occurred. Only a detailed investigation will reveal these underlying reasons.

Ratios can be expressed in various forms, for example as a percentage, as a fraction, or as a proportion. The way that a particular ratio is presented will depend on the needs of those who will use the information. Although it is possible to calculate a large number of ratios, only a relatively few, based on key relationships, may be helpful to the user. Many ratios that could be calculated from the financial statements (for example, rent payable in relation to current assets) may not be considered because there is no clear or meaningful relationship between the two items.

There is no generally accepted list of ratios that can be applied to the financial statements, nor is there a standard method of calculating many ratios. Variations in both the choice of ratios and their calculation will be found in practice. However, it is important to be consistent in the way in which ratios are calculated for comparison purposes. The ratios discussed below are those that are widely used because many consider them to be among the more important for decision-making purposes.

Financial ratio classification

Ratios can be grouped into certain categories, each of which reflects a particular aspect of financial performance or position. The following broad categories provide a useful basis for explaining the nature of the financial ratios to be dealt with. There are five of them:

■ *Profitability*. Businesses come into being with the primary purpose of creating wealth for their owners. Profitability ratios provide an insight to the degree of success in achieving this purpose. They express the profits made (or figures bearing on profit, such as overheads) in relation to other key figures in the financial statements or to some business resource.

■ *Efficiency*. Ratios may be used to measure the efficiency with which certain resources have been utilised within the business. These ratios are also referred to as *activity* ratios.

■ *Liquidity*. It is vital to the survival of a business for there to be sufficient liquid resources available to meet maturing obligations. Certain ratios may be calculated that examine the relationship between liquid resources held and creditors due for payment in the near future.

■ *Gearing*. This is the relationship between the amount financed by the owners of the business and the amount contributed by outsiders. It has an important effect on the degree of risk associated with a business, as we shall see. Gearing is, therefore, something that managers must consider when making financing decisions. Gearing ratios tend to highlight the extent to which the business uses finance supplied by outsiders.

■ *Investment*. Certain ratios are concerned with assessing the returns and performance of shares held in a particular business from the perspective of shareholders who are not involved with the management of the business.

The analyst must be clear *who* the target users are and *why* they need the information.

Different users of financial information are likely to have different information needs, which will in turn determine the ratios that they find useful. For example, shareholders are likely to be interested in their returns in relation to the level of risk associated with their investment. Thus profitability, investment and gearing ratios will be of particular interest. Long-term lenders are concerned with the long-term viability of the business and to help them to assess this, the profitability and gearing ratios of the business are also likely to be of particular interest. Short-term lenders, such as suppliers of goods and services on credit, may be interested in the ability of the business to repay the amounts owing in the short term. As a result, the liquidity ratios should be of interest.

We shall consider ratios falling into each of the five categories (profitability, efficiency, liquidity, gearing and investment) later in the chapter.

The need for comparison

Calculating a ratio by itself will not tell us very much about the position or performance of a business. For example, if a ratio revealed that the business was generating £100 in sales per square metre of counter space, it would not be possible to deduce from this information alone whether this particular level of performance was good, bad or indifferent. It is only when we compare this ratio with some 'benchmark' that the information can be interpreted and evaluated.

> **Activity 6.1**
>
> **Can you think of any bases that could be used to compare a ratio you have calculated from the financial statements of a particular period?**
>
> ---
>
> In answering this activity you may have thought of the following bases:
>
> - *Past periods*. By comparing the ratio we have calculated with the ratio of a previous period, it is possible to detect whether there has been an improvement or deterioration in performance. Indeed, it is often useful to track particular ratios over time (say, five or ten years) in order to see whether it is possible to detect trends. However, the comparison of ratios from different time periods brings certain problems. In particular, there is always the possibility that trading conditions may have been quite different in the periods being compared. There is the further problem that, when comparing the performance of a single business over time, operating inefficiencies may not be clearly exposed. For example, the fact that net profit per employee has risen by 10 per cent over the previous period may at first sight appear to be satisfactory; however, this may not be the case if similar businesses have shown an improvement of 50 per cent for the same period. Finally, there is the problem that inflation may have distorted the figures on which the ratios are based. Inflation can lead to an overstatement of profit and an understatement of asset values.
> - *Planned performance*. Ratios may be compared with the targets that management developed before the commencement of the period under review. The comparison of planned performance with actual performance may therefore be a useful way of revealing the level of achievement attained. However, the planned levels of performance must be based on realistic assumptions if they are to be useful for comparison purposes.
> - *Similar businesses*. In a competitive environment, a business must consider its performance in relation to that of other businesses operating in the same industry. Survival may depend on the ability to achieve comparable levels of performance. Thus a very useful basis for comparing a particular ratio is the ratio achieved by similar businesses during the same period. This basis is not, however, without its problems. Competitors may have different year ends, and therefore trading conditions may not be identical. They may also have different accounting policies, which can have a significant effect on reported profits and asset values (for example, different methods of calculating depreciation, or different methods of valuing stock). Finally, it may be difficult to get hold of the financial statements of competitor businesses. Sole proprietorships and partnerships, for example, are not obliged to make their financial statements available to the public. In the case of limited companies, there is a legal obligation to do so. However, a diversified business may not provide a detailed breakdown of activities sufficient for analysts to compare them with the activities of other businesses.

Calculating the ratios

Probably the best way to explain financial ratios is to go through an example. Example 6.1 provides a set of financial statements from which we can calculate important ratios.

Example 6.1

The following financial statements relate to Alexis plc, which operates a wholesale carpet business:

Balance sheets as at 31 March

	2003 £m	2003 £m	2004 £m	2004 £m
Fixed assets *(at cost less depreciation)*				
Freehold land and buildings	381		427	
Fixtures and fittings	129		160	
		510		587
Current assets				
Stock at cost	300		406	
Trade debtors	240		273	
Bank	3		–	
	543		679	
Creditors due within one year				
Trade creditors	(221)		(314)	
Dividends proposed	(40)		(40)	
Corporation tax due	(30)		(5)	
Bank overdraft	–		(74)	
	(291)	252	(433)	246
		762		833
Creditors due beyond one year				
9% debentures (secured)		(200)		(300)
		562		533
Capital and reserves				
£0.50 ordinary shares (Note 1)		300		300
Retained profit		262		233
		562		533

Profit and loss accounts for the year ended 31 March

	2003 £m	2004 £m
Sales (Note 2)	2,240	2,681
Less Cost of sales (Note 3)	1,745	2,272
Gross profit	495	409
Less Operating costs	252	362
Net profit before interest and tax	243	47
Less Interest payable	18	32
Net profit before tax	225	15
Less Corporation tax	61	4
Net profit after tax	164	11
Add Retained profit brought forward	138	262
	302	273
Less Dividends proposed	40	40
Retained profit carried forward	262	233

Notes:

1 The market value of the shares of the business at the end of the year was £2.50 for 2003 and £1.50 for 2004.
2 All sales and purchases are made on credit.
3 The cost of sales figure can be analysed as follows:

	2003	2004
	£m	£m
Opening stock	241	300
Purchases (Note 2)	1,804	2,378
	2,045	2,678
Less Closing stock	300	406
Cost of sales	1,745	2,272

4 The business employed 13,995 staff in 2003 and 18,623 in 2004.
5 The business expanded its capacity during 2004 by setting up a new warehouse and distribution centre in the north of England.

Profitability

The following ratios may be used to evaluate the profitability of the business:

- return on ordinary shareholders' funds;
- return on capital employed;
- net profit margin;
- gross profit margin.

We shall now look at each of these in turn.

Return on ordinary shareholders' funds (ROSF)

The **return on ordinary shareholders' funds** compares the amount of profit for the period available to the owners with the owners' stake in the business. For a limited company, the ratio (which is normally expressed in percentage terms) is as follows:

$$\text{ROSF} = \frac{\text{Net profit after taxation and preference dividend (if any)}}{\text{Ordinary share capital plus reserves}} \times 100$$

The net profit after taxation and any preference dividend is used in calculating the ratio, as this figure represents the amount of profit available to the owners.

In the case of Alexis plc, the ratio for the year ended 31 March 2003 is:

$$\text{ROSF} = \frac{164}{562} \times 100 = 29.2\%$$

Note that in calculating the ROSF, the figure for ordinary shareholders' funds as at the end of the year has been used. However, it can be argued that it is preferable to use an average figure for the year, as this would be more representative of the amount invested by owners during the period. The easiest approach to calculating the average amount invested by ordinary shareholders would be to take a simple average based on the opening and closing figures for the year. However, where these figures are not available, it is usually acceptable to use the year end figures, provided that this approach is consistently adopted.

Activity 6.2

Calculate the ROSF for Alexis plc for the year to 31 March 2004.

The ROSF for the following year will be as follows:

$$\text{ROSF} = \frac{11}{533} \times 100 = 2.1\%$$

Broadly, businesses would seek to generate as high as possible a value for this ratio, provided that it is not achieved at the expense of potential future returns by, for example, taking on more risky activities. In view of this, the 2004 ratio is very poor by any standards; a bank deposit account will yield a better return than this. We need to try to find out why things went so badly wrong in 2004. As we look at other ratios, we should find some clues.

Return on capital employed (ROCE)

The **return on capital employed** is a fundamental measure of business performance. This ratio expresses the relationship between the net profit generated by the business and the long-term capital invested in the business.

The ratio is expressed in percentage terms and is as follows:

$$\text{ROCE} = \frac{\text{Net profit before interest and taxation}}{\text{Share capital + Reserves + Long-term loans}} \times 100$$

Note, in this case, that the profit figure used in the ratio is the net profit *before* interest and taxation. This figure is used because the ratio attempts to measure the returns to all suppliers of long-term finance before any deductions for interest payable to lenders or payments of dividends to shareholders are made.

For the year to 31 March 2003, the ratio for Alexis plc is:

$$\text{ROCE} = \frac{243}{762} \times 100 - 31.9\%$$

ROCE is considered by many to be a primary measure of profitability. It compares inputs (capital invested) with outputs (profit). This comparison is vital in assessing the effectiveness with which funds have been deployed. Once again, an average figure for capital employed may be used where the information is available.

Activity 6.3

Calculate the ROCE for Alexis plc for the year to 31 March 2004.

For the year ended 31 March 2004, the ratio is:

$$\text{ROCE} = \frac{47}{833} \times 100 = 5.6\%$$

This ratio tells much the same story as ROSF; namely a poor performance, with the return on the assets being less than the rate that the business has to pay for most of its borrowed funds (that is, 9% for the debentures).

Net profit margin

The **net profit margin ratio** relates the net profit for the period to the sales during that period. The ratio is expressed as follows:

$$\textbf{Net profit margin} = \frac{\textbf{Net profit before interest and taxation}}{\textbf{Sales}} \times \textbf{100}$$

The net profit before interest and taxation is used in this ratio as it represents the profit from trading operations before the interest costs are taken into account. This is often regarded as the most appropriate measure of operational performance, when used as a basis of comparison, because differences arising from the way in which the business is financed will not influence the measure.

For the year ended 31 March 2003, Alexis plc's net profit margin ratio is:

$$\text{Net profit margin} = \frac{243}{2,240} \times 100 = 10.8\%.$$

This ratio compares one output of the business (profit) with another output (sales). The ratio can vary considerably between types of business. For example, a supermarket will often operate on low prices and, therefore, low profit margins in order to stimulate sales and thereby increase the total amount of profit generated. A jeweller, on the other hand, may have a high net profit margin, but have a much lower level of sales volume. Factors such as the degree of competition, the type of customer, the economic climate and industry characteristics (such as the level of risk) will influence the net profit margin of a business.

Activity 6.4

Calculate the net profit margin for Alexis plc for the year to 31 March 2004.

The net profit margin for the year to 31 March 2004 will be:

$$\text{Net profit margin} = \frac{47}{2,681} \times 100 = 1.8\%$$

Once again a very weak performance compared with that of 2003. Whereas in 2003 for every £1 of sales an average of 10.8p (that is, 10.8%) was left as profit, after paying the cost of the carpets sold and other expenses of operating the business, for 2004 this had fallen to only 1.8p for every £1. Thus the reason for the poor ROSF and ROCE ratios was partially, perhaps wholly, a high level of expenses relative to sales. The next ratio should provide us with a clue as to how the sharp decline in this ratio occurred.

Gross profit margin

The **gross profit margin ratio** relates the gross profit of the business to the sales generated for the same period. Gross profit represents the difference between sales and the cost of sales. The ratio is therefore a measure of profitability in buying (or producing) and selling goods before any other expenses are taken into account. As cost of sales represents a major expense for retailing, wholesaling and manufacturing businesses, a change in this ratio can have a significant effect on the 'bottom line' (that is, the net profit for the year). The gross profit ratio margin is calculated as follows:

$$\text{Gross profit margin} = \frac{\text{Gross profit}}{\text{Sales}} \times 100$$

For the year to 31 March 2003, the ratio for Alexis plc is as follows:

$$\text{Gross profit margin} = \frac{495}{2{,}240} \times 100 = 22.1\%$$

Activity 6.5

Calculate the gross profit margin for Alexis plc for the year to 31 March 2004.

The gross profit margin for the year to 31 March 2004 is as follows:

$$\text{Gross profit margin} = \frac{409}{2{,}681} \times 100 = 15.3\%$$

The decline in this ratio means that gross profit was lower *relative* to sales in 2004 than it had been in 2003. Bearing in mind that:

Gross profit = Sales less cost of sales (or cost of goods sold)

this means that cost of sales was higher *relative* to sales in 2004, than in 2003. This could mean that sales prices were lower or the purchase cost of goods sold had increased. It is possible that both sales prices and goods sold prices had reduced, but the former at a greater rate than the latter. Similarly they may both have increased, but with sales prices having increased at a lesser rate than costs of the goods sold.

Clearly part of the decline in the net profit margin ratio is linked to the dramatic decline in the gross profit margin ratio. Whereas, after paying for the carpets sold, for each £1 of sales 22.1p was left to cover other operating expenses and leave a profit in 2003, this was only 15.3p in 2004.

The profitability ratios for the business over the two years can be set out as follows:

	2003	2004
	%	%
ROSF	29.2	2.1
ROCE	31.9	5.6
Net profit margin	10.8	1.8
Gross profit margin	22.1	15.3

Activity 6.6

What do you deduce from a comparison of the declines in the net profit and gross profit margin ratios?

It occurs to us that the decline in the net profit margin was 9 per cent (that is, 10.8% to 1.8%), whereas that of the gross profit margin was only 6.8 per cent (that is, from 22.1% to 15.3%). This can only mean that operating expenses were greater, compared with sales in 2004, than they had been in 2003. Thus, the declines in both ROSF and ROCE were caused partly by the business incurring higher stock purchasing costs relative to sales and partly through higher operating expenses to sales.

The analyst must now carry out some investigation to discover what caused the increases in both cost of sales and operating costs, relative to sales, from 2003 to 2004. This will involve checking on what has happened with sales and stock prices over the two years. Similarly, it will involve looking at each of the individual expenses that make up operating costs to discover which ones were responsible for the increase, relative to sales. Here further ratios, for example staff costs (wages and salaries) to sales, could be calculated in an attempt to isolate the cause of the change from 2003 to 2004.

Efficiency

Efficiency ratios examine the ways in which various resources of the business are managed. The following ratios consider some of the more important aspects of resource management:

- average stock turnover period;
- average settlement period for debtors;
- average settlement period for creditors;
- sales to capital employed;
- sales per employee.

We shall now look at each of these in turn.

Average stock turnover period

Stocks often represent a significant investment for a business. For some types of business (for example, manufacturers), stocks may account for a substantial proportion of the total assets held. The **average stock turnover period** measures the average period for which stocks are being held. The ratio is calculated thus:

$$\text{Stock turnover period} = \frac{\text{Average stock held}}{\text{Cost of sales}} \times 365$$

The average stock for the period can be calculated as a simple average of the opening and closing stock levels for the year. However, in the case of a highly seasonal business, where stock levels may vary considerably over the year, a monthly average may be more appropriate.

In the case of Alexis plc, the stock turnover period for the year ended 31 March 2003 is:

$$\text{Stock turnover period} = \frac{(241 + 300)/2}{1,745} \times 365 = 56.6 \text{ days}$$

This means that, on average, the stock held is being 'turned over' every 56.6 days. A business will normally prefer a low stock turnover period to a high period, as funds tied up in stocks cannot be used for other purposes. In judging the amount of stock to carry, the business must consider such things as the likely future demand, the possibility of future shortages, the likelihood of future price rises, the amount of storage space available and the perishability of the product. The management of stocks will be considered in more detail in Chapter 11.

This ratio is sometimes expressed in terms of months rather than days. Multiplying by 12 rather than 365 will achieve this.

Activity 6.7

Calculate the average stock turnover period for Alexis plc for the year ended 31 March 2004.

The stock turnover period for the year to 31 March 2004 will be:

$$\text{Stock turnover period} = \frac{(300 + 406)/2}{2,272} \times 365 = 56.7 \text{ days}$$

Thus the stock turnover period is virtually the same in both years.

Average settlement period for debtors

A business will usually be concerned with how long it takes for customers to pay the amounts owing. The speed of payment can have a significant effect on the cash flow of the business. The **average settlement period for debtors** calculates how long, on average, credit customers take to pay the amounts that they owe to the business. The ratio is as follows:

$$\text{Average settlement period for debtors} = \frac{\text{Trade debtors}}{\text{Credit sales}} \times 365$$

A business will normally prefer a shorter average settlement period to a longer one as, once again, funds are being tied up that may be used for more profitable purposes. Though this ratio can be useful, it is important to remember that it produces an *average* figure for the number of days for which debts are outstanding. This average may be badly distorted by, for example, a few large customers who are very slow or very fast payers.

Since all sales made by Alexis plc are on credit, the average settlement period for debtors for the year ended 31 March 2003 is:

$$\text{Average settlement period for debtors} = \frac{240}{2,240} \times 365 = 39.1 \text{ days}$$

As no figures for opening debtors are available, the year end debtors figure only is used. This is common practice.

Activity 6.8

Calculate the average settlement period for Alexis plc's debtors for the year ended 31 March 2004. (In the interests of consistency, use the year end debtors figure rather than an average figure.)

The average settlement period for the year to 2004 is:

$$\text{Average settlement period for debtors} = \frac{273}{2,681} \times 365 = 37.2 \text{ days}$$

On the face of it, this reduction in the settlement period is welcome. It means that fewer funds were tied up in debtors for each £1 of sales in 2004 than in 2003. Only if the reduction were achieved at the expense of customer goodwill, for example chasing customers too vigorously, or as a result of incurring higher costs, for example allowing discounts to customers who pay quickly, might the desirability of the reduction be questioned.

Average settlement period for creditors

The **average settlement period for creditors** measures how long, on average, the business takes to pay its trade creditors. The ratio is calculated as follows:

$$\text{Average settlement period for creditors} = \frac{\text{Trade creditors}}{\text{Credit purchases}} \times 365$$

This ratio provides an average figure, which, like the average settlement period for debtors ratio, can be distorted by the payment period for one or two large suppliers.

As trade creditors provide a free source of finance for the business, it is perhaps not surprising that some businesses attempt to increase their average settlement period for trade creditors. However, such a policy can be taken too far and result in a loss of goodwill of suppliers. We shall return to the issues concerning the management of trade debtors and trade creditors in Chapter 11.

For the year ended 31 March 2003, Alexis plc's average creditors settlement period is:

$$\text{Average settlement period for creditors} = \frac{221}{1,804} \times 365 = 44.7 \text{ days}$$

Once again, the year end figure rather than an average figure for creditors has been used in the calculations.

Activity 6.9

Calculate the average settlement period for creditors for Alexis plc for the year ended 31 March 2004. (For the sake of consistency, use a year end figure for creditors.)

The average settlement period for creditors is:

$$\text{Average settlement period for creditors} = \frac{314}{2,378} \times 365 = 48.2 \text{ days}$$

There was an increase, between 2003 and 2004, in the average length of time that elapsed between buying stock and paying for it. On the face of it, this is beneficial because the business is using free finance provided by suppliers. If, however, this is leading to a loss of supplier goodwill that could have adverse consequences for Alexis plc, it is not necessarily advantageous.

Sales to capital employed

The **sales to capital employed ratio** (or asset turnover ratio) examines how effectively the assets of the business are generating sales revenue. It is calculated as follows:

$$\textbf{Sales to capital employed ratio} = \frac{\textbf{Sales}}{\substack{\textbf{Long-term capital employed} \\ \textbf{(shareholders' funds + long-term loans)}}}$$

Generally speaking, a higher asset turnover ratio is preferred to a lower one. A higher ratio will normally suggest that assets are being used more productively in the generation of revenue. However, a very high ratio may suggest that the business is 'overtrading on its assets', that is, it has insufficient assets to sustain the level of sales achieved. When comparing this ratio between businesses, such factors as the age and condition of assets held, the valuation bases for assets and whether assets are rented or purchased outright can complicate interpretation.

A variation of this formula is to use the total assets less current liabilities (which is equivalent to long-term capital employed) in the denominator (lower part of the fraction) – the identical result is obtained.

For the year ended 31 March 2003 this ratio for Alexis plc is as follows:

$$\text{Sales to capital employed} = \frac{2,240}{(562 + 200)} = 2.94 \text{ times}$$

Once again, year end figures have been used, though an average figure for total assets could also be used if sufficient information were available.

Activity 6.10

Calculate the sales to long-term capital employed ratio for Alexis plc for the year ended 31 March 2004. (For consistency, use a year end figure for total assets.)

The sales to long-term capital employed ratio for the year ended 31 March 2003 will be:

$$\text{Sales to capital employed} = \frac{2,681}{(533 + 300)} = 3.22 \text{ times}$$

This seems to be an improvement, since in 2004 more sales were being generated per £1 of capital employed in 2004 (£3.22) than was the case in 2003 (£2.94). Provided that overtrading is not an issue, this is to be welcomed.

Sales per employee

This ratio relates sales generated to a particular business resource, that is, labour. It provides a measure of the productivity of the workforce. The ratio is:

$$\text{Sales per employee} = \frac{\text{Sales}}{\text{Number of employees}}$$

Generally, businesses would prefer to have a high value for this ratio, implying that they are using their staff effectively.

For the year ended 31 March 2003, the ratio for Alexis plc is:

$$\text{Sales per employee} = \frac{£2,240m}{13,995} = £160,057$$

Activity 6.11

Calculate the sales per employee for Alexis plc for the year ended 31 March 2004.

The ratio for the year ended 31 March 2004 is:

$$\text{Sales per employee} = \frac{£2,681m}{18,623} = £143,962$$

This represents a fairly significant decline and probably one that merits further investigation. The number of employees had increased quite notably over the two years and the analyst will probably try to discover why this had not generated sufficient additional sales to maintain the ratio at its 2003 level.

The activity ratios may be summarised as follows:

	2003	*2004*
Average stock turnover period	56.6 days	56.7 days
Average settlement period for debtors	39.1 days	37.2 days
Average settlement period for creditors	44.7 days	48.2 days
Sales to capital employed (asset turnover)	2.94 times	3.22 times
Sales per employee	£160,057	£143,962

The relationship between profitability and efficiency

In our earlier discussions concerning profitability ratios on page 153, we saw that return on capital employed (ROCE) is regarded as a key ratio by many businesses. The ratio is:

$$\text{ROCE} = \frac{\textbf{Net profit before interest and taxation}}{\textbf{Long-term capital employed}} \times 100$$

(where long-term capital comprises share capital plus reserves plus long-term loans). This ratio can be broken down into two elements, as shown in Figure 6.1. The first ratio is the net profit margin ratio, and the second ratio is the sales to capital employed (asset turnover) ratio, which we discussed earlier.

By breaking down the ROCE ratio in this manner, we highlight the fact that the overall return on funds employed within the business will be determined both by the profitability of sales and by efficiency in the use of capital.

Example 6.2

Consider the following information concerning two different businesses operating in the same industry:

	Business A	*Business B*
Profit before interest and tax	£20m	£15m
Long-term capital employed	£100m	£75m
Sales	£200m	£300m

The ROCE for each business is identical (20 per cent). However, the manner in which the return was achieved by each business was quite different. In the case of Business A, the net profit margin is 10 per cent and the sales to capital employed ratio is 2 times (hence ROCE = 10% × 2 = 20%). In the case of Business B, the net profit margin is 5 per cent and the sales to capital employed ratio is 4 times (hence ROCE = 5% × 4 = 20%).

Figure 6.1 The main elements comprising the ROCE ratio

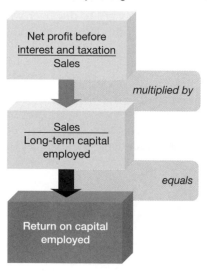

The ROCE ratio can be divided into two elements: net profit to sales, and sales to capital employed. By analysing ROCE in this way we can see the influence of both profitability and efficiency on this important ratio.

Example 6.2 demonstrates that a relatively low net profit margin can be compensated for by a relatively high sales to capital employed ratio, and a relatively low sales to capital employed ratio can be compensated for by a relatively high net profit margin. In many areas of retail and distribution (for example, supermarkets and delivery services) the net profit margins are quite low but the ROCE can be high, provided the assets are used productively.

Activity 6.12

Show how the ROCE ratio for Alexis plc can be analysed into the two elements for each of the years 2003 and 2004.

What conclusions can we draw from your figures?

	ROCE	=	Net profit margin	×	Asset turnover
2003	31.9%		10.8%		2.94
2004	5.6%		1.8%		3.22

Though the business was more effective at generating sales (asset turnover ratio increased) from 2003 to 2004, it fell well below the level necessary to compensate for the sharp decline in the effectiveness of each sale (net profit margin). Thus the 2004 ROCE was well below the 2003 value.

Liquidity

Liquidity ratios are concerned with the ability of the business to meet its short-term financial obligations. The following ratios are widely used:

- current ratio;
- acid test ratio.

These two will now be considered.

Current ratio

The **current ratio** compares the 'liquid' assets (that is, cash and those assets held that will soon be turned into cash) of the business with the short-term liabilities (creditors due within one year). The ratio is calculated as follows:

$$\text{Current ratio} = \frac{\text{Current assets}}{\text{Current liabilities (creditors due within one year)}}$$

In some texts the notion of an 'ideal' current ratio (usually 2 times or 2:1) is suggested for all businesses. However, this fails to take into account the fact that different types of business require different current ratios. For example, a manufacturing business will often have a relatively high current ratio because it is necessary to hold stocks of finished goods, raw materials and work in progress. It will also normally sell goods on credit, thereby incurring debtors. A supermarket chain, on the other hand, will have a relatively low ratio, as it will hold only fast-moving stocks of finished goods and will generate mostly cash sales. (See Exhibit 11.1 on p. 321.)

The higher the ratio, the more liquid the business is considered to be. As liquidity is vital to the survival of a business, a higher current ratio might be thought to be preferable to a lower one. If a business has a very high ratio, however, it may be that funds are tied up in cash of other liquid assets and are not, therefore, being used as productively as they might otherwise be.

As at 31 March 2003, the current ratio of Alexis plc was:

$$\text{Current ratio} = \frac{543}{291} = 1.9 \text{ times (or 1.9:1)}$$

Activity 6.13

Calculate the current ratio for Alexis plc as at 31 March 2004.

The current ratio as at 31 March 2004 is:

$$\text{Current ratio} = \frac{679}{433} = 1.6 \text{ times (or 1.6:1)}$$

Though this is a decline from 2003 to 2004, it is not necessarily a matter of concern. The next ratio may provide a clue as to whether there seems to be a problem.

Acid test ratio

→ The **acid test ratio** represents a more stringent test of liquidity. It can be argued that, for many businesses, the stock in hand cannot be converted into cash quickly. (Note that, in the case of Alexis plc, the stock turnover period was about 57 days in both years (see p. 157). As a result, it may be better to exclude this particular asset from any measure of liquidity.)

The minimum level for this ratio is often stated as 1.0 times (or 1:1 – that is, current assets (excluding stock) equals current liabilities). In many highly successful businesses that are regarded as having adequate liquidity, however, it is not unusual for the acid test ratio to be below 1.0 without causing particular liquidity problems. (See Exhibit 11.1 on p. 321.)

The acid test ratio is calculated as follows:

$$\text{Acid test ratio} = \frac{\text{Current assets (excluding stock)}}{\text{Current liabilities (creditors due within one year)}}$$

The acid test ratio for Alexis plc as at 31 March 2003 is:

$$\text{Acid test ratio} = \frac{543 - 300}{291} = 0.8 \text{ times (or 0.8:1)}$$

We can see that the 'liquid' current assets do not quite cover the current liabilities, and so the business may be experiencing some liquidity problems.

Activity 6.14

Calculate the acid test ratio for Alexis plc as at 31 March 2004.

The acid test ratio as at 31 March 2004 is:

$$\text{Acid test ratio} = \frac{679 - 406}{433} = 0.6 \text{ times}$$

The 2004 ratio is significantly below that for 2003. The 2004 level may well be a cause for concern. The rapid decline in this ratio should lead to steps being taken, at least to stop further decline.

Both the current ratio and the acid test ratio derive the relevant figures from the balance sheet. As the balance sheet is simply a 'snapshot' of the financial position of the business at a single moment in time, care must be taken when interpreting the ratios. It is possible that the balance sheet figures are not representative of the liquidity position during the year. This may be due to exceptional factors, or simply to the fact that the business is seasonal in nature and the balance sheet figures represent the position at one particular point in the seasonal cycle only.

The liquidity ratios for the two-year period may be summarised as follows:

	2003	*2004*
Current ratio	1.9	1.6
Acid test ratio	0.8	0.6

Gearing

Gearing occurs when a business is financed, at least in part, by borrowing, instead of by finance provided by the owners (the shareholders). A business's level of gearing (that is, the extent to which it is financed from sources that require a fixed return) is an important factor in assessing risk. Where a business borrows heavily, it takes on a commitment to pay interest charges and make capital repayments. This can be a significant financial burden, and can increase the risk of the business becoming insolvent. Nevertheless, most businesses are geared to some extent.

Given the risks involved, we may wonder why a business would want to take on gearing (that is, to borrow). One reason may be that the owners have insufficient funds, and therefore the only way to finance the business adequately is to borrow from others. Another reason is that gearing can be used to increase the returns to owners. This is possible provided the returns generated from borrowed funds exceed the cost of paying interest. Example 6.3 illustrates this point.

Example 6.3

The long-term capital structures of two new businesses, Lee Ltd and Nova Ltd, are as follows:

	Lee Ltd	*Nova Ltd*
	£	£
£1 ordinary shares	100,000	200,000
10% loan	200,000	100,000
	300,000	300,000

In their first year of operations, they each make a profit before interest and taxation of £50,000. The tax rate is 30 per cent of the net profit after interest.

Lee Ltd would probably be considered highly geared as it has a high proportion of borrowed funds in its long-term capital structure. Nova Ltd is much lower geared. The profit available to the shareholders of each business in the first year of operations will be:

	Lee Ltd	*Nova Ltd*
	£	£
Profit before interest and taxation	50,000	50,000
Interest payable	(20,000)	(10,000)
Profit before taxation	30,000	40,000
Taxation (30%)	(9,000)	(12,000)
Profit available to ordinary shareholders	21,000	28,000

The return on ordinary shareholders' funds (ROSF) for each business will be:

Lee Ltd

$$\frac{21{,}000}{100{,}000} \times 100 = 21\%$$

Nova Ltd

$$\frac{28{,}000}{200{,}000} \times 100 = 14\%$$

We can see that Lee Ltd, the more highly geared business, has generated a better ROSF than Nova Ltd.

An effect of gearing is that returns to shareholders become more sensitive to changes in profits. For a highly geared business, a change in profits can lead to a proportionately greater change in the ROSF ratio.

Activity 6.15

Assume that the profit before interest and tax was 20 per cent higher for each business than stated above (that is, a profit of £60,000). What would be the effect of this on ROSF?

The revised profit available to the shareholders of each business in the first year of operations will be:

	Lee Ltd	Nova Ltd
	£	£
Profit before interest and taxation	60,000	60,000
Interest payable	(20,000)	(10,000)
Profit before taxation	40,000	50,000
Taxation (30%)	(12,000)	(15,000)
Profit available to ordinary shareholders	28,000	35,000

The ROSF for each business will now be:

Lee Ltd

$$\frac{28{,}000}{100{,}000} \times 100 = 28\%$$

Nova Ltd

$$\frac{35{,}000}{200{,}000} \times 100 = 17.5\%$$

We can see that for Lee Ltd, the higher-geared business, the returns to shareholders have increased by a third (from 21 per cent to 28 per cent), whereas for the lower-geared business, Nova Ltd, the benefits of gearing are less pronounced, only increasing by a quarter (from 14 per cent to 17.5 per cent). The effect of gearing, of course, can work in both directions. Thus, for a highly geared business a small decline in profits may bring about a much greater decline in the returns to shareholders.

The reason that gearing tends to be beneficial to shareholders is that loan interest rates are relatively low, compared with the returns that the typical business can earn. On top of this, interest costs are tax deductible, in the way shown in Example 6.3 and Activity 6.15, making the effective cost of borrowing quite cheap. It is debatable whether the apparent low interest rates really are beneficial to the shareholders. Some argue that since borrowing increases the risk to shareholders, there is a hidden cost of borrowing. What are not illusory, however, are the benefits to the shareholders of the tax deductibility of loan interest.

The effect of gearing is like the effect of two intermeshing cogwheels of unequal size (see Figure 6.2). The movement in the larger cog (profit before interest and tax) causes a more than proportionate movement in the smaller cog (returns to ordinary shareholders). The subject of gearing is discussed further in Chapter 12 on p. 364.

There are two ratios widely used to assess gearing:

- gearing ratio;
- interest cover ratio.

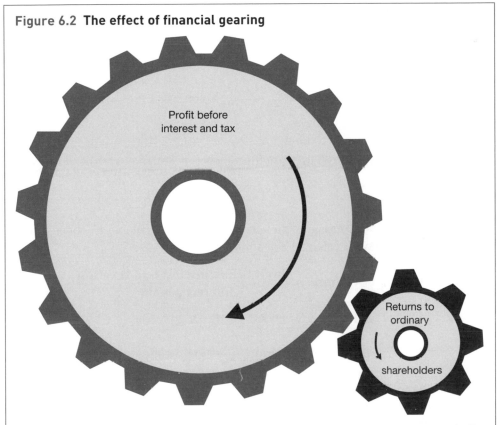

Figure 6.2 The effect of financial gearing

Profit before interest and tax

Returns to ordinary shareholders

The two wheels are linked by the cogs, so that a relatively small circular movement in the large wheel (profit before interest and tax) leads to a relatively large circular movement in the small wheel (returns to ordinary shareholders).

Gearing ratio

➡ The **gearing ratio** measures the contribution of long-term lenders to the long-term capital structure of a business:

$$\text{Gearing ratio} = \frac{\text{Long-term liabilities}}{\text{Share capital} + \text{Reserves} + \text{Long-term liabilities}} \times 100$$

The gearing ratio for Alexis plc, as at 31 March 2003, is:

$$\text{Gearing ratio} = \frac{200}{(562 + 200)} \times 100 = 26.2\%$$

This ratio reveals a level of gearing that would not normally be considered to be very high.

Activity 6.16

Calculate the gearing ratio of Alexis plc as at 31 March 2004.

The gearing ratio as at 31 March 2004 will be:

$$\text{Gearing ratio} = \frac{300}{(533 + 300)} \times 100 = 36.0\%$$

This ratio reveals a substantial increase in the level of gearing over the year.

Interest cover ratio

➡ The **interest cover ratio** measures the amount of profit available to cover interest payable. The ratio may be calculated as follows:

$$\text{Interest cover ratio} = \frac{\text{Profit before interest and taxation}}{\text{Interest payable}}$$

The ratio for Alexis plc for the year ended 31 March 2003 is:

$$\text{Interest cover ratio} = \frac{243}{18} = 13.5 \text{ times}$$

This ratio shows that the level of profit is considerably higher than the level of interest payable. Thus a significant fall in profits could occur before profit levels failed to cover interest payable. The lower the level of profit coverage, the greater the risk to lenders that interest payments will not be met, and the greater the risk to the shareholders that the lenders will take action against the business to recover the interest due.

Activity 6.17

Calculate the interest cover ratio of Alexis plc for the year ended 31 March 2004.

The interest cover ratio for the year ended 31 March 2004 is:

$$\text{Interest cover ratio} = \frac{47}{32} = 1.5 \text{ times}$$

The gearing ratios are:

	2003	2004
Gearing ratio	26.2%	36.0%
Interest cover ratio	13.5 times	1.5 times

Activity 6.18

What do you deduce from a comparison of the gearing ratios over the two years?

The gearing ratio altered significantly. This is mainly due to the substantial increase in the long-term loan during 2004, which has had the effect of increasing the relative contribution of long-term lenders to the financing of the business.

The interest cover ratio has declined dramatically from a position where profit covered interest 13.5 times in 2003, to one where profit covered interest only 1.5 times in 2004. This was partly caused by the increase in borrowings in 2004, but mainly caused by the dramatic decline in profitability in that year. The later situation looks hazardous; only a small decline in future profitability in 2005 would leave the business with insufficient profit to cover the interest payments.

The gearing ratio at 31 March 2004 would not necessarily be considered to be very high for a business that was trading successfully. It is the low profitability that is the problem.

Investment ratios

There are various ratios available that are designed to help investors assess the returns on their investment. The following are widely used:

- dividend payout ratio;
- dividend yield ratio;
- earnings per share;
- price/earnings ratio.

Dividend payout ratio

→ The **dividend payout ratio** measures the proportion of earnings that a business pays out to shareholders in the form of dividends. The ratio is calculated as follows:

$$\text{Dividend payout ratio} = \frac{\text{Dividends announced for the year}}{\text{Earnings for the year available for dividends}} \times 100$$

In the case of ordinary shares, the earnings available for dividend will normally be the net profit after taxation and after any preference dividends announced during the period. This ratio is normally expressed as a percentage.

The dividend payout ratio for Alexis plc for the year ended 31 March 2003 is:

$$\text{Dividend payout ratio} = \frac{40}{164} \times 100 = 24.4\%$$

The information provided by this ratio is often expressed slightly differently as the dividend cover ratio. Here the calculation is:

$$\text{Dividend cover ratio} = \frac{\text{Earnings for the year available for dividend}}{\text{Dividend announced for the year}}$$

In the case of Alexis plc, (for 2003) it would be 164/40 = 4.1 times. That is to say, the earnings available for dividend cover the actual dividend by just over four times.

Activity 6.19

Calculate the dividend payout ratio of Alexis plc for the year ended 31 March 2004.

Your answer to this activity should be as follows:

$$\text{Dividend payout ratio} = \frac{40}{11} \times 100 = 363.6\%$$

This would normally be considered to be a very alarming decline in the ratio over the two years. Paying a dividend of £40m in 2004 would be regarded as very imprudent.

Dividend yield ratio

→ The **dividend yield ratio** relates the cash return from a share to its current market value. This can help investors to assess the cash return on their investment in the business. The ratio is:

$$\text{Dividend yield} = \frac{\text{Dividend per share}/(1-t)}{\text{Market value per share}} \times 100$$

This ratio is also expressed as a percentage.

The numerator (the top part) of this ratio requires some explanation. In the UK, investors who receive a dividend from a business also receive a tax credit. This tax credit is equal to the amount of tax that would be payable on the dividends received by a lower-rate taxpayer. As this tax credit can be offset against any tax liability arising from the dividends received, the dividends are effectively issued net of tax to lower-rate income tax payers.

Investors may wish to compare the returns from shares with the returns from other forms of investment. As these other forms of investment are often quoted on a 'gross' (that is, pre-tax) basis it is useful to 'gross up' the dividend to make comparison easier. This can be done by dividing the dividend per share by $(1 - t)$, where t is the 'lower' rate of income tax.

Assuming a lower rate of income tax of 10 per cent, the dividend yield for Alexis plc for the year ended 31 March 2003 is:

$$\text{Dividend yield} = \frac{0.067^*/(1 - 0.10)}{2.50} \times 100 = 3.0\%$$

* Dividend proposed/Number of shares = 40/(300 × 2) = £0.067 dividend per share (the 300 is multiplied by 2 because they are £0.50 shares).

Activity 6.20

Calculate the dividend yield for Alexis plc for the year ended 31 March 2004.

Your answer to this activity should be as follows:

$$\text{Dividend yield} = \frac{0.067^{**}/(1 - 0.10)}{1.50} \times 100 = 5.0\%$$

** 40/(300 × 2) = £0.067

Earnings per share

The **earnings per share** (EPS) ratio relates the earnings generated by the business, and available to shareholders, during a period to the number of shares in issue. For equity (ordinary) shareholders, the amount available will be represented by the net profit after tax (less any preference dividend, where applicable). The ratio for equity shareholders is calculated as follows:

$$\textbf{Earnings per share} = \frac{\textbf{Earnings available to ordinary shareholders}}{\textbf{Number of ordinary shares in issue}}$$

In the case of Alexis plc, the earnings per share for the year ended 31 March 2003 will be as follows:

$$\text{EPS} = \frac{164}{600} = 27.3\text{p}$$

Many investment analysts regard the EPS ratio as a fundamental measure of share performance. The trend in earnings per share over time is used to help assess the investment potential of a business's shares. Though it is possible to make total profits rise through ordinary shareholders investing more in the business, this will not necessarily mean that the profitability *per share* will rise as a result.

It is not usually very helpful to compare the earnings per share of one business with those of another. Differences in capital structure (level of gearing) can render any such comparison meaningless. However, it can be very useful to monitor the changes that occur in this ratio for a particular business over time.

Activity 6.21

Calculate the earnings per share of Alexis plc for the year ended 31 March 2004.

The earnings per share for the year ended 31 March 2004 will be:

$$\text{EPS} = \frac{11}{600} = 1.8\text{p}$$

Price/earnings (P/E) ratio

The **price/earnings ratio** relates the market value of a share to the earnings per share. This ratio can be calculated as follows:

$$\textbf{P/E ratio} = \frac{\textbf{Market value per share}}{\textbf{Earnings per share}}$$

The P/E ratio for Alexis plc as at 31 March 2003 will be:

$$\text{P/E ratio} = \frac{£2.50}{27.3\text{p*}} = 9.2 \text{ times}$$

* The EPS figure (27.3p) was calculated on p. 171.

This ratio reveals that the capital value of the share is 9.2 times higher than its current level of earnings. The ratio is a measure of market confidence in the future of a business. The higher the P/E ratio, the greater the confidence in the future earning power of the business and, consequently, the more investors are prepared to pay in relation to the earnings stream of the business.

P/E ratios provide a useful guide to market confidence concerning the future and they can, therefore, be helpful when comparing different businesses. However, differences in accounting conventions between businesses can lead to different profit and earnings per share figures, and this can distort comparisons.

Activity 6.22

Calculate the P/E ratio of Alexis plc as at 31 March 2004.

Your answer to this activity should be as follows:

$$\text{P/E ratio} = \frac{£1.50}{1.8p} = 83.3 \text{ times}$$

The investment ratios for Alexis plc over the two-year period are as follows:

	2003	2004
Dividend payout ratio	24.4%	363.6%
Dividend yield ratio	3.0%	5.0%
Earnings per share	27.3p	1.8p
P/E ratio	9.2 times	83.3 times

Activity 6.23

What do you deduce from the investment ratios set out above?

Can you offer an explanation why the share price has not fallen as much as it might have done, bearing in mind the very poor (relative to 2003) trading performance in 2004?

We thought that, though the EPS figure has fallen dramatically and the dividend payment for 2004 seems very impudent, the share price seems to have held up remarkably well (fallen from £2.50 to £1.50, see p. 152). This means that dividend yield and P/E value for 2004 look better than those for 2003. This is an anomaly of these two ratios, which stems from using a forward-looking value (the share price) in conjunction with historic data (dividends and earnings). Share prices are based on investors' assessments of the business's future. It seems with Alexis plc that at the end of 2004 the 'market' was not happy with the business, relative to 2003, evidenced by the fact that the share price had fallen by £1 a share. On the other hand, the share price has not fallen as much as profits. It appears that investors believe that the business will perform better in the future than it did in 2004. This may well be because they believe that the large expansion in assets and employee numbers that occurred in 2004 will yield benefits in the future, benefits that the business was not able to generate during 2004.

Exhibit 6.1

Investment ratios can vary significantly between businesses and between industries. To give some indication of the range of variations that occur, the average dividend yield ratios and average P/E ratios for listed businesses in 12 different industries are shown in Figures 6.3 and 6.4 respectively.

Exhibit 6.1 continued

These ratios are calculated from the current market value of the shares and the most recent year's dividend paid (dividend yield) or earnings per share (P/E).

Some industries tend to pay out lower dividends than others, leading to lower dividend yield ratios. Pharmaceutical businesses tend to invest heavily in developing new drugs, hence their tendency to pay low dividends compared with their share prices. Electricity businesses probably tend to invest less heavily than pharmaceuticals, hence their rather higher level of dividend yields. Some of the inter-industry differences in the dividend yield ratio can be explained by the nature of the calculation of the ratio. The prices of shares at any given moment are based on future expectations of their economic futures; dividends are actual past events. A business that had a good trading year recently may have paid a dividend that, in the light of investors' assessment on the business's economic future, may be high (a high dividend yield).

Businesses that have a high share price relative to their recent historic earnings have high P/E ratios. This may be because their future is regarded as economically bright because, for example, they invest heavily in the future to some extent at the expense of current profits (earnings). On the other hand, high P/Es also arise where businesses have recent low earnings, but investors believe that their future is brighter.

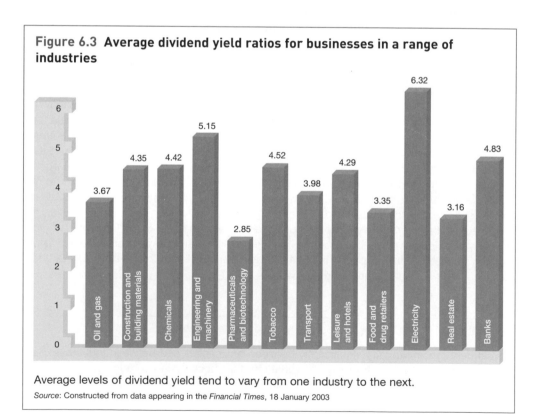

Figure 6.3 Average dividend yield ratios for businesses in a range of industries

Average levels of dividend yield tend to vary from one industry to the next.

Source: Constructed from data appearing in the *Financial Times*, 18 January 2003

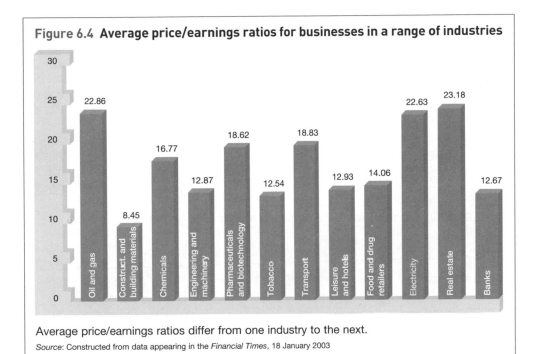

Figure 6.4 **Average price/earnings ratios for businesses in a range of industries**

Average price/earnings ratios differ from one industry to the next.

Source: Constructed from data appearing in the *Financial Times*, 18 January 2003

? Self-assessment question 6.1

Ali plc and Bhaskar plc each operates electrical stores throughout the UK. The financial statements of each business for the year ended 30 June 2004 are as follows:

Balance sheets as at 30 June 2004

	Ali plc		Bhaskar plc	
	£m	£m	£m	£m
Fixed assets (cost less depreciation)				
Freehold land and buildings at cost		360.0		510.0
Fixtures and fittings at cost		87.0		91.2
		447.0		601.2
Current assets				
Stock at cost	592.0		403.0	
Debtors	176.4		321.9	
Cash at bank	84.6		91.6	
	853.0		816.5	
Creditors due within one year				
Trade creditors	(271.4)		(180.7)	
Dividends	(135.0)		(95.0)	
Corporation tax	(16.0)		(17.4)	
	(422.4)	430.6	(293.1)	523.4
		877.6		1,124.6

▶

Self-assessment question 6.1 continued

	Ali plc		Bhaskar plc	
	£m	£m	£m	£m
Creditors due beyond one year				
Debentures		(190.0)		(250.0)
		687.6		874.6
Capital and reserves				
£1 ordinary shares		320.0		250.0
General reserves		355.9		289.4
Retained profit		11.7		335.2
		687.6		874.6

Trading and profit and loss accounts for the year ended 30 June 2004

	Ali plc		Bhaskar plc	
	£000	£000	£000	£000
Sales		1,478.1		1,790.4
Less Cost of sales				
Opening stock	480.8		372.6	
Purchases	1,129.5		1,245.3	
	1,610.3		1,617.9	
Less Closing stock	592.0	1,018.3	403.0	1,214.9
Gross profit		459.8		575.5
Less Operating expenses		308.5		408.6
Net profit before interest and tax		151.3		166.9
Less Interest payable		19.4		27.5
Net profit before tax		131.9		139.4
Less Corporation tax		32.0		34.8
Net profit after taxation		99.9		104.6
Add Retained profit brought forward		46.8		325.6
		146.7		430.2
Less Dividends proposed		135.0		95.0
Retained profit carried forward		11.7		335.2

All purchases and sales were on credit. The market values of a share in each business at the end of the year were £6.50 and £8.20 respectively.

Required:
For each business, calculate two ratios that are concerned with liquidity, gearing and invest-ment (six ratios in total). What can you conclude from the ratios that you have calculated?

Trend analysis

It is important to see whether there are trends occurring that can be detected from the use of ratios. Thus key ratios can be plotted on a graph to provide users with a simple visual display of changes occurring over time. The trends occurring within

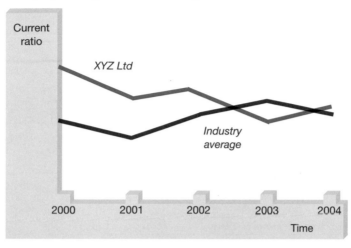

Figure 6.5 Graph plotting current ratio against time

The current ratio for a particular business (XYZ Ltd) is plotted over time. On the same graph the same ratio for the average of businesses in the same industry is also plotted, enabling comparison to be made between the ratio for the particular business and the industry average.

a business may be plotted against trends occurring within the industry as a whole for comparison purposes. An example of trend analysis is shown in Figure 6.5. Here the current ratio of a particular business (XYZ Ltd) at various dates is plotted against the average current ratio for other businesses in the same industry as XYZ Ltd. This enables a comparison of the business and similar businesses to be tracked over time.

Many larger businesses publish certain key financial ratios as part of their annual reports to help users identify significant trends. These ratios typically cover several years' activities. Exhibit 6.2 shows part of the table of 'key performance measures' of Marks and Spencer plc (M and S), the well-known UK high street store. After many years of profitable growth, M and S had suffered a decline in its fortunes during the late 1990s. This was seen by the directors, and by many independent commentators, as arising from allowing itself to be drawn away from its traditional areas of strength into such activities as operating overseas businesses. Steps were taken to deal with the problem and the business now seems to have 'turned the corner'. M and S seems to have reached its low point in the year ended March 2001 when it incurred a significant overall loss, with a trading profit only about 40% of what had been achieved in 1998. We can see from the table that it seems not to have been the gross (profit) margin that was the cause of the problem. In fact turnover was down in that year and expenses were up. The improvements in 2002 are very clear–gross (profit) margin is the highest over the five years and both net (profit) margin and return on equity (ordinary shareholders' funds) the best since 1998.

Exhibit 6.2 Key performance measures

		2002 £m 52 weeks	2001 £m 52 weeks	2000 £m 53 weeks	1999 £m 52 weeks	1998 £m 52 weeks
Gross margin	$\dfrac{\text{Gross profit}}{\text{Turnover}}$	35.8%	34.3%	31.8%	31.1%	33.3%
Net margin	$\dfrac{\text{Operating profit}}{\text{Turnover}}$	8.3%	6.2%	6.6%	8.0%	14.4%
Net margin excluding exceptional items		8.3%	6.5%	7.5%	8.4%	13.7%
Profitability	$\dfrac{\text{Profit before tax}}{\text{Turnover}}$	9.0%	5.2%	6.3%	8.6%	15.4%
Profitability excluding exceptional items		8.5%	6.7%	7.3%	8.8%	14.7%
Earnings per share	$\dfrac{\text{Standard earnings}}{\substack{\text{Weighted average ordinary}\\ \text{shares in issue}}}$	5.4p	(0.2)p	9.6p	13.0p	28.8p
Earnings per share adjusted for exceptional items		16.3p	11.2p	13.8p	15.6p	27.6p
Dividend per share		9.5p	9.0p	9.0p	14.4p	14.3p
Dividend cover	$\dfrac{\text{Profit attributable to shareholders}}{\text{Dividends}}$	2.2x	n/a	1.1x	0.9x	2.0x
Return on equity	$\dfrac{\text{Profit after tax and minority interests}}{\text{Average shareholders' funds}}$	11.1%	(0.1)%	5.7%	7.8%	18.3%

Source: Reproduced by kind permission of Marks & Spencer p.l.c., Annual Report 2002

Ratios and prediction models

Financial ratios, based on current or past performance, are often used to help predict the future, though both the choice of ratios and the interpretation of results are normally dependent on the judgement of the analyst. Attempts have been made, however, to develop a more rigorous and systematic approach to the use of ratios for prediction purposes. In particular, researchers have shown an interest in the use of ratios to predict financial distress in a business. Several methods and models using ratios have been developed that are claimed to predict future financial distress. Researchers have also developed ratio-based models with which to assess the supposed vulnerability of a business to takeover by another business. These areas, of course, are of interest to all those connected with the business. In the future, it is likely that further ratio-based models will be developed that predict other aspects of future performance.

Limitations of ratio analysis

Although ratios offer a quick and useful method of analysing the position and performance of a business, they are not without their problems and limitations. Some of the more important limitations are as follows:

■ *Quality of financial statements.* It must always be remembered that ratios are based on financial statements, and the results of ratio analysis are dependent on the quality of these underlying statements. Ratios will inherit the limitations of the financial statements on which they are based. A significant example of this arises from the application of the prudence convention to internally generated intangible fixed assets (as compared with purchased ones). This convention tends to lead to assets of considerable value, like goodwill and brand names, being excluded from the balance sheet. This can mean that ratios, like ROSF, ROCE and the gearing ratio, fail to take account of these assets.

■ *The restricted vision of ratios.* It is important not to rely exclusively on ratios, thereby losing sight of information contained in the underlying financial statements. Some items reported in these statements can be vital in assessing position and performance. For example, the total sales, capital employed and profit figures may be useful in assessing changes in absolute size that occur over time, or differences in scale between businesses. Ratios do not provide such information. In comparing one figure with another, ratios measure *relative* performance and position, and therefore provide only part of the picture. Thus, when comparing two businesses, it will often be useful to assess the absolute size of profits, as well as the relative profitability of each business. For example, Business A may generate £1 million profit and have a ROCE of 15 per cent, and Business B may generate £100,000 profit and have a ROCE of 20 per cent. Although Business B has a higher level of *profitability*, as measured by ROCE, it generates lower total profits.

■ *The basis for comparison.* We saw earlier that for ratios to be useful they require a basis for comparison. Moreover, it is important that the analyst compares like with like. When comparing businesses, however, no two businesses will be identical, and the greater the differences between the businesses being compared, the greater the limitations of ratio analysis. Also, when comparing businesses, differences in such matters as accounting policies, financing policies and financial year ends will add to the problems of evaluation.

■ *Balance sheet ratios.* Because the balance sheet is only a 'snapshot' of the business at a particular moment in time, any ratios based on balance sheet figures, such as the liquidity ratios above, may not be representative of the financial position of the business for the year as a whole. For example, it is common for a seasonal business to have a financial year end that coincides with a low point in business activity. Thus stocks and debtors may be low at the balance sheet date, and the liquidity ratios may also be low as a result. A more representative picture of liquidity can only really be gained by taking additional measurements at other points in the year.

Exhibit 6.3 points out another way in which ratios are limited.

Exhibit 6.3 **Remember it's people that really count . . .**

Lord Weinstock was an influential industrialist whose management style and philosophy helped to shape management practice in many UK businesses. During his long reign at GEC plc, a major engineering business, Lord Weinstock relied heavily on financial ratios to assess performance and to exercise control. In particular, he relied on ratios relating to sales, costs, debtors, profit margins and stock turnover. However, he was keenly aware of the limitations of ratios and recognised that, ultimately, people produce profits.

In a memo written to GEC managers he pointed out that ratios are an aid to, rather than a substitute for, good management. He wrote:

> The operating ratios are of great value as measures of efficiency but they are only the measures and not efficiency itself. Statistics will not design a product better, make it for a lower cost or increase sales. If ill-used, they may so guide action as to diminish resources for the sake of apparent but false signs of improvement.
>
> Management remains a matter of judgement, of knowledge of products and processes and of understanding and skill in dealing with people. The ratios will indicate how well all these things are being done and will show comparison with how they are done elsewhere. But they will tell us nothing about how to do them. That is what you are meant to do.

Source: Extract from *Arnold Weinstock and the making of GEC*, by S. Aris, Arum Press (1998), published in *Sunday Times*, 22 February 1998, p. 3

Summary

- *Ratio analysis*:
  - compares two related figures, usually both from the same set of financial statements;
  - is an aid to understanding what the financial statements are saying;
  - is an inexact science so results must be interpreted cautiously;
  - past periods, planned performance and the performance of similar businesses are often used to provide benchmark ratios.

- *Profitability ratios – concerned with effectiveness at generating profit*:
  - return on ordinary shareholders' funds (ROSF);
  - return on capital employed (ROCE);
  - net profit margin;
  - gross profit margin.

- *Efficiency ratios – concerned with efficiency of using assets/resources*:
  - average stock turnover period;
  - average settlement period for debtors;
  - average settlement period for creditors;
  - sales to capital employed;
  - sales per employee.
- *Liquidity ratios – concerned with the ability to meet short-term obligations*:
  - current ratio;
  - acid test ratio.

- *Gearing ratios – concerned with relationship between equity and debt financing*:
  - ❏ gearing ratio;
  - ❏ interest cover ratio.

- *Investment ratios – concerned with returns to shareholders*:
  - ❏ dividend payout ratio;
  - ❏ dividend yield ratio;
  - ❏ earnings per share;
  - ❏ price/earnings ratio.

- *Individual ratios can be plotted to detect trends.*

- *Ratios can be used to predict financial failure.*

- *Limitations of ratio analysis*:
  - ❏ ratios are only as reliable as the financial statements from which they derive;
  - ❏ ratios have restricted vision;
  - ❏ it can be difficult to find a suitable benchmark (for example, another business) to compare with;
  - ❏ some ratios could mislead due to the 'snapshot' nature of the balance sheet.

→ Key terms

return on ordinary shareholders' funds (ROSF)　*p 152*	sales to capital employed ratio　*p 159*
return on capital employed (ROCE)　*p 153*	current ratio　*p 163*
	acid test ratio　*p 164*
net profit margin ratio　*p 154*	gearing　*p 165*
gross profit margin ratio　*p 155*	gearing ratio　*p 168*
average stock turnover period　*p 157*	interest cover ratio　*p 168*
average settlement period for debtors　*p 157*	dividend payout ratio　*p 170*
	dividend yield ratio　*p 170*
average settlement period for creditors　*p 158*	earnings per share　*p 171*
	price/earnings ratio　*p 172*

? Review questions

Answers to these questions can be found on the students' side of the Companion Website.

6.1 Some businesses operate on a low net profit margin (for example, a supermarket chain). Does this mean that the return on capital employed from the business will also be low?

6.2 What potential problems arise for the external analyst from the use of balance sheet figures in the calculation of financial ratios?

6.3 Two businesses operate in the same industry. One has a stock turnover period that is higher than the industry average. The other has a stock turnover period that is lower than the industry average. Give three possible explanations for each business's stock turnover period ratio.

6.4 Identify and discuss three reasons why the P/E ratio of two businesses operating within the same industry may differ.

? Exercises

Exercises 6.4 and 6.5 are more advanced than 6.1–6.3. Those with a coloured number have an answer at the back of the book.

6.1 Jiang Ltd has recently produced its financial statements for the current year. The directors are concerned that the return on capital employed (ROCE) had decreased from 14 per cent last year to 12 per cent for the current year.

The following reasons were suggested as to why this reduction in ROCE had occurred:

(i) an increase in the gross profit margin;
(ii) a reduction in sales;
(iii) an increase in overhead expenses;
(iv) an increase in amount of stock held;
(v) the repayment of a loan at the year end;
(vi) an increase in the time taken for debtors to pay.

Required:
Taking each of these six suggested reasons in turn, state, with reasons, whether each of them could lead to a reduction in ROCE.

6.2 Business A and Business B are both engaged in retailing, but they seem to take a different approach to it according to the following information:

Ratio	Business A	Business B
Return on capital employed (ROCE)	20%	17%
Return on ordinary shareholders' funds (ROSF)	30%	18%
Average settlement period for debtors	63 days	21 days
Average settlement period for creditors	50 days	45 days
Gross profit margin	40%	15%
Net profit margin	10%	10%
Stock turnover period	52 days	25 days

Required:
Describe what this information indicates about the differences in approach between the two businesses. If one of them prides itself on personal service and one of them on competitive prices, which do you think is which and why?

6.3 Conday and Co. Ltd has been in operation for three years and produces antique reproduction furniture for the export market. The most recent set of financial statements for the business is set out as follows:

Balance sheet as at 30 November

	£000	£000	£000
Fixed assets			
Freehold land and buildings at cost			228
Plant and machinery at cost		942	
Less Accumulated depreciation		180	762
			990

	£000	£000	£000
Current assets			
Stocks		600	
Trade debtors		820	
		1,420	
Less Creditors: amounts falling due			
within one year			
Trade creditors	665		
Taxation	48		
Bank overdraft	432	1,145	275
			1,265
Less Creditors: amounts falling due			
in more than one year			
12% debentures (Note 1)			200
			1,065
Capital and reserves			
Ordinary shares of £1 each			700
Retained profits			365
			1,065

Profit and loss account for the year ended 30 November

	£000	£000
Sales		2,600
Less Cost of sales		1,620
Gross profit		980
Less Selling and distribution expenses (Note 2)	408	
Administration expenses	174	
Finance expenses	78	660
Net profit before taxation		320
Less Corporation tax		95
Net profit after taxation		225
Less Proposed dividend		160
Retained profit for the year		65

Notes
1 The debentures are secured on the freehold land and buildings.
2 Selling and distribution expenses include £170,000 in respect of bad debts.

The directors have approached an investor, to invest £200,000 by taking up a new issue of ordinary shares in the business at £6.40 each. The directors wish to use the funds to finance a programme of further expansion.

Required:
(a) Analyse the financial position and performance of the business and comment on any features that you consider to be significant.
(b) State, with reasons, whether or not the investor should invest in the business on the terms outlined.

6.4 The directors of Helena Beauty Products Ltd have been presented with the following abridged financial statements:

Helena Beauty Products Ltd
Profit and loss account for the year ended 30 September

	2003		2004	
	£000	£000	£000	£000
Sales		3,600		3,840
Less Cost of sales				
Opening stock	320		400	
Purchases	2,240		2,350	
	2,560		2,750	
Less Closing stock	400	2,160	500	2,250
Gross profit		1,440		1,590
Less Expenses		1,360		1,500
Net profit		80		90

Balance sheet as at 30 September

	2003		2004	
	£000	£000	£000	£000
Fixed assets		1,900		1,860
Current assets				
Stock	400		500	
Debtors	750		960	
Bank	8		4	
	1,158		1,464	
Less Creditors: amounts due				
within one year	390	768	450	1,014
		2,668		2,874
Financed by				
£1 ordinary shares		1,650		1,766
Reserves		1,018		1,108
		2,668		2,874

Required:
Using six ratios, comment on the profitability (three ratios) and efficiency (three ratios) of the business as revealed by the statements shown above.

6.5 Threads Limited manufactures nuts and bolts, which are sold to industrial users. The abbreviated financial statements for 2003 and 2004 are as follows:

Profit and loss account for the year ended 30 June

	2003		2004	
	£000	£000	£000	£000
Sales		1,180		1,200
Cost of sales		(680)		(750)
Gross profit		500		450
Operating expenses	(200)		(208)	
Depreciation	(66)		(75)	

	2003		2004	
	£000	£000	£000	£000
Interest	(–)		(8)	
		(266)		(291)
Profit before tax		234		159
Tax		(80)		(48)
Profit after tax		154		111
Dividend – proposed		(70)		(72)
Retained profit for year		84		39

Balance sheet as at 30 June

	2003		2004	
	£000	£000	£000	£000
Fixed assets		702		687
Current assets				
Stocks	148		236	
Debtors	102		156	
Cash	3		4	
	253		396	
Creditors: amounts due within one year				
Trade creditors	(60)		(76)	
Other creditors and accruals	(18)		(16)	
Dividend	(70)		(72)	
Tax	(40)		(24)	
Bank overdraft	(11)		(50)	
	(199)		(238)	
Net current assets		54		158
Creditors: amounts due after more than one year				
Bank loan		–		(50)
		756		795
Share capital and reserves				
Ordinary share capital of £1 (fully paid)		500		500
Retained profits		256		295
		756		795

Required:
(a) Calculate the following financial ratios for *both* 2003 and 2004:
   (i)   Return on capital employed
   (ii) Net profit margin
   (iii) Gross profit margin
   (iv) Current ratio
   (v)   Acid test ratio
   (vi) Settlement period for debtors
   (vii) Settlement period for creditors
   (viii) Stock turnover period
(b) Comment on the performance of Threads Limited from the viewpoint of a business considering supplying a substantial amount of goods to Threads Limited on usual trade credit terms.

Chapter 7

Cost–volume–profit analysis

Introduction

This chapter is concerned with the relationship between volume of activity, costs and profit. Broadly, costs can be analysed between those that are fixed, relative to the volume of activity, and those that vary with the volume of activity. We shall consider how we can use knowledge of this relationship to make decisions and assess risk, particularly in the context of short-term decisions. Though the distinction between financial and management accounting is rather blurred, and much relating to the financial statements that we have discussed so far in the book relates to providing information to managers, this chapter is the first one that is clearly in the area of management accounting.

Objectives

On completion of this chapter, you should be able to:

- distinguish between fixed costs and variable costs
- use knowledge of this distinction to deduce the break-even point for some activity
- make decisions on the use of spare capacity, using knowledge of the relationship between fixed and variable costs
- make decisions about the acceptance (or continuance) or rejection of a particular contract or activity, based on knowledge of the relationship between fixed and variable costs.

The behaviour of costs

Costs represent the resources that have to be sacrificed to achieve a business objective. The objective may be to make a particular product, to provide a particular service and so on. Costs may be broadly classified as:

■ those that stay fixed (the same) when changes occur to the volume of activity; and
■ those that vary according to the volume of activity.

These are known as **fixed costs** and **variable costs** respectively.

A restaurant manager's salary would normally provide an example of a fixed cost of operating the restaurant. The cost to the restaurant of buying the raw food would be a typical variable cost of operating the restaurant.

We shall see in this chapter that knowledge of how much of each type of cost is associated with some particular activity can be of great value to the decision maker.

Fixed costs

The way in which fixed costs behave can be depicted as in Figure 7.1. The distance OF represents the amount of fixed costs, and this stays the same irrespective of the volume of activity.

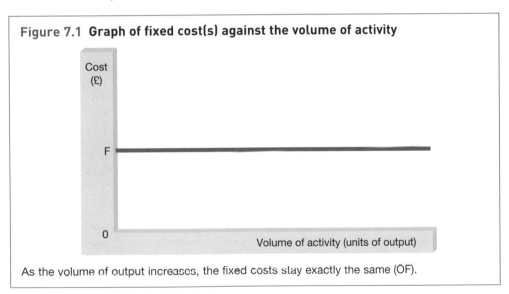

Figure 7.1 Graph of fixed cost(s) against the volume of activity

As the volume of output increases, the fixed costs stay exactly the same (OF).

Activity 7.1

A business operates a small chain of hairdressing salons. Can you give some examples of costs that are likely to be fixed for this business?

We came up with the following:

■ rent
■ insurance
■ cleaning costs
■ staff salaries.

These costs seem likely to be the same irrespective of alterations in the number of customers having their hair cut or styled.

Staff salaries and wages are sometimes automatically assumed always to be variable costs. In practice, they tend to be fixed. People are generally not paid according to the volume of output, and it is not normal to sack staff when there is a short-term downturn in activity. If there is a long-term downturn in activity, or at least if it looks that way to management, redundancies may occur, with fixed cost savings. This, however, is true of all costs. If there is seen to be a likely reduction in demand the business may decide to close some branches and make rental cost savings. Thus 'fixed' does not mean set in stone for all time; it usually means fixed over the short to medium term.

Nevertheless, in some circumstances, labour costs are variable (for example, where employees are paid according to how much output they produce), but probably in a minority of cases.

It is important to be clear that 'fixed', in this context, means only that the cost is not altered by changes in the volume of activity. Fixed costs are likely to be affected by inflation. If rent (a typical fixed cost) goes up because of inflation, a fixed cost will have increased, but not because of a change in the volume of activity.

The level of fixed costs does not stay the same, irrespective of the time period involved. Fixed costs are almost always *time-based*: that is, they vary with the length of time concerned. The rental charge for two months is normally twice that for one month. Thus fixed costs normally vary with time, but (of course) not with the volume of output. We should note that when we talk of fixed costs being, say, £1,000, we must add the period concerned, say, £1,000 a month.

Activity 7.2

Do fixed costs stay the same irrespective of the volume of output, even where there is a massive rise in that volume?
    Think in terms of the rent cost for the hairdressing business.

In fact, the rent is only fixed over a particular range (known as the 'relevant' range). If the number of people wanting to have their hair cut by the business increased, and the business wished to meet this increased demand, it would eventually have to expand its physical size. This might be achieved by opening additional branches, or perhaps by moving existing branches to larger premises in the same vicinity. It may be possible to cope with relatively minor increases in activity by using existing space more efficiently, or by having longer opening hours. If activity continued to expand, increased rent charges would seem inevitable.

In practice, the situation described in Activity 7.2 would look something like Figure 7.2.

At lower volumes of activity, the rent cost shown in Figure 7.2 would be OR. As the volume of activity expands, the accommodation becomes inadequate and further expansion requires an increase in premises and, therefore, cost. This higher level of accommodation provision will enable further expansion to take place. Eventually, further costs will need to be incurred if further expansion is to occur. Fixed costs that behave like this are often referred to as **stepped fixed costs**.

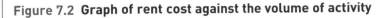

Figure 7.2 Graph of rent cost against the volume of activity

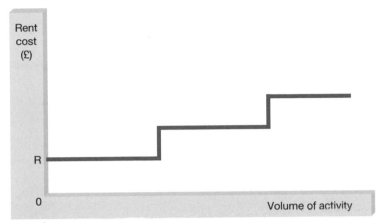

As the volume of activity increases from zero, the rent (a fixed cost) is unaffected. At a particular point, the volume of activity cannot increase further without additional space being rented. The cost of renting the additional space will cause a 'step' in the rent cost. The higher rent cost will continue unaffected if volume rises further until eventually another step point is reached.

Variable costs

Variable costs are costs that vary with the volume of activity. In a manufacturing business, for example, this would include raw materials used.

Activity 7.3

Can you think of some examples of variable costs in the hairdressing business?

We can think of a couple:

- lotions and other materials used
- laundry costs to wash towels used to dry customers' hair.

As with many types of business activity, variable costs of hairdressers tend to be relatively light in comparison with fixed costs: that is, fixed costs tend to make up the bulk of total costs.

Variable costs can be represented graphically as in Figure 7.3. At zero volume of activity the variable cost is zero. The cost increases in a straight line as activity increases.

The straight line for variable cost on this graph implies that the variable cost will normally be the same per unit of activity, irrespective of the volume of activity concerned. We shall consider the practicality of this assumption a little later in this chapter.

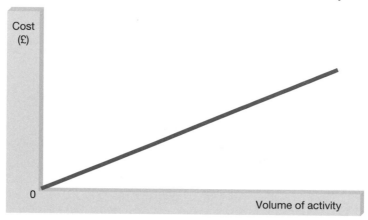

Figure 7.3 **Graph of variable costs against the volume of activity**

The graph shows that, at zero activity, there are no variable costs. However, as the volume of activity increases, so does the variable cost.

Semi-fixed (semi-variable) costs

In some cases, costs have both an element of fixed and of variable cost about them. They can be described as **semi-fixed (semi-variable) costs**. An example might be the electricity cost for the hairdressing business. Some of this will be for heating and lighting, and this part is probably fixed, at least until the volume of activity expands to a point where longer opening hours or larger premises are necessary. The other part of the cost will vary with the volume of activity. Here we are talking about such things as power for hairdryers, and so on.

Activity 7.4

Can you suggest another cost for a hairdressing business that is likely to be semi-fixed (semi-variable)?

We thought of telephone charges for landlines. These tend to have a rental element, which is fixed, and there may also be certain calls that have to be made irrespective of the volume of activity involved. However, increased business would be likely to lead to the need to make more telephone calls and hence increased call charges.

Usually, it is not obvious how much of each element a particular cost contains. It is normally necessary to look at past experience. If we have data on what the

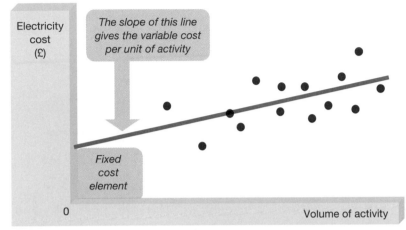

Figure 7.4 Graph of electricity cost against the volume of activity

Here the electricity bill for a time period (for example, three months) is plotted against the volume of activity for that same period. This is done for a series of periods. A line is then drawn that best 'fits' the various points on the graph. From this line we can then deduce both the cost at zero activity (the fixed element) and the slope of the line (the variable element).

electricity cost has been for various volumes of activity, say the relevant data over several three-month periods (electricity is usually billed by the quarter), we can estimate the fixed and variable portions. This may be done graphically, as shown in Figure 7.4. We tend to use past data here purely because it provides us with an estimate of future costs; past costs are not, of course, relevant for their own sake.

Each of the dots in Figure 7.4 is a reading of the electricity charge for a particular volume of activity (probably measured in terms of sales revenue). The diagonal line on the graph is the *line of best fit*. This means that, to us, this was the line that best seemed to represent the data. A better estimate can usually be made using a statistical technique (*least squares regression*), which does not involve drawing graphs and making estimates. In practice though, it probably makes little difference which approach is taken.

From the graph we can say that the fixed element of the electricity cost is the amount represented by the vertical distance from the origin at zero (bottom left-hand corner) to the point where the line of best fit crosses the vertical axis of the graph. The variable cost per unit is the amount that the graph rises for each increase in the volume of activity.

By analysing semi-fixed costs into their fixed and variable elements, in this way, we are left with just two types of cost. This means that we can use the information for further analysis.

Now that we have considered the nature of fixed and variable costs, we can go on to do something useful with that knowledge – carry out a **break-even analysis**.

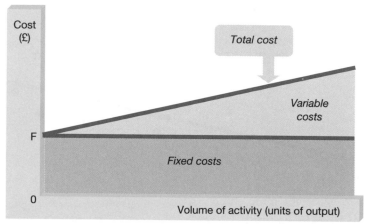

Figure 7.5 **Graph of total cost against the volume of activity**

The bottom part of the graph represents the fixed cost element. To this is added the wedge-shaped top portion, which represents the variable costs. The two parts together represent total cost. At zero activity, the variable costs are zero, so total costs equal fixed costs. As activity increases so does total cost, but only because variable costs increase. We are assuming that there are no steps in the fixed costs.

Break-even analysis

If, in respect of a particular activity, we know the total fixed costs for a period and the total variable cost per unit, we can produce a graph like Figure 7.5.

The bottom part of Figure 7.5 shows the fixed cost area. Added to this is the variable cost, the wedge-shaped portion at the top of the graph. The uppermost line represents the total cost at any particular volume of activity. This total is the vertical distance between the graph's horizontal axis and the uppermost line for the particular volume of activity concerned. Logically enough, the total cost at zero activity is the amount of the fixed costs. This is because, even where there is nothing going on, the business will still be paying rent, salaries, and so on, at least in the short term. The fixed cost is augmented by the amount of the relevant variable costs, as the volume of activity increases.

If we superimpose, onto this total cost graph in Figure 7.5, a line representing total revenue for each volume of activity, we obtain the **break-even chart** shown in Figure 7.6. Note in Figure 7.6 that, at zero volume of activity (zero sales), there is zero sales revenue. The profit (total sales revenue less total cost) at various volumes of activity is the vertical distance between the total sales revenue line and the total cost line at that particular volume of activity. Where the volume of activity is at **break-even point**, there is no vertical distance between these two lines (total sales revenue equals total costs) and so there is no profit or loss; that is, the activity breaks even. Where the volume of activity is below break-even point, a loss will be incurred

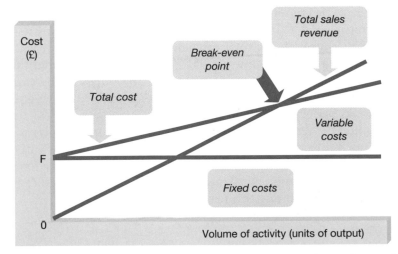

Figure 7.6 **Break-even chart**

The sloping line starting at zero represents the sales revenue at various volumes of activity. The point at which this finally catches up with the sloping total cost line, which starts at F, is the break-even point. Below this point a loss is made, above it a profit.

because total costs exceed total sales revenue. Where the business operates at a volume of activity above break-even point, there will be a profit because total sales revenue will exceed total costs. The further below break-even point, the higher the loss. The further above, the higher the profit.

As we may imagine, deducing break-even points by graphical means is a laborious business. Since the relationships in the graph are all linear (that is, the lines are all straight), it would be easy to calculate the break-even point, however.

We know that at break-even point (but not at any other point):

Total sales revenue = Total costs

That is,

Total sales revenue = Fixed costs + Total variable costs

If we call the number of units of output at break-even point b, then

$b \times$ Sales revenue per unit = Fixed costs + ($b \times$ Variable costs per unit)

Thus:

($b \times$ Sales revenue per unit) − ($b \times$ Variable costs per unit) = Fixed costs

and:

$b \times$ (Sales revenue per unit − Variable costs per unit) = Fixed costs

giving:

$$b = \frac{\text{Fixed costs}}{\text{Sales revenue per unit} - \text{Variable costs per unit}}$$

If we look back at the break-even chart in Figure 7.6, this seems logical. The total cost line starts off at point F, higher than the starting point for the total sales revenues line (zero) by amount F (the amount of the fixed costs). Because the sales revenue per unit is greater than the variable cost per unit, the sales revenue line will gradually catch up with the total cost line. The rate at which it will catch up is dependent on the relative steepness of the two lines and the amount that it has to catch up (the fixed costs). Bearing in mind that the slopes of the two lines are the variable cost per unit and the selling price per unit, the above equation for calculating b looks perfectly logical.

Though the break-even point can be calculated quickly and simply, as shown, it does not mean that the graphical approach of the break-even chart is without value. The chart shows the relationship between cost, volume and profit in a form that can easily be understood by non-financial managers. The break-even chart can therefore be a useful device for explaining this relationship.

Example 7.1

Cottage Industries Ltd makes baskets. The fixed costs of operating the workshop for a month total £500. Each basket requires materials that cost £2. Each basket takes two hours to make, and the business pays the basket makers £5 an hour. The basket makers are all on contracts such that if they do not work for any reason, they are not paid. The baskets are sold to a wholesaler for £14 each.

What is the break-even point for basket making for the business?

The break-even point (in number of baskets):

$$= \frac{\text{Fixed costs}}{\text{(Sales revenue per unit − Variable costs per unit)}}$$

$$= £500/[£14 − (2 + 10)] = 250 \text{ baskets per month.}$$

Note that the break-even point must be expressed with respect to a period of time.

Exhibit 7.1 shows how one well-known business uses break-even analysis.

Exhibit 7.1 BE at BA

British Airways plc (BA) regularly reports the break-even level for its operations on a year-to-year basis. For 2002, BA reports that, in general terms, had its planes flown at 65.0% full, the business would have broken even. In fact they flew at an average 64.0% full, leading to a small operating loss for the year. In each of the four preceding years, the actual volume had exceeded the break-even point and BA had, therefore, generated operating profits.

The fact that BA reports this information implies that it uses cost–volume relationships when assessing its financial performance. It seems likely that many other businesses also look at these relationships.

Source: Taken from information contained in the British Airways plc Annual Report 2002

Activity 7.5

Can you think of reasons why the managers of a business might find it useful to know the break-even point of some activity that they are planning to undertake?

The usefulness of being able to deduce the break-even point is that it makes it possible to compare the planned or expected volume of activity with the break-even point and so make a judgement about risk. Planning to operate only just above the volume of activity necessary in order to break even may indicate that it is a risky venture, since only a small fall from the planned volume of activity could lead to a loss.

Activity 7.6

Cottage Industries Ltd (see Example 7.1) expects to sell 500 baskets a month. The business has the opportunity to rent a basket-making machine. Doing so would increase the total fixed costs of operating the workshop for a month to £3,000. Using the machine would reduce the labour time to one hour per basket. The basket makers would still be paid £5 an hour.

(a) How much profit would the business make each month from selling baskets (i) assuming that the basket-making machine is not rented and (ii) assuming that it is rented?
(b) What is the break-even point if the machine is rented?
(c) What do you notice about the figures that you calculate?

(a) Estimated profit, per month, from basket making:

	Without the machine		With the machine	
	£	£	£	£
Sales (500 × £14)		7,000		7,000
Less Materials (500 × £2)	1,000		1,000	
Labour (500 × 2 × £5)	5,000			
(500 × 1 × £5)			2,500	
Fixed costs	500		3,000	
		6,500		6,500
Profit		500		500

(b) The break-even point (in number of baskets) with the machine:

$$= \frac{\text{Fixed costs}}{\text{Sales revenue per unit} - \text{Variable costs per unit}}$$

$$= £3,000/[£14 - (£2 + £5)] = 429 \text{ baskets per month}$$

The break-even point without the machine is 250 baskets per month (see Example 7.1). ▶

Activity 7.6 continued

(c)   There seems to be nothing to choose between the two manufacturing strategies regarding profit, at the estimated sales volume. There is, however, a distinct difference between the two strategies regarding the break-even point. Without the machine, the actual volume of sales could fall by a half of that which is expected (from 500 to 250) before the business would fail to make a profit. With the machine, however, a 14 per cent fall (from 500 to 429) would be enough to cause the business to fail to make a profit. On the other hand, for each additional basket sold above the estimated 500, an additional profit of only £2 (that is, £14 − (£2 + £10)) would be made without the machine, whereas £7 (that is, £14 − (£2 + £5)) would be made with the machine. (Note that knowledge of the break-even point and the planned volume of activity gives some basis for assessing the riskiness of the activity.)

We shall take a closer look at the relationship between fixed costs, variable costs and break-even together with any advice that we might give the management of Cottage Industries Ltd after we have briefly considered the notion of **contribution**.

Contribution

The bottom part of the break-even formula (sales revenue per unit less variable costs per unit) is known as the 'contribution' per unit. Thus for the basket-making activity, without the machine the contribution per unit is £2, and with the machine it is £7. This can be quite a useful figure to know in a decision-making context. It is called 'contribution' because it contributes to meeting the fixed costs and, if there is any excess, it also contributes to profit.

We shall see, a little later in this chapter, how knowing the amount of the contribution generated by a particular activity can be valuable in making short-term decisions of various types, as well as being useful in the break-even point calculation.

Margin of safety and operating gearing

The **margin of safety** is the extent to which the planned volume of output or sales lies above the break-even point. Going back to Activity 7.6, we saw that the following situation exists:

	Without the machine (number of baskets)	With the machine (number of baskets)
Expected volume of sales	500	500
Break-even point	250	429
Difference (margin of safety):		
Number of baskets	250	71
Percentage of estimated volume of sales	50%	14%

Activity 7.7

What advice would you give Cottage Industries Ltd about renting the machine, on the basis of the values for margin of safety?

It is a matter of personal judgement, which in turn is related to individual attitudes to risk, as to which strategy to adopt. Most people, however, would prefer the strategy of not renting the machine, since the margin of safety between the expected volume of activity and the break-even point is much greater. Thus, for the same level of return the risk will be lower without renting the machine.

The relative margins of safety are directly linked to the relationship between the selling price per basket, the variable costs per basket, and the fixed costs per month. Without the machine the contribution (selling price less variable costs) per basket is £2; with the machine it is £7. On the other hand, without the machine the fixed costs are £500 a month; with the machine they are £3,000. This means that, with the machine, the contributions have more fixed costs to 'overcome' before the activity becomes profitable. However, the rate at which the contributions can overcome fixed costs is higher with the machine, because variable costs are lower. This means that one more, or one less, basket sold has a greater impact on profit than it does if the machine is not rented. The contrast between the two scenarios is shown graphically in Figures 7.7(a) and 7.7(b).

The relationship between contribution and fixed costs is known as **operating gearing**. An activity with relatively high fixed costs compared with its variable costs is said to have high operating gearing. Thus, Cottage Industries Ltd is more highly operationally geared using the machine than not using it. Renting the machine increases the level of operating gearing quite dramatically because it causes an increase in fixed costs, but at the same time it leads to a reduction in variable costs per basket.

The reason why the word 'gearing' is used in this context is that, as with intermeshing gear wheels of different circumferences, a movement in one of the factors (volume of output) causes a more-than-proportionate movement in the other (profit) as illustrated by Figure 7.8.

Increasing the level of operating gearing tends to make profits more sensitive to changes in the volume of activity. We can demonstrate operating gearing with Cottage Industries Ltd's basket-making activities as follows:

	Without the machine			With the machine		
Volume	500	1,000	1,500	500	1,000	1,500
	£	£	£	£	£	£
Contributions*	1,000	2,000	3,000	3,500	7,000	10,500
Less Fixed costs	500	500	500	3,000	3,000	3,000
Profit	500	1,500	2,500	500	4,000	7,500

* £2 per basket without the machine and £7 per basket with it.

Figure 7.7 Break-even charts for Cottage Industries' basket-making activities (a) without the machine and (b) with the machine

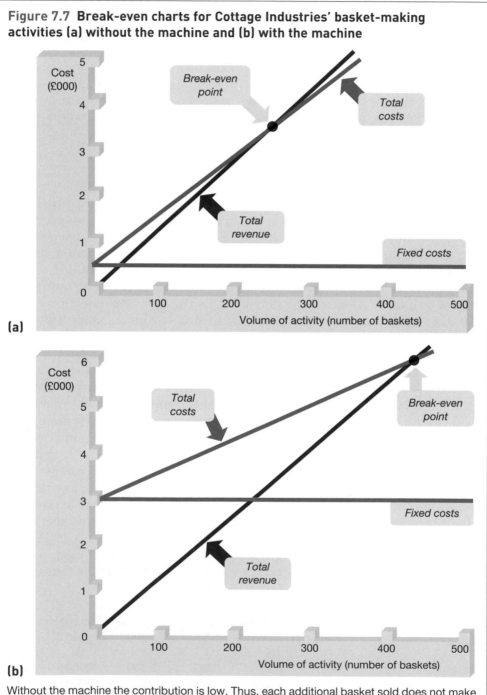

(a)

(b)

Without the machine the contribution is low. Thus, each additional basket sold does not make a dramatic difference to the profit or loss. With the machine, however, the opposite is true, and small increases or decreases in the sales volume will have a marked effect on the profit or loss.

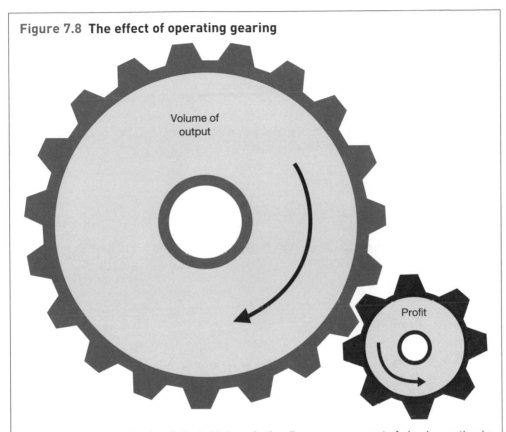

Figure 7.8 The effect of operating gearing

Where operating gearing is relatively high, as in the diagram, an amount of circular motion in the volume wheel causes a greater amount of circular motion in the profit wheel. An increase in volume would cause a disproportionately greater increase in profit. The equivalent would also be true of a decrease in activity, however.

Note that, without the machine (low operating gearing), a doubling of the output from 500 to 1,000 units brings a trebling of the profit. With the machine (high operating gearing), doubling output causes profit to rise by eight times. At the same time reductions in the volume of output tend have a more damaging effect on profit where the operating gearing is higher.

Operating gearing is quite similar in nature and effect to the financial gearing that we met in Chapter 6.

Activity 7.8

In general terms, what types of business activity tend to be most highly operationally geared?

Hint: Cottage Industries Ltd might give you some idea.

In general, activities that are capital intensive tend to be more highly operationally geared. This is because renting or owning capital equipment gives rise to additional fixed costs, but it can also give rise to lower variable costs.

Profit–volume charts

➡ A slight variant of the break-even chart is the **profit–volume (PV) chart**. A typical PV chart is shown in Figure 7.9.

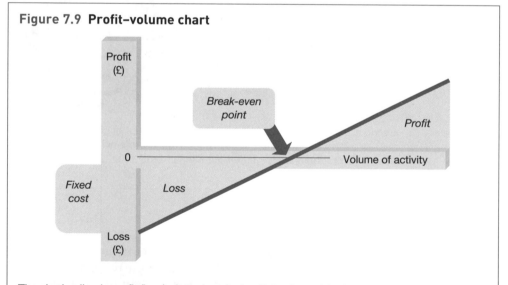

Figure 7.9 Profit–volume chart

The sloping line is profit (loss) plotted against activity. As activity increases, so does total contribution (sales revenue less variable costs). At zero activity there are no contributions, so there will be a loss equal in amount to the total fixed costs.

The profit–volume chart is obtained by plotting loss or profit against volume of activity. The slope of the graph is equal to the contribution per unit, since each additional unit sold decreases the loss, or increases the profit, by the sales revenue per unit less the variable cost per unit. At zero volume of activity there are no contributions, so there is a loss equal to the amount of the fixed costs. As the volume of activity increases, the amount of the loss gradually decreases until break-even point is reached. Beyond break-even point, profits increase as activity increases.

As we can see, the profit–volume chart does not tell us anything not shown by the break-even chart. On the other hand, information is perhaps more easily absorbed from the profit–volume chart. This is particularly true of the profit at any volume of activity. This information is provided by the break-even chart as the vertical distance between the total cost and total sales revenue lines. The profit–volume chart, in effect, combines the total sales revenue and total variable cost lines, which means that profit (or loss) is plotted directly.

Weaknesses of break-even analysis

As we have seen, break-even analysis can provide some useful insights to the important relationship between fixed costs, variable costs and the volume of activity. It does, however, have its weaknesses. There are three general problems:

- *Non-linear relationships*. The normal approach to break-even analysis assumes that the relationships between sales revenues, variable costs and volume are strictly straight-line ones. In real life this is unlikely to be so.

   This is probably not a major problem, since break-even analysis is normally conducted in advance of the activity actually taking place. Our ability to predict future costs, revenues and so on is somewhat limited: hence what are probably minor variations from strict linearity are unlikely to be significant, compared with other forecasting errors.
- *Stepped fixed costs*. Most fixed costs are not fixed over all volumes of activity. They tend to be 'stepped' in the way depicted in Figure 7.2. This means that, in practical circumstances, great care must be taken in making assumptions about fixed costs. The problem is particularly heightened because most activities will probably involve fixed costs of various types (rent, supervisory salaries, administration costs), all of which are likely to have steps at different points.
- *Multi-product businesses*. Most businesses do not offer just one product or service. This is a problem for break-even analysis since it raises the question of the effect of additional sales of one product or service on sales of another of the business's products or services. There is also the problem of identifying the fixed costs of one particular activity. Fixed costs tend to relate to more than one activity – for example, two activities may be carried out in the same rented premises. There are ways of dividing fixed costs between activities, but these tend to be arbitrary, which calls into question the value of the break-even analysis.

Marginal analysis

When we are trying to decide between two or more possible courses of action, and where economic costs and benefits are the decision-making criteria, *only costs that vary with the decision should be included in the decision analysis.*

Example 7.2

A householder wants a room decorated. Two decorators have been asked to price the job. One of them will do the work for £250, the other one wants £300, in both cases on the basis that the householder will supply the materials. It is believed that the two decorators will do an equally good job. The materials will cost £200 irrespective of which decorator does the work. Assuming that the householder wants the room decorated at the lower cost, which decorator should be asked to do the work? Is the cost of the materials relevant to the decision?

Clearly the first of the two decorators should be selected. The cost of the materials is irrelevant because it will be the same in each case. It is only possible to distinguish rationally between courses of action on the basis of differences between them.

For many decisions that involve relatively small variations from existing practice and/or are for relatively limited periods of time, fixed costs are not relevant to the decision, because they will be the same irrespective of the decision made. This is because either:

■ fixed costs tend to be impossible to alter in the short term; or
■ managers are reluctant to alter them in the short term.

Activity 7.9

Ali plc occupies premises that it owns in order to provide a service. There is a downturn in demand for the service, and it would be possible for Ali plc to carry on the business from smaller, cheaper premises.

Can you think of any reasons why the business might not immediately move to smaller, cheaper premises?

We thought of broadly two reasons:

1 It is not usually possible to find a buyer for premises at very short notice, and it may be difficult to move premises quickly where there is, say, delicate equipment to be moved.
2 Management may feel that the downturn might not be permanent, and would thus be reluctant to take such a dramatic step and deny itself the opportunity to benefit from a possible revival of trade.

The business's premises in Activity 7.9 may provide an example of the more inflexible types of cost, but most fixed costs tend to be broadly similar in this context.

We shall now consider some decision-making areas where fixed costs can be regarded as irrelevant, and analyse decisions in those areas. The fact that the decisions that we are considering here are short term means that the objective of wealth enhancement will be promoted by trying to generate as much net cash inflow as possible. In **marginal analysis** we concern ourselves just with costs and revenues that vary with the decision. This often means that fixed costs are ignored.

The variable cost per unit will usually be equal to the **marginal cost**, that is, the additional cost of producing one more unit of output. Where producing one more will involve a step in the fixed costs, the marginal cost is not just the variable cost, it will include the increment, or step, in the fixed costs.

Accepting/rejecting special contracts

Activity 7.10

Cottage Industries Ltd (see Example 7.1) has spare capacity in that it has spare basket makers. An overseas retail chain has offered the business an order for 300 baskets at a price of £13 each.

Without considering any wider issues, should the business accept the order? (Assume that the business does not rent the machine.)

Since the fixed costs will be incurred in any case, they are not relevant to this decision. All we need to do is see whether the price offered will yield a contribution. If it will, the business will be better off by accepting the contract than by refusing it.

	£
Additional revenue per unit	13
Less Additional cost per unit	12
Additional contribution per unit	1

For 300 units, the additional contribution will be £300 (that is, 300 × £1). Since no fixed cost increase is involved, irrespective of what else is happening to the business, it will be £300 better off by taking this contract than by refusing it.

As ever with decision making, there are other factors that are either difficult or impossible to quantify. These should be taken into account before reaching a final decision. In the case of Cottage Industries Ltd's decision on the overseas customer, these could include the following:

- The possibility that spare capacity will have been 'sold off' cheaply when there might be another potential customer who will offer a higher price, but, by which time, the capacity will be fully committed. It is a matter of commercial judgement as to how likely this will be.
- The problem that selling the same product, but at different prices, could lead to a loss of customer goodwill. The fact that a different price will be set for customers in different countries (that is, in different markets) may be sufficient to avoid this potential problem.
- If the business is going to suffer continually from being unable to sell its full production potential at the 'regular' price, it might be better, in the long run, to

reduce capacity and make fixed cost savings. Using the spare capacity to produce marginal benefits may lead to the business failing to address this issue.

■ On a more positive note, the business may see this as a way of breaking into the overseas market. This is something that might be impossible to achieve if the business charges its regular price.

The most efficient use of scarce resources

We tend to think in terms of the size of the market being the brake on output. This is to say that the ability of a business to sell will limit production, rather than the ability to produce will limit sales. In some cases, however, it is a limit on what can be produced that limits sales. Limited production might stem from a shortage of any factor of production – labour, raw materials, space, machinery and so on.

The most profitable combination of products will occur where the *contribution per unit of the scarce factor* is maximised. Example 7.3 should illustrate this point.

Example 7.3

A business provides three different services, the details of which are as follows:

Service (code name)	AX107	AX109	AX220
	£	£	£
Selling price per unit	50	40	65
Variable cost per unit	(25)	(20)	(35)
Contribution per unit	25	20	30
Labour time per unit	5 hours	3 hours	6 hours

Within reason, the market will take as many units of each service as can be provided, but the ability to provide the service is limited by the availability of labour, all of which needs to be skilled. Fixed costs are not affected by the choice of service provided because all three services use the same production facilities.

The most profitable service is AX109 because it generates a contribution of £6.67 (£20/3) per hour. The other two generate only £5.00 each per hour (£25/5 and £30/6). So, to maximise profit, priority should be given to the production that maximises the contribution per unit of limiting factor.

Our first reaction may have been that the business should provide only service AX220, because this is the one that yields the highest contribution per unit sold. If so, we should have been making the mistake of thinking of the ability to sell as being the limiting factor. If the above analysis is not convincing, we can take an imaginary number of available labour hours and ask ourselves what is the maximum contribution (and, therefore, profit) that could be made by providing each service exclusively. Bear in mind that there is no shortage of anything else, including market demand, just a shortage of labour.

Activity 7.11

A business makes three different products, the details of which are as follows:

Product (code name)	B14	B17	B22
Selling price per unit (£)	25	20	23
Variable cost per unit (£)	10	8	12
Weekly demand (units)	25	20	30
Machine time per unit	4 hours	3 hours	4 hours

Fixed costs are not affected by the choice of product because all three products use the same machine. Machine time is limited to 148 hours a week.

Which combination of products should be manufactured if the business is to produce the highest profit?

Product (code name)	B14	B17	B22
	£	£	£
Selling price per unit	25	20	23
Variable cost per unit	(10)	(8)	(12)
Contribution per unit (£)	15	12	11
Machine time per unit	4 hours	3 hours	4 hours
Contribution per machine hour	£3.75	£4.00	£2.75
Order of priority	2nd	1st	3rd

Therefore:

Produce	20 units of product B17 using	60 hours
	22 units of product B14 using	88 hours
		148 hours

This leaves unsatisfied the market demand for a further 3 units of product B14 and 30 units of product B22.

Activity 7.12

What steps could be contemplated that could lead to a higher level of contribution for the business in Activity 7.11?

The possibilities for improving matters that occurred to us are as follows:

- Consider obtaining additional machine time. This could mean obtaining a new machine, subcontracting the machining to another business, or perhaps squeezing a few more hours per week out of the business's own machine. Perhaps a combination of two or more of these is a possibility.
- Redesign the products in a way that requires less time per unit on the machine.
- Increase the price per unit of the three products. This might well have the effect of dampening demand, but the existing demand cannot be met at present, and it may be more profitable in the long run to make a greater contribution on each unit sold than to take one of the other courses of action to overcome the problem.

Activity 7.13

Going back to Activity 7.11, what is the maximum price that the business concerned would logically be prepared to pay to have the remaining B14s machined by a subcontractor, assuming that no fixed or variable costs would be saved as a result of not doing the machining 'in-house'?

Would there be a different maximum if we were considering the B22s?

If the remaining three B14s were subcontracted at no cost, the business would be able to earn a contribution of £15, which it would not otherwise be able to gain. Therefore, any price up to £15 per unit would be worth paying a subcontractor to undertake the machining. Naturally, the business would prefer to pay as little as possible, but anything up to £15 would still make it worthwhile subcontracting the machining.

This would not be true of the B22s because they have a different contribution per unit; £11 would be the relevant figure in their case.

Make-or-buy decisions

Businesses are frequently confronted by the need to decide whether to produce the product or service that they sell themselves, or to buy it in from some other business. Thus, a producer of electrical appliances might decide to subcontract the manufacture of one of its products to another business, perhaps because there is a shortage of production capacity in the producer's own factory, or because it believes it to be cheaper to subcontract than to make the appliance itself.

It might just be part of a product that is subcontracted. For example, the producer may have a component for the appliance made by another manufacturer. In principle, there is hardly any limit to the scope of make-or-buy decisions. Virtually any part, component or service that is required in production of the main product or service, or the main product or service itself, could be the subject of a make-or-buy decision. So, for example, the personnel function of a business, which is normally performed 'in-house', could be subcontracted. At the same time, electrical power, which is typically provided by an outside electrical utility business, could be generated 'in-house'.

Example 7.4

Shah Ltd needs a component for one of its products. It can subcontract production of the component to a subcontractor who will provide the components for £20 each. The business can produce the components internally for total variable costs of £15 per component. Shah Ltd has spare capacity.

Should the component be subcontracted or produced internally?

The answer is that Shah Ltd should produce the component internally, since the variable cost of subcontracting is greater by £5 than the variable cost of internal manufacture.

Activity 7.14

Now assume that Shah Ltd (Example 7.4) has no spare capacity, so it can only produce the component internally by reducing its output of another of its products. While
it is making each component, it will lose contributions of £12 from the other product.
   Should the component be subcontracted or produced internally?

The answer is to subcontract.
   The relevant cost of internal production of each component is:

	£
Variable cost of production of the component	15
Opportunity cost of lost production of the other product	12
	27

This is obviously more costly than the £20 per component that will have to be paid to the
subcontractor.

Activity 7.15

What factors, other than the immediately financially quantifiable, would you consider
when making a make-or-buy decision?

We feel that there are two major factors:

1 The general problems of subcontracting:
   (a) loss of control of quality;
   (b) potential unreliability of supply.
2 Expertise and specialisation. It is possible for most businesses, with sufficient determination, to do virtually everything 'in house'. This may, however, require a level of
   skill and facilities that most businesses neither have nor feel inclined to acquire. For
   example, though it is true that most businesses could generate their own electricity, their
   managements tend to take the view that this is better done by a specialist generator
   business. Specialists can often do things more cheaply, with less risk of things going
   wrong.

Closing or continuation decisions

It is quite common for businesses to account separately for each department or section, to try to assess the relative effectiveness of each one.

Example 7.5

Goodsports Ltd is a retail shop that operates through three departments, all in the same premises. The three departments occupy roughly equal areas of the premises. The trading results for the year just finished showed the following:

	Total	Sports equipment	Sports clothes	General clothes
	£000	£000	£000	£000
Sales	534	254	183	97
Costs	(482)	(213)	(163)	(106)
Profit/(loss)	52	41	20	(9)

It would appear that if the general clothes department were to close, the business would be more profitable, by £9,000 a year, assuming last year's performance to be a reasonable indication of future performance.

When the costs are analysed between those that are variable and those that are fixed, however, the contribution of each department can be deduced and the following results obtained:

	Total	Sports equipment	Sports clothes	General clothes
	£000	£000	£000	£000
Sales	534	254	183	97
Variable costs	(344)	(167)	(117)	(60)
Contribution	190	87	66	37
Fixed costs (rent, and so on)	138	46	46	46
Profit/(loss)	52	41	20	(9)

Now it is obvious that closing the general clothes department, without any other developments, would make the business worse off by £37,000 (the department's contribution). The department should not be closed, because it makes a positive contribution. The fixed costs would continue whether the department were closed or not. As can be seen from the above analysis, distinguishing between variable and fixed costs, and deducing the contribution, can make the picture a great deal clearer.

Activity 7.16

In considering Goodsports Ltd (in Example 7.5), we saw that the general clothes department should not be closed 'without any other developments'.

What 'other developments' could affect this decision, making continuation either more attractive or less attractive?

Activity 7.16 continued

The things that we could think of are as follows:

■ Expansion of the other departments or replacing the general clothes department with a completely new activity. This would make sense only if the space currently occupied by the general clothes department could generate contributions totalling at least £37,000 a year.
■ Subletting the space occupied by the general clothes department. Once again, this would need to generate a net rent greater than £37,000 a year to make it more financially beneficial than keeping the department open.
■ Keeping the department open even if it generated no contribution whatsoever (assuming that there is no other use for the space) may be beneficial if customers are attracted into the shop because it has general clothing and they may then buy something from one of the other departments. In the same way, the activity of a subtenant might attract customers into the shop. (On the other hand, it might drive them away!)

? Self-assessment question 7.1

Khan Ltd can make three products (Alpha, Beta and Gamma) using the same machines. Various estimates for next year have been made as follows:

Product	Alpha	Beta	Gamma
	£/unit	£/unit	£/unit
Selling price	30	39	20
Variable material cost	15	18	10
Other variable production costs	6	10	5
Share of fixed overheads	8	12	4
Time per unit required on machines (hours)	2	3	1

Fixed overhead costs for next year are expected to total £40,000.

Required:
(a) If the business were to make only product Alpha next year, how many units would it need to make in order to break even? (Assume for this part of the question that there is no effective limit to market size and production capacity.)
(b) If the business has maximum machine capacity for next year of 10,000 hours, in which order of preference would the three products come?
(c) If the maximum market for next year for the three products is as follows:

Alpha   3,000 units
Beta   2,000 units
Gamma   5,000 units

what quantities of which product should the business make next year and how much profit would this be expected to yield?

Summary

The main points in this chapter may be summarised as follows:

■ *Behaviour of costs:*
  ❑ fixed costs are those that are independent of the level of activity (for example, rent);
  ❑ variable costs are those that vary with the level of activity (for example, raw materials);
  ❑ semi-fixed (semi-variable) costs are a mixture of the two (for example, electricity).

■ *Break-even analysis:*
  ❑ the break-even point (BEP) is the level of activity (in units of output or sales revenue) at which total costs (fixed + variable) = total sales revenue;
  ❑ calculation of BEP is as follows:

$$\text{BEP (in units of output)} = \frac{\text{Fixed costs for the period}}{\text{Contribution per unit}}$$

  ❑ use of knowledge of BEP for a particular activity – risk assessment;
  ❑ contribution per unit = sales revenue per unit less variable cost per unit;
  ❑ margin of safety = excess over BEP of planned volume of activity;
  ❑ operating gearing = the extent to which the total costs of some activity are fixed rather than variable;
  ❑ profit–volume (PV) chart an alternative approach to BE chart.

■ *Weaknesses of BE analysis:*
  ❑ non-linear relationships;
  ❑ stepped fixed costs;
  ❑ multi-product businesses.

■ *Marginal analysis* (ignores fixed costs where these are not affected by the decision):
  ❑ accepting/rejecting special contracts – consider only the effect on contributions;
  ❑ using scarce resources – the limiting factor is most effectively used by maximising contribution per unit of it;
  ❑ make-or-buy decisions – take the action that leads to the higher total contributions;
  ❑ closing/continuing an activity – should be assessed by net effect on total contributions.

→ **Key terms**

costs *p 186*	break-even point *p 192*
fixed costs *p 187*	contribution *p 196*
variable costs *p 187*	margin of safety *p 196*
stepped fixed costs *p 188*	operating gearing *p 197*
semi-fixed (semi-variable) costs *p 190*	profit–volume (PV) chart *p 200*
break-even analysis *p 191*	marginal analysis *p 203*
break-even chart *p 192*	marginal cost *p 203*

? Review questions

Answers to these questions can be found on the students' side of the Companion Website.

7.1   Define the terms *fixed cost* and *variable cost*. Explain how an understanding of the distinction between fixed costs and variable costs can be useful to managers.

7.2   What is meant by the *break-even point* for an activity? How is the break-even point calculated? Why is it useful to know the break-even point?

7.3   When we say that some business activity has *high operating gearing*, what do we mean? What are the implications for the business of high operating gearing?

7.4   If there is a scarce resource that is restricting sales, how will the business maximise its profit? Explain the logic of the approach that you have identified for maximising profit.

? Exercises

Exercises 7.4 and 7.5 are more advanced than 7.1–7.3. Those with a coloured number have answers at the back of the book.

7.1   The management of a business is concerned at its inability to obtain enough fully trained labour to enable it to meet its present budget projection.

Product:	*Alpha*	*Beta*	*Gamma*	*Total*
	£000	*£000*	*£000*	*£000*
Variable costs				
Materials	6	4	5	15
Labour	9	6	12	27
Expenses	3	2	2	7
Allocated fixed costs	13	8	12	33
Total cost	31	20	31	82
Profit	8	9	2	19
Sales	39	29	33	101

The amount of labour likely to be available amounts to £20,000. All of the variable labour is paid at the same hourly rate. You have been asked to prepare a statement of production plans ensuring that at least 50 per cent of the budget sales are achieved for each product, and the balance of labour is used to produce the greatest profit.

Required:
(a)   Prepare a statement, with explanations, showing the greatest profit available from the limited amount of skilled labour available, within the constraint stated. *Hint*: Remember that all labour is paid at the same rate.
(b)   What steps could the business take in an attempt to improve profitability, in the light of the labour shortage?

7.2 Lannion and Co is engaged in providing and marketing a standard cleaning service. Summarised results for the past two months reveal the following:

	October	November
Sales (units of the service)	200	300
Sales (£)	5,000	7,500
Operating profit (£)	1,000	2,200

There were no price changes of any description during these two months.

Required:
(a) Deduce the break-even point (in units of the service) for Lannion.
(b) State why the business might find it useful to know its break-even point.

7.3 A hotel group prepares accounts on a quarterly basis. The senior management is reviewing the performance of one hotel and making plans for next year.

   They have in front of them the results for this year (based on some actual results and some forecasts to the end of this year):

Quarter	Sales	Profit/(loss)
	£000	£000
1	400	(280)
2	1,200	360
3	1,600	680
4	800	40
Total	4,000	800

The total estimated number of visitors (guest nights) for this year is 50,000. The results follow a regular pattern; there are no unexpected cost fluctuations beyond the seasonal trading pattern exhibited. The management intends to incorporate into its plans for next year an anticipated increase in unit variable costs of 10 per cent and a profit target for the hotel of £1 million.

Required:
(a) Calculate the total variable and total fixed costs of the hotel for this year. Show the provisional annual results for this year in total, showing variable and fixed costs separately. Show also the revenue and costs per visitor.
(b) (i) If there is no increase in visitors for next year, what will be the required revenue rate per hotel visitor to meet the profit target?
    (ii) If the required revenue rate per visitor is not raised above this year's level, how many visitors will be required to meet the profit target?
(c) Outline and briefly discuss the assumptions that are made in typical PV or break-even analysis, and assess whether they limit its usefulness.

7.4 A business makes three products, A, B and C. All three products require the use of two types of machine: cutting machines and assembling machines. Estimates for next year include the following:

Product	A	B	C
Selling price (£ per unit)	25	30	18
Sales demand (units)	2,500	3,400	5,100
Material cost (£ per unit)	12	13	10
Variable production cost (£ per unit)	7	4	3
Time required per unit on cutting machines (hours)	1.0	1.0	0.5
Time required per unit on assembling machines (hours)	0.5	1.0	0.5

Fixed overhead costs for next year are expected to total £42,000. It is the business's policy for each unit of production to absorb these in proportion to its total variable costs.

The business has cutting machine capacity of 5,000 hours a year and assembling machine capacity of 8,000 hours a year.

Required:
(a) State, with supporting workings, which products in which quantities the business should plan to make next year on the basis of the above information. *Hint*: First determine which machines will be a limiting factor (scarce resource).
(b) State the maximum price per product that it would be worth the business paying a subcontractor to carry out that part of the work that could not be done internally.

7.5 Darmor Ltd has three products, which require the same production facilities. Information about the production costs for one unit of its products is as follows:

Product	X	Y	Z
	£	£	£
Labour: Skilled	6	9	3
Unskilled	2	4	10
Materials	12	25	14
Other variable costs	3	7	7
Fixed costs	5	10	10

All labour and materials are variable costs. Skilled labour is paid a basic rate of £6 an hour, and unskilled labour is paid a basic rate of £5 an hour. The labour costs per unit, shown above, are based on basic rates of pay. Skilled labour is scarce, which means that the business could sell more than the maximum that it is able to make of any of the three products.

Product X is sold in a regulated market, and the regulators have set a price of £30 per unit for it.

Required:
(a) State, with supporting workings, the price that must be charged for Products Y and Z, such that the business would find it equally profitable to make and sell any of the three products.
(b) State, with supporting workings, the maximum rate of overtime premium that the business would logically be prepared to pay its skilled workers to work beyond the basic time.

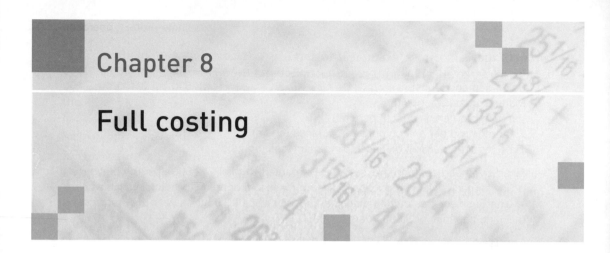

Chapter 8

Full costing

Introduction

In this chapter we continue our consideration of management accounting by looking at an approach to deducing the cost of a unit of output that takes account of all of the costs. This contrasts with the approach that we looked at in Chapter 7, where we concentrated just on the variable costs. This full-costing approach, as it is called, is very widely used in practice. Many businesses base their selling prices on the full cost. Also, in deriving a business's profit for a period, we need (as we saw in Chapter 3) to know the cost of the goods or services sold. We shall look at the traditional approach to full costing and at activity-based costing which represents an alternative approach. Finally, having considered how full costing is achieved, we shall consider its usefulness for management purposes. One of the uses relates closely to the problem of measuring accounting profit that we encountered in Chapter 3.

Objectives

When you have completed this chapter, you should be able to:

- deduce the full cost of a unit of output in a single-product environment
- distinguish between direct and indirect costs and use this distinction to deduce the full cost of a job in a multi-product environment
- discuss the problem of charging overheads to jobs in a multi-product environment
- explain the role and nature of activity-based costing.

The nature of full costing

With **full costing** we are concerned with all costs involved with achieving some objective, such as making a particular product. The logic of full costing is that all of the costs of running a particular facility, say a factory, are part of the cost of the output of that factory. For example, the rent may be a cost that will not alter merely because we make one more unit of production, but if the factory were not rented there would be nowhere for production to take place, so rent is an important element of the cost of each unit of output.

Full cost is the total amount of resources, usually measured in monetary terms, sacrificed to achieve a particular objective. It takes account of all resources sacrificed to achieve the objective. Thus, if the objective were to supply a customer with a service or product, the delivery of the service or product to the customer's premises would normally be included as part of the full cost.

If a business is trying to set prices for its output that will lead to the business making a profit, the prices charged must cover all costs. As we shall see later, pricing is one of the uses to which full cost information is put in practice.

Deriving full costs in a single-product operation

The simplest case for which to deduce the full cost per unit is where the business has only one product line, that is, each unit of its product is identical. Here it is simply a question of adding up all the costs of production incurred in the period (materials, labour, rent, fuel and power and so on) and dividing this total by the total number of units of output for the period.

Activity 8.1

Fruitjuice Ltd has just one product, a sparkling orange drink that is marketed as 'Orange Fizz'. During last month the business produced 7,300 litres of the drink. The costs incurred were as follows:

	£
Ingredients (oranges and so on)	390
Fuel	85
Rent of premises	350
Depreciation of equipment	75
Labour	880

What is the full cost per litre of producing 'Orange Fizz'?

This is found simply by taking all of the costs and dividing by the number of litres produced:

£(390 + 85 + 350 + 75 + 880)/7,300 – £0.24 per litre.

There can be problems in deciding exactly how much cost was incurred. In the case of Fruitjuice Ltd, for example, how is the cost of depreciation deduced? It is certainly an estimate, and so its reliability is open to question. Should we use the 'relevant' cost of the raw materials (almost certainly the replacement cost), or the actual price paid for the stock used? If it is worth calculating the cost per litre, it must be because this information will be used for some decision-making purpose, so the replacement cost is probably more logical. In practice, however, it seems that historic costs are more often used to deduce full costs.

There can also be problems in deciding precisely how many units of output there were. If making Orange Fizz is not a very fast process, at any given moment there is likely to be some of the drink that is in the process of being made. This, in turn, means that some of the costs incurred last month were in respect of some Orange Fizz that was work in progress at the end of the month and are not therefore included in the output quantity of 7,300 litres. Similarly, part of the 7,300 litres was started and incurred costs in the previous month, yet all of those litres were included in the 7,300 litres that we used in our calculation of the cost per litre. Work in progress is not a serious problem, but account does need to be taken of it if reliable full cost information is to be obtained.

This approach to full costing, which can be taken with identical, or near identical units of output, is often referred to as **process costing**.

Deriving full costs in multi-product operations

Where the units of output of the product, or service, are not identical, for the purposes for which full cost is used, it will not be acceptable to adopt the approach that we used with litres of 'Orange Fizz' in Activity 8.1. It is clearly reasonable to ascribe an identical cost to units of output that are identical; it is not reasonable where the units of output are obviously different. Whereas customers would expect to pay the same price for each litre of 'Orange Fizz' that they buy, most people would not expect to pay the same price for each car repair carried out by a particular garage, irrespective of the complexity and size of the repair. So, while it is reasonable to price litres of 'Orange Fizz' equally because the litres are identical, it is not acceptable to price car repairs equally where they are widely different.

Direct and indirect costs

Where the units of output are not identical, we normally separate costs into two categories. These are:

- **Direct costs.** These are costs that can be identified with specific cost units. That is to say, the effect of the cost can be measured in respect of each particular unit of output. The main examples of these are direct materials and direct labour. In costing a motor car repair by a garage, both the cost of spare parts used in the repair and the cost of the mechanic's time would be direct costs. Collecting direct costs is a simple matter of having a cost-recording system that is capable of capturing the cost of direct material used on each job and the cost, based on the hours worked and the rate of pay, of direct workers.
- **Indirect costs** (or **overheads**). These are all other costs, that is, those that cannot be directly measured in respect of each particular unit of output. Thus the rent of the garage premises would be an indirect cost of a motor car repair.

We shall use the terms 'indirect costs' and 'overheads' interchangeably for the remainder of this book. Overheads are sometimes known as **common costs** because they are common to all production of the production unit (for example, factory or department) for the period.

Exhibit 8.1 provides some insight into the direct/indirect cost balance in the real world.

Exhibit 8.1 **Direct and indirect costs in practice**

A survey of 176 fairly large UK businesses, conducted during 1999, revealed that, on average, total costs of businesses are in the following proportions:

- Direct costs   70 per cent
- Indirect costs   30 per cent

Perhaps surprisingly, these proportions did not vary greatly between manufacturers, retailers and service businesses. The only significant variation from the 70/30 proportions was with financial and commercial businesses, which had an average 52/48 split.

Source: Based on information taken from Drury and Tayles (see References section at the end of the chapter)

Job costing

The term **job costing** is used to describe the way in which we identify the full cost per unit of output (job) where the units of output differ. To cost (that is, deduce the full cost of) a particular unit of output (job), we usually ascribe the direct costs to the job, which, by the definition of direct costs, is capable of being done. We then seek to 'charge' each unit of output with a fair share of indirect costs. This is shown graphically in Figure 8.1.

Figure 8.1 **The relationship between direct costs and indirect costs**

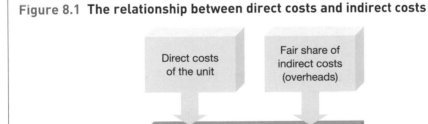

The full cost of any particular job is the sum of those costs that can be measured specifically in respect of the job (direct costs) and a share of those costs that create the environment in which production (of an object or service) can take place, but which do not relate specifically to any particular job (overheads).

Activity 8.2

Sparky Ltd is a business that employs a number of electricians. The business undertakes a range of work for its customers, from repairing fuses to installing complete wiring systems in new houses.

In respect of a particular job done by Sparky Ltd, into which category, direct or indirect, would each of the following costs fall?

- the wages of the electrician who did the job;
- depreciation (wear and tear) of the tools used by the electrician;
- the salary of Sparky Ltd's accountant;
- the cost of cable and other materials used on the job;
- rent of the premises where Sparky Ltd stores its stock of cable and other materials.

Only the electrician's wages earned while working on the particular job and the cost of the materials used on the job are direct costs. This is because it is possible to measure how much time (and therefore the labour cost) was spent on the particular job and how much materials were used in the job.

All of the other costs are general costs of running the business and, as such, must form part of the full cost of doing the job, but they cannot be directly measured in respect of the particular job.

It is important to note that whether a cost is a direct one or an indirect one depends on the item being costed, the cost objective. People tend to refer to overheads without stating what the cost objective is; this is incorrect.

Activity 8.3

Into which category, direct or indirect, would each of the costs listed in Activity 8.2 fall if we were seeking to find the cost of operating the entire business of Sparky Ltd for a month?

The answer is that all of them will be direct costs, since they can all be related to, and measured in respect of, running the business for a month.

Naturally, broader-reaching cost units, such as operating Sparky Ltd for a month, tend to include a higher proportion of direct costs than do more limited ones, such as a particular job done by Sparky Ltd. As we shall see shortly, this makes costing broader cost units rather more straightforward than costing narrower ones, since direct costs are easier to deal with.

Full costing and the behaviour of costs

We saw in Chapter 7 that the full cost of doing something (or total cost, as it is usually known in the context of marginal analysis) can be analysed between the fixed and the variable elements. This is illustrated in Figure 8.2.

Figure 8.2 The relationship between fixed costs, variable costs and total costs

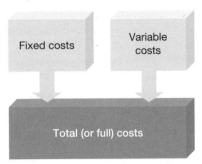

The total cost of a job is the sum of those costs that remain the same irrespective of the level of activity (fixed costs) and those that vary according to the level of activity (variable costs).

The similarity of what is shown in Figure 8.2 to that depicted in Figure 8.1 seems to lead some people to believe, mistakenly, that variable costs and direct costs are the same and that fixed costs and overheads are the same. This is incorrect.

The notions of fixed and variable are concerned entirely with **cost behaviour** in the face of changes to the volume of activity. Directness of costs, on the other hand, is entirely concerned with collecting together the elements that make up full cost, that is, with the extent to which costs can be measured directly in respect of particular units of output or jobs. These are two entirely different concepts. Though it may be true that there is a tendency for fixed costs to be indirect costs (overheads) and for variable costs to be direct costs, there is no link, and there are many exceptions to this tendency. For example, most activities have variable overheads. Labour, a major element of direct cost in most types of business activity, is usually a fixed cost, certainly over the short term.

The relationship between the reaction of costs to volume changes (cost behaviour), on the one hand, and how costs need to be gathered to deduce the full cost (cost collection), on the other, in respect of a particular job is shown in Figure 8.3.

Total cost is the sum of direct and indirect costs. It is also the sum of fixed and variable costs. These two facts are independent of one another. Thus a particular cost may, for example, be fixed relative to the level of output on the one hand, and be either direct or indirect on the other.

The problem of indirect costs

The notion of distinguishing between direct and indirect costs is related only to deducing full cost in a job-costing environment. As we saw when we were considering costing a litre of 'Orange Fizz' drink earlier in Activity 8.1, whether particular elements of cost were direct or indirect was of absolutely no consequence. This was because all costs were shared equally between the litre of 'Orange Fizz'. Where we

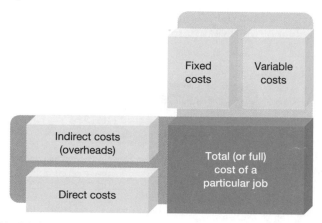

Figure 8.3 **The relationship between direct, indirect, variable and fixed costs of a particular job**

Fixed costs	Variable costs

Indirect costs (overheads)

Total (or full) cost of a particular job

Direct costs

A particular job's full (or total) cost will be made up of some variable and some fixed cost elements. It will also be made up of some direct and some indirect (overhead) elements.

have units of output that are not identical, we have to look more closely at the make-up of the costs to achieve a fair measure of the full cost of a particular job.

Indirect costs of any activity must form part of the cost of each unit of output. By definition, however, they cannot be directly related to individual **cost units**. This raises a major practical issue: how are indirect costs to be apportioned to individual cost units?

Overheads as service renderers

It is reasonable to view the overheads as rendering a service to the cost units. A manufactured product can be seen as being rendered a service by the factory in which the product is made. In this sense, it is reasonable to charge each cost unit with a share of the costs of running the factory (rent, lighting, heating, cleaning, building maintenance, and so on). It also seems reasonable to relate the charge for the 'use' of the factory to the level of service that the product has received from the factory.

The next step is the difficult one. How might the cost of running the factory, which is a cost of all production, be divided between individual products that are not similar in size and complexity of manufacture?

One possibility is sharing this overhead cost equally between each cost unit produced in the period. Most of us would not propose this method unless the cost units were close to being identical, in terms of the extent to which they had 'benefited' from the overheads.

If we are not to propose equal shares, we must identify something observable and measurable about the cost units that we feel provides a reasonable basis for distinguishing between one cost unit and the next in this context.

In practice, time spent working on the cost unit by direct labour is the basis that is most popular. It must be stressed that this is not the 'correct' way, and it certainly is not the only way. We could, for example, use relative size of products as measured by weight or by relative material cost. Possibly, we could use the relative lengths of time during which each unit of output was worked on by machines.

Job costing: a worked example

To see how job costing, as it is usually called, works let's consider Example 8.1.

Example 8.1

Johnson Ltd, a business that provides a television repair service to its customers, has overheads of £10,000 each month. Each month 1,000 direct labour hours are worked and charged to units of output (repairs carried out by the business). A particular repair undertaken by the business used direct materials costing £15. Direct labour worked on the repair was 3 hours and the wage rate is £8 an hour. Overheads are charged to jobs on a direct labour hour basis. What is the full cost of the repair?

First, let us establish the **overhead absorption (recovery) rate**, that is, the rate at which individual repairs will be charged with overheads. This is £10 (that is, £10,000/1,000) per direct labour hour.

Thus, the full cost of the repair is:

	£
Direct materials	15
Direct labour (3 × £8)	24
	39
Overheads (3 × £10)	30
Full cost of the job	69

Note, in Example 8.1, that the number of labour hours (3 hours) appears twice in deducing the full cost: once to deduce the direct labour cost and a second time to deduce the overheads to be charged to the repair. These are really two separate issues, though they are both based on the same number of labour hours.

Note also that if all of the repair jobs that are undertaken during the month are assigned overheads in a similar manner, all £10,000 of overheads will be charged to the jobs between them. Jobs that involve a lot of direct labour will be assigned a large share of overheads, and those that involve little direct labour will be assigned a small share of overheads.

Activity 8.4

Can you think of reasons why direct labour hours is regarded as the most logical basis for sharing overheads between cost units?

Activity 8.4 continued

The reasons that occurred to us are as follows:

■ Large jobs should logically attract large amounts of overheads because they are likely to have been rendered more 'service' by the overheads than small ones. The length of time that they are worked on by direct labour may be seen as a rough and ready way of measuring relative size, though other means of doing this may be found – for example, relative physical size, where the cost unit is a physical object, like a manu-factured product.

■ Most overheads are related to time. Rent, heating, lighting, fixed asset depreciation, supervisors' and managers' salaries and loan interest, which are all typical overheads, are all more or less time based. That is to say that the overhead cost for one week tends to be about half of that for a similar two-week period. Thus, a basis of apportioning overheads to jobs that takes account of how long the units of output benefited from the 'service' rendered by the overheads seems logical.

■ Direct labour hours are capable of being measured in respect of each job. They will normally be measured to deduce the direct labour element of cost in any case. Thus, a direct labour hour basis of dealing with overheads is practical to apply in the real world.

It cannot be emphasised enough that there is no 'correct' way to apportion over-heads to jobs. Overheads (indirect costs), by definition, do not naturally relate to individual jobs. If, nevertheless, we wish to take account of the fact that overheads are part of the cost of all jobs, we must find some acceptable way of including a share of the total overheads in each job. If a particular means of doing this is accepted by those who are affected by the full cost deduced, then the method is as good as any other method. Accounting is concerned only with providing useful information to decision makers. In practice, the method that gains the most acceptability as being useful is the direct labour hour method.

Activity 8.5

Marine Suppliers Ltd undertakes a range of work, including making sails for small sailing boats on a made-to-measure basis.

The business expects to incur the following costs during the next month:

Indirect labour cost	£9,000
Direct labour time	6,000 hours
Depreciation (wear and tear) of machinery	£3,000
Rent and rates	£5,000
Direct labour costs	£30,000
Heating, lighting and power	£2,000
Machine time	2,000 hours
Indirect materials	£500
Other miscellaneous indirect costs	£200
Direct materials cost	£3,000

Activity 8.5 continued

The business has received an enquiry about a sail, and it is estimated that the sail will take 12 direct labour hours to make and will require 20 square metres of sailcloth, which costs £2 per square metre.

The business normally uses a direct labour hour basis of charging overheads to individual jobs.

What is the full cost of making the sail?

First we need to identify which are the indirect costs and total them as follows:

	£
Indirect labour	9,000
Depreciation	3,000
Rent and rates	5,000
Heating, lighting and power	2,000
Indirect materials	500
Other miscellaneous indirect costs	200
Total indirect costs	19,700

(Note that this list does not include the direct costs. We shall deal with these separately.)

Since the business uses a direct labour hour basis of charging overheads to jobs, we need to deduce the indirect cost or overhead recovery rate per direct labour hour. This is simply:

£19,700/6,000 = £3.28 per direct labour hour.

Thus, the full cost of the sail would be expected to be:

	£
Direct materials (20 × £2)	40.00
Direct labour (12 × (£30,000/6,000))	60.00
Indirect costs (12 × £3.28)	39.36
Total cost	139.36

Activity 8.6

Suppose that Marine Suppliers Ltd (Activity 8.5) used a machine hour basis of charging overheads to jobs. What would be the cost of the job detailed if it was expected to take 5 machine hours (as well as 12 direct labour hours)?

The total overheads will of course be the same irrespective of the method of charging them to jobs. Thus, the overhead recovery rate, on a machine hour basis, will be:

£19,700/2,000 = £9.85 per machine hour

Thus, the full cost of the sail would be expected to be:

	£
Direct materials (20 × £2)	40.00
Direct labour (12 × (£30,000/6,000))	60.00
Indirect costs (5 × £9.85)	49.25
Total cost	149.25

Selecting a basis for charging overheads

A question now presents itself as to which of the two costs for this sail is the correct one, or simply the better one. The answer is that neither is the correct one, as was pointed out earlier. Which is the better one is a matter of judgement. This judgement is concerned entirely with usefulness of information, which in this context is probably concerned with the attitudes of those who will be affected by the figure used. Thus fairness, as those people perceive it, is likely to be the important issue.

Probably, most people would feel that the nature of the overheads should influence the choice of the basis of charging the overheads to jobs. Where, because the operation is a capital-intensive one, the overheads are dominated by those relating to machinery (depreciation, machine maintenance, power and so on), machine hours might be favoured. Otherwise direct labour hours might be preferred.

It could appear that one of these bases might be preferred to the other one simply because it apportions either a higher or a lower amount of overheads to a particular job. This would probably be irrational, however. Since the total overheads are the same irrespective of the method of charging the total to individual jobs, a method that gives a higher share of overheads to one particular job must give a lower share to the remaining jobs. There is one cake of fixed size. If one person is to be given a relatively large slice, the other people, between them, must receive relatively smaller slices. To illustrate further this issue of apportioning overheads, consider Example 8.2.

Example 8.2

A business, that provides a service, expects to incur overheads totalling £20,000 next month. The total direct labour time worked is expected to be 1,600 hours and machines are expected to operate for a total of 1,000 hours.

During next month, the business expects to do just two large jobs. Information concerning each job is as follows:

	Job 1	Job 2
Direct labour hours	800	800
Machine hours	700	300

How much of the total overheads will be charged to each job if overheads are to be charged on:

(a) a direct labour hour basis; and
(b) a machine hour basis?

What do you notice about the two sets of figures that you calculate?

(a) Direct labour hour basis
Overhead recovery rate = £20,000/1,600 = £12.50 per direct labour hour.

$$\text{Job 1} \quad £12.50 \times 800 = \underline{£10,000}$$
$$\text{Job 2} \quad £12.50 \times 800 = \underline{£10,000}$$

(b) Machine hour basis
Overhead recovery rate = £20,000/1,000 = £20.00 per machine hour.

$$\text{Job 1} \quad £20.00 \times 700 = \underline{£14,000}$$
$$\text{Job 2} \quad £20.00 \times 300 = \underline{£6,000}$$

It is clear from these calculations that the total of the overheads charged to jobs is the same (that is, £20,000) whichever method is used. So, whereas the machine hour basis gives job 1 a higher share than does the direct labour hour method, the opposite is true for Job 2.

It is not possible to charge overheads on one basis to one job and on the other basis to the other job. This is because either total overheads will not be fully charged to the jobs, or the jobs will be overcharged with overheads. For example, the direct labour hour method for Job 1 (£10,000) and the machine hour basis for Job 2 (£6,000) will mean that only £16,000 of a total £20,000 of overheads will be charged to jobs. As a result, the objective of full costing, which is to charge all overheads to jobs done, will not be achieved. In this particular case, if selling prices are based on full costs, the business may not charge prices high enough to cover all of its costs.

Exhibit 8.2 provides some insight to the basis of overhead recovery in the real world.

Exhibit 8.2 Overhead recovery rates in practice

A survey of 303 UK manufacturing businesses, published in 1993, showed that the direct labour hour basis of charging overheads to cost units was overwhelmingly the most popular, used by 73% of the respondents to the survey. Where the work has a strong labour element this seems reasonable, but the survey also showed that 68% of businesses used this basis for automated activities. It is surprising that direct labour hours should have been used as the basis of charging overheads in an environment dominated by machines and machine-related costs.

Though this survey is not very recent and applied only to manufacturing businesses, in the absence of other information, it provides some impression of the real world. There is no particular reason to believe that current practice is very different from that which applied at the beginning of the 1990s.

Source: Based on information taken from Drury, Braund, Osborne and Tayles (see References section at the end of the chapter)

Segmenting the overheads

As we have just seen, charging the same overheads to different jobs on different bases is not possible. It is possible, however, to charge one segment of the overheads on one basis and another segment, or other segments, on another basis.

Activity 8.7

Taking the same business as in Example 8.2, on closer analysis we find that of the overheads totalling £20,000 next month, £8,000 relate to machines (depreciation, maintenance, rent of the space occupied by the machines, and so on) and the remainder to more general overheads. The other information about the business is exactly as it was before.

How much of the total overheads will be charged to each job if the machine-related overheads are to be charged on a machine hour basis and the remaining overheads are charged on a direct labour hour basis?

Direct labour hour basis

Overhead recovery rate = £12,000/1,600 = £7.50 per direct labour hour

Machine hour basis

Overhead recovery rate = £8,000/1,000 = £8.00 per machine hour

Overheads charged to jobs

	Job 1 £	Job 2 £
Direct labour hour basis		
£7.50 × 800	6,000	
£7.50 × 800		6,000
Machine hour basis		
£8.00 × 700	5,600	
£8.00 × 300		2,400
Total	11,600	8,400

We can see from this that the total expected overheads of £20,000 is charged in total.

Segmenting the overheads in this way may well be seen as providing a better basis of charging overheads to jobs. This is quite often found in practice, usually by dividing a business into separate 'areas' for costing purposes, charging overheads differently from one area to the next.

Remember that there is no correct basis of charging overheads to jobs, so our frequent reference to the direct labour and machine hour bases should not be taken to imply that these are the correct methods. However, it should be said that these two methods do have something to commend them and are popular in practice. As we have already discussed, a sensible method does need to identify something about each job that can be measured and which distinguishes it from other jobs. There is also a lot to be said for methods that are concerned with time because most overheads are time related.

Dealing with overheads on a departmental basis

In general, all but the smallest businesses are divided into departments. Normally, each department deals with a separate activity.

The reasons for dividing a business into departments include the following:

- Many businesses are too large and complex to manage as a single unit, and it is more practical to operate them as a series of relatively independent units with each one having its own manager.
- Each department normally has its own area of specialism and is managed by a specialist.
- Each department can have its own accounting records that enable its performance to be assessed, which can lead to greater motivation among the staff.

Very many businesses deal with charging overheads to cost units on a department-by-department basis. They do this in the expectation that it will give rise to a fairer means of charging overheads. It is probably often the case that it does not lead to any great improvement in the fairness of the resulting full costs. Though it may not be of enormous benefit in many cases, it is probably not an expensive exercise to apply overheads on a departmental basis. Since costs are collected department by department for other purposes (particularly control), to apply overheads on a department-by-department basis is a relatively simple matter.

We shall now take a look at how the departmental approach to deriving full costs works, in a service-industry context, through Example 8.3.

Example 8.3

Autosparkle Ltd offers a motor vehicle paint-respray service. The jobs that it undertakes range from painting a small part of a saloon car, usually following a minor accident, to a complete respray of a double-decker bus.

Each job starts life in the Preparation Department, where it is prepared for the Paintshop. In the Preparation Department the job is worked on by direct workers, in most cases taking some direct materials from the stores with which to treat the old paintwork to render the vehicle ready for respraying. Thus the job will be charged with direct materials, direct labour and with a share of the Preparation Department's overheads. The job then passes into the Paintshop Department, already valued at the costs that it picked up in the Preparation Department.

In the Paintshop, the staff draws direct materials from the stores and direct workers spend time respraying the job, using a sophisticated spraying apparatus as well as working by hand. So, in the Paintshop, the job is charged with direct materials, direct labour plus a share of that department's overheads. The job now passes into the Finishing Department, valued at the cost of the materials, labour and overheads that it accumulated in the first two departments.

In the Finishing Department, jobs are cleaned and polished ready to go back to the customers. Further direct labour and, in some cases, materials are added. All jobs also pick up a share of that department's overheads. The job, now complete, passes back to the customer.

Figure 8.4 shows graphically how this works for a particular job.

The basis of charging overheads to jobs (for example direct labour hours) might be the same for all three departments, or it might be different from one department to another. It is possible that spraying apparatus costs dominate the Paintshop costs, so overheads might well be charged to jobs on a machine hour basis. The other two departments are probably labour intensive, so that direct labour hours may be seen as being appropriate there.

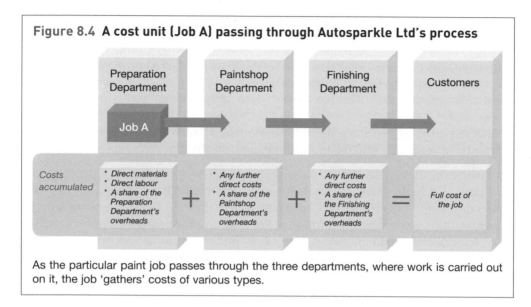

Figure 8.4 A cost unit (Job A) passing through Autosparkle Ltd's process

As the particular paint job passes through the three departments, where work is carried out on it, the job 'gathers' costs of various types.

The passage of the job through the departments can be compared to a snowball being rolled across snow: as it rolls, it picks up more and more snow.

Where costs are dealt with departmentally, each department is known as a **cost centre**. A cost centre can be defined as some physical area or some activity or function for which costs are separately identified. Charging direct costs to jobs, in a departmental system, is exactly the same as where the whole business is one single cost centre. It is simply a matter of keeping a record of:

- the number of hours of direct labour worked on the particular job and the grade of labour, assuming that there are different grades with different rates of pay;
- the cost of the direct materials taken from stores and applied to the job; and
- any other direct costs, for example some subcontracted work, associated with the job.

This record keeping will normally be done departmentally in a departmental system.

It is obviously necessary to identify the production overheads of the entire organisation on a departmental basis. This means that the total overheads of the business must be divided between the departments, such that the sum of the departmental overheads equals the overheads for the entire business. By charging all of their overheads to jobs, between them the departments will charge all of the overheads of the business to jobs.

Exhibit 8.3 provides some information on the extent of 'departmentalisation' of overheads in the real world.

Exhibit 8.3 Departmentalisation of overheads in practice

A survey of 303 UK manufacturing businesses, published in 1993, showed that 69% of respondents to the survey used some form of departmentalisation of overheads in deriving the overhead recovery rate to be applied in deriving full costs. This seems to lead to many different rates being used – presumably one for each department.

As mentioned earlier, this survey is not very recent and applied only to manufacturing businesses, in the absence of other information, it provides some impression of the real world. There is no particular reason to believe that current practice is very different from that which applied at the beginning of the 1990s.

Source: Based on information taken from Drury, Braund, Osborne and Tayles (see References section at the end of the chapter)

Batch costing

The production of many types of goods and services (particularly goods) involves producing in a batch of identical, or nearly identical, units of output, but where each batch is distinctly different from other batches. For example, a theatre may put on a production whose nature (and therefore costs) is very different from that of other productions. On the other hand, ignoring differences in the desirability of the various types of seating, all of the individual units of output (tickets to see the production) are identical.

In these circumstances, we should normally deduce the cost per ticket by using a job costing approach (taking account of direct and indirect costs and so on) to find the cost of mounting the production and then we should simply divide this by the number of tickets expected to be sold to find the cost per ticket. This is known as **batch costing**.

Full cost as the break-even price

We should have recognised that if all goes according to plan (so that direct costs, overheads and the basis of charging overheads, for example direct labour hours, prove to be as expected), then selling the output for its full cost should cause the business to break even exactly. Therefore, whatever profit (in total) is loaded onto full cost to set actual selling prices will result in that level of profit being earned for the period.

The forward-looking nature of full costing

Though deducing full costs can be done after the work has been completed, it is often done in advance. In other words, costs are frequently predicted. Where, for example, full costs are needed as a basis on which to set selling prices, it is usually the case that prices need to be set before the customer will accept the job being done. Even where no particular customer has been identified, some idea of the ultimate price will need to be known before the business will be able to make a judgement as to whether potential customers will buy the product, and in what quantities. There is a risk, of course, that the actual outcome will differ from that which was predicted. If this occurs, corrections are subsequently made.

?　Self-assessment question 8.1

Promptprint Ltd, a printing business, has received an enquiry from a potential customer for a quotation for the price of a job. The pricing policy of the business will be based on the plans for the next financial year shown below:

	£
Sales (billings to customers)	196,000
Materials (direct)	(38,000)
Labour (direct)	(32,000)
Variable overheads	(2,400)
Advertising (for business)	(3,000)
Depreciation	(27,600)
Administration	(36,000)
Interest	(8,000)
Profit (before tax)	49,000

An estimate of the direct costs for the job is:

	£
Direct materials	4,000
Direct labour	3,600

Required:

(a) Prepare a recommended price for the job based on the plans, commenting on your method.

(b) Comment on the validity of using financial plans in pricing and recommend any improvements you would consider desirable for the business's pricing policy used in (a).

Activity-based costing (ABC)

What we have considered so far in this chapter is the traditional, and still very widely used, approach to job costing (deriving the full cost of output where one unit of output differs from another). This approach is to collect for each job those costs that can be unequivocally linked to, and measured in respect of, the particular job (direct costs). All other costs (overheads) are thrown into a pool of costs and charged to individual jobs according to some formula. Traditionally, this formula has been on the basis of the number of direct labour hours worked on each individual job.

The background to traditional full costing

The traditional approach to job costing developed when the notion of trying to cost industrial production first emerged, probably around the time of the Industrial Revolution. At that time, manufacturing industry was characterised by the following features:

■ *Direct labour-intensive and direct labour-paced production.* Labour was at the heart of production. To the extent that machinery was used, it was to support the efforts of direct labour, and the speed of production was dictated by direct labour.
■ *A low level of overheads relative to direct costs.* Little was spent on power, personnel services, machinery (therefore, low depreciation charges) and other areas typical of the overheads of modern businesses.
■ *A relatively uncompetitive market.* Transport difficulties, limited industrial production worldwide and lack of knowledge among customers of competitors' prices meant that businesses could prosper without being too scientific in pricing their output.

Since overheads then represented a pretty small element of total costs, it was acceptable and practical to deal with overheads in a fairly arbitrary manner. Not too much effort was devoted to trying to control the cost of overheads because the rewards of better control were relatively small, certainly when compared with the rewards from controlling direct labour and material costs. It was also reasonable to charge overheads to individual jobs on a direct labour hour basis. Most of the overheads were incurred directly in support of direct labour: providing direct workers with a place to work, heating and lighting that workplace, employing people to supervise the direct workers, and so on. At the same time, direct workers, perhaps aided by machinery, undertook all production.

The current full costing environment

In more recent years, the world of industrial production has fundamentally altered. Most of it is now characterised by:

■ *Capital-intensive and machine-paced production.* Machines are now at the heart of production. Most labour supports the efforts of machines, for example technically maintaining them, and the speed of production is dictated by machines.
■ *A high level of overheads relative to direct costs.* Modern industrial businesses tend to have very high depreciation, servicing and power costs. There are also high costs of a nature scarcely envisaged in the early days of industrial production, such as personnel and staff welfare costs. At the same time, there are very low (sometimes no) direct labour costs. The proportion of total cost accounted for by direct materials has typically not altered too much, but more efficient production tends to lead to less waste and therefore less material cost, again tending to make overheads more dominant.

■ *A highly competitive international market.* Industrial production, much of it highly sophisticated, is carried out worldwide. Transport, including fast airfreight, is relatively cheap. Fax, telephone, the Internet and so on ensure that potential customers can quickly and cheaply know the prices of a range of suppliers. The market is therefore likely to be highly competitive. This means that businesses need to know their costs with a greater degree of accuracy than historically has been the case.

Whereas, in the past, overhead recovery rates (that is, the rate at which overheads are absorbed by jobs) were typically much less per direct labour hour than the actual rate paid to direct workers, it is now becoming increasingly common for overhead recovery rates to be a multiple of the hourly rate of pay because overheads are much more significant. When production is dominated by direct labour paid £5 an hour, it might be reasonable to have a recovery rate of £1 an hour. When, however, direct labour plays a relatively small part in production, to have overhead recovery rates of £50 per direct labour hour is likely to lead to very arbitrary costing. Just a small change in the amount of direct labour worked on a job could massively affect the cost deduced. This is not because the direct worker is massively well paid, but – for no better reason – overheads, not particularly related to labour, are charged on a direct labour hour basis.

An alternative approach to full costing

The whole question of overheads, what causes them and how they are charged to jobs has been receiving closer attention recently, as a result of changes in the environment in which manufacturers operate. Historically, businesses have been content to accept that overheads exist and, therefore, they must be dealt with, for costing purposes, in as practical a way as possible. In recent years, there has been a growing realisation that overheads do not just happen; they must be caused by something.

Example 8.4

Modern Producers Ltd has, like virtually all manufacturers, a stock storage area (known as the 'stores'). The costs of running the stores include a share of the factory rent and other establishment costs, such as heating and lighting. These costs also include the salaries of staff employed to look after the stock, and the cost of financing the stock held in the stores.

The business has two product lines, Product A and Product B. Production of both of these uses raw materials that are held in the stores. Product A tends to be made in small batches and so low levels of finished goods stock are held. The business prides itself on its ability to supply Product B in relatively large quantities instantly. As a consequence, much of the finished goods stores is filled with finished stocks of Product B ready to be dispatched as an order is received.

Traditionally, the whole cost of operating the stores has been treated as a general overhead and included in the total of overheads charged to jobs, on a direct labour hour basis. This means that, when assessing the cost of Products A and B, the cost of operating the stores has fallen on them according to the number of direct labour hours worked on each one. In fact, most of the stores cost should be charged to Product B, since this product causes (and benefits from) the stores cost much more than is true of Product A. Failure to account more precisely for the costs of running the stores is masking the fact that Product B is not as profitable as it seems to be; it may even be making a loss as a result of the relatively high cost of operating the stores that it causes, but which so far has been charged partly to Product A, without regard to the fact that Product A causes little of the cost. In fact, traditionally the products would absorb stores costs in proportion to the number of direct labour hours used in production, a factor that has nothing to do with storage.

Cost drivers

Realisation that overheads do not just occur, but that they are caused by activities, such as holding products in stores, that 'drive' the costs, is at the heart of **activity-based costing** (ABC). The traditional approach is that direct labour hours are a **cost driver**, which probably used to be true. It is now recognised to be no longer the case.

There is a basic philosophical difference between the traditional and ABC approaches. Traditionally, we tend to think of overheads as rendering a service to cost units, the cost of which must be charged to those units. ABC sees overheads as being *caused* by cost units, and those cost units must be charged with the costs that they cause.

Example 8.5

The accountant at Modern Producers Ltd (see Example 8.4) has estimated that the costs of running the finished goods stores for next year will be £90,000. (In the jargon of ABC, this £90,000 is known as the finished goods stores **cost pool**, that is the total of all of the costs relating to running that stores.) It is also estimated that each unit of Product A will spend an average of one week in the stores before being sold. With Product B, the equivalent period is four weeks. Both products are of roughly similar size and have very similar storage needs. It is felt, therefore, that the quantity of each product and the period spent in the stores are the cost drivers.

It is estimated that next year 50,000 units of Product A and 25,000 units of Product B will pass through the stores. The total number of 'product weeks' in the stores will therefore be:

$$\begin{array}{lll} \text{Product A} & 50,000 \times 1 \text{ week} = & 50,000 \\ \text{Product B} & 25,000 \times 4 \text{ weeks} = & \underline{100,000} \\ & & \underline{\underline{150,000}} \end{array}$$

The stores cost per 'product week' is given by

$$£90,000/150,000 = £0.60$$

Therefore each unit of Product A will be charged with £0.60 for finished stores costs and each unit of Product B with £2.40 (that is, £0.60 × 4).

Activity 8.8

Can you think of any other purpose that identification of the cost drivers serves, apart from deriving more accurate costs?

Identification of the activities that cause costs puts management in a position where it may well be able to control them.

The opaque nature of overheads has traditionally rendered them difficult to control, relative to the much more obvious direct labour and material costs. If, however, analysis of overheads can identify the cost drivers, questions can be asked about whether the activity that is driving certain costs is necessary at all, and whether the cost justifies the benefit. In our example, it may be a good marketing ploy that Product B can be supplied immediately from stock, but there is an associated cost, and that cost should be recognised and assessed against the benefit.

Advocates of activity-based costing argue that most overheads can be analysed and cost drivers identified. If this is true, it means that it is possible to gain much clearer insights into the costs that are caused activity by activity. As a result, fairer and more accurate product costs can be identified, and costs can be controlled more effectively.

ABC and service industries

Much of the discussion of ABC so far in this chapter has concentrated on manufacturing industry, perhaps because early users of ABC were manufacturing businesses. In fact, ABC is possibly even more relevant to service industries because, in the absence of a direct materials element, its total costs are likely to be particularly heavily affected by overheads. There is certainly evidence that ABC has been adopted by many businesses that sell services rather than goods (see Exhibit 8.4, below).

Activity 8.9

What is the difference in the way in which direct costs are accounted for when using ABC, relative to their treatment taking a traditional approach to full costing?

The answer is no difference at all. ABC is concerned only with the way in which overheads are charged to jobs to derive the full cost.

Criticisms of ABC

Critics of ABC argue that analysis of overheads in order to identify cost drivers is very time consuming and costly, and that the benefit of doing so, in terms of more accurate costing and the potential for cost control, does not justify the cost of carrying out the analysis.

ABC is also criticised for the same reason that full costing generally is criticised. This is that it does not provide very relevant information for decision making. This point will be addressed shortly.

Despite the criticisms of ABC it has gained some popularity in practice, though it has not made the progress in popularity that its advocates might have expected. This is shown in Exhibit 8.4.

Exhibit 8.4 **ABC in practice**

A survey of 176 fairly large UK businesses, conducted during 1999, revealed that, on average, 15 per cent of businesses fully used an ABC approach to deriving full costs. A further 8 per cent used it partially. The remaining 77 per cent did not use ABC at all. Even so, there was a surprising range in the level of usage of ABC from industry to industry (see diagram). It is particularly surprising that so few manufacturers use ABC. The survey shows, not surprisingly, that larger businesses tend to use ABC more than smaller ones.

ABC implementation in practice

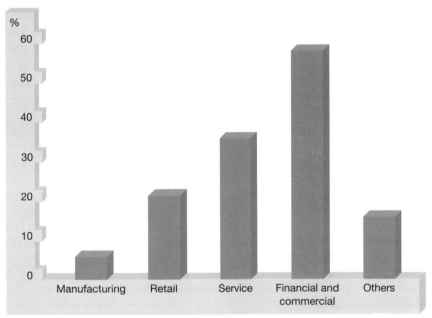

Source: Adapted from Table 7.10 from *Cost System Design and Profitability Analysis in UK Manufacturing Companies, p. 55*, CIMA Publishing, by C. Drury and M. Tayles (2000), reprinted by permission of Elsevier Ltd (see References section at the end of the chapter)

There is no evidence of an increase in the use of ABC, possibly the opposite. A study conducted in the early 1990s by Drury, Braund, Osborne and Tayles showed that 13 per cent of manufacturing businesses had adopted it at that time.

Uses of full-cost information

Why do we need to deduce full-cost information? There are probably two main reasons:

- *For pricing purposes*. In some industries and circumstances, full costs are used as the basis of pricing. Here, the full cost is deduced and a percentage is added on for profit. This is known as *cost-plus* pricing. Garages, carrying out vehicle repairs, typically operate in this way.

    In many circumstances, suppliers are not in a position to deduce prices on a cost-plus basis, however. Where there is a competitive market, a supplier will usually have to accept the price that the market offers: that is, most suppliers are *price takers* not *price makers*.

- *For income measurement purposes*. As we saw in Chapter 3, to provide a valid means of measuring a business's income it is necessary to match expenses with the revenues realised in the same accounting period. Where manufactured stock is made or partially made in one period but sold in the next, or where a service is partially rendered in one accounting period but the revenue is realised in the next, the full cost (including an appropriate share of overheads) must be carried from one accounting period to the next. Unless we are able to identify the full cost of work done in one period that is the subject of a sale in the next, the profit figures of the periods concerned will become meaningless. This will mean that users of accounting information will not have reliable means of assessing the effectiveness of the business as a whole, or the effectiveness of individual parts of it. This second reason for needing full cost information can be illustrated by Example 8.6.

Example 8.6

During the accounting year that ended on 31 December last year, Engineers Ltd made a special machine for a customer. At the beginning of this year, after having a series of tests successfully completed by a subcontractor, the machine was delivered to the customer. The business's normal practice (typical of most businesses and following the realisation convention) is to take account of sales when the product passes to the customer. The sale price of the machine was £25,000.

During last year, materials costing £3,500 were used on making the machine and 1,200 hours of direct labour, costing £9,300, were worked on the machine. The business uses a direct labour hour basis of charging overheads to jobs, which is believed to be fair because most of its work is labour intensive. The total manufacturing overheads for the business for last year were £77,000, and the total direct labour hours worked were 22,000. Testing the machine cost £1,000.

How much profit or loss did the business make on the machine during last year? How much profit or loss did the business make on the machine during this year? At what value should the business have included the machine on its balance sheet at the end of last year, so that the correct profit will be recorded for each of the two years?

No profit or loss was made during last year, following the business's (and the generally accepted) approach to recognising revenues (sales). If the sale were not to be recognised until this year it would be illogical (and in contravention of the matching convention) to treat the costs of making the machine as expenses until that time.

During this year, the sale would be recognised and all of the costs, including a reasonable share of overheads, would be set against it in this year's profit and loss account, as follows:

	£	£
Sales price		25,000
Costs:		
Direct labour	(9,300)	
Direct materials	(3,500)	
Overheads (1,200 × (£77,000/22,000))	(4,200)	
Total incurred last year	(17,000)	
Testing cost	(1,000)	
Total cost		(18,000)
This year's profit from the machine		7,000

The machine needs to be shown as an asset of the business (valued at £17,000) in the balance sheet as at 31 December last year.

Unless all production costs are charged in the same accounting period as that in which the sale is recognised in the profit and loss account, distortions will occur that will render the profit and loss account much less useful. Thus it is necessary to deduce the full cost of any production undertaken completely or partially in one accounting period, but sold in a subsequent one.

Criticisms of full costing

Full costing is widely criticised because, in practice, it tends to use past costs and to restrict its consideration of future costs to outlay costs. It can be argued that past costs are irrelevant, irrespective of the purpose for which the information is to be used. This is basically because it is not possible to make decisions about the past, only about the future. Advocates of full costing would argue that it provides an informative long-run average cost.

Despite the criticisms that are made of full costing, it is, according to research evidence, very widely practised.

Summary

The main points in this chapter may be summarised as follows:

- *Full costing = the total amount of resources sacrificed to achieve a particular objective.*

- *Single-product operations:*

$$\text{cost per unit} = \frac{\text{total cost of output}}{\text{number of units produced}}$$

- *Multi-product operations – job costing.*
  - ❑ Direct costs = costs that can be identified with specific cost units (for example, labour of a garage mechanic).
  - ❑ Indirect costs (overheads) = costs that cannot be directly measured in respect of particular cost units (for example, the rent of a garage).
  - ❑ Full cost = direct cost + indirect cost.
  - ❑ Direct/indirect is not linked to variable/fixed.
  - ❑ Indirect costs difficult to relate to individual cost units – arbitrary bases used, no correct method.
  - ❑ Traditionally indirect costs seen as the costs of providing a 'service' to cost units.
  - ❑ Direct labour hour basis of applying indirect costs to cost units is the most popular.
  - ❑ Indirect costs can be segmented – usually on departmental basis – each department has its own overhead recovery rate.
  - ❑ Batch costing = a variation of job costing where each job consists of a number of identical (or near identical) cost units:

$$\text{cost per unit} = \frac{\text{cost of the batch (direct + indirect)}}{\text{number of units in the batch}}$$

- *If the full cost is charged as the sales price, the business will break even.*

- *ABC = an approach to dealing with indirect costs that treats all costs as being caused or 'driven' by activities – advocates argue that it is more relevant to the modern commercial environment.*
  - ❑ Identification of the cost drivers can lead to more relevant indirect cost treatment in full costing.
  - ❑ Critics argue that ABC is time consuming and expensive to apply – not justified by the possible improvement in the quality of the information.

- *Uses of full cost information:*
  1 pricing (full cost) on a cost-plus basis;
  2 income measurement.

- *Full cost information is seen by some as not very useful because it can be backward looking, it includes information irrelevant to decision making, but excludes some relevant information.*

→ **Key terms**

full costing *p 214*
process costing *p 216*
direct costs *p 216*
indirect costs *p 216*
overheads *p 216*
common costs *p 217*
job costing *p 217*
cost behaviour *p 219*

cost units *p 220*
overhead absorption (recovery)
  rate *p 221*
cost centre *p 228*
batch costing *p 229*
activity-based costing *p 233*
cost driver *p 233*
cost pool *p 233*

References

Drury, C. and Tayles, M. *Cost systems design and profitability analysis in UK manufacturing companies*, CIMA Publishing, 2000.

Drury, C., Braund, S., Osborne, P. and Tayles, M. *A survey of management accounting practices in UK manufacturing companies*, Chartered Association of Certified Accountants, 1993.

? Review questions

Answers to these questions can be found on the students' side of the Companion Website.

8.1 What problem does the existence of work in progress cause in process costing?

8.2 What is the point of distinguishing direct costs from indirect ones? Why is this not necessary in process costing environments?

8.3 Are direct costs and variable costs the same thing? Explain your answer.

8.4 It is sometimes claimed that the full cost of pursuing some objective represents the long-run break-even selling price. Why is this said, and what does it mean?

? Exercises

Exercise 8.5 is more advanced than exercises 8.1–8.4. Those with a coloured number have answers at the back of the book.

8.1 Distinguish between:

- job costing;
- process costing;
- batch costing.

What tend to be the problems specifically associated with each of these?

8.2 Bodgers Ltd, a business that provides a market research service, operates a job costing system. Towards the end of each financial year, the overhead recovery rate (the rate at which overheads will be charged to jobs) is established for the forthcoming year.

(a) Why does the business bother to predetermine the recovery rate in the way outlined?

(b) What steps will be involved in predetermining the rate?

(c) What problems might arise with using a predetermined rate?

8.3 'In a job costing system, it is necessary to divide up the business into departments. Fixed costs (or overheads) will be collected for each department. Where a particular fixed cost relates to the business as a whole, it must be divided between the departments. Usually this is done on the basis of area of floor space occupied by each department relative to the entire business. When the total fixed costs for each department have been identified, this will be divided by the number of hours that were worked in each department to deduce an overhead recovery rate. Each job that was worked on in a department will have a share of fixed costs allotted to it according to how long it was worked on. The total cost for each job will therefore be the sum of the variable costs of the job and its share of the fixed costs. It is essential that this approach is taken in order to deduce a selling price for the business's output.'

You are required to prepare a table of two columns. In the first column you should show any phrases or sentences with which you do not agree (in the above statement), and in the second column you should show your reason for disagreeing with each one.

8.4 Pieman Products Ltd makes road trailers to the precise specifications of individual customers.

The following are predicted to occur during the forthcoming year, which is about to start:

Direct materials cost	£50,000
Direct labour costs	£80,000
Direct labour time	16,000 hours
Indirect labour cost	£25,000
Depreciation (wear and tear) of machinery	£8,000
Rent and rates	£10,000
Heating, lighting and power	£5,000
Indirect materials	£2,000
Other indirect costs	£1,000
Machine time	3,000 hours

All direct labour is paid at the same hourly rate.

A customer has asked the business to build a trailer for transporting a racing motorcycle to races. It is estimated that this will require materials and components that will cost £1,150. It will take 250 direct labour hours to do the job, of which 50 will involve the use of machinery.

Required:

Deduce a logical cost for the job, and explain the basis of dealing with overheads that you propose.

8.5 Athena Ltd is an engineering business doing work for its customers to their particular requirements and specifications. It determines the full cost of each job taking a 'job costing' approach, accounting for overheads on a departmental basis. It bases its prices to customers on this full cost figure. The business has two departments: a Machining Department, where each job starts, and a Fitting Department, which completes all of the jobs. Machining Department overheads are charged to jobs on a machine hour basis and those of the Fitting Department on a direct labour hour basis. The budgeted information for next year is as follows:

Heating and lighting	£25,000	(allocated equally between the two departments)
Machine power	£10,000	(all allocated to the Machining Department)
Direct labour	£200,000	(£150,000 allocated to the Fitting Department and £50,000 to the Machining Department. All direct workers are paid £5 an hour)
Indirect labour	£50,000	(apportioned to the departments in proportion to the direct labour cost)
Direct materials	£120,000	(all applied to jobs in the Machining Department)
Depreciation	£30,000	(all relates to the Machining Department)
Machine time	£200,000 hours	(all worked in the Machining Department)

Required:

(a) Prepare a statement showing the budgeted overheads for next year, analysed between the two departments. This should be in the form of three columns: one for the total figure for each type of overhead and one column each for the two departments, where each type of overhead is analysed between the two departments. Each column should show the total of overheads for the year.

(b) Derive the appropriate rate for charging the overheads of each department to jobs (that is, a separate rate for each department).

(c) Athena Ltd has been asked by a customer to specify the price that it will charge for a particular job that will, if the job goes ahead, be undertaken early next year. The job is expected to use direct materials costing Athena Ltd £1,200, to need 50 hours of machining time, 10 hours of Machine Department direct labour and 40 hours of Fitting Department direct labour. Athena Ltd charges a profit loading of 20 per cent to the full cost of jobs to determine the selling price.

Show workings to derive the proposed selling price for this job.

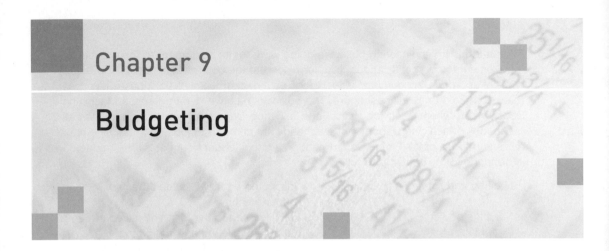

Chapter 9

Budgeting

Introduction

This chapter is concerned with budgets. Budgeting is an activity that most business managers see as one of the most crucial in which they are engaged. We shall consider the purpose of budgets and how they fit into the decision-making and planning process. We shall also consider how budgets are prepared. Preparing budgets relies on knowledge of the financial statements (balance sheet and profit and loss account) that we considered in Chapters 2 and 3. It also picks up many of the issues relating to the behaviour of costs and full costing, topics that we explored in Chapters 7 and 8, respectively. Lastly, we shall take a look at how budgets are used to help exercise control over the business to try to ensure that its objectives are achieved.

Objectives

On completion of this chapter, you should be able to:

- define a budget and show how budgets, corporate objectives and long-term plans are related
- explain the interlinking of the various budgets within the business
- indicate the uses of budgeting, and construct various budgets, including the cash budget, from relevant data
- use a budget to provide a means of exercising control over the business.

Budgets, long-term plans and corporate objectives

We saw in Chapter 1 that it is vital that businesses develop plans for the future. Whatever a business is trying to achieve, it is unlikely to be successful unless its managers have clear in their minds what the future direction of the business is going to be. Thus the starting point is to identify, as precisely as possible, the long-term objectives to be pursued. Once this has been done, the various options available to

Figure 9.1 The planning process

The figure shows the planning sequence within a business. Once the objectives of the business have been identified, the various options that can fulfil these objectives must be evaluated. A long-term plan is then developed to achieve these objectives. The budget is a short-term plan for the business, which is prepared within the framework of the long-term plan.

fulfil these objectives should be evaluated. The most appropriate option(s) should be selected and plans developed on the basis of this selection.

Businesses typically produce a long-term plan, perhaps going five years into the future, and a short-term plan normally looking at the following 12 months.

The planning sequence can be shown graphically, as in Figure 9.1. We can see that the overall objectives are first defined; they are then translated into long-term plans of action, whose achievement is through working towards short-term plans or **budgets**.

The long-term plan would define the general direction of the business over the next five or so years and would deal, in broad terms, with such matters as:

- the market that the business will seek to serve;
- production/service rendering methods;
- what the business will offer to its customers;
- levels of profit and returns to shareholders sought;
- financial requirements and financing methods;
- personnel requirements;
- bought-in goods and services requirements and sources.

The budget is essentially a financial plan for the short term. It is likely to be expressed mainly in financial terms, and is designed to convert the long-term plan into an actionable blueprint for the future. The budget will define precise targets for:

- sales and expenses;
- cash receipts and payments;
- short-term credit to be given or taken;

- stock-in-trade requirements;
- personnel requirements.

Clearly, the relationship between objectives, long-term plans and budgets is that the objectives, once set, are likely to last for quite a long time, perhaps throughout the life of the business (though changes can and do occur). A series of long-term plans identify how the objectives are to be pursued, and budgets identify how the long-term plan is to be fulfilled.

An analogy might be found in terms of someone enrolling on a course of study. His, or her, objective might be to have a working career that is rewarding in various ways. The person might have identified the course as the most effective way to work towards this objective. In working towards achievement of the objective, passing a particular stage of the course might be identified as the target for the forthcoming year. Here the intention to complete the entire course is analogous to a long-term plan, and passing each stage is analogous to the budget. Having achieved the 'budget' for the first year, the 'budget' for the second year becomes passing the second stage. It should be emphasised that planning is the role of management rather than of accountants. Traditionally, the role of the management accountant has been simply to provide technical advice and assistance to managers in order to help them plan. However, things are changing. Increasingly, the management accountant is seen as a member of the management team and, in this management role, is expected to contribute towards the planning process.

Time horizon of plans and budgets

It need not necessarily be the case that long-term plans are set for five years and that budgets are set for 12 months – it is up to the management of the business concerned – though these are fairly typical of the time periods found in practice. Businesses involved in certain industries, say, information technology, may feel that five years is too long a planning period since new developments can, and do, occur virtually overnight. Nor need it be the case that a budget is set for one year. However, this appears to be a widely used time horizon.

Activity 9.1

Can you think of any reason why most businesses prepare detailed budgets for the forthcoming year, rather than for a shorter or longer period?

The reason is probably that a year represents a long enough period for the budget preparation exercise to be worthwhile, yet short enough into the future for detailed plans to be made. As we shall see later in this chapter, the process of formulating budgets can be time consuming, but there are economies of scale: for example, preparing the budget for the next 12 months would not normally take twice as much time and effort as preparing the budget for the next six months.

The annual budget sets targets for the forthcoming year for all levels of the business. It is usually broken down into monthly budgets that define monthly targets. In many cases the annual budget will, in any case, be built up from monthly figures. For example, the sales staff will be required to make sales targets for each month of the budget period.

There will always be some aspect of the business that will stop it achieving its objectives to the maximum extent. This is often a limited ability of the business to sell its products. Sometimes, it is some production shortage (labour, materials and plant) that is the **limiting factor**. It is important that the limiting factor is identified. Ultimately, most, if not all, budgets will be affected by the limiting factor, so if it can be identified at the outset, all managers can be informed of the restriction early in the process.

Budgets and forecasts

We saw earlier that a budget is a financial plan for a future period of time. Note particularly that a budget is a plan, not a forecast. To talk of a plan suggests an intention or determination to achieve the planned targets. Forecasts tend to be predictions of the future state of the environment.

Clearly forecasts are very helpful to the planner/budget setter. If a reputable forecaster has forecast the particular number of new cars to be purchased in the United Kingdom during next year, it will be valuable for a manager in a car manufacturing business to obtain and take account of this forecast figure when setting sales budgets. However, a forecast and a budget are distinctly different.

The interrelationship of various budgets

For a particular business, for a particular period, there is more than one budget. Each one will relate to a specific aspect of the business. It is generally considered that the ideal situation is that there should be a separate budget for each person who is in a managerial position, no matter how junior. The contents of all of the individual budgets are, in effect, summarised in **master budgets**, which would typically be a budgeted income statement (profit and loss account) and balance sheet. However, the cash flow statement (in summarised form) may also be considered part of the master budget.

Figure 9.2 illustrates the interrelationship and interlinking of the individual budgets, in this particular case using a manufacturing business as an example. The sales budget is usually the first budget to be prepared, as this will determine the overall level of activity for the forthcoming period. The finished stock requirement would be dictated largely by the level of sales; it would also be dictated by the policy of the business on finished stock holding. The requirement for finished stock would define the required production levels, which would in turn dictate the

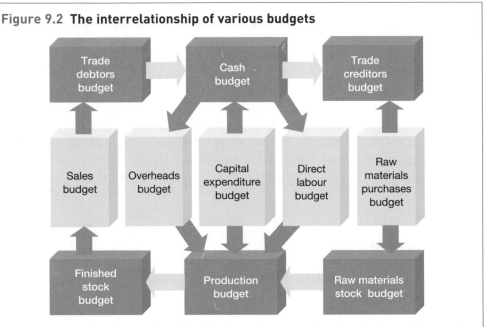

Figure 9.2 The interrelationship of various budgets

The figure shows the interrelationship of budgets for a manufacturing business. The starting point is usually the sales budget. The expected level of sales normally defines the overall level of activity for the business, and the other budgets will be drawn up in accordance with this. Thus, the sales budget will largely define the finished stock requirements, and from this we can define the production requirements and so on.

requirements of the individual production departments or sections. The demands of manufacturing, in conjunction with the business's policy on raw material stock holding, define the raw materials stock budget. The purchases budget will be dictated by the raw materials stock budget, which will, in conjunction with the policy of the business on creditor payment, dictate the trade creditors budget. One of the determinants of the cash budget will be the trade creditors budget; another will be the trade debtors budget, which itself derives through the debtor policy of the business from the sales budget. Cash will also be affected by overheads and by direct labour costs (themselves linked to production) and by capital expenditure. The factors that affect policies on matters such as stock holding, debtor and creditor collection periods will be discussed in some detail in Chapter 10.

Assuming that the budgeting process takes the order just described, it might be found in practice that there is some constraint to achieving the sales target. For example, the production facilities of the business may be incapable of meeting the necessary levels of output to match the sales budget for one or more months. In this case, it might be reasonable to look at ways of overcoming the problem. As a last resort, it might be necessary to revise the sales budget to a lower level to enable production to meet the target.

Activity 9.2

Can you think of any ways in which a short-term shortage of production facilities might be capable of being overcome?

We thought of the following:

- Higher production in previous months and stockpiling to meet the higher demand period(s).
- Increasing the production facility might be possible, perhaps by working overtime and/or acquiring (buying or leasing) additional plant.
- Subcontracting some production.
- Encouraging potential customers to change the timing of their buying by offering discounts, or other special terms, during the months that have been identified as being quiet.

You may well have thought of other approaches.

There will not only be the horizontal relationships between budgets that we have just looked at, but usually vertical ones as well. For example, the sales budget may be broken down into a number of subsidiary budgets, perhaps one for each regional sales manager. Thus the overall sales budget will be a summary of the subsidiary ones. The same may be true of virtually all of the other budgets, most particularly the production budget. Figure 9.2, that we considered earlier, gives a very simplified outline of the budgetary framework of the typical manufacturing business.

All of the operating budgets that we have just reviewed have to be consistent with the overall short-term plans laid out in the master budgets: that is, the budgeted profit and loss account and balance sheet.

The uses of budgets

Budgets are generally regarded as having four areas of usefulness. We shall explain these below:

- *They tend to promote forward thinking and the possible identification of short-term problems.* We saw earlier that a shortage of production capacity may be identified during the budgeting process. Making this discovery, in plenty of time, could leave a number of means of overcoming the problem open to exploration. Take, for example, the problem of a shortage of production at a particular part of the year. If the potential problem is picked up early enough, all of the suggestions in the answer to Activity 9.2 and, possibly, other ways of overcoming the problem can be explored and considered rationally. Budgeting should help to achieve this.
- *They can be used to help co-ordination between various sections of the business.* It is crucial that the activities of the various departments and sections of the business are linked so that the activities of one department are complementary to those of

another. For example, the activities of the purchasing/procurement department of a manufacturing business should dovetail with the raw materials needs of the production departments. If this is not the case, production could run out of stock, leading to expensive production stoppages. Alternatively, excessive stocks could be bought, leading to large and unnecessary stock holding costs.

■ *They can motivate managers to better performance.* Having a stated task can motivate performance. It is a well established view that simply to tell a manager to do his or her best is not very motivating, but to define a required level of achievement is likely to motivate. It is felt by some that managers are better motivated by being able to relate their particular role in the business to the overall objectives of the business. Since budgets are directly derived from corporate objectives, budgeting makes this possible.

It might seem that requiring managers to work towards predetermined targets will stifle skill, flair and enthusiasm. There is this danger if targets are badly set. If, however, the budgets are set in such a way as to offer challenging, yet achievable, targets, the manager is still required to show these qualities.

It is obviously not possible to allow managers to operate in an unconstrained environment. Having to operate in a way that matches the goals of the business is a price of working in an effective business.

■ *They can provide a basis for a system of control.* **Control** is concerned with ensuring that events conform to plans. If senior management wishes to control the performance of more junior staff, it needs some standard or yardstick against which the performance can be compared and assessed. It is possible to compare current performance with that which happened last month or last year, or perhaps with what happens in another business. However, the most logical yardstick is often planned performance.

Activity 9.3

What is wrong with comparing actual performance with past performance or the performance of others in an effort to exercise control?

The answer is that there is no automatic reason to believe that what happened in the past, or is happening elsewhere, represents a sensible target for this year in this business. Considering what happened last year, and in other businesses, may help in the formulation of plans, but past events and the performance of others should not automatically be seen as the target.

If there are data available concerning the actual performance for a period (say, a month) that can be compared with the planned performance, then a basis for control will have been established. Such a basis will enable the use of **management by exception**, a technique whereby senior managers concentrate their energy on areas where things are not going according to plan (the exceptions – it is to be hoped). Junior managers who are performing to budget can be left to get on with the job.

Budgets should also allow junior managers to exercise self-control, since by knowing what is expected of them and what they have actually achieved, they can assess how well they are performing and take steps to correct matters where they are failing to achieve.

We shall consider the effect of making plans, and being held accountable for their achievement, later in the chapter.

The extent that budgets are prepared

There is no recent survey evidence of the extent to which budgeting is used by larger businesses, but it seems a fair assumption that most, if not all, of them prepare and use budgets in the manner that we have discussed so far. A fairly recent survey of budgeting practice in small and medium-sized enterprises (SMEs) (see Exhibit 9.1) revealed that not all such businesses fully use budgeting. It seems that some smaller businesses prepare budgets only for what they see as key areas. The budget that is most frequently prepared by such businesses is the sales budget, followed by the budgeted profit and loss account and the overheads budget. Perhaps surprisingly, the cash budget was shown to be prepared by less than two-thirds of the small businesses surveyed.

Exhibit 9.1 Preparation of budgets in SMEs

A recent study of budgeting practice in small and medium-sized enterprises (SMEs) revealed that the most frequently prepared budget is the sales budget, followed by the budgeted profit and loss account and the overheads budget.

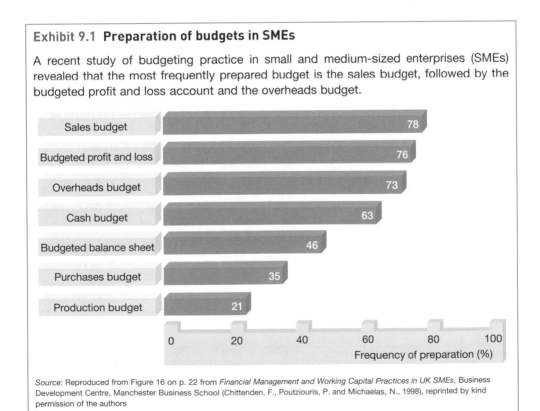

Source: Reproduced from Figure 16 on p. 22 from *Financial Management and Working Capital Practices in UK SMEs*, Business Development Centre, Manchester Business School (Chittenden, F., Poutziouris, P. and Michaelas, N., 1998), reprinted by kind permission of the authors

An example of a budget – the cash budget

We shall now look in some detail at one particular budget, the cash budget. We shall use this as our first example because:

- it is a key budget–most economic aspects of a business are reflected in cash sooner or later, so that the cash budget reflects the whole business more than any other single budget for the typical business;
- very small, unsophisticated businesses (for example, a corner shop) may feel that full-scale budgeting is not appropriate to their needs, but almost certainly they should prepare a cash budget as a minimum, despite the evidence in Exhibit 9.1.

We shall consider other budgets later in the chapter.

Since budgets are documents that are to be used only internally by the business, their style and format is a question of management choice, and will therefore vary from one business to the next. However, since managers, irrespective of the business, are likely to be using budgets for similar purposes, there is a tendency for some consistency of approach to exist across most businesses. We can probably say that, in most businesses, the cash budget would possess the following features:

1 The budget period would be broken down into sub-periods, typically months.
2 The budget would be in columnar form, with one column for each month.
3 Receipts of cash would be identified under various headings and a total for each month's receipts shown.
4 Payments of cash would be identified under various headings and a total for each month's payments shown.
5 The surplus of total cash receipts over payments, or of payments over receipts, for each month would be identified.
6 The running cash balance would be identified by taking the balance at the end of the previous month and adjusting it for the surplus or deficit of receipts over payments for the current month.

Typically, all of the pieces of information in items 3 to 6 in the above list would be useful to management for one reason or another.

The best way to deal with this topic is through an example.

Example 9.1

Suppliers Ltd is a wholesale business. The budgeted profit and loss account for the next six months is as follows:

	Jan	Feb	Mar	Apr	May	June
	£000	£000	£000	£000	£000	£000
Sales	52	55	55	60	55	53
Cost of goods sold	30	31	31	35	31	32
Salaries and wages	10	10	10	10	10	10

	Jan £000	Feb £000	Mar £000	Apr £000	May £000	June £000
Electricity	5	5	4	3	3	3
Depreciation	3	3	3	3	3	3
Other overheads	2	2	2	2	2	2
Total expenses	50	51	50	53	49	50
Net profit	2	4	5	7	6	3

The business allows all of its customers one month's credit (that is, goods sold in January will be paid for in February). Sales during December had been £60,000.

The business plans to maintain stocks at their existing level until some time in March, when they are to be reduced by £5,000. Stocks will remain at this lower level indefinitely. Stock purchases are made on one month's credit (the December purchases were £30,000). Salaries, wages and 'other overheads' are paid in the month concerned. Electricity is paid quarterly in arrears in March and June. The business plans to buy and pay for a new delivery van in March. This will cost a total of £15,000, but an existing van will be traded in for £4,000 as part of the deal. The business expects to start January with £12,000 in cash.

Show the cash budget for the six months ending in June.

Solution

Cash budget for the six months ending 30 June:

	Jan £000	Feb £000	Mar £000	Apr £000	May £000	June £000
Receipts						
Debtors (Note 1)	60	52	55	55	60	55
Payments						
Creditors (Note 2)	30	30	31	26	35	31
Salaries and wages	10	10	10	10	10	10
Electricity			14			9
Other overheads	2	2	2	2	2	2
Van purchase			11			
Total payments	42	42	68	38	47	52
Cash surplus	18	10	(13)	17	13	3
Cash balance (Note 3)	30	40	27	44	57	60

Notes

1 The cash receipts lag a month behind sales because customers are given a month in which to pay for their purchases. So, December purchases will be paid for in January and so on.

2 In most months, the purchases of stock will equal the cost of goods sold. This is because the business maintains a constant level of stock. For stock to remain constant at the end of each month, the business must replace exactly the amount of stock that has been used. During March, however, the business plans to reduce its stock by £5,000. This means that stock purchases will be lower than stock usage in that month. The payments for stock purchases lag a month behind purchases because the business expects to be allowed a month to pay for what it buys.

3 Each month's cash balance is the previous month's figure plus the cash surplus (or minus the cash deficit) for the current month. The balance at the start of January is £12,000, according to the information provided above.

4 Depreciation does not give rise to a cash payment.

Activity 9.4

Looking at the cash budget of Suppliers Ltd (above), what conclusions do you draw, and what possible course of action do you recommend, regarding the cash balance over the period concerned?

For the size of the business, there appears to be a fairly large and increasing cash balance. Management might give consideration to putting some of the cash into an income-yielding deposit. Alternatively, it could be used to expand the trading activities of the business by, for example, increasing the investment in fixed assets.

Activity 9.5

Suppliers Ltd, the wholesale business that was the subject of Example 9.1, now wishes to prepare its cash budget for the second six months of the year. The budgeted profit and loss account for the second six months is as follows:

	July £000	Aug £000	Sept £000	Oct £000	Nov £000	Dec £000
Sales	57	59	62	57	53	51
Cost of goods sold	32	33	35	32	30	29
Salaries and wages	10	10	10	10	10	10
Electricity	3	3	4	5	6	6
Depreciation	3	3	3	3	3	3
Other overheads	2	2	2	2	2	2
Total expenses	50	51	54	52	51	50
Net profit	7	8	8	5	2	1

The business will continue to allow all of its customers one month's credit (that is, goods sold in July will be paid for in August).

The business plans to increase stocks from the 30 June level by £1,000 each month until, and including, September. During the following three months, stock levels will be decreased by £1,000 each month.

Stock purchases, which had been made on one month's credit until the June payment, will, starting with the purchases made in June, be made on two months' credit.

Salaries and wages and 'other overheads' will continue to be paid in the month concerned. Electricity is paid quarterly in arrears in September and December.

At the end of December, the business intends to pay off part of a loan. This payment is to be such that it will leave the business with a cash balance of £5,000 with which to start next year.

Remember, any information that you need relating to the first six months of the year, including the cash balance that is expected to be brought forward on 1 July, is given in Example 9.1.

Have a go at the cash budget for the six months ending in December.

Activity 9.5 continued

Cash budget for the six months ending 31 December:

	July £000	Aug £000	Sept £000	Oct £000	Nov £000	Dec £000
Receipts						
Debtors	53	57	59	62	57	53
Payments						
Creditors (Note 1)	–	32	33	34	36	31
Salaries and wages	10	10	10	10	10	10
Electricity			10			17
Other overheads	2	2	2	2	2	2
Loan repayment (Note 2)						131
Total payments	12	44	55	46	48	191
Cash surplus	41	13	4	16	9	(138)
Cash balance	101	114	118	134	143	5

Notes

1 There will be no payment to creditors in July because the June purchases will be made on two months' credit, and will therefore be paid in August. The July purchases, which will equal the July cost of sales figure plus the increase in stock made in July, will be paid for in September, and so on.

2 The repayment is simply the amount that will cause the balance at 31 December to be £5,000.

Preparing other budgets

Though each one will have its own particular features, other budgets will tend to follow the same sort of pattern as the cash budget, that is, they will show inflows and outflows during each month and the opening and closing balances in each month.

Example 9.2

To illustrate some of the other budgets, we shall continue to use the example of Suppliers Ltd that we considered in Example 9.1, on p. 250. To the information given there, we need to add the fact that the stock balance at 1 January was £30,000.

Show the debtors, creditors and stock budgets for the six months.

Solution

Debtors budget

This would normally show the planned amount owing from credit sales to the business at the beginning and at the end of each month, the planned total sales for each month, and the planned total cash receipts from debtors. The layout would be something like the following:

	Jan £000	Feb £000	Mar £000	Apr £000	May £000	June £000
Opening balance	60	52	55	55	60	55
Add: Sales	52	55	55	60	55	53
	112	107	110	115	115	108
Less: Cash receipts	60	52	55	55	60	55
Closing balance	52	55	55	60	55	53

The opening and closing balances represent the amount that the business plans to be owed (in total) by debtors at the beginning and end of the month, respectively.

Creditors budget

Typically this shows the planned amount owed to suppliers by the business at the beginning and at the end of each month, the planned purchases for each month, and the planned total cash payments to creditors. The layout would be something like the following:

	Jan £000	Feb £000	Mar £000	Apr £000	May £000	June £000
Opening balance	30	30	31	26	35	31
Add: Purchases	30	31	26	35	31	32
	60	61	57	61	66	63
Less: Cash payment	30	30	31	26	35	31
Closing balance	30	31	26	35	31	32

The opening and closing balances represent the amount planned to be owed (in total) by the business to creditors, at the beginning and end of the month respectively.

Stock budget

This would normally show the planned amount of stock to be held by the business at the beginning and at the end of each month, the planned total stock purchases for each month, and the planned total monthly stock usage. The layout would be something like the following:

	Jan £000	Feb £000	Mar £000	Apr £000	May £000	June £000
Opening balance	30	30	30	25	25	25
Add: Purchases	30	31	26	35	31	32
	60	61	56	60	56	57
Less: Stock used	30	31	31	35	31	32
Closing balance	30	30	25	25	25	25

The opening and closing balances represent the amount of stock, at cost, planned to be held by the business at the beginning and end of the month respectively.

A *raw materials stock budget*, for a manufacturing business, would follow a similar pattern, with the 'stock usage' being the cost of the stock put into production. A *finished stock budget* for a manufacturer would also be similar to the above, except that 'stock manufactured' would replace 'purchases'. A manufacturing business would normally produce both a raw materials stock budget and a finished stock budget.

The stock budget will normally be expressed in financial terms, but may also be expressed in physical terms (for example, kg or metres) for individual stock items.

Activity 9.6

Have a go at preparing the debtors budget for Suppliers Ltd for the six months July to December (see Activities 9.4 and 9.5).

Debtors budget for the six months ended 31 December:

	July £000	Aug £000	Sept £000	Oct £000	Nov £000	Dec £000
Opening balance (Note 1)	53	57	59	62	57	53
Add: Sales (Note 2)	57	59	62	57	53	51
	110	116	121	119	110	104
Less: Cash receipts (Note 3)	53	57	59	62	57	53
Closing balance (Note 4)	57	59	62	57	53	51

This budget could of course be set out in any manner that would have given the sort of information that management would require in respect of planned levels of debtors and associated transactions. Note that if we knew three of the four figures for any month, we could deduce the fourth.

Notes

1   The opening balances will be the sales figures for the previous month, since the business plans to allow its credit customers one month's credit.
2   The sales figures are the current month's figures.
3   The cash received each month is equal to the previous month's sales figure.
4   The closing balance is equal to the current month's sales figure.

Note how the debtors budget links to the cash budget; the cash receipts row of figures is the same. The debtors budget would similarly link to the sales budget. This is how the linking that was discussed earlier in this chapter (p. 247) is achieved.

Activity 9.7

Have a go at preparing the creditors budget for Suppliers Ltd for the six months July to December (see Activity 9.5).

Hint: Remember that the creditor payment period alters from the June purchases onwards.

Creditors budget for the six months ending 31 December:

	July £000	Aug £000	Sept £000	Oct £000	Nov £000	Dec £000
Opening balance (Note 1)	32	65	67	70	67	60
Add: Purchases	33	34	36	31	29	28
	65	99	103	101	96	88
Less: Cash payments (Note 2)	–	32	33	34	36	31
Closing balance	65	67	70	67	60	57

Activity 9.7 continued

This again could be set out in any manner that would have given the sort of information that management would require in respect of planned levels of creditors and associated transactions.

Notes

1   The opening balance for July will be the planned purchases figures for the previous month (June), since the business plans, until the June purchases, to take one month's credit from its suppliers. The opening balances for July to December will represent the planned purchases for the previous two months.

2   There will be no payment to creditors planned in July because creditors will be paid two months after the month of purchase, starting with the June purchases which will be paid for in August.

? Self-assessment question 9.1

Antonio Ltd has planned production and sales for the next nine months as follows:

	Production (units)	Sales (units)
May	350	350
June	400	400
July	500	400
August	600	500
September	600	600
October	700	650
November	750	700
December	750	800
January	750	750

During the period, the business plans to advertise heavily to generate these increases in sales. Payments for advertising of £1,000 and £1,500 will be made in July and October respectively.

The selling price per unit will be £20 throughout the period. Forty per cent of sales are normally made on two months' credit. The other 60 per cent are settled within the month of the sale.

Raw material will be held in stock for one month before it is taken into production. Purchases of raw materials will be on one month's credit (buy one month, pay the next). The cost of raw material is £8 per unit of production.

Other direct production expenses, including labour, are planned to be £6 per unit of production. These will be paid in the month concerned.

Various production overheads, which during the period to 30 June had run at £1,800 per month, are expected to rise to £2,000 each month from 1 July to 31 October. These are expected to rise again from 1 November to £2,400 per month and to remain at that level for the foreseeable future. These overheads include a steady £400 each month for depreciation. Overheads are planned to be paid 80 per cent in the month of production and 20 per cent in the following month.

Self-assessment question 9.1 continued

To help to meet the planned increased production, a new item of plant will be bought and will be delivered in August. The cost of this item is £6,600; the contract with the supplier will specify that this will be paid in three equal amounts in September, October and November.

Raw material stock is planned to be 500 units on 1 July. The balance at the bank the same day is planned to be £7,500.

You are required to draw up:

■ a raw materials budget, showing both physical quantities and financial values
■ a creditors budget
■ a cash budget

for the six months ending 31 December.

The cash budget reveals a potential cash deficiency during October and November. Can you suggest any ways in which a modification of plans could overcome this problem?

Using budgets for control – flexible budgets

Earlier in this chapter, we saw that budgets can provide a useful basis for exercising control over the business. This is because control is usually seen as making events conform to a plan. Since the budget represents the plan, making events conform to it is the obvious way to try to control the business. Using budgets in this way is popular in practice.

As we saw in Chapter 1, for most businesses the routine is as shown in Figure 9.3.

These steps in the control process are fairly easy to understand. The point is that, if plans are drawn up sensibly, we have a basis for exercising control over the business. This also requires that we have the means of measuring actual performance, in the same terms as those in which the budget is stated. If they are not in the same terms, comparison will not usually be possible.

Taking steps to exercise control means finding out where and why things did not go according to plan and seeking ways to put things right for the future. One of the reasons why things may have gone wrong is that the plans may, in reality, prove to be unachievable. In this case, if budgets are to be a useful basis for exercising control in the future, it may be necessary to revise the budgets for future periods to bring targets into the realms of achievability.

This last point should not be taken to mean that budget targets can simply be ignored if the going gets tough; rather that they should be flexible. Budgets may prove to be totally unrealistic targets, however, for a variety of reasons, including unexpected changes in the commercial environment (for example, an unexpected collapse in demand for services of the type that the business provides). In this case, nothing whatsoever will be achieved by pretending that the targets can be met.

By having a system of budgetary control, through **flexible budgets** a position can be established where decision making and responsibility can be delegated to junior

Figure 9.3 The planning and control process

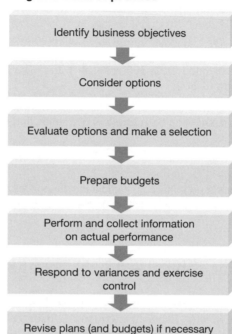

The figure shows the planning and control sequence within a business and extends Figure 9.1 to include the control aspect. Once the objectives have been determined, the various options that can fulfil these objectives must be evaluated in order to prepare the long-term plan. The budget is a short-term plan set within the framework of the long-term plan. Control can be exercised through a comparison of budgeted and actual performance. Where a significant divergence emerges, some form of corrective action should be taken. If the budget figures prove to be based on incorrect assumptions about the future, it may be necessary to revise the budget.

management, yet control can still be retained by senior management. This is because senior managers can use the budgetary control system to ascertain which junior managers are meeting targets and, therefore, working towards the objectives of the business.

Comparison of the actual performance with the budget

Since the principal objective of most private-sector businesses is to enhance their shareholders' wealth, and remembering that profit is the net increase in wealth as a result of trading, the most important budget target to meet is the profit target. In view of this, we shall begin with that aspect in our consideration of making the comparison between the budget and the actual results. Example 9.3 shows the budgeted and actual profit and loss account for Baxter Ltd for the month of May.

Example 9.3

The following are the budgeted and actual profit and loss accounts for Baxter Ltd for the month of May:

	Budget	Actual
Output	1,000 units	900 units
(production and sales)		
	£	£
Sales	100,000	92,000
Raw materials	(40,000) (40,000 metres)	(36,900) (37,000 metres)
Labour	(20,000) (2,500 hours)	(17,500) (2,150 hours)
Fixed overheads	(20,000)	(20,700)
Operating profit	20,000	16,900

From these figures, it is clear that the budgeted profit was not achieved. As far as May is concerned, this is a matter of history. However, the business (or at least one aspect of it) is out of control. Senior management must discover where things went wrong during May and try to ensure that these mistakes are not repeated in later months. Thus it is not enough to know that, overall, things went wrong; we need to know where and why. The approach taken is to compare the budgeted and actual figures for the various items (sales, raw materials and so on) in the above statement.

Activity 9.8

Can you see any problems in comparing the various items (sales, raw materials and so on) for the budget and the actual performance of Baxter Ltd in order to draw conclusions as to which aspects were out of control?

The problem is that the actual level of output was not as budgeted. The actual level of output was 10 per cent less than budget. This means that we cannot, for example, say that there was a labour cost saving of £2,500 (that is, £20,000 – £17,500) and conclude that all is well in that area.

Flexing the budget

One practical way to overcome our difficulty is to 'flex' the budget to what it would have been had the planned level of output been 900 units rather than 1,000 units. Flexing the budget simply means revising it, assuming a different volume of output.

In the context of control, the budget is usually flexed to reflect the volume that actually occurred, where this is higher or lower than the originally planned volume. To be able to do this we need to know which items are fixed and which are variable, relative to the volume of output. Once we have this knowledge, flexing is a simple operation. We shall assume that sales revenue, material cost and labour cost vary strictly with volume. Fixed overheads, by definition, will not. Whether in real life labour cost does vary with the volume of output is not so certain, but it will serve well enough as an assumption for our purposes.

On the basis of the assumptions regarding the behaviour of revenues and costs, the flexed budget would be as follows:

	Flexed budget
Output	900 units
(production and sales)	
	£
Sales	90,000
Raw materials	(36,000) (36,000 metres)
Labour	(18,000) (2,250 hours)
Fixed overheads	(20,000)
Operating profit	16,000

This is simply the original budget, with the sales, raw materials and labour figures scaled down by 10% (the same factor as the actual output fell short of the budgeted one).

Putting the original budget, the flexed budget and the actual for May together, we obtain the following:

	Original budget	Flexed budget	Actual
Output	1,000 units	900 units	900 units
(production and sales)			
	£	£	£
Sales	100,000	90,000	92,000
Raw materials	(40,000)	(36,000) (36,000m)	(36,900) (37,000m)
Labour	(20,000)	(18,000) (2,250 hrs)	(17,500) (2,150 hrs)
Fixed overheads	(20,000)	(20,000)	(20,700)
Operating profit	20,000	16,000	16,900

We can now make a more valid comparison between budget (using the flexed figures) and actual. We can now see that there was a genuine labour cost saving, even after allowing for the output shortfall.

Sales volume variance

It may seem to you as if we are saying that it does not matter if there are volume shortfalls, because we just revise the budget and carry on as if nothing had happened. This must be an invalid approach, because losing sales means losing profit. The first point we must pick up, therefore, is the loss of profit arising from the loss of sales of 100 units of the product.

Activity 9.9

What will be the loss of profit arising from the sales shortfall, assuming that everything except sales volume was as planned?

The answer is simply the difference between the original and flexed budget profit figures. The only difference between these two profit figures is the assumed volume of sales; everything else was the same. Thus the figure is £4,000 (that is, £20,000 – £16,000).

As we saw in Chapter 7, when we considered the relationship between cost, volume and profit, selling one unit less will result in one less contribution to profit. The contribution is sales revenue per unit less variable cost per unit. We can see from the original budget that the sales revenue per unit is £100 (that is, £100,000/1,000), raw material cost per unit is £40 (that is, £40,000/1,000) and labour cost per unit is £20 (that is, £20,000/1,000). Thus the contribution per unit is £40 (that is, £100 – (£40 + £20)).

If, therefore, 100 units of sales are lost, £4,000 (that is, 100 × £40) of contributions, and therefore profit, are foregone. This would be an alternative means of finding the sales volume variance, instead of taking the difference between the original and flexed budget profit figures; nevertheless once we have produced the flexed budget, it is generally easier simply to compare the two profit figures.

The difference between the original and flexed budget profit figures is called the *sales volume variance*. It is an **adverse variance** because, taken alone, it has the effect of making the actual profit lower than that which was budgeted. A variance that has the effect of increasing profit above that which is budgeted is known as a **favourable variance**. We can therefore say that a **variance** is the effect of that factor on the budgeted profit. When looking at some particular aspect, such as sales volume, we assume that all other factors went according to plan. This is shown in Figure 9.4.

Sales volume variance

The difference between the profit as shown in the original budget and the profit as shown in the flexed budget for the period.

Activity 9.10

What else does the senior management of Baxter Ltd need to know about the May sales volume variance?

It needs to know why the volume of sales fell below the budgeted figure. Only by discovering this information will management be in a position to try to see that it does not occur again.

Figure 9.4 **Relationship between the budgeted and actual profit**

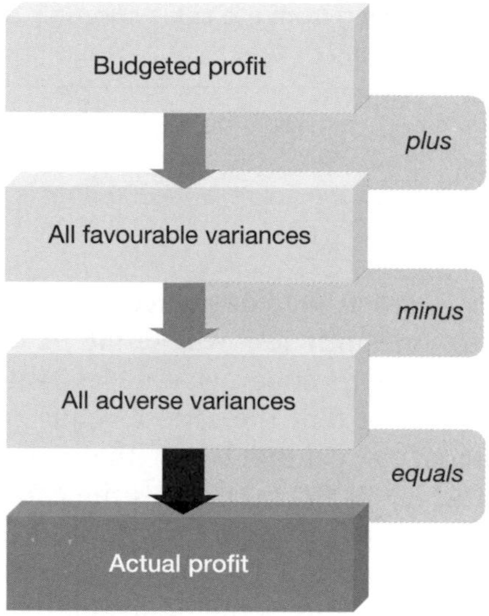

The variances represent the differences between the budgeted and actual profit, and can be used to reconcile the two profit figures.

Who should be asked about this sales volume variance? The answer would probably be the sales manager: the person who should know precisely why the departure from budget has occurred. This is not the same as saying that it was the sales manager's fault. The reason for the problem could easily have been that production was at fault in not having produced the budgeted quantities, meaning that there were not sufficient items to sell. What is not in doubt is that, in the first instance, it is the sales manager who should know the reason for the problem.

The budget and actual figures for Baxter Ltd for June are given below. They will be used as the basis for a series of activities, which you should work through, as we look at variance analysis. Note that the business had budgeted for a higher level of output for June than it did for May.

Activity 9.11

	Budget for June	Actual for June
Output (production and sales)	1,100 units	1,150 units
	£	£
Sales	110,000	113,500
Raw materials	(44,000) (44,000 metres)	(46,300) (46,300 metres)
Labour	(22,000) (2,750 hours)	(23,200) (2,960 hours)
Fixed overheads	(20,000)	(19,300)
Operating profit	24,000	24,700

Activity 9.11 continued

Try flexing the June budget, comparing it with the original June budget and so find the sales volume variance.

	Flexed budget	
Output	1,150 units	
(production and sales)		
	£	
Sales	115,000	
Raw materials	(46,000)	(46,000 metres)
Labour	(23,000)	(2,875 hours)
Fixed overheads	(20,000)	
Operating profit	26,000	

The sales volume variance is £2,000 (favourable) (that is, £26,000 – £24,000). It is favourable since the original budget profit was lower than the flexed budget profit. This is because more sales were actually made than were budgeted.

Having dealt with the sales volume variance, we have picked up the profit difference caused by any variation between the budgeted and the actual volumes of sales. This means that, for the remainder of the analysis of the difference between the actual and budgeted profits, we can ignore the original budget and concentrate exclusively on the differences between the figures in the flexed budget and the actual figures.

Sales price variance

Going back to May, it is now a matter of comparing the actual figures with the flexed budget ones to find out the other causes of the £3,100 (that is, £20,000 – £16,900) profit shortfall.

Starting with the sales revenue figure, we can see that there is a difference of £2,000 (favourable) between the flexed budget and the actual figures. This can only arise from higher prices being charged than were envisaged in the original budget, because any variance arising from the volume difference has already been 'stripped out' in the flexing process. This difference is known as the *sales price variance*. Higher sales prices will, all other things being equal, mean more profit. Hence, a favourable variance.

Sales price variance

The difference between the actual sales figure for the period and the sales figure as shown in the flexed budget.

Activity 9.12

Using the figures in Activity 9.11, what is the sales price variance for June?

The sales price variance for June is £1,500 (adverse) (that is, £115,000 − £113,500). Actual sales prices, on average, must have been lower than those budgeted. The actual price averaged £98.70 (that is, £113,500/1,150) whereas the budgeted price was £100. Selling output at a lower price than the budgeted one must tend to reduce profit, hence an adverse variance.

We shall now move on to look at the expenses.

Materials variances

In May, there was an overall or *total direct materials variance* of £900 (adverse) (that is, £36,900 − £36,000). It is adverse because the actual material cost was higher than the budgeted one, which has an adverse effect on profit. Who should be held accountable for this variance? The answer depends on whether the difference arises from excess usage of the raw material, in which case it is the production manager, or whether it is a higher-than-budgeted price per metre being paid, in which case it is the responsibility of the buying manager.

Total direct material variance

The difference between the actual direct material cost and the direct material cost according to the flexed budget (budgeted usage for the actual output).

Fortunately, we have the means available to go beyond this total variance. We can see from the figures that there was a 1,000 metre excess usage of the raw material (that is, 37,000 metres − 36,000 metres). All other things being equal, this alone would have led to a profit shortfall of £1,000, since clearly the budgeted price per metre is £1. The £1,000 (adverse) variance is known as the *direct materials usage variance*. Normally, this variance would be the responsibility of the production manager.

Direct material usage variance

The difference between the actual quantity of direct material used and the quantity of direct material according to the flexed budget (budgeted usage for actual output). This quantity is multiplied by the budgeted direct material cost per unit.

Activity 9.13

Using the figures in Activity 9.11, what was the direct materials usage variance for June?

The direct materials usage variance for June was £300 (adverse) (that is, (46,300 – 46,000) × £1). It is adverse because more material was used than was budgeted for an output of 1,150 units. Excess usage of material will tend to reduce profit.

The other aspect of direct materials is the *direct materials price variance*. Here we simply take the actual cost of materials used and compare it with the cost that was allowed, given the quantity used. In May the actual cost of direct materials used was £36,900, whereas the allowed cost of the 37,000 metres was £37,000. Thus we have a favourable variance of £100. Paying less than the budgeted price will tend to increase profit, hence a favourable variance.

Direct material price variance

The difference between the actual cost of the direct material used and the direct material cost allowed (actual quantity of material used at the budgeted direct material cost).

Activity 9.14

Using the figures in Activity 9.11, what was the direct materials price variance for June?

The direct materials price variance for June was zero (that is, (46,300 – 46,300) × £1).

As we have just seen, the total direct materials variance is the sum of the usage variance and the price variance. This is illustrated in Figure 9.5.

Labour variances

Direct labour variances are similar in form to those for raw materials. The *total direct labour variance* for May was £500 (favourable) (that is, £18,000 – £17,500). It is favourable because £500 less was spent on labour than was budgeted for the actual level of output achieved. Again, this information is not particularly helpful, and needs to be analysed further, since the responsibility for the rate of pay lies primarily with the personnel manager, whereas the number of hours taken to complete a particular quantity of output is the responsibility of the production manager.

Total direct labour variance

The difference between the actual direct labour cost and the direct labour cost according to the flexed budget (budgeted direct labour hours for the actual output).

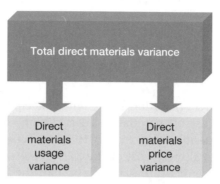

Figure 9.5 Relationship between the total, usage and price variances of direct materials

Total direct materials variance

Direct materials usage variance

Direct materials price variance

The total direct materials variance is the sum of the direct materials usage variance and the price variance, and can be analysed into those two.

The *direct labour efficiency variance* compares the number of hours that would be allowed for the achieved level of production with the actual number of hours, and then costs the difference at the allowed hourly rate. Thus, for May, it was (2,250 − 2,150) × £8 = £800 (favourable). We know that the budgeted hourly rate is £8 because the original budget shows that 2,500 hours were budgeted to cost £20,000. The variance is favourable because fewer hours were used than would have been allowed for the actual level of output. Working more quickly would tend to lead to higher profit.

Direct labour efficiency variance

The difference between the actual direct labour hours worked and the number of direct labour hours according to the flexed budget (budgeted direct labour hours for the actual output). This figure is multiplied by the budgeted direct labour rate per hour.

Activity 9.15

Using the figures in Activity 9.11, what was the direct labour efficiency variance for June?

The direct labour efficiency variance for June was £680 (adverse) (that is, (2,960 − 2,875) × £8). It is adverse because the work took longer than the budget allowed. This would tend to lead to less profit.

The *direct labour rate variance* compares the actual cost of the hours worked with the allowed cost. For 2,150 hours worked in May, the allowed cost would be £17,200 (that is, $2,150 \times £8$). So, the direct labour rate variance is £300 adverse (that is, $£17,500 - £17,200$).

Direct labour rate variance

The difference between the actual cost of the direct labour hours worked and the direct labour cost allowed (actual direct labour hours worked at the budgeted labour rate).

Activity 9.16

Using the figures in Activity 9.11, what was the direct labour rate variance for June?

The direct labour rate variance for June was £480 (favourable) (that is, $(2,960 \times £8) - 23,200$). It is favourable because a lower rate was paid than the budgeted one. Paying a lower wage rate will, of itself, tend to increase profit.

Fixed overhead variance

The remaining area is that of fixed overheads. Here the *fixed overhead spending variance* is simply the difference between the flexed budget and the actual figures. For May, this was £700 (adverse) (that is, $£20,700 - £20,000$). It is adverse because more overheads cost was actually incurred than was budgeted. This would tend to lead to less profit. In theory, this is the responsibility of whoever controls overheads expenditure. In practice, this tends to be a very slippery area, and one that is notoriously difficult to control.

Fixed overhead spending variance

The difference between the actual fixed overhead cost and the fixed overhead cost according to the flexed (and the original) budget.

Activity 9.17

Using the figures in Activity 9.11, what was the fixed overhead spending variance for June?

The fixed overhead spending variance for June was £700 (favourable) (that is, $£20,000 - £19,300$). It was favourable because less was spent on overheads than was budgeted, tending to increase profit.

We are now in a position to reconcile the original May budget profit with the actual profit, as follows:

	£	£
Budgeted profit		20,000
Add **Favourable variances**		
Sales price variance	2,000	
Direct materials price	100	
Direct labour efficiency	800	2,900
		22,900
Less **Adverse variances**		
Sales volume	4,000	
Direct material usage	1,000	
Direct labour rate	300	
Fixed overhead spending	700	6,000
Actual profit		16,900

Activity 9.18

Using the figures in Activity 9.11, try reconciling the original profit figure for June with the actual June figure.

	£	£
Budgeted profit		24,000
Add **Favourable variances**		
Sales volume	2,000	
Fixed overhead spending	700	
Direct labour rate	480	
		3,180
		27,180
Less **Adverse variances**		
Sales price	1,500	
Direct material usage	300	
Direct labour efficiency	680	
		2,480
Actual profit		24,700

Activity 9.19

The following are the budgeted and actual profit and loss accounts for Baxter Ltd for the month of July:

	Budget		Actual	
Output (production and sales)	1,000 units		1,050 units	
	£		£	
Sales	100,000		104,300	
Raw materials	(40,000)	(40,000 metres)	(41,200)	(40,500 metres)
Labour	(20,000)	(2,500 hours)	(21,300)	(2,600 hours)
Fixed overheads	(20,000)		(19,400)	
Operating profit	20,000		22,400	

Activity 9.19 continued

Produce a reconciliation of the budgeted and actual operating profit, going into as much detail as possible with the variance analysis.

The original budget, the flexed budget and the actual are as follows:

	Original budget 1,000 units	Flexed budget 1,050 units	Actual 1,050 units
Output (production and sales)			
	£	£	£
Sales	100,000	105,000	104,300
Raw materials	(40,000)	(42,000)	(41,200)
Labour	(20,000)	(21,000)	(21,300)
Fixed overheads	(20,000)	(20,000)	(19,400)
Operating profit	20,000	22,000	22,400

Reconciliation of the budgeted and actual operating profits for July

	£	£
Budgeted profit		20,000
Add Favourable variances:		
Sales volume (22,000 − 20,000)	2,000	
Direct material usage {[(1,050 × 40) − 40,500] × £1}	1,500	
Direct labour efficiency {[(1,050 × 2.50) − 2,600] × £8}	200	
Fixed overhead spending (20,000 − 19,400)	600	4,300
		24,300
Less Adverse variances:		
Sales price variance (105,000 − 104,300)	700	
Direct materials price [(40,500 × £1) − 41,200]	700	
Direct labour rate [(2,600 × £8) − 21,300]	500	1,900
Actual profit		22,400

Standard quantities and costs

The budget is a financial plan for a future period of time. It is built up from standards. **Standard quantities and costs** (or revenues) are those planned for individual units of input or output. Thus standards are the building blocks of the budget.

We can say about Baxter Ltd's operations that:

- the standard selling price is £100 per unit of output;
- the standard raw material cost is £40 per unit of output;
- the standard raw material usage is 40 metres per unit of output;
- the standard raw material price is £1 per metre (that is, per unit of input);
- the standard labour cost is £20 per unit of output;
- the standard labour time is 2.50 hours per unit of output;
- the standard labour rate is £8 per hour (that is, per unit of input).

The standards, like the budgets to which they are linked, represent targets and, therefore, yardsticks by which actual performance is measured. They are derived from experience of what is a reasonable quantity of input (for labour time and materials usage) and from assessments of the market for the product (standard selling price) and the market for the inputs (labour rate and material price). These should be subject to frequent review and, where necessary, revision. It is vital, if they are to be used as part of the control process, that they represent realistic targets.

Calculation of most variances is, in effect, based on standards. For example, the material usage variance is the difference between the standard materials usage for the level of output and the actual usage, costed at the standard materials price.

Standards can have uses other than in the context of budgetary control. The existence of a database of costs, usages, selling prices and so on, that are known to be broadly realistic, provides decision makers with a ready set of information for their decision making and income measurement purposes.

Reasons for adverse variances

A constant possible reason why variances occur is that the standards against which performance is being measured are not reasonable targets. This is certainly not to say that the immediate reaction to an adverse variance should be that the standard is unreasonably harsh. On the other hand, standards that are not achievable are useless.

Activity 9.20

The variances that we have considered are:

- sales volume
- sales price
- direct materials usage
- direct materials price
- direct labour efficiency
- direct labour rate
- fixed overhead spending.

Ignoring the possibility that standards may be unreasonable, jot down any ideas that occur to you as possible practical reasons for adverse variances in each case.

The reasons that we thought of included the following:

Sales volume

- Poor performance by sales personnel.
- Deterioration in market conditions between the setting of the budget and the actual event.
- Lack of stock to sell as a result of some production problem.

Activity 9.20 continued

Sales price

■ Poor performance by sales personnel.
■ Deterioration in market conditions between the setting of the budget and the actual event.

Direct materials usage

■ Poor performance by production department staff, leading to high rates of scrap.
■ Substandard materials, leading to high rates of scrap.
■ Faulty machinery, causing high rates of scrap.

Direct materials price

■ Poor performance by buying department staff.
■ Change in market conditions between setting the standard and the actual event.

Labour efficiency

■ Poor supervision.
■ A low skill grade of worker taking longer to do the work than was envisaged for the correct skill grade.
■ Low-grade materials, leading to high levels of scrap and wasted labour time.
■ Problems with machinery, leading to labour time being wasted.
■ Dislocation of materials supply, leading to workers being unable to proceed with production.

Labour rate

■ Poor performance by the personnel function.
■ Using a higher grade of worker than was planned.
■ Change in labour market conditions between setting the standard and the actual event.

Fixed overheads

■ Poor supervision of overheads.
■ General increase in costs of overheads not taken into account in the budget.

Though we have tended to use the example of a manufacturing business to explain variance analysis, this should not be taken to imply that variance analysis is not equally applicable and useful in service sector businesses.

Investigating variances

It is unreasonable to expect budget targets to be met precisely each month. Whatever the reason for a variance, finding it will take time, and time is costly. Given that small variances are almost inevitable, and that **investigating variances** can be expensive, management needs to establish a policy on which variances to investigate and which to accept. For example, for Baxter Ltd (Example 9.3 on p. 259) the budgeted usage of materials during May was 40,000 metres at a cost of £1 per metre. Suppose that production had been the same as the budgeted quantity of output, but that 40,005 metres of material, costing £1 a metre, had actually been used. Would this adverse variance of £5 be investigated? Probably not. What though if the variance were £50 or £500 or £5,000?

Activity 9.21

What broad approach do you feel should be taken on whether to spend money investigating a particular variance?

The general approach to this policy must be concerned with cost and benefit. What benefit there is likely to be from knowing why a variance exists needs to be balanced against the cost of obtaining that knowledge.

Knowing the reason for a variance can have a value only when it might provide management with the means to bring things back under control, so that future targets can be met. It should be borne in mind here that variances will normally either be zero, or very close to zero. This is to say that achieving targets, give or take small variances, should be normal.

Broadly, we suggest the following:

- Significant adverse variances should be investigated because the continuation of the fault that they represent could be very costly. Management must decide what 'significant' means. A certain amount of science, in the form of statistical models, ultimately can be brought to bear in making this decision, but it must be a matter of managerial judgement as to what is significant. Perhaps a variance of 5 per cent from the budgeted figure would be deemed to be significant.
- Significant *favourable* variances should probably be investigated as well as those that are unfavourable. Though such variances would not cause such immediate management concern as adverse ones, they still represent things not going according to plan. If actual performance is significantly better than target, it may well mean that the target is unrealistically low.
- Insignificant variances, though not triggering immediate investigation, should be kept under review. For each aspect of operations, the cumulative sum of variances, over a series of control periods, should be zero, with small adverse variances in some periods being compensated for by small favourable ones in other periods. This should be the case with variances that are caused by chance factors, which will not necessarily repeat themselves.

Where a variance is caused by a more systematic factor, which will repeat itself, the cumulative sum of the periodic variances will not be zero but an increasing figure. Where the increasing figure represents a set of adverse variances it may well be worth investigating the situation, even though the individual variances may be insignificant. Even where the direction of the cumulative total points to favourable variances, investigation may still be considered to be valuable.

Exhibit 9.2 is taken from the research of Drury, Braund, Osborne and Tayles, which was mentioned in Chapter 8. The table shows the methods used by respondents to the survey to make the decision on whether to investigate a particular variance.

Exhibit 9.2 Methods used to make decisions on investigation of variances

	% 'Often' or 'Always'
Decisions based on managerial judgement	75
Variance exceeds a specific monetary amount	41
Variance exceeds a given percentage of standard	36
Statistical models	3

Source: Reproduced from Table 5.7 on p. 39 from *A survey of management accounting practices in UK manufacturing companies*, Chartered Association of Certified Accountants (Drury, C., Braund, S., Osborne, P. and Tayles, M.,1993). Copyright © 1993 The Association of Chartered Certified Accountants.

It is interesting to note the large extent, revealed by this survey, to which decisions on whether to investigate variances are made on the basis of some, presumably subjective, judgement rather than using a more systematic approach. The survey is not very recent and it may well be that a more scientific approach is more common now.

Compensating variances

There is superficial appeal in the idea of **compensating variances**, that is, trading off linked favourable and adverse variances against each other without further consideration. For example, a sales manager believes that she could sell more of the product if prices were lowered, and that this would feed through to increased net operating profit. This would lead to a favourable sales volume variance, but also to an adverse sales price variance. On the face of it, provided that the former is greater than the latter, all would be well.

Activity 9.22

What possible reason is there why the sales manager mentioned above should not go ahead with the price reduction?

The change in policy will have ramifications for other areas of the business, including the following:

- The need for more goods to be available to sell. Production might not be able to supply them, and it might not be possible to buy the stock in from elsewhere.
- Increased sales would involve an increased need for finance to pay for increased production.

Thus 'trading off' variances is not automatically acceptable, without a more far-reaching consultation and revision of plans.

Making budgetary control effective

It is obvious from what we have seen of **budgetary control** that if it is to be success-ful, a system, or a set of routines, must be established to enable the potential benefits to be gained. Most businesses that operate successful budgetary control systems tend to share some common factors. These include the following:

- A serious attitude taken to the system by all levels of management, right from the very top. For example, senior managers need to make clear to junior managers that they take notice of the monthly variance reports and base some of their actions on them.
- Clear demarcation between areas of managerial responsibility so that accountabil-ity can more easily be ascribed for any area that seems to be going out of control. It needs to be clear which manager is responsible for each aspect of the business.
- Budget targets being reasonable, so that they represent a rigorous yet achievable tar-get. This may be promoted by managers being involved in setting their own targets. It is argued that this can promote the managers' commitment and motivation.
- Established data collection, analysis and dissemination routines, which take the actual results, the budget figures, and calculate and report the variances. This should be part of the business's regular accounting information system, so that the required reports are automatically produced each month.
- Reports aimed at individual managers, rather than general-purpose documents. This avoids managers having to wade through reams of reports to find the part that is relevant to them.
- Fairly short reporting periods, typically a month, so that things cannot go too far wrong before they are picked up.
- Variance reports being produced and disseminated shortly after the end of the relevant reporting period. If it is not until the end of June that a manager is informed that the performance in May was below the budgeted level, it is quite likely that the performance for June will be below it as well. Reports on the per-formance in May ideally need to emerge in early June.
- Action being taken to get operations back under control if they are shown to be out of control. The report will not change things by itself. Managers need to take action to try to ensure that significant adverse variances being reported leads to action to put things right for the future.

Limitations of the traditional approach to control through variances and standards

Budgetary control, of the type that we have reviewed in this chapter, has obvious appeal and, judging by the wide extent of its use in practice, it has value as well. It is somewhat limited at times, however. Some of its limitations are as follows:

- Vast areas of most business and commercial activities simply do not have the same direct relationship between inputs and outputs as is the case with, say, level of output and the amount of raw materials used. Many of the expenses of a modern business are in areas such as training and advertising, where the expense is discretionary and not linked to the level of output in a direct way.
- Standards can quickly become out of date as a result of both technological change and price changes. This does not pose insuperable problems, but it does require that the potential problem is systematically addressed. Standards that are unrealistic are, at best, useless. At worst, they could have adverse effects on performance. A buyer who knows that it is impossible to meet price targets, because of price rises, may have a reduced incentive to minimise costs.
- Sometimes factors that are outside the control of the manager concerned can affect the calculation of the variance for which that manager is held accountable. This is likely to have an adverse effect on the manager's performance. The situation can often be overcome by a more considered approach to the calculation of the variance, resulting in those factors controllable by the manager being separated from those that are not.
- In practice, creating clear lines of demarcation between the areas of responsibility of various managers may be difficult. Thus, one of the prerequisites of good budgetary control is lost.

Behavioural aspects of budgetary control

Budgets, perhaps more than any other accounting statement, are prepared with the objective of affecting the attitudes and behaviour of managers. The point was made earlier in this chapter that budgets are intended to motivate managers. In practice, research evidence generally shows that they are successful. More specifically, the research shows that:

- The existence of budgets generally tends to improve performance.
- Demanding, yet achievable, budget targets tend to motivate better than less demanding targets. It seems that setting the most demanding targets that will be accepted by managers is a very effective way to motivate them.
- Unrealistically demanding targets tend to have an adverse effect on managers' performance.
- The participation of managers in setting their targets tends to improve motivation and performance. This is probably because those managers feel a sense of commitment to the targets and a moral obligation to achieve them.

It has been suggested that allowing managers to set their own targets will lead to 'slack' being introduced, so making achievement of the target that much easier. On the other hand, in an effort to impress, a manager may select a target that is not really achievable. These points imply that care must be taken in the extent to which managers have unfettered choice of their own targets. Evidence tends to suggest that where managers work in an environment where they are expected to meet the targets represented in the budget, they will, almost irrespective of other factors, try to introduce slack into the budget. Where there is a more relaxed attitude, or other factors (for example, staff morale) are considered alongside the analysis of variances, managers are less inclined to seek to build in slack.

Where a manager fails to meet a budget, care must be taken by that manager's senior in dealing with the failure. A harsh, critical approach may demotivate the manager. Adverse variances may imply that the manager needs help from the senior.

The existence of budgets gives senior managers a ready means to assess the performance of their subordinates. Where promotion or bonuses depend on the absence of variances, senior management must be very cautious.

? Self-assessment question 9.2

Toscanini Ltd makes a standard product, which is budgeted to sell at £4.00 per unit, in a competitive market. It is made by taking a budgeted 0.4 kg of material, budgeted to cost £2.40/kg, and working on it by hand by an employee, paid a budgeted £8.00/hour, for a budgeted 6 minutes. Monthly fixed overheads are budgeted at £4,800. The output for May was budgeted at 4,000 units.

The actual results for May were as follows:

	£
Sales (3,500 units)	13,820
Materials (1,425 kg)	(3,420)
Labour (345 hours)	(2,690)
Fixed overheads	(4,900)
Actual operating profit	2,810

No stocks of any description existed at the beginning and end of the month.

Required:
(a) Deduce the budgeted profit for May, and reconcile it with the actual profit in as much detail as the information provided will allow.
(b) State which manager should be held accountable, in the first instance, for each variance calculated.
(c) Assuming that the standards were all well set in terms of labour times and rates and material usage and price, suggest at least one feasible reason for each of the variances that you identified in (a), given what you know about the business's performance for May.
(d) If it were discovered that the actual total world market demand for the business's product was 10 per cent lower than estimated when the May budget was set, state how and why the variances that you identified in (a) could be revised to provide information that would be potentially more useful.

Summary

The main points of this chapter may be summarised as follows:

- *Budget = a short-term financial plan.*
  - Budgets are the short-term means of working towards the business's objectives.
  - Usually for 12 months with subperiods of a month.
  - Uses are to:
    1. promote forward thinking;
    2. help co-ordinate the various aspects;
    3. motivate performance;
    4. provide the basis of a system of control.

- *Controlling through budgets*:
  - flexing the budget to match actual volume of output;
  - variance = increase (favourable) or decrease (adverse) in profit, relative to the budgeted profit, as a result of some aspect of the business's activities taken alone;
  - budgeted profit plus all favourable variances less all adverse variances equals actual profit;
  - commonly calculated variances:
    - Sales volume variance = difference between budgeted and actual volume (in units) multiplied by the contribution per unit.
    - Sales price variance = difference between actual sales revenue and actual volume at the budgeted sales price per unit.
    - Direct materials usage variance = difference between actual usage and budgeted usage, for the actual volume of output, multiplied by the budgeted material cost per unit of material.
    - Direct material price variance = difference between the actual material cost and the actual usage multiplied by the budgeted cost per unit of material.
    - Direct labour efficiency variance = difference between actual labour time and budgeted time, for the actual volume of output, multiplied by the budgeted labour rate.
    - Direct labour rate variance = difference between the actual labour cost and the actual labour time multiplied by the budgeted labour rate.
    - Fixed overhead spending variance – difference between the actual and budgeted spending on fixed overheads.
  - Standards = budgeted physical quantities and financial values for one unit of inputs and outputs.
  - Standards are useful in providing data for decision making.
  - Significant and/or persistent variances need to be investigated to establish their cause.
  - Good budgetary control requires establishing systems and routines to ensure such things as clear distinction between individual managers' areas of responsibility, prompt, frequent and relevant variance reporting and senior management commitment.

❏ Not all activities can usefully be controlled through traditional variance analysis, etc.

❏ There is a behavioural aspect of control and this should be taken into account by senior managers.

→ Key terms

budgets p 243
limiting factor p 245
master budgets p 245
control p 248
management by exception p 248
flexible budgets p 257
flexing the budget p 259

adverse variance p 261
favourable variance p 261
variance p 261
standard quantities and costs p 269
investigating variances p 271
compensating variances p 273
budgetary control p 274

? Review questions

Answers to these questions can be found on the students' side of the Companion Website.

9.1 Define a *budget*. How is a budget different from a forecast?

9.2 What were the four uses of budgets that were identified in the chapter?

9.3 What is meant by a *variance*? What approaches might be used to decide whether a variance should be investigated?

9.4 What is the point in flexing the budget in the context of variance analysis? Does flexing imply that differences between budget and actual in the volume of output are ignored in variance analysis?

? Exercises

Exercises 9.4 and 9.5 are more advanced than Exercises 9.1–9.3. Those with a coloured number have an answer at the back of the book.

9.1 You have overheard the following statements:

(a) 'A budget is a forecast of what is expected to happen in a business during the next year.'

(b) 'Budgets must be prepared with a column for each month so that you can see the whole year at a glance, month by month.'

(c) 'Budgets are OK but they stifle all initiative. No manager worth employing would work for a business which seeks to control through budgets.'

(d) 'Any sensible person would start with the sales budget and build up the other budgets from there.'

Required:
Critically discuss these statements, explaining any technical terms.

9.2 Daniel Chu Ltd, a new business, will start production on 1 April, but sales will not commence until 1 May. Planned sales for the next nine months are as follows:

	Sales units
May	500
June	600
July	700
August	800
September	900
October	900
November	900
December	800
January	700

The selling price per unit will be a consistent £100, and all sales will be made on one month's credit. It is planned that sufficient finished goods stock for each month's sales should be available at the end of the previous month.

Raw material purchases will be such that there will be sufficient raw materials stock available at the end of each month to meet the following month's planned production precisely. This planned policy will operate from the end of April. Purchases of raw materials will be on one month's credit. The cost of raw material is £40 per unit of finished product.

The direct labour cost, which is variable with the level of production, is planned to be £20 per unit of finished production. Production overheads are planned to be £20,000 each month, including £3,000 for depreciation. Non-production overheads are planned to be £11,000 per month, of which £1,000 will be depreciation. Various fixed assets costing £250,000 will be bought and paid for during April.

Except where specified otherwise, assume that all payments take place in the same month as the cost is incurred.

The business will raise £300,000 in cash from a share issue in April.

Required:
Draw up:

- a finished stock budget, showing just physical quantities
- a raw materials stock budget, showing both physical quantities and financial values
- a trade creditors budget
- a trade debtors budget
- a cash budget

for the six months ending 30 September.

9.3 Antonio plc makes a product, the Gadget, the standard cost of which is:

	£
Sales revenue	31
Direct labour (2 hours)	(11)
Direct materials (1 kg)	(10)
Fixed overheads	(3)
Standard profit	7

The budgeted output for March was 1,000 units of the Gadget; the actual output was 1,100 units, which was sold for £34,950. There were no stocks of any description at either end of March.

The actual production costs were:

	£
Direct labour (2,150 hours)	12,210
Direct materials (1,170 kg)	11,630
Fixed overheads	3,200

Calculate the variances for March as fully as you are able to from the available information, and use the variances calculated to reconcile the budgeted and actual profit figures.

9.4 Lewisham Ltd manufactures one product line – the Zenith. Sales of Zeniths over the next few months are planned as follows:

1 **Demand**

	units
July	180,000
August	240,000
September	200,000
October	180,000

Each Zenith sells for £3.

2 **Debtor receipts**
Debtors are expected to pay as follows:

70% during the month of sale
28% during the following month

The remainder of debtors are expected to go bad (that is, to be uncollectable).

Debtors who pay in the month of sale are entitled to deduct a 2 per cent discount from the invoice price.

3 **Finished goods stocks**
Stocks of finished goods are expected to be 40,000 units at 1 July. The business's policy is that, in future, the stock at the end of each month should equal 20 per cent of the following month's planned sales requirements.

4 **Raw materials stock**
Stock of raw materials is expected to be 40,000 kg on 1 July. The business's policy is that, in future, the stock at the end of each month should equal 50 per cent of the following month's planned production requirements. Each Zenith requires 0.5 kg of the raw material, which costs £1.50 per kg.

Raw materials are paid for in the month after purchase.

5 **Labour and overheads**

The direct labour cost of each Zenith is £0.50. The variable overhead element of each Zenith is £0.30. Fixed overheads, including depreciation of £25,000, total £47,000 per month.

All labour and overheads are paid during the month in which they arise.

6 **Cash in hand**

The business plans to have a bank balance (in funds) at 1 August of £20,000.

Required:

Prepare the following budgets:

(a) Finished stock budget (expressed in units of Zenith) for each of the three months July, August and September.

(b) Raw materials budget (expressed in kg of the raw material) for the two months July and August.

(c) Cash budget for August and September.

9.5 Mowbray Ltd makes and sells one standard product, the standard costs of which are as follows:

	£
Direct materials: 3 kg at £2.50 per kg	7.50
Direct labour: 15 minutes at £9.00 per hour	2.25
Fixed overheads	3.60
	13.35
Selling price	20.00
Standard profit margin	6.65

The monthly production and sales are planned to be 1,200 units. The actual results for May were as follows:

	£
Sales	18,000
Less Direct materials	(7,400) (2,800 kg used)
Direct labour	(2,300) (255 hours)
Fixed overheads	(4,100)
Operating profit	4,200

There were no stocks of any description at either the start or the end of the month. As a result of poor sales demand during May, the business had reduced the price of all sales by 10 per cent.

Required:

Calculate the budgeted profit for May and reconcile it to the actual profit through variances, going into as much detail as is possible from the information available.

Chapter 10

Making capital investment decisions

Introduction

In this chapter we shall look at how businesses can make decisions involving investments in new plant, machinery, buildings and similar long-term assets. Though we shall be considering this topic in the context of businesses making decisions about the type of assets that were just mentioned, the general principles can equally well be applied to investments in the shares of businesses, irrespective of whether the investment is being considered by a business or by a private individual. This chapter is the first of the three that deal with the area generally known as *business finance* or *financial management*.

Objectives

When you have completed your study of this chapter you should be able to:

- explain the nature and importance of investment decision making
- identify the four main investment appraisal methods used in practice
- use each method to reach a decision on a particular practical investment opportunity
- discuss the attributes and defects of each of the methods.

The nature of investment decisions

The essential feature of investment decisions is the time factor. Investment involves making an outlay of something of economic value, usually cash, at one point in time, which is expected to yield economic benefits to the investor at some other point in time. Typically, the outlay precedes the benefits. Also, the outlay is typically one large amount and the benefits arrive in a stream of smaller amounts over a fairly protracted period.

Investment decisions tend to be crucial to the business because:

- *Large amounts of resources are often involved.* Many investments made by a business involve laying out a significant proportion of its total resources (see Exhibit 10.1 below). If mistakes are made with the decision, the effects on the business could be significant, if not catastrophic.
- *It is often difficult and/or expensive to 'bail out' of an investment once it has been undertaken.* It is often the case that investments made by a business are specific to its needs. For example, a hotel business may invest in a new, purposely designed hotel complex. The specialist nature of this complex will probably lead to it having a rather limited second-hand value to another potential user with different needs. If the business found, after having made the investment, that room occupancy rates were not as buoyant as was planned, the only possible course of action might be to close down and sell the complex. This would probably mean that much less could be recouped from the investment than it had originally cost, particularly if the costs of design are included as part of the cost, as they logically should be.

Exhibit 10.1 indicates the level of annual investment for a number of randomly selected, well-known UK businesses. It can be seen that the scale of investment varies from one business to another. (It also tends to vary from one year to the next for a particular business.) In nearly all of these businesses the scale of investment is very significant. The exhibit is limited to considering the fixed asset investment, but most fixed asset investment also requires a level of current asset investment to support it (additional stock-in-trade, for example), meaning that the real scale of investment is even greater than indicated by the exhibit.

Exhibit 10.1

Business	*Expenditure on additional fixed assets as a percentage of:*	
	Annual sales	*Start of year fixed assets*
Associated British Foods plc	10.1	28.6
The Boots Company plc	3.2	7.6
British Airways plc	9.3	7.0
BT plc	19.9	17.0
British Sky Broadcasting Group plc	5.0	5.8
J D Wetherspoon plc	25.1	24.1
Manchester United plc	27.5	20.5
Stagecoach Group plc	6.0	5.4
Tesco plc	8.5	20.1
Vodafone Group plc	79.4	11.8

Source: Annual reports of the businesses concerned for the accounting years ending in 2002

When managers are making decisions involving capital investments, what should the decision seek to achieve?

The answer to this question must be that any decision must be made in the context of the objectives of the business concerned. For a private-sector business, this is likely to include increasing the wealth of the shareholders of the business through long-term profitability.

Methods of investment appraisal

Given the importance of investment decisions to the viability of the business, it is essential that proper screening of investment proposals takes place. An important part of this screening process is to ensure that the business uses appropriate methods of evaluation.

Research shows that there are basically four methods used in practice by businesses throughout the world to evaluate investment opportunities.

They are:

- accounting rate of return (ARR);
- payback period (PP);
- net present value (NPV);
- internal rate of return (IRR).

It is possible to find businesses that use variants of these four methods. It is also possible to find businesses, particularly smaller ones, that do not use any formal appraisal method, but rely more on the 'gut feeling' of their managers. Most businesses, however, seem to use one of the four methods listed above that we shall now review.

We are going to assess the effectiveness of each of these methods and we shall see that only one of them (NPV) is not flawed to some extent. We shall also see how popular these four methods seem to be in practice.

To help us to examine each of the methods, it might be useful to consider how each of them would cope with a particular investment opportunity. Let us consider the following example.

Example 10.1

Billingsgate Battery Company has carried out some research that shows that it could manufacture and sell a product that the business has recently developed.

Production would require investment in a machine that would cost £100,000, payable immediately. Production and sales would take place throughout the next five years. At the end of that time, it is estimated that the machine could be sold for £20,000.

Production and sales of the product would be expected to occur as follows:

	Number of units
Next year	5,000
Second year	10,000
Third year	15,000
Fourth year	15,000
Fifth year	5,000

It is estimated that the new product can be sold for £12 a unit, and that the relevant material and labour costs will total £8 a unit.

To simplify matters, we shall assume that the cash from sales and for the costs of production are paid and received, respectively, at the end of each year. (This is clearly unlikely to be true in real life – money will have to be paid to employees on a weekly or a monthly basis, and customers will pay within a month or two of buying the product. On the other hand, it is probably not a serious distortion. It is a simplifying assumption that is often made in real life, and it will make things more straightforward for us now. We should be clear, however, that there is nothing about any of the four approaches that *demands* this assumption being made.)

Bearing in mind that each product sold will give rise to a net cash inflow of £4 (that is £12 – £8), the total net cash flows (receipts less payments) for each year of the life of the product will be as follows:

Time		£000
Immediately	Cost of machine	(100)
1 year's time	Net profit before depreciation (£4 × 5,000)	20
2 years' time	Net profit before depreciation (£4 × 10,000)	40
3 years' time	Net profit before depreciation (£4 × 15,000)	60
4 years' time	Net profit before depreciation (£4 × 15,000)	60
5 years' time	Net profit before depreciation (£4 × 5,000)	20
5 years' time	Disposal proceeds from the machine	20

Note that, broadly speaking, the net profit before deducting depreciation (that is, before non-cash items) equals the net amount of cash flowing into the business. Apart from depreciation, all of this business's expenses cause cash to flow out of the business. Sales revenues lead to cash flowing in.

Having set up the example, we shall go on to look at the techniques used to assess investment opportunities and see how they deal with this particular decision.

Accounting rate of return (ARR)

The **accounting rate of return** method takes the average accounting profit that the investment will generate and expresses it as a percentage of the average investment in the project as measured in accounting terms.

Thus:

$$ARR = \frac{\text{Average annual profit}}{\text{Average investment to earn that profit}} \times 100\%$$

We can see that to calculate the ARR, we need to deduce two pieces of information:

- the annual average profit;
- the average investment for the particular project.

In our example, the average profit before depreciation over the five years is £40,000 [that is, £(20 + 40 + 60 + 60 + 20)/5]. Assuming straight-line depreciation (that is, equal annual amounts), the annual depreciation charge will be £16,000 [that is, £(100,000 – 20,000)/5]. Thus the average annual profit is £24,000 (that is, £40,000 – £16,000).

The average investment over the five years can be calculated as follows:

$$\text{Average investment} = \frac{\text{Cost of machine + disposal value}}{2}$$

$$= \frac{£100,000 + £20,000}{2}$$

$$= £60,000$$

Thus, the ARR of the investment is:

$$ARR = \frac{£24,000}{£60,000} \times 100\%$$

$$= 40\%$$

To decide whether the 40 per cent return is acceptable, we need to compare this percentage with the minimum required by the business.

Activity 10.2

Chaotic Industries is considering an investment in a fleet of ten delivery vans to take its products to customers. The vans will cost £15,000 each to buy, payable immediately. The annual running costs are expected to total £20,000 for each van (including the driver's salary). The vans are expected to operate successfully for six years, at the end of which period they will all have to be sold, with disposal proceeds expected to be about £3,000 per van. At present, the business uses a commercial carrier for all of its deliveries. It is expected that this carrier will charge a total of £230,000 each year for the next five years to undertake the deliveries.

What is the ARR of buying the vans? (Note that cost savings are as relevant a benefit from an investment as are actual net cash inflows.)

The vans will save the business £30,000 a year (that is, £230,000 – (£20,000 × 10)), before depreciation, in total.

Activity 10.2 continued

Thus, the inflows and outflows will be:

Time		£000
Immediately	Cost of vans	(150)
1 year's time	Net saving before depreciation	30
2 years'. time	Net saving before depreciation	30
3 years' time	Net saving before depreciation	30
4 years' time	Net saving before depreciation	30
5 years' time	Net saving before depreciation	30
6 years' time	Net saving before depreciation	30
6 years' time	Disposal proceeds from the vans (10 × 3)	30

The total annual depreciation expense (assuming a straight-line approach) will be £20,000 (that is, (£150,000 − £30,000)/6). Thus, the average annual saving, after depreciation, is £10,000 (that is, £30,000 − £20,000).

The average investment will be

$$\text{Average investment} = \frac{£150,000 + £30,000}{2}$$

$$= £90,000$$

Thus, the ARR of the investment is

$$\text{ARR} = \frac{£10,000}{£90,000} \times 100\% = 11.1\%$$

ARR and the return on capital employed (ROCE) ratio take the same approach to performance measurement, in that they both relate accounting profit to the cost of the assets invested to generate that profit. We may recall from Chapter 6 that ROCE is a popular means of assessing the performance of a business, as a whole, *after* it has performed. ARR is an approach that assesses the potential performance of a particular investment, taking the same approach as ROCE, *before* it has performed.

Since private-sector businesses are normally seeking to increase the wealth of their owners, ARR may seem to be a sound method of appraising investment opportunities. Profit can be seen as a net increase in wealth over a period, and relating it to the size of investment made to achieve it seems a logical approach.

A user of ARR would require that any investment undertaken by the business would be able to achieve a minimum ARR. Perhaps the minimum would be the rate that previous investments had actually achieved (as measured by ROCE). Perhaps it would be the industry-average ROCE.

Where there are competing projects that all seem capable of exceeding this minimum rate, the one with the higher or highest ARR would normally be selected.

ARR is said to have a number of advantages as a method of investment appraisal. It was mentioned earlier that ROCE seems a widely used measure of business performance. Shareholders seem to use this ratio to evaluate management performance, and sometimes the financial objective of a business will be expressed in terms of a target ROCE. It therefore seems sensible to use a method of investment appraisal that is consistent with this overall approach to measuring business performance. ARR is also a measure of profitability that many believe is the correct way to evaluate investments, and it gives the result expressed as a percentage. It seems that some managers feel comfortable with using measures expressed in percentage terms.

Activity 10.3

ARR suffers from a very major defect as a means of assessing investment opportunities. Can you reason out what this is? Consider the three competing projects whose cash flows are shown below. All three of these involve investment in a machine that is expected to have no residual value at the end of the five years. Note that all of the projects have the same total net profits over the five years.

Project		A	B	C
Time		£000	£000	£000
Immediately	Cost of machine	(200)	(200)	(200)
1 year's time	Net profit after depreciation	20	10	160
2 years' time	Net profit after depreciation	40	10	10
3 years' time	Net profit after depreciation	60	10	10
4 years' time	Net profit after depreciation	60	10	10
5 years' time	Net profit after depreciation	20	160	10

Hint: The defect is not concerned with the ability of the decision maker to forecast future events, though this too can be a problem. Try to remember what was the essential feature of investment decisions that we identified at the beginning of this chapter.

The problem with ARR is that it almost completely ignores the time factor. In the Billingsgate Battery example, exactly the same ARR would have been computed under any of the three scenarios.

Since the same total profit over the five years arises in all three of these projects (that is, £200,000) and the average investment in each project is £100,000 (that is, £200,000/2), this means that each case will give rise to the same ARR of 40 per cent (that is, £40,000/£100,000).

Given a financial objective of increasing the wealth of the business, any rational decision maker faced with these three scenarios as a choice between the three separate investments, set out in Activity 10.3, would strongly prefer Project C. This is because most of the benefits from the investment come in within 12 months of investing the £200,000 to establish the project. Project A would rank second, and Project B would come a poor third in the rankings. Any appraisal technique that is not capable of distinguishing between these three situations is seriously flawed.

Clearly the use of ARR can easily cause poor decisions to be made. We shall look in more detail at the reason for timing being so important later in this chapter.

There are other defects associated with the ARR method. For investment appraisal purposes, it is cash flows rather than accounting profits that are important. Cash is the ultimate measure of the economic wealth generated. This is because it is cash that is used to acquire resources and for distribution to shareholders. Accounting profit is more appropriate for reporting achievement over the short term. It is a useful measure of productive effort for a relatively short period, such as a year, rather than for a long period. ARR also fails to take account of the fact that pounds received at a later date are worth less than pounds received at an earlier date.

The ARR method can also create problems when considering competing investments of different size.

Activity 10.4

Sinclair Wholesalers plc is currently considering opening a new sales outlet in Coventry. Two possible sites have been identified for the new outlet. Site A has a capacity of 30,000 sq. metres. It will require an average investment of £6 million, and will produce an average profit of £600,000 a year. Site B has a capacity of 20,000 sq. metres. It will require an average investment of £4 million, and will produce an average profit of £500,000 a year.

What is the ARR of each investment opportunity? Which site would you select, and why?

The ARR of Site A is £600,000/£6 million = 10 per cent. The ARR of Site B is £500,000/£4 million = 12.5 per cent. Thus, Site B has the higher ARR. However, in terms of the absolute profit generated, Site A is the more attractive. If the ultimate objective is to maximise the wealth of the shareholders of Sinclair Wholesalers plc, it might be better to choose Site A even though the percentage return is lower. It is the absolute size of the return rather than the relative (percentage) size that is important.

Payback period (PP)

The **payback period** method seems to go some way to overcoming the timing problem of ARR, or at least at first glance it does.

It might be useful to consider PP in the context of the Billingsgate Battery example. We should recall that essentially the project's costs and benefits can be summarised as:

Time		£000
Immediately	Cost of machine	(100)
1 year's time	Net profit before depreciation	20
2 years' time	Net profit before depreciation	40
3 years' time	Net profit before depreciation	60
4 years' time	Net profit before depreciation	60
5 years' time	Net profit before depreciation	20
5 years' time	Disposal proceeds	20

Note that all of these figures are amounts of cash to be paid or received (we saw earlier that net profit before depreciation is a rough measure of the cash flows from the project).

The payback period is the length of time it takes for the initial investment to be repaid out of the net cash inflows from the project. In this case, it will be nearly three years before the £100,000 outlay is covered by the inflows, still assuming that the cash flows occur at year ends. The payback period can be derived by calculating the cumulative cash flows as follows:

Time		Net cash flows £000	Cumulative cash flows £000	
Immediately	Cost of machine	(100)	(100)	
1 year's time	Net profit before depreciation	20	(80)	(−100 + 20)
2 years' time	Net profit before depreciation	40	(40)	(−80 + 40)
3 years' time	Net profit before depreciation	60	20	(−40 + 60)
4 years' time	Net profit before depreciation	60	80	(20 + 60)
5 years' time	Net profit before depreciation	20	100	(80 + 20)
5 years' time	Disposal proceeds	20	120	(100 + 20)

We can see that the cumulative cash flows become positive at the end of the third year. Had we assumed that the cash flows arise evenly over the year, the precise payback period would be:

$$2 \text{ years} + (40/60) = 2\frac{2}{3} \text{ years}$$

(where 40 represents the cash flow still required at the beginning of the third year to repay the initial outlay, and 60 is the projected cash flow during the third year). Again we must ask how to decide whether $2\frac{2}{3}$ years is acceptable. A manager using PP would need to have a minimum payback period in mind. For example, if Billingsgate Battery had a minimum payback period of three years it would accept the project, but it would not go ahead if its minimum payback period were two years. If there were two competing projects that both met the minimum payback period requirement, the decision maker should select the project with the shorter payback period.

Activity 10.5

What is the payback period of the Chaotic Industries project from Activity 10.2?

The inflows and outflows are expected to be:

Time		Net cash flows £000	Cumulative net cash flows £000	
Immediately	Cost of vans	(150)	(150)	
1 year's time	Net saving before depreciation	30	(120)	(−150 + 30)
2 years' time	Net saving before depreciation	30	(90)	(−120 + 30)
3 years' time	Net saving before depreciation	30	(60)	(−90 + 30)
4 years' time	Net saving before depreciation	30	(30)	(−60 + 30)
5 years' time	Net saving before depreciation	30	0	(−30 + 30)
6 years' time	Net saving before depreciation	30	30	(0 + 30)
6 years' time	Disposal proceeds from the machine	30	60	(30 + 30)

The payback period here is five years; that is, it is not until the end of the fifth year that the vans will pay for themselves out of the savings that they are expected to generate.

The PP approach has certain advantages. It is quick and easy to calculate, and can be easily understood by managers. The logic of using PP is that projects that can recoup their cost quickly are economically more attractive than those with longer payback periods, that is, it emphasises liquidity. PP is probably an improvement on ARR in respect of the timing of the cash flows. PP is not, however, the whole answer to the problem.

Activity 10.6

In what respect, in your opinion, is PP not the whole answer as a means of assessing investment opportunities? Consider the cash flows arising from three competing projects:

Time		Project 1 £000	Project 2 £000	Project 3 £000
Immediately	Cost of machine	(200)	(200)	(200)
1 year's time	Net profit before depreciation	40	10	80
2 years' time	Net profit before depreciation	80	20	100
3 years' time	Net profit before depreciation	80	170	20
4 years' time	Net profit before depreciation	60	20	200
5 years' time	Net profit before depreciation	40	10	500
5 years' time	Disposal proceeds	40	10	20

Hint: Again, the defect is not concerned with the ability of the manager to forecast future events. This is a problem, but it is a problem whatever approach we take.

Any rational manager would prefer Project 3 to either of the other two projects, yet PP sees all three of them as being equally attractive in that they all have a three-year payback period. The method cannot distinguish between those projects that pay back a significant amount before the three-year payback period and those that do not. Project 3 is by far the best bet because the cash flows come in earlier and they are greater in total, yet PP would not identify it as the best.

The cumulative cash flows of each project in Activity 10.6 are set out in Figure 10.1.

Within the payback period, PP ignores the timing of the cash flows. Beyond the payback period, the method totally ignores both the size and the timing of the cash flows. While ignoring cash flows beyond the payback period neatly avoids the practical problems of forecasting cash flows over a long period, it means that relevant information may be ignored.

The PP approach is often seen as a means of dealing with the problem of risk by favouring projects with a short payback period. However, this is a fairly crude approach to the problem. There are more systematic approaches to dealing with risk that can be used.

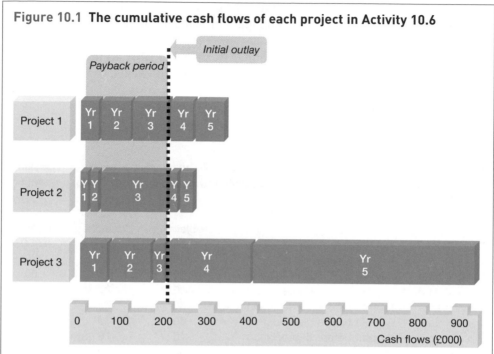

Figure 10.1 **The cumulative cash flows of each project in Activity 10.6**

The payback method of investment appraisal would view Projects 1, 2 and 3 as being equally attractive. In doing so, the method completely ignores the fact that Project 3 provides the payback cash earlier in the three-year period and goes on to generate large benefits in later years.

It seems that PP has the advantage of taking some note of the timing of the costs and benefits from the project, but it suffers from the disadvantage of ignoring relevant information. ARR ignores timing to a great extent, but it does take account of all benefits and costs. What we really need to help us to make sensible decisions is a method of appraisal that takes account of all of the costs and benefits of each investment opportunity, but which also makes a logical allowance for the timing of those costs and benefits.

Net present value (NPV)

What we really need to help us to make sensible investment decisions is a method of appraisal that takes account of *all* of the costs and benefits of each investment opportunity and that also makes a logical allowance for the *timing* of those costs and benefits. The **net present value** method provides us with this.

Consider the Billingsgate Battery example, which we should recall can be summarised as follows:

Time		£000
Immediately	Cost of machine	(100)
1 year's time	Net profit before depreciation	20
2 years' time	Net profit before depreciation	40
3 years' time	Net profit before depreciation	60
4 years' time	Net profit before depreciation	60
5 years' time	Net profit before depreciation	20
5 years' time	Disposal proceeds	20

Given that the principal financial objective of the business is probably to increase wealth, it would be very easy to assess this investment if all of the cash flows were to occur now (all at the same time). All that we should need to do would be to add up the benefits (total £220,000) and compare them with the cost (£100,000). This would lead us to the conclusion that the project should go ahead, because the business would be better off by £120,000. Of course, it is not as easy as this, because time is involved. The cash outflow (payment) will occur immediately if the project is undertaken. The inflows (receipts) will arise at a range of later times.

The time factor arises because normally people do not see £100 paid out now as equivalent in value to £100 receivable in a year's time. If we were to be offered £100 in 12 months, provided that we paid £100 now, we should not be prepared to do so, unless we wished to do someone (perhaps a friend or relation) a favour.

Activity 10.7

Why would you see £100 to be received in a year's time as unequal in value to £100 to be paid immediately? (There are basically three reasons.)

The reasons are:

- interest lost
- risk
- effects of inflation.

We shall now take a closer look at these three reasons in turn.

Interest lost

If we are to be deprived of the opportunity to spend your money for a year, we could equally well be deprived of its use by placing it on deposit in a bank or building society. In this case, at the end of the year we could have our money back and have interest as well. Thus, unless the opportunity to invest will offer similar returns, we shall be incurring an *opportunity cost*. An opportunity cost occurs where one course of action, for example making an investment in, say, a computer, deprives us of the opportunity to derive some benefit from an alternative action, for example putting the money in the bank.

From this we can see that any investment opportunity must, if it is to make us wealthier by taking it than by ignoring it, do better than the returns that are available from the next best opportunity. Thus, if Billingsgate Battery Company sees putting the money in the bank on deposit as the alternative to investment in the machine, the return from investing in the machine must be better than that from investing in the bank. If the bank offered a better return, the business would become wealthier by putting the money on deposit.

Risk

Buying a machine to manufacture a product to be sold in the market, on the strength of various estimates made in advance of buying the machine, exposes the business to **risk**. Things may not turn out as expected.

Activity 10.8

Can you suggest some areas where things could go other than according to plan in the Billingsgate Battery Company example?

We have come up with the following:

- The machine might not work as well as expected; it might break down, leading to loss of production and to loss of sales.
- Sales of the product may not be as buoyant as expected.
- Labour costs may prove to be higher than was expected.
- The sale proceeds of the machine could prove to be less than was estimated.

It is important to remember that the decision as to whether or not to invest in the machine must be taken *before* any of these things are known. It is only after the machine has been purchased that we could discover that the level of sales that had been estimated before the event is not going to be achieved. It is not possible to wait until we know for certain whether the market will behave as we expected before we buy the machine. We can study reports and analyses of the market. We can commission sophisticated market surveys, and these may give us more confidence in the likely outcome. We can advertise strongly and try to expand sales. Ultimately, however, we have to decide whether or not to jump off into the dark and accept the risk if we want the opportunity to make profitable investments.

Normally, people expect to receive greater returns where they perceive risk to be a factor. Examples of this in real life are not difficult to find. One such example is that banks tend to charge higher rates of interest to borrowers whom the bank perceives as more risky than to those who can offer good security for a loan and who can point to a regular source of income.

Going back to Billingsgate Battery Company's investment opportunity, it is not enough to say that we should not advise making the investment unless the returns from it are higher than those from investing in a bank deposit. Clearly we should want returns above the level of bank deposit interest rates, because the logical equivalent to investing in the machine is not putting the money on deposit but making an alternative investment that seems to have a risk similar to that of the investment in the machine.

In practice, we tend to expect a higher rate of return from investment projects where the risk is perceived as being higher. How risky a particular project is, and therefore how large this **risk premium** should be, are matters that are difficult to handle. In practice, it is necessary to make some judgement on these questions.

Inflation

If we are to be deprived of £100 for a year, when we come to spend that money it will not buy as much in the way of goods and services as it would have done a year earlier. Generally, we shall not be able to buy as many tins of baked beans or loaves of bread or bus tickets for a particular journey as we could have done a year earlier. Clearly, the investor needs this loss of purchasing power to be compensated for if the investment is to be made. This is on top of a return that takes account of the returns that could have been gained from an alternative investment of similar risk.

In practice, interest rates observable in the market tend to take **inflation** into account. Rates that are offered to potential building society and bank depositors include an allowance for the rate of inflation that is expected in the future.

Actions of a logical investor

To summarise these factors, we can say that the logical investor, who is seeking to increase his or her wealth, will only be prepared to make investments that will compensate for the loss of interest and purchasing power of the money invested and for the fact that the returns expected may not materialise (risk). This is usually assessed by seeing whether the proposed investment will yield a return that is greater than the basic rate of interest (which would include an allowance for inflation) plus a risk premium.

These three factors (interest lost, risk and inflation) are set out in Figure 10.2.

Naturally, investors need at least the minimum returns before they are prepared to invest. However, it is in terms of the effect on their wealth that they should logically assess an investment project. Usually it is the investment with the highest percentage return that will make the investor most wealthy, but we shall see later in this chapter that this is not always the case. For the time being, therefore, we shall concentrate on wealth.

Let us now return to the Billingsgate Battery Company example and assume that instead of making this investment the business could make an alternative investment with similar risk and obtain a return of 20 per cent a year.

We should recall that we have seen that it is not sufficient just to compare the basic figures for the investment. It would therefore be useful if we could express each of these cash flows in similar terms so that we could make a direct comparison between the sum of the inflows over time and the immediate £100,000 investment. In fact, we can do this.

Figure 10.2 The factors influencing the discount rate to be applied to a project

The figure shows the three factors influencing the opportunity cost of finance that were discussed earlier.

Activity 10.9

We know that Billingsgate Battery Company could alternatively invest its money at a rate of 20 per cent a year. How much do you judge the present (immediate) value of the expected first year receipt of £20,000 to be? In other words, if instead of having to wait a year for the £20,000, and being deprived of the opportunity to invest it at 20 per cent, you could have some money now, what sum to be received now would you regard as exactly equivalent to getting £20,000, but having to wait a year for it?

We should obviously be happy to accept a lower amount if we could get it immediately than if we had to wait a year. This is because we could invest it at 20 per cent (in the alternative project). Logically, we should be prepared to accept the amount that with a year's income will grow to £20,000. If we call this amount PV (for present value) we can say:

$$PV + (PV \times 20\%) = £20,000$$

that is, the amount plus income from investing the amount for the year equals the £20,000.
   If we rearrange this equation we find:

$$PV \times (1 + 0.2) = £20,000$$

Note that 0.2 is the same as 20 per cent, but expressed as a decimal.
   Further rearranging gives:

$$PV = £20,000/(1 + 0.2)$$

$$PV = £16,667$$

Thus, rational investors who have the opportunity to invest at 20 per cent a year would not mind whether they have £16,667 now or £20,000 in a year's time. In this sense we can say that, given a 20 per cent investment opportunity, the present value of £20,000 to be received in one year's time is £16,667.

If we could derive the present value (PV) of each of the cash flows associated with Billingsgate's machine investment, we could easily make the direct comparison between the cost of making the investment (£100,000) and the various benefits that will derive from it in years 1 to 5. Fortunately we can do precisely this.

We can make a more general statement about the PV of a particular cash flow. It is:

PV of the cash flow of year n = Actual cash flow of year n divided by $(1 + r)^n$

where n is the year of the cash flow (that is, how many years into the future) and r is the opportunity investing rate expressed as a decimal (instead of as a percentage).

We have already seen how this works for the £20,000 inflow for year 1. For year 2 the calculation would be:

$$\text{PV of year 2 cash flow (£40,000)} = £40,000/(1 + 0.2)^2$$

$$PV = £40,000/(1.2)^2 = £40,000/1.44 = £27,778$$

Thus the present value of the £40,000 to be received in two years' time is £27,778.

Activity 10.10

See if you can show that an investor would be indifferent to £27,778 receivable now, or £40,000 receivable in two years' time, assuming that there is a 20 per cent investment opportunity.

The reasoning goes like this:

	£
Amount available for immediate investment	27,778
Add Interest for year 1 (20% × 27,778)	5,556
	33,334
Add Interest for year 2 (20% × 33,334)	6,667
	40,001

(The extra £1 is only a rounding error.)

Thus because the investor can turn £27,778 into £40,000 in two years, these amounts are equivalent, and we can say that £27,778 is the present value of £40,000 receivable after two years (given a 20 per cent rate of return).

Now let us deduce the present values of all of the cash flows associated with the Billingsgate machine project and hence the *net present value* of the project as a whole.

The relevant cash flows and calculations are as follows:

Time	Cash flow	Calculation of PV	PV
	£000		£000
Immediately (time 0)	(100)	$(100)/(1 + 0.2)^0$	(100.00)
1 year's time	20	$20/(1 + 0.2)^1$	16.67
2 years' time	40	$40/(1 + 0.2)^2$	27.78
3 years' time	60	$60/(1 + 0.2)^3$	34.72
4 years' time	60	$60/(1 + 0.2)^4$	28.94
5 years' time	20	$20/(1 + 0.2)^5$	8.04
5 years' time	20	$20/(1 + 0.2)^5$	8.04
			24.19

(Note that $(1 + 0.2)^0 = 1$)

Once again, we must ask how we can decide whether the machine project is acceptable to the business. In fact, the decision rule is simple. If the NPV is positive we accept the project; if it is negative we reject the project. In this case, the NPV is positive, so we accept the project and buy the machine.

Investing in the machine will make the business £24,190 better off. What the above is saying is that the benefits from investing in this machine are worth a total of £124,190 today. Since the business can 'buy' these benefits for just £100,000 the investment should be made. If, however, the benefits were below £100,000 they would be less than the cost of 'buying' them.

Activity 10.11

What is the *maximum* the Billingsgate Battery Company would be prepared to pay for the machine, given the potential benefits of owning it?

The business would be prepared to pay up to £124,190 since the wealth of the owners of the business would be increased up to this price – though the business would prefer to pay as little as possible.

Using discount tables

Deducing the present values of the various cash flows is a little laborious using the approach that we have just taken. To deduce each PV we took the relevant cash flow and multiplied it by $1/(1 + r)^n$. Fortunately, there is a quicker way. Tables exist that show values of this **discount factor** for a range of values of r and n. Such a table is appended at the end of this chapter on p. 317. Take a look at it.

Look at the column for 20 per cent and the row for one year. We find that the factor is 0.833. Thus the PV of a cash flow of £1 receivable in one year is £0.833. So a cash flow of £20,000 receivable in one year's time is £16,660 (that is, 0.833 × £20,000), the same result as we found doing it in longhand.

Activity 10.12

What is the NPV of the Chaotic Industries project from Activity 10.2, assuming a 15 per cent opportunity cost of finance (discount rate)? You should use the discount table on p. 317.

Remember that the inflows and outflow are expected to be:

Time		£000
Immediately	Cost of vans	(150)
1 year's time	Net saving before depreciation	30
2 years' time	Net saving before depreciation	30
3 years' time	Net saving before depreciation	30
4 years' time	Net saving before depreciation	30
5 years' time	Net saving before depreciation	30
6 years' time	Net saving before depreciation	30
6 years' time	Disposal proceeds from the machine	30

The calculation of the NPV of the project is as follows:

Time	Cash flows	Discount factor (15% – from the table)	Present value
	£000		£000
Immediately	(150)	1.000	(150.00)
1 year's time	30	0.870	26.10
2 years' time	30	0.756	22.68
3 years' time	30	0.658	19.74
4 years' time	30	0.572	17.16
5 years' time	30	0.497	14.91
6 years' time	30	0.432	12.96
6 years' time	30	0.432	12.96
		Net present value	(23.49)

Activity 10.13

How would you interpret this result?

The fact that the project has a negative NPV means that the present value of the benefits from the investment are worth less than the cost of entering into it. Any cost up to £126,510 (the present value of the benefits) would be worth paying, but not £150,000.

The discount tables reveal how the value of £1 diminishes as its receipt goes further into the future. Assuming an opportunity cost of finance of 20 per cent a year, £1 to be received immediately, obviously, has a present value of £1. However, as the time before it is to be received extends, the present value diminishes significantly, as is shown in Figure 10.3.

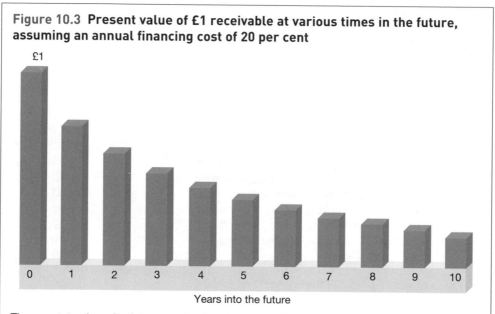

Figure 10.3 Present value of £1 receivable at various times in the future, assuming an annual financing cost of 20 per cent

Years into the future

The present value of a future receipt (or payment) of £1 depends on how far in the future it will occur. Those that will occur in the near future will have a larger present value than those whose occurrence is more distant in time.

Why NPV is superior to ARR and PP

From what we have seen, NPV seems to be a better method of appraising investment opportunities than either ARR or PP. This is because it fully addresses each of the following issues:

■ *The timing of the cash flows.* By discounting the various cash flows associated with each project according to when it is expected to arise, the fact that cash flows do not all occur simultaneously is taken into account by NPV. Associated with this is the fact that by discounting, using the opportunity cost of finance (that is, the return that the next best alternative opportunity would generate), the net benefit after financing costs have been met is identified (as the NPV of the project).

■ *The whole of the relevant cash flows.* NPV includes all of the relevant cash flows, irrespective of when they are expected to occur. It treats them differently according to their date of occurrence, but they are all taken into account in the NPV, and they all have an influence on the decision.

■ *The objectives of the business.* NPV is the only method of appraisal in which the output of the analysis has a direct bearing on the wealth of the business. (Positive NPVs enhance wealth; negative ones reduce it.) Since most private-sector businesses seek to maximise shareholders' wealth, NPV is superior to the methods previously discussed.

We saw earlier that a business should take on all projects with positive NPVs, when their cash flows are discounted at the opportunity cost of finance. Where a choice has to be made among projects, a business should normally select the one with the highest NPV.

Internal rate of return (IRR)

This is the last of the four major methods of investment appraisal that are found in practice. It is quite closely related to the NPV method in that, like NPV, it also involves discounting future cash flows. The **internal rate of return** of a particular investment is the discount rate that, when applied to its future cash flows, will pro-duce an NPV of precisely zero. In essence, it represents the yield from the project.

We should recall that when we discounted the cash flows of the Billingsgate Battery Company machine investment opportunity at 20 per cent, we found that the NPV was a positive figure of £24,190 (see p. 298).

Activity 10.14

What does the NPV of the machine project (that is, £24,190 (positive)) tell us about the rate of return that the investment will yield for the business?

The fact that the NPV is positive when discounting at 20 per cent implies that the rate of return that the project generates is more than 20 per cent. The fact that the NPV is a pretty large figure implies that the actual rate of return is quite a lot above 20 per cent. We should expect increasing the size of the discount rate to reduce NPV, because a higher discount rate gives a lower discounted figure. Thus future inflows are more heavily discounted, which will reduce their impact on the NPV.

It is somewhat laborious to deduce the IRR by hand, since it cannot usually be calculated directly. Thus iteration (trial and error) is the only approach.

Let us try a higher rate and see what happens, say, 30 per cent:

Time	Cash flow £000	Discount factor 30%	PV £000
Immediately (time 0)	(100)	1.000	(100.00)
1 year's time	20	0.769	15.38
2 years' time	40	0.592	23.68
3 years' time	60	0.455	27.30
4 years' time	60	0.350	21.00
5 years' time	20	0.269	5.38
5 years' time	20	0.269	5.38
			(1.88)

Figure 10.4 The relationship between the NPV and IRR methods

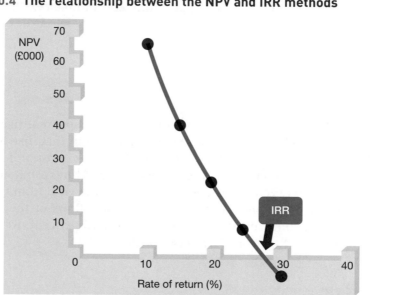

If the discount rate were zero, the NPV would be the sum of the net cash flows. In other words, no account would be taken of the time value of money. However, if we assume increasing discount rates, there is a corresponding decrease in the NPV of the project. When the NPV line crosses the horizontal axis there will be a zero NPV, and the point where it crosses is the IRR.

In increasing the discount rate from 20 per cent to 30 per cent, we have reduced the NPV from £24,190 (positive) to £1,880 (negative). Since the IRR is the discount rate that will give us an NPV of exactly zero, we can conclude that the IRR of Billingsgate Battery Company's machine project is very slightly below 30 per cent. Further trials could lead us to the exact rate, but there is probably not much point, given the likely inaccuracy of the cash flow estimates. It is probably good enough, for practical purposes, to say that the IRR is about 30 per cent.

The relationship between the NPV method discussed earlier and the IRR is shown graphically in Figure 10.4 using the information relating to the Billingsgate Battery Company.

We can see that, where the discount rate is zero, the NPV will be the sum of the net cash flows. In other words, no account is taken of the time value of money. However, as the discount rate increases there is a corresponding decrease in the NPV of the project. When the NPV line touches the horizontal axis there will be a zero NPV, and that will also represent the IRR.

Activity 10.15

What is the internal rate of return of the Chaotic Industries project from Activity 10.2? You should use the discount table at the end of this chapter. *Hint*: Remember that you already know the NPV of this project at 15 per cent.

Since we know (from a previous activity) that, at a 15 per cent discount rate, the NPV is a relatively large negative figure, our next trial is using a lower discount rate, say 10 per cent:

Time	Cash flows £000	Discount factor (10% – from the table)	Present value £000
Immediately	(150)	1.000	(150.00)
1 year's time	30	0.909	27.27
2 years' time	30	0.826	24.78
3 years' time	30	0.751	22.53
4 years' time	30	0.683	20.49
5 years' time	30	0.621	18.63
6 years' time	30	0.565	16.95
6 years' time	30	0.565	16.95
		Net present value	(2.40)

We can see that NPV increased by about £21,000 (£23,490 – £2,400) for a 5 per cent drop in the discount rate: that is, about £4,200 for each 1 per cent. We need to know the discount rate for a zero NPV: that is, a fall of a further £2,400. This logically would be roughly 0.6 per cent (that is, 2,400/4,200). Thus the IRR is close to 9.4 per cent. However, to say that the IRR is about 9 per cent is near enough for most purposes.

Users of the IRR approach should apply the following decision rules:

- For any project to be acceptable, it must meet a minimum IRR requirement. Logically, this minimum should be the opportunity cost of finance.
- Where there are competing projects (for example, the business can choose one of the projects only) the one with the higher or highest IRR would be selected.

IRR has certain attributes in common with NPV. All cash flows are taken into account, and their timing is logically handled. The main disadvantage with IRR is the fact that it does not address the question of wealth generation. It could therefore lead to the wrong decision being made. This is because IRR would, for example, always see a return of 25 per cent being preferable to a 20 per cent IRR, assuming an opportunity cost of finance of, say, 15 per cent. Though this may well lead to the project being taken that could most effectively increase wealth, this may not always be the case. This is because IRR completely ignores the *scale of investment*. With a 15 per cent cost of finance, £15 million invested at 20 per cent would make us richer than £5 million invested at 25 per cent. IRR does not recognise this. It should be acknowledged that it is not usual for projects to be competing where there is such a large difference in scale.

Even though the problem may be rare and, typically, IRR will give the same signal as NPV, a method (NPV) that is always reliable must be better to use than IRR.

A further problem with the IRR method is that it has difficulty handling projects with unconventional cash flows. In the examples studied so far, each project has a negative cash flow arising at the start of its life and then positive cash flows thereafter. However, in some cases, a project may have both positive and negative cash flows at future points in its life. Such a pattern of cash flows can result in the IRR method providing more than one solution, or even no solution at all.

Some practical points

When undertaking an investment appraisal, there are several practical points that we should bear in mind:

- *Relevant costs.* As with all decision making, we should only take account of cash flows that vary according to the decision in our analysis. Thus cash flows that will be the same, irrespective of the decision under review, should be ignored. For example, overheads that will be incurred in equal amount whether or not the investment is made should be ignored, despite the fact that the investment could not be made without the infrastructure that the overhead costs create. Similarly, past costs should be ignored as they are not affected by, and do not vary with, the decision.

- *Opportunity costs.* Opportunity costs arising from benefits foregone must be taken into account. Thus, for example, when considering a decision concerning whether or not to continue to use a machine already owned by the business, for producing a new product, the realisable value of the machine may be an important opportunity cost.

- *Taxation.* Tax will usually be affected by an investment decision. The profits will be taxed, the capital investment may attract tax relief, and so on. Tax is levied on these at significant rates. This means that, in real life, unless tax is formally taken into account, the wrong decision could easily be made.

- *Cash flows not profit flows.* We have seen that for the NPV, IRR and PP methods, it is cash flows rather than profit flows that are relevant to the evaluation of investment projects. In a problem requiring the application of any of these methods we may be given details of the profits for the investment period, and will be required to adjust these in order to derive the cash flows. Remember, the net profit before depreciation is an approximation to the cash flows for the period, and so we should work back to this figure.

  When the data are expressed in profit rather than cash flow terms, an adjustment in respect of working capital may also be necessary. Some adjustment should be made to take account of changes to working capital. For example, launching a new product may give rise to an increase in the net cash investment (or divestment) made in trade debtors, stock and creditors, requiring an immediate outlay of cash.

This outlay for additional working capital should be shown in the NPV calculations as part of the initial cost. However, the additional working capital will be released by the end of the life of the project, so the resulting inflow of cash at the end of the life of the project should also be taken into account. ⌣

■ *Interest payments*. When using discounted cash flow techniques, interest payments should not be taken into account in deriving the cash flows for the period. The discount factor already takes account of the costs of financing, so to take account of interest charges in deriving cash flows for the period would be double counting.

■ *Other factors*. Investment decision making must not be viewed as simply a mechanical exercise. The results derived from a particular investment appraisal method will be only one input to the decision-making process. There may be broader issues connected to the decision that have to be taken into account, but which may be difficult or impossible to quantify. The reliability of the forecasts and the validity of the assumptions used in the evaluation will also have a bearing on the final decision.

Activity 10.16

The directors of Manuff (Steel) Ltd have decided to close one of its factories. There has been a reduction in the demand for the products made at the factory in recent years, and the directors are not optimistic about the long-term prospects for these products. The factory is situated in the north of England, in an area where unemployment is high.

The factory is leased, and there are still four years of the lease remaining. The directors are uncertain as to whether the factory should be closed immediately or at the end of the period of the lease. Another business has offered to sublease the premises from Manuff at a rental of £40,000 a year for the remainder of the lease period.

The machinery and equipment at the factory cost £1,500,000, and have a balance sheet value of £400,000. In the event of immediate closure, the machinery and equipment could be sold for £220,000. The working capital at the factory is £420,000, and could be liquidated for that amount immediately, if required. Alternatively, the working capital can be liquidated in full at the end of the lease period. Immediate closure would result in redundancy payments to employees of £180,000.

If the factory continues in operation until the end of the lease period, the following operating profits (losses) are expected:

	Year 1 £000	Year 2 £000	Year 3 £000	Year 4 £000
Operating profit (loss)	160	(40)	30	20

The above figures include a charge of £90,000 per year for depreciation of machinery and equipment. The residual value of the machinery and equipment at the end of the lease period is estimated at £40,000.

Redundancy payments are expected to be £150,000 at the end of the lease period if the factory continues in operation. The business has an annual cost of capital of 12 per cent. Ignore taxation.

Activity 10.16 continued

Required:
(a) Calculate the relevant cash flows arising from a decision to continue operations until the end of the lease period rather than to close immediately.
(b) Calculate the net present value of continuing operations until the end of the lease period, rather than closing immediately.
(c) What other factors might the directors take into account before making a final decision on the timing of the factory closure?
(d) State, with reasons, whether or not the business should continue to operate the factory until the end of the lease period.

Your answer to this activity should be as follows:

(a) Relevant cash flows

	0	*1*	*2*	*3*	*4*
			Years		
	£000	*£000*	*£000*	*£000*	*£000*
Operating cash flows (Note 1)		250	50	120	110
Sale of machinery (Note 2)	(220)				40
Redundancy costs (Note 3)	180				(150)
Sublease rentals (Note 4)		(40)	(40)	(40)	(40)
Working capital invested (Note 5)	(420)				420
	(460)	210	10	80	380

Notes:
1 Each year's operating cash flows are calculated by adding back the depreciation charge for the year to the operating profit for the year. In the case of the operating loss, the depreciation charge is deducted.
2 In the event of closure, machinery could be sold immediately. Thus an opportunity cost of £220,000 is incurred if operations continue.
3 By continuing operations, there will be a saving in immediate redundancy costs of £180,000. However, redundancy costs of £150,000 will be paid in four years' time.
4 By continuing operations, the opportunity to sublease the factory will be foregone.
5 Immediate closure would mean that working capital could be liquidated. By continuing operations this opportunity is foregone. However, working capital can be liquidated in four years' time.

(b)

Discount rate 12 per cent	1.000	0.893	0.797	0.712	0.636
Present value	(460)	187.5	8.0	57.0	241.7
Net present value	34.2				

(c) Other factors that may influence the decision include:

■ *The overall strategy of the business*. The business may need to set the decision within a broader context. It may be necessary to manufacture the products made at the factory because they are an integral part of the business's product range. The business may wish to avoid redundancies in an area of high unemployment for as long as possible.

Activity 10.16 continued

- *Flexibility*. A decision to close the factory is probably irreversible. If the factory continues, however, there may be a chance that the prospects for the factory will brighten in the future.
- *Creditworthiness of sublessee*. The business should investigate the creditworthiness of the sublessee. Failure to receive the expected sublease payments would make the closure option far less attractive.
- *Accuracy of forecasts*. The forecasts made by the business should be examined carefully. Inaccuracies in the forecasts or any underlying assumptions may change the expected outcomes.

(d) The NPV of the decision to continue operations rather than close immediately is positive. Hence, shareholders would be better off if the directors took this course of action. The factory should therefore continue in operation rather than close down. This decision is likely to be welcomed by employees, as unemployment is high in the area.

? Self-assessment question 10.1

Beacon Chemicals plc is considering buying some equipment to produce a chemical named X14. The new equipment's capital cost is estimated at £100,000, and if its purchase is approved now, the equipment can be bought and commence production by the end of this year. £50,000 has already been spent on research and development work. Estimates of revenues and costs arising from the operation of the new equipment appear below:

	Year 1	Year 2	Year 3	Year 4	Year 5
Sales price (£ per unit)	100	120	120	100	80
Sales volume (units)	800	1,000	1,200	1,000	800
Variable costs (£ per unit)	50	50	40	30	40
Fixed costs (£000)	30	30	30	30	30

If the equipment is bought, sales of some existing products will be lost, and this will result in a loss of contribution of £15,000 a year over its life.

The accountant has informed you that the fixed costs include depreciation of £20,000 a year on the new equipment. They also include an allocation of £10,000 for fixed overheads. A separate study has indicated that if the new equipment were bought, additional overheads, excluding depreciation, arising from producing the chemical would be £8,000 a year. Production would require additional working capital of £30,000.

For the purposes of your initial calculations ignore taxation.

Required:
(a) Deduce the relevant annual cash flows associated with buying the equipment.
(b) Deduce the payback period.
(c) Calculate the net present value using a discount rate of 8 per cent.

Hint: You should deal with the investment in working capital by treating it as a cash outflow at the start of the project and an inflow at the end.

Investment appraisal in practice

Many surveys have been conducted in the UK into the methods of investment appraisal used in practice. They have tended to show the following features:

■ businesses using more than one method to assess each investment decision, increasingly so over time;
■ an increased use of the discounting methods (NPV and IRR) over time, with these two becoming the most popular in recent years;
■ continued popularity of ARR and PP, despite their theoretical shortcomings and the rise in popularity of the discounting methods;
■ a tendency for larger businesses to use the discounting methods and to use more than one method in respect of each decision.

Exhibit 10.2 shows the results of the most recent (1997) survey conducted of UK businesses regarding their use of investment appraisal methods.

Exhibit 10.2

Method	Percentage of businesses using the method
Net present value	80
Internal rate of return	81
Payback period	70
Accounting rate of return	56

Source: Reproduced by kind permission of Blackwell Publishing Ltd

---

Activity 10.17

How do you explain the popularity of the PP method, given the theoretical limitations discussed earlier in this chapter?

A number of possible reasons may explain this finding:

■ PP is easy to understand and use.
■ It can avoid the problems of forecasting far into the future.
■ It gives emphasis to the early cash flows when there is greater certainty concerning their accuracy.
■ It emphasises the importance of liquidity. Where a business has liquidity problems, a short payback period for a project is likely to appear attractive.

The popularity of PP may suggest a lack of sophistication among managers concerning investment appraisal. This criticism is most often made against managers of smaller business. In fact, the Arnold and Hatzopoulos and other surveys found that smaller businesses were much less likely to use discounted cash flow methods (NPV and IRR) than larger businesses.

IRR may be as popular as NPV, despite IRR's theoretical weaknesses, because it expresses outcomes in percentage terms rather than in absolute terms. This form of expression appears to be more acceptable to managers. This may be because managers are used to using percentage figures as targets (for example, return on capital employed).

The sum of percentage usage for each appraisal method is 287 per cent (see Exhibit 10.2), which indicates that many businesses use more than one method to appraise investments. Exhibit 10.2 suggests that most businesses use one of the two discounted cash flow methods.

Generally survey evidence has shown a strong increase in the rate of usage of both NPV and IRR, in the UK, over the years.

Exhibit 10.3 shows extracts from the 2001 annual report of a well-known business: Rolls-Royce plc, the builder of engines for aircraft and other purposes.

Exhibit 10.3 The use of NPV at Rolls-Royce

In its 2001 annual report, Rolls-Royce said:

> The Group continues to subject all investments to rigorous examination of risks and future cash flows to ensure that they create shareholder value. All major investments require Board approval.
> The Group has a portfolio of projects at different stages of their life-cycles. Discounted cash flow analysis of the remaining life of projects is performed on a regular basis.

Source: Rolls-Royce plc, *Annual Report* 2001

Rolls-Royce makes clear that it uses NPV (the report refers to creating shareholder value and to discounted cash flow, which strongly implies NPV). It is interesting to note that Rolls-Royce not only assesses new projects but also reassesses existing ones. This must be a sensible commercial approach. Businesses should not continue with existing projects unless those projects have a positive NPV based on future cash flows. Just because a project seemed to have a positive NPV before it started does not mean that this will persist, in the light of changing circumstances.

Summary

- *Payback period (PP) = the length of time that it takes for the cash outflow for the initial investment to be repaid out of resulting cash inflows.*
  - ☐ Decision rule – projects with a PP up to defined maximum period are acceptable, the shorter the PP, the more desirable.

- ❑ Conclusion on PP:
  - – does not relate to shareholders' wealth, ignores inflows after the payback date;
  - – takes little account of the timing of cash flows;
  - – ignores much relevant information;
  - – does not always provide clear signals and can be impractical to use;
  - – much inferior to NPV, but it is easy to understand and can offer a liquidity insight, which might be the reason for its widespread use.

- ■ *Accounting rate of return (ARR) = the average accounting profit from the project expressed as a percentage of the average (or initial) investment.*
  - ❑ Decision rule – projects with an ARR above a defined minimum are acceptable; the greater the ARR, the more attractive the project becomes.
  - ❑ Conclusion on ARR:
    - – it does not relate directly to shareholders' wealth – can lead to illogical conclusions;
    - – takes almost no account of the timing of cash flows;
    - – ignores some relevant information and may take account of some irrelevant;
    - – relatively simple to use;
    - – much inferior to NPV.

- ■ *Net present value (NPV) = the sum of the discounted values of the cash flows from the investment.*
  - ❑ Money has a time value.
  - ❑ Decision rule – all positive NPV investments enhance shareholders' wealth; the greater the NPV, the greater the enhancement and the more desirable.
  - ❑ PV of a cashflow = cashflow $\times 1/(1 + r)^n$, assuming a constant discount rate.
  - ❑ The act of discounting brings cash flows at different points in time to a common valuation basis (their present value), which enables them to be directly compared.
  - ❑ Conclusion on NPV:
    - – relates directly to shareholders' wealth objective;
    - – takes account of the timing of cash flows;
    - – takes all relevant information into account;
    - – provides clear signals and practical to use.

- ■ *Internal rate of return (IRR) = the discount rate that causes a project to have a zero NPV.*
  - ❑ Represents the average percentage return on the investment, taking account of the fact that cash may be flowing in and out of the project at various points in its life.
  - ❑ Decision rule – projects that have an IRR greater than the cost of capital are acceptable; the greater the IRR, the more attractive the project.
  - ❑ Usually cannot be calculated directly; a trial and error approach is usually necessary.

❑ Conclusion on IRR:
  – does not relate directly to shareholders' wealth. Usually gives the same signals as NPV – can mislead where there are competing projects of different scales;
  – takes account of the timing of cash flows;
  – takes all relevant information into account;
  – does not always provide clear signals and can be impractical to use;
  – with unconventional cash flows, problems of multiple or no IRR;
  – inferior to NPV.

■ *Use of appraisal methods in practice*:
  ❑ all four methods are widely used;
  ❑ the discounting methods (NPV and IRR) show a strong increase in usage over time;
  ❑ many businesses use more than one method;
  ❑ larger businesses seem to be more sophisticated than smaller ones.

→ **Key terms**

accounting rate of return (ARR) *p 285*   risk premium *p 295*
payback period (PP) *p 289*   inflation *p 295*
net present value (NPV) *p 292*   discount factor *p 298*
risk *p 294*   internal rate of return *p 301*

? **Review questions**

Answers to these questions can be found on the students' side of the Companion Website.

10.1 Why is the net present value method of investment appraisal considered to be theoretically superior to other methods that are found in practice?

10.2 The payback method has been criticised for not taking the time value of money into account. Could this limitation be overcome? If so, would this method then be preferable to the NPV method?

10.3 Research indicates that the IRR method is a more popular method of investment appraisal than the NPV method. Why might this be?

10.4 Why are cash flows rather than profit flows used in the IRR, NPV and PP methods of investment appraisal?

? **Exercises**

Exercise 10.5 is more advanced than 10.1–10.4. Those with a coloured number have an answer at the back of the book.

10.1 The directors of Mylo Ltd are currently considering two mutually exclusive investment projects. Both projects are concerned with the purchase of new plant. The following data are available for each project:

	Project 1 £	Project 2 £
Cost (immediate outlay)	100,000	60,000
Expected annual net profit (loss):		
Year 1	29,000	18,000
2	(1,000)	(2,000)
3	2,000	4,000
Estimated residual value of the plant	7,000	6,000

The business has an estimated cost of capital of 10 per cent, and uses the straight-line method of depreciation for all fixed assets when calculating net profit. Neither project would increase the working capital of the business. The business has sufficient funds to meet all capital expenditure requirements.

Required:
(a) Calculate for each project:
   (i)   The net present value.
   (ii) The approximate internal rate of return.
   (iii) The payback period.
(b) State which, if any, of the two investment projects the directors of Mylo Ltd should accept, and why.
(c) State, in general terms, which method of investment appraisal you consider to be most appropriate for evaluating investment projects, and why.

10.2 C. George (Controls) Ltd manufactures a thermostat that can be used in a range of kitchen appliances. The manufacturing process is, at present, semi-automated. The equipment used costs £540,000, and has a written-down (balance sheet) value of £300,000. Demand for the product has been fairly stable, and output has been maintained at 50,000 units a year in recent years.

The following data, based on the current level of output, have been prepared in respect of the product:

	Per unit £	Per unit £
Selling price		12.40
Less		
Labour	3.30	
Materials	3.65	
Overheads: Variable	1.58	
Fixed	1.60	
		10.13
Profit		2.27

Although the existing equipment is expected to last for a further four years before it is sold for an estimated £40,000, the business has recently been considering purchasing new equipment that would completely automate much of the production process. The new equipment would cost £670,000 and would have an expected life of four years, at the end of which it would be sold for an estimated £70,000. If the new equipment is purchased, the old equipment could be sold for £150,000 immediately.

The assistant to the business's accountant has prepared a report to help assess the viability of the proposed change, which includes the following data:

	Per unit	
	£	£
Selling price		12.40
Less		
Labour	1.20	
Materials	3.20	
Overheads: Variable	1.40	
Fixed	3.30	
		9.10
Profit		3.30

Depreciation charges will increase by £85,000 a year as a result of purchasing the new machinery; however, other fixed costs are not expected to change.

In the report the assistant wrote:

The figures shown above that relate to the proposed change are based on the current level of output and take account of a depreciation charge of £150,000 a year in respect of the new equipment. The effect of purchasing the new equipment will be to increase the net profit to sales ratio from 18.3% to 26.6%. In addition, the purchase of the new equipment will enable us to reduce our stock level immediately by £130,000.

In view of these facts, I recommend purchase of the new equipment.

The business has a cost of capital of 12 per cent.
Ignore taxation.

Required:
(a) Prepare a statement of the incremental cash flows arising from the purchase of the new equipment.
(b) Calculate the net present value of the proposed purchase of new equipment.
(c) State, with reasons, whether the business should purchase the new equipment.
(d) Explain why cash flow forecasts are used rather than profit forecasts to assess the viability of proposed capital expenditure projects.

10.3 The accountant of your business has recently been taken ill through overwork. In his absence his assistant has prepared some calculations of the profitability of a project, which are to be discussed soon at the board meeting of your business. His workings, which are set out below, include some errors of principle. You can assume that the statement below includes no arithmetical errors.

	Year 1 £000	Year 2 £000	Year 3 £000	Year 4 £000	Year 5 £000	Year 6 £000
Sales revenue		450	470	470	470	470
Less Costs						
Materials		126	132	132	132	132
Labour		90	94	94	94	94
Overheads		45	47	47	47	47
Depreciation		120	120	120	120	120
Working capital	180					
Interest on working capital		27	27	27	27	27
Write-off of development costs		30	30	30		
Total costs	180	438	450	450	420	420
Profit/(loss)	(180)	12	20	20	50	50

$$\frac{\text{Total profit (loss)}}{\text{Cost of equipment}} = \frac{(£28,000)}{£600,000} = \text{Return on investment (4.7\%)}$$

You ascertain the following additional information:

■ The cost of equipment contains £100,000, being the book value of an old machine. If it were not used for this project it would be scrapped with a zero net realisable value. New equipment costing £500,000 will be purchased on 31 December Year 0. You should assume that all other cash flows occur at the end of the year to which they relate.
■ The development costs of £90,000 have already been spent.
■ Overheads have been costed at 50 per cent of direct labour, which is the business's normal practice. An independent assessment has suggested that incremental overheads are likely to amount to £30,000 per year.
■ The business's cost of capital is 12 per cent.

Ignore taxation in your answer.

Required:
(a) Prepare a corrected statement of the incremental cash flows arising from the project. Where you have altered the assistant's figures you should attach a brief note explaining your alterations.
(b) Calculate:
  (i) The project's payback period.
  (ii) The project's net present value as at 31 December Year 0.
(c) Write a memo to the board advising on the acceptance or rejection of the project.

10.4 Arkwright Mills plc is considering expanding its production of a new yarn, code name X15. The plant is expected to cost £1 million and have a life of five years and a nil residual value. It will be bought, paid for and ready for operation on 31 December Year 0. £500,000 has already been spent on development costs of the product, and this has been charged to revenue in the year it was incurred.

The following profit and loss statements for the new yarn are forecast:

	Year 1 £m	Year 2 £m	Year 3 £m	Year 4 £m	Year 5 £m
Sales	1.2	1.4	1.4	1.4	1.4
Costs, including depreciation	1.0	1.1	1.1	1.1	1.1
Profit before tax	0.2	0.3	0.3	0.3	0.3

Tax is charged at 50 per cent on annual profits (before tax and after depreciation) and paid one year in arrears. Depreciation of the plant has been calculated on a straight-line basis. Additional working capital of £0.6 million will be required at the beginning of the project and released at the end of Year 5. You should assume that all cash flows occur at the end of the year in which they arise.

Required:
(a) Prepare a statement showing the incremental cash flows of the project relevant to a decision concerning whether or not to proceed with the construction of the new plant.
(b) Compute the net present value of the project using a 10 per cent discount rate.
(c) Compute the payback period to the nearest year. Explain the meaning of this term.

10.5 Newton Electronics Ltd has incurred expenditure of £5 million over the past three years researching and developing a miniature hearing aid. The hearing aid is now fully developed, and the directors are considering which of three mutually exclusive options should be taken to exploit the potential of the new product. The options are as follows:

1 The business could manufacture the hearing aid itself. This would be a new departure for the business, which has so far concentrated on research and development
projects. However, the business has manufacturing space available that it currently
rents to another business for £100,000 a year. The business would have to purchase
plant and equipment costing £9 million and invest £3 million in working capital
immediately for production to begin.

A market research report, for which the business paid £50,000, indicates that
the new product has an expected life of five years. Sales of the product during this
period are predicted as follows:

	Predicted sales for the year ended 30 November				
	Year 1	Year 2	Year 3	Year 4	Year 5
Number of units (000s)	800	1,400	1,800	1,200	500

The selling price per unit will be £30 in the first year but will fall to £22 in the following three years. In the final year of the product's life, the selling price will fall to £20.
Variable production costs are predicted to be £14 a unit, and fixed production costs
(including depreciation) will be £2.4 million a year. Marketing costs will be £2 million
a year.

The business intends to depreciate the plant and equipment using the straight-
line method and based on an estimated residual value at the end of the five years
of £1 million. The business has a cost of capital of 10 per cent.

2   Newton Electronics Ltd could agree to another business manufacturing and marketing the product under licence. A multinational business, Faraday Electricals plc, has offered to undertake the manufacture and marketing of the product, and in return will make a royalty payment to Newton Electronics Ltd of £5 per unit. It has been estimated that the annual number of sales of the hearing aid will be 10 per cent higher if the multinational business, rather than if Newton Electronics Ltd, manufactures and markets the product.

3   Newton Electronics Ltd could sell the patent rights to Faraday Electricals plc for £24 million, payable in two equal instalments. The first instalment would be payable immediately and the second at the end of two years. This option would give Faraday Electricals the exclusive right to manufacture and market the new product.

Ignore taxation.
Assume it is now 30 November Year 0.

Required:
(a) Calculate the net present value of each of the options available to Newton Electronics Ltd.
(b) Identify and discuss any other factors that Newton Electronics Ltd should consider before arriving at a decision.
(c) State what you consider to be the most suitable option, and why.

Appendix: present value table

Present value of £1, that is, $1/(1 + r)^n$

where r = discount rate
      n = number of periods until payment

Periods (n)				Discount rates (r)						
	1%	2%	3%	4%	5%	6%	7%	8%	9%	10%
1	0.990	0.980	0.971	0.962	0.952	0.943	0.935	0.926	0.917	0.909	1
2	0.980	0.961	0.943	0.925	0.907	0.890	0.873	0.857	0.842	0.826	2
3	0.971	0.942	0.915	0.889	0.864	0.840	0.816	0.794	0.772	0.751	3
4	0.961	0.924	0.888	0.855	0.823	0.792	0.763	0.735	0.708	0.683	4
5	0.951	0.906	0.863	0.822	0.784	0.747	0.713	0.681	0.650	0.621	5
6	0.942	0.888	0.837	0.790	0.746	0.705	0.666	0.630	0.596	0.564	6
7	0.933	0.871	0.813	0.760	0.711	0.665	0.623	0.583	0.547	0.513	7
8	0.923	0.853	0.789	0.731	0.677	0.627	0.582	0.540	0.502	0.467	8
9	0.914	0.837	0.766	0.703	0.645	0.592	0.544	0.500	0.460	0.424	9
10	0.905	0.820	0.744	0.676	0.614	0.558	0.508	0.463	0.422	0.386	10
11	0.896	0.804	0.722	0.650	0.585	0.527	0.475	0.429	0.388	0.350	11
12	0.887	0.788	0.701	0.625	0.557	0.497	0.444	0.397	0.356	0.319	12
13	0.879	0.773	0.681	0.601	0.530	0.469	0.415	0.368	0.326	0.290	13
14	0.870	0.758	0.661	0.577	0.505	0.442	0.388	0.340	0.299	0.263	14
15	0.861	0.743	0.642	0.555	0.481	0.417	0.362	0.315	0.275	0.239	15

	11%	12%	13%	14%	15%	16%	17%	18%	19%	20%	
1	0.901	0.893	0.885	0.877	0.870	0.862	0.855	0.847	0.840	0.833	1
2	0.812	0.797	0.783	0.769	0.756	0.743	0.731	0.718	0.706	0.694	2
3	0.731	0.712	0.693	0.675	0.658	0.641	0.624	0.609	0.593	0.579	3
4	0.659	0.636	0.613	0.592	0.572	0.552	0.534	0.516	0.499	0.482	4
5	0.593	0.567	0.543	0.519	0.497	0.476	0.456	0.437	0.419	0.402	5
6	0.535	0.507	0.480	0.456	0.432	0.410	0.390	0.370	0.352	0.335	6
7	0.482	0.452	0.425	0.400	0.376	0.354	0.333	0.314	0.296	0.279	7
8	0.434	0.404	0.376	0.351	0.327	0.305	0.285	0.266	0.249	0.233	8
9	0.391	0.361	0.333	0.308	0.284	0.263	0.243	0.225	0.209	0.194	9
10	0.352	0.322	0.295	0.270	0.247	0.227	0.208	0.191	0.176	0.162	10
11	0.317	0.287	0.261	0.237	0.215	0.195	0.178	0.162	0.148	0.135	11
12	0.286	0.257	0.231	0.208	0.187	0.168	0.152	0.137	0.124	0.112	12
13	0.258	0.229	0.204	0.182	0.163	0.145	0.130	0.116	0.104	0.093	13
14	0.232	0.205	0.181	0.160	0.141	0.125	0.111	0.099	0.088	0.078	14
15	0.209	0.183	0.160	0.140	0.123	0.108	0.095	0.084	0.074	0.065	15

Managing working capital

Introduction

In this chapter we consider the factors that must be taken into account when managing the working capital of a business. Each element of working capital will be identified, and the major issues surrounding them will be discussed. As we saw in Chapter 10, working capital represents a significant aspect of most business investment decisions. Important tools in the management of working capital are accounting ratios, which we explored in Chapter 6, and budgets, which were considered in Chapter 9.

Objectives

When you have completed this chapter you should be able to:

- identify the main elements of working capital
- discuss the purpose of working capital and the nature of the working capital cycle
- explain the importance of establishing policies for the control of working capital
- explain the factors that have to be taken into account when managing each element of working capital.

The nature and purpose of working capital

Working capital is usually defined as current assets less current liabilities (creditors due within one year).

The major elements of current assets are:

- stocks;
- trade debtors;
- cash (in hand and at bank).

Figure 11.1 **The working capital cycle**

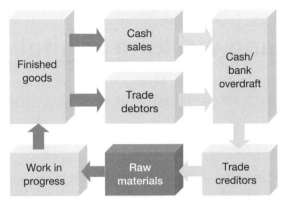

Cash is used to pay trade creditors for raw materials, or raw materials are bought for immediate cash settlement; cash is spent on labour and other aspects that turn raw materials into work in progress and, finally, into finished goods. The finished goods are sold either for cash or on credit. In the case of credit customers, there will be a delay before the cash is received from the sales. Receipt of cash completes the cycle.

The major elements of current liabilities are:

- trade creditors;
- bank overdrafts.

The size and composition of working capital can vary between industries. For some types of business, the investment in working capital can be substantial. For example, a manufacturing business will typically invest heavily in raw material, work in progress and finished goods, and will often sell its goods on credit, thereby generating trade debtors. A retailer, on the other hand, will hold only one form of stock (finished goods), and will usually sell goods for cash. Most businesses buy goods and services on credit, giving rise to trade creditors. Few businesses operate without a cash balance, though in some cases it is a negative one (bank overdraft).

Working capital represents a net investment in short-term assets. These assets are continually flowing into and out of the business, and are essential for day-to-day operations. The various elements of working capital are interrelated, and can be seen as part of a short-term cycle. For a manufacturing business, the working capital cycle can be depicted as shown in Figure 11.1.

Managing working capital

The management of working capital is an essential part of the business's short-term planning process. It is necessary for management to decide how much of each element should be held. As we shall see later, there are costs associated with holding either too much or too little of each element. Management must be aware of these costs in order to manage effectively. Management must also be aware that there may be other, more profitable, uses for the funds of the business. Hence, the potential benefits must be weighed against the likely costs in order to achieve the optimum investment.

The working capital needs of a particular business are likely to change over time as a result of changes in the business environment. This means that working capital decisions are constantly being made. Managers must try to identify changes in an attempt to ensure that the level of investment in working capital is appropriate.

Activity 11.1

What kind of changes in the commercial environment might lead to a decision to change the level of investment in working capital? Try to identify four possible changes that could affect the working capital needs of a business.

We thought of the following:

- changes in interest rates
- changes in market demand
- changes in the seasons
- changes in the state of the economy.

You may have also thought of others.

In addition to changes in the external environment, changes arising within the business such as using different production methods (resulting, perhaps, in a need to hold less stock) and changes in the level of risk managers are prepared to take could alter the required level of investment in working capital.

The scale of working capital

It is tempting to form the impression that, compared with the scale of investment in fixed assets by the typical business, the amounts involved with working capital are pretty trivial. This would be a false assessment of reality – the scale of working capital for most businesses is vast.

Exhibit 11.1 gives some impression of the working capital involvement for five UK businesses that are either very well known by name, or whose products are everyday commodities for most of us.

The totals for current assets are pretty large when compared with the total long-term investment. The amounts vary considerably from one type of business to the next. Rolls-Royce is the only one of the five businesses that is a manufacturer. Debenhams and Somerfield are both retailers and these three are the only ones that hold significant amounts of stock. The other two are service providers. Rolls-Royce is also the only one of the five that sells a significant amount on credit and so has a substantial investment in trade debtors. It is interesting to note that Somerfield's trade creditors are much higher than its stock. Since most of these creditors will be suppliers of stock, it means that the business is able, on average, to have the cash from a particular sale in the bank before it needs to pay for the goods concerned.

These types of variation in the amounts and types of working capital elements are typical of other businesses.

Exhibit 11.1

A summary of the balance sheets of five UK businesses

Business	Debenhams plc	Rolls-Royce plc	Somerfield plc	Stagecoach Group plc	Vodafone Group plc
Balance sheet date	31.8.02	31.12.01	27.4.02	30.4.02	31.3.02
	%	%	%	%	%
Fixed assets	111	64	117	102	103
Current assets					
Stock	24	28	40	3	–
Trade debtors	2	24	–	6	2
Other debtors	5	33	14	9	3
Cash and near cash	3	20	11	8	–
	34	105	65	26	5
Current liabilities					
Trade creditors	8	13	60	6	2
Tax and dividends	8	12	3	3	2
Other short-term liabilities	17	38	19	15	3
Overdrafts and short-term loans	12	6	–	4	1
	45	69	82	28	8
Working capital	(11)	36	(17)	(2)	(3)
Total long-term investment	100	100	100	100	100

Source: The table was constructed from information appearing in the annual reports of the five businesses concerned

The fixed assets, current assets and current liabilities (creditors: amounts falling due within one year) are expressed as a percentage of the total net investment of the business concerned. The businesses were randomly selected, except that they were deliberately taken from different industries. Debenhams is a major UK department store chain. Rolls-Royce builds engines for aircraft and for other purposes. Somerfield is one of the major UK supermarkets, trading under both the Somerfield and KwikSave names. Stagecoach is a major passenger transport provider, principally through buses, coaches and trains. It owns South West Trains, and has a major stake in Virgin trains. Vodafone is a major mobile phone and other mobile communications provider.

In the sections that follow, we shall consider each element of working capital separately and how they might be properly managed.

Managing stocks

A business may hold stocks for various reasons, the most common of which is to meet the immediate day-to-day requirements of customers and production. However, a business may hold more than is necessary for this purpose if it is believed that future supplies may be interrupted or scarce. Similarly, if the business believes that the cost of stocks will rise in the future, it may decide to stockpile.

For some types of business the stock held may represent a substantial proportion of the total assets held. For example, a car dealership that rents its premises may have nearly all of its total assets in the form of stock. As we have seen, manufacturing businesses' stock levels tend to be higher than in many other types of business. For some types of business, the level of stock held may vary substantially over the year owing to the seasonal nature of the industry, for example greetings card manufacturers, whereas for other businesses stock levels may remain fairly stable throughout the year.

Where a business holds stock simply to meet the day-to-day requirements of its customers and production, it will normally seek to minimise the amount of stock held. This is because there are significant costs associated with holding stocks. These include storage and handling costs, financing costs, the risks of pilferage and obsolescence, and the opportunities forgone in tying up funds in this form of asset. However, a business must also recognise that, if the level of stocks held is too low, there will also be associated costs.

Activity 11.2

What costs might a business incur as a result of holding too low a level of stocks? Try to jot down at least three types of cost.

In answering this activity you may have thought of the following costs:

- loss of sales, from being unable to provide the goods required immediately;
- loss of goodwill from customers, for being unable to satisfy customer demand;
- high transport costs incurred to ensure that stocks are replenished quickly;
- lost production due to shortage of raw materials;
- inefficient production scheduling due to shortages of raw materials;
- purchasing stocks at a higher price than might otherwise have been possible in order to replenish stocks quickly.

Before we go on to deal with the various approaches that can be taken to managing stock, Exhibit 11.2 provides an example of how badly things can go wrong if stock is not adequately controlled.

Exhibit 11.2

Pallets lost at Brambles

Brambles Industries plc (BI) is an Anglo-Australian industrial services business formed in 2001 when the industrial services subsidiary of GKN plc, the UK engineering business, was merged with the Australian business Brambles Ltd.

BI uses 'pallets' on which it delivers its products to customers. These are returnable by customers so BI holds a stock or 'pool' of pallets. Each pallet costs the business about £10. Unfortunately, BI lost 14 million pallets during the year ended in June 2002 as a result of poor stock control and this led to a significant decline in the business's profits and share price.

At BI's annual general meeting in Sydney, Australia, one of the shareholders was quoted as saying: 'Running a pallet pool is not rocket science. I can teach one of my employees about pallets in 20 minutes.'

Source: Information taken from an article appearing in the *Financial Times*, 27 November 2002

To try to ensure that the stocks are properly managed, a number of procedures and techniques may be used. These are reviewed below.

Budgeting future demand

One of the best means of a business trying to ensure that there will be stock available to meet future production requirements and sales is to make appropriate plans. These budgets should deal with each product that the business makes and/or sells. It is important that every attempt is made to ensure their accuracy, as they will determine future ordering and production levels. The budgets may be derived in various ways. They may be developed using statistical techniques such as time series analysis, or they may be based on the judgement of the sales and marketing staff. We considered stock budgets, and their link to sales and production budgets, in Chapter 9.

Financial ratios

One ratio that can be used to help monitor stock levels is the stock turnover period, which we examined in Chapter 6. As we should recall, this ratio is calculated as follows:

$$\text{Stock turnover period} = \frac{\text{Average stock held}}{\text{Cost of sales}} \times 365$$

This will provide a picture of the average period for which stocks are held, and can be useful as a basis for comparison. It is possible to calculate the stock turnover period for individual product lines as well as for stocks as a whole.

Recording and reordering systems

The management of stocks in a business of any size requires a sound system of recording stock movements. There must be proper procedures for recording stock purchases and sales. Periodic stock checks may be required to ensure that the amount of physical stocks held is consistent with what the stock records indicate is held.

There should also be clear procedures for the reordering of stocks. Authorisation for both the purchase and the issue of stocks should be confined to a few senior staff if problems of duplication and lack of co-ordination are to be avoided. To determine the point at which stock should be reordered, information will be required concerning the lead time (that is, the time between the placing of an order and the receipt of the goods) and the likely level of demand.

Activity 11.3

An electrical retailer keeps a particular type of light switch in stock. The annual demand for the light switch is 10,400 units, and the lead time for orders is four weeks. Demand for the stock is steady throughout the year. At what level of stock should the business reorder, assuming that it is confident of the figures mentioned above?

The average weekly demand for the stock item is 10,400/52 = 200 units. During the time between ordering the stock and receiving the goods the stock sold will be 4 × 200 units = 800 units. So the business should reorder no later than when the stock level reaches 800 units, in order to avoid a 'stockout'.

In most businesses, there will be some uncertainty surrounding the above factors and so a buffer or safety stock level may be maintained in case problems occur. The amount of safety stock to be held is really a matter of judgement, and will depend on the degree of uncertainty concerning the above factors. However, the likely costs of running out of stock must also be taken into account.

Levels of control

Management must make a commitment to the management of stocks. However, the cost of controlling stocks must be weighed against the potential benefits. It may be possible to have different levels of control according to the nature of the stocks held. The **ABC system of stock control** is based on the idea of selective levels of control.

A business may find that it is possible to divide its stock into three broad categories: A, B and C. Each category will be based on the value of stock held, as is illustrated in Example 11.1.

Example 11.1

Alascan Products plc makes door handles and door fittings. It makes them in brass, in steel and in plastic. The business finds that brass fittings account for 10 per cent of the physical volume of the finished stocks that it holds and that these represent 65 per cent of the total finished stock value. These are treated as Category A stocks. There are sophisticated recording procedures, tight control is exerted over stock movements and there is a high level of security at the stocks' location. This is economic because the stock represents a relatively small proportion of the total volume.

The business finds that steel fittings account for 30 per cent of the total volume of finished stocks, representing 25 per cent of the total value of finished stocks held. These are treated as Category B stocks with a lower level of recording and management control being applied.

The remaining 60 per cent of the volume of stocks are plastic fittings, which represent the least valuable items that account for only 10 per cent of the total value of finished stocks held. For these stocks the level of recording and management control would be lower still. These are treated as Category C stocks. Applying the level of control to these stocks as is applied to Category A or even Category B stocks would be uneconomic.

Categorising stocks in this way seeks to direct management effort to the most important areas, and tries to ensure that the costs of controlling stocks are appropriate to their importance.

Figure 11.2 graphically shows the logic of the ABC approach to stock control.

Figure 11.2 ABC method of analysing and controlling stock

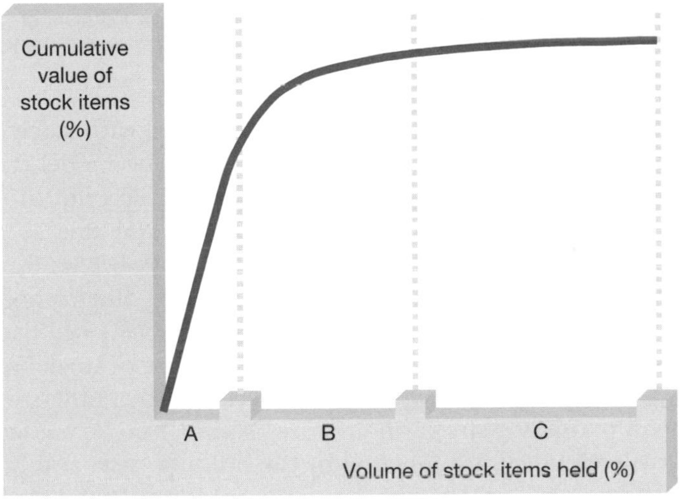

Category A contains stocks that, though relatively few in quantity, account for a large proportion of the total value of stocks. Category B stocks are those items that are less valuable, but more numerous. Category C comprises those stock items that are very numerous, but relatively low in value. Different stock control rules would be applied to each category. For example, only Category A stocks would attract the more expensive and sophisticated controls.

Stock management models

→ It is possible to use decision models to help manage stocks. The **economic order quantity (EOQ)** model is concerned with answering the question 'How much stock should be ordered?' In its simplest form, the EOQ model assumes that demand is constant, so that stocks will be depleted evenly over time, and replenished just at the point that the stock runs out. These assumptions would lead to a 'saw tooth' pattern to represent stock movements within a business, as shown in Figure 11.3.

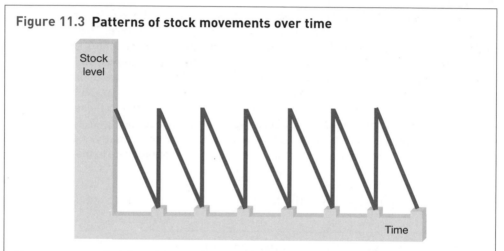

Figure 11.3 Patterns of stock movements over time

Here we assume that there is a constant rate of usage of the stock item, and that stocks are reduced to zero just as new stock arrives. At time zero there is a full level of stock. This is steadily used as time passes; just as it falls to zero it is replaced. This pattern is then repeated.

The EOQ model recognises that the key costs associated with stock management are the costs of holding it and the cost of ordering it. The model can be used to calculate the optimum size of a purchase order by taking account of both of these cost elements. The cost of holding stock can be substantial, and so management may try to minimise the average amount of stock held. However, by reducing the level of stock held, and therefore the holding costs, there will be a need to increase the number of orders during the period, and so ordering costs will rise.

Figure 11.4 shows how, as the level of stock and the size of stock orders increase, the annual costs of placing orders will decrease because fewer orders will be placed. However, the cost of holding stock will increase, as there will be higher stock levels. The total costs curve, which is a function of the holding costs and ordering costs, will fall until the point E, which represents the minimum total cost. Thereafter, total costs begin to rise. The EOQ model seeks to identify the point E at which total costs are minimised. This will represent half of the optimum amount that should be ordered on each occasion. Assuming, as we are doing, that stock is used evenly over time and that stock falls to zero before being replaced, the average stock level equals half of the order size.

Figure 11.4 **Stockholding and stock order costs**

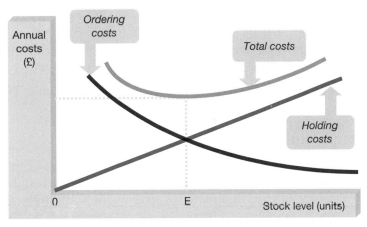

Small stock levels imply frequent reordering and high annual ordering costs. Small stock levels also imply relatively low stock-holding costs. High stock levels imply exactly the opposite. There is, in theory, an optimum order size that will lead to the sum of ordering and stock-holding costs (total costs) being at a minimum.

The EOQ model, which can be used to derive the most economic order quantity, is:

$$EOQ = \sqrt{\frac{2DC}{H}}$$

where:
D = the annual demand for the item of stock
C = the cost of placing an order
H = the cost of holding one unit of stock for one year.

Activity 11.4

HLA Ltd sells 2,000 bags of cement each year. It has been estimated that the cost of holding one bag of cement for a year is £4. The cost of placing an order for stock is estimated at £250.
Calculate the EOQ for bags of cement.

Your answer to this activity should be as follows:

$$EOQ = \sqrt{\frac{2 \times 2{,}000 \times 250}{4}}$$

$$= 500 \text{ units}$$

This will mean that the business will have to order bags of cement four times each year to enable sales demand to be met.

The basic EOQ model has a number of limiting assumptions. In particular, it assumes that demand for the product can be predicted with accuracy, and that this demand is even over the period and does not fluctuate through seasonality or other reasons. It also assumes that no 'buffer' stock is required. However, these limiting assumptions do not mean we should dismiss the model as being of little value. The model can be developed to accommodate the problems of uncertainty and uneven demand. Many businesses use this model (or a development of it) to help in the management of stocks.

Materials requirement planning systems

→ A **materials requirement planning (MRP) system** takes forecasts of sales demand as its starting point. It then uses computer technology to help schedule the timing of deliveries of bought-in parts and materials to coincide with production requirements. It is a co-ordinated approach that links materials and parts deliveries to their scheduled input to the production process. By ordering only those items that are necessary to ensure the flow of production, stock levels may therefore be reduced. MRP is really a 'top-down' approach to stock management, which recognises that stock ordering decisions cannot be viewed as being independent from production decisions. In recent years, this approach has been extended so as to provide a fully integrated approach to production planning. The approach also takes account of other manufacturing resources such as labour and machine capacity.

Just-in-time stock management

In recent years, some manufacturing businesses have tried to eliminate the need → to hold stocks by adopting **'just-in-time' (JIT) stock management**. This approach was first used in the United States defence industry during the Second World War, but in more recent times it has been widely used, particularly by Japanese businesses. The essence of JIT is, as the name suggests, to have supplies delivered to a business just in time for them to be used in the production process. By adopting this approach the stockholding problem rests with suppliers rather than with the business itself.

For JIT to be successful, it is important that the business informs suppliers of its production plans and requirements in advance, and that suppliers, in their turn, deliver materials of the right quality at the agreed times. Failure to do so could lead to a dislocation of production and could be very costly. Thus a close relationship is required between the business and its suppliers.

Though a business will not have to hold stocks, there may be certain costs associated with this approach. As the suppliers will be required to hold stocks for the business, they may try to recoup this additional cost through increased prices. The close relationship necessary between the business and its suppliers may also prevent the business from taking advantage of cheaper sources of supply if they become available.

Many people view JIT as more than simply a stock control system. The philosophy underpinning this method is concerned with eliminating waste and striving for excellence. There is an expectation that suppliers will always deliver parts on time and that there will be no defects in the parts supplied. There is also an expectation that the production process will operate at maximum efficiency. This means there will be no production breakdowns and the queuing and storage times of products manufactured will be eliminated, as only that time spent directly on processing the products is seen as adding value. While these expectations may be impossible to achieve, they do help to create a culture that is dedicated to the pursuit of excellence and quality.

Exhibit 11.3 shows how a very well-known UK business uses JIT to advantage.

Exhibit 11.3

JIT at Tesco

Tesco plc is one of the leading supermarket chains in the UK. To gain an advantage in the intensely competitive market, the business has invested heavily in technology to support its JIT system and other stock management systems. Laser technology is used to improve its distribution flow and to replenish stocks quickly. As a result, Tesco plc now holds less than two weeks of stock and almost half of the goods received from suppliers are sent immediately to the stores rather than to the warehouse.

The improvement in distribution procedures has allowed stores to reduce the amount of each line of stock held which, in turn, has made it possible to increase the number of lines of stock held by each store. It has also made it possible to convert storage space at the supermarkets into selling space.

Source: Information taken from an article appearing in *The Economist*, 1995

Managing debtors

Selling goods or services on credit results in costs being incurred by a business. These costs include credit administration costs, bad debts, and opportunities forgone in using the funds for more profitable purposes. However, these costs must be weighed against the benefits of increased sales resulting from the opportunity for customers to delay payment.

Selling on credit is very widespread, and appears to be the norm outside the retail trade. When a business offers to sell its goods or services on credit, it must have clear policies concerning:

- which customers it is prepared to offer credit to;
- what length of credit it is prepared to offer;
- whether discounts will be offered for prompt payment;
- what collection policies should be adopted.

In this section, we shall consider each of these issues.

Which customers should receive credit?

A business offering credit runs the risk of not receiving payment for goods or services supplied. Thus, care must be taken over the type of customer to whom credit facilities are offered. When considering a proposal from a customer for the supply of goods or services on credit, the business must take a number of factors into account. The following **five Cs of credit** provide a business with a useful checklist.

- *Capital.* The customer must appear to be financially sound before any credit is extended. Where the customer is a business, its financial statements should be examined. Particular regard should be given to the profitability and liquidity of the customer. In addition, any onerous financial commitments must be taken into account.
- *Capacity.* The customer must appear to have the capacity to pay amounts owing. Where possible, the payment record of the customer to date should be examined. If the customer is a business, the type of business operated and the physical resources of the business will be relevant. The value of goods that the customer wishes to buy on credit must be related to the total financial resources of the customer.
- *Collateral.* On occasions, it may be necessary to ask for some kind of security for goods supplied on credit. When this occurs, the business must be convinced that the customer is able to offer a satisfactory form of security.
- *Conditions.* The state of the industry in which the customer operates, and the general economic conditions of the particular region or country, may have an important influence on the ability of a customer to pay the amounts outstanding on the due date.
- *Character.* It is important for a business to make some assessment of the character of the customer. The willingness to pay will depend on the honesty and integrity of the individual with whom the business is dealing. Where the customer is a limited company this will mean assessing the characters of its directors. The business must feel satisfied that the customer will make every effort to pay any amounts owing.

Once a customer has been considered creditworthy, credit limits for the customer should be established, and procedures should be laid down to ensure that these are adhered to.

Activity 11.5

Assume that you are the credit manager of a business and that a limited company approaches you with a view to buying goods on credit. What sources of information might you decide to use to help assess the financial health of the potential customer?

There are various possibilities. You may have thought of some of the following:

- *Trade references.* Some businesses ask potential customers to supply them with references from other suppliers who have made sales on credit to them. This may

Activity 11.5 continued

> be extremely useful, provided that the references supplied are truly representative of the opinions of a customer's suppliers. There is a danger that a potential customer will attempt to be selective when giving details of other suppliers, in order to gain a more favourable impression than is deserved.
>
> ■ *Bank references.* It is possible to ask the potential customer for a bank reference. Though banks are usually prepared to supply references, the contents of such a reference are not always very informative. If customers are in financial difficulties, the bank may be unwilling to add to their problems by supplying poor references.
>
> ■ *Published financial statements.* A limited company is obliged by law to file a copy of its annual accounts with the Registrar of Companies. The financial statements are available for public inspection and provide a useful source of information.
>
> ■ *The customer.* You may wish to interview the directors of the customer business and visit its premises in an attempt to gain some impression about the way that the customer conducts its business. Where a significant amount of credit is required, the business may ask the customer for access to internal budgets and other unpublished financial information to help assess the level of risk involved.
>
> ■ *Credit agencies.* Specialist agencies exist to provide information that can be used to assess the creditworthiness of a potential customer. The information that a credit agency supplies may be gleaned from various sources, including the accounts of the customer, court judgements, and news items relating to the customer from both published and unpublished sources.

Length of credit period

A business must determine what credit terms it is prepared to offer its customers. The length of credit offered to customers can vary significantly between businesses, and may be influenced by such factors as:

■ the typical credit terms operating within the industry;
■ the degree of competition within the industry;
■ the bargaining power of particular customers;
■ the risk of non-payment;
■ the capacity of the business to offer credit;
■ the marketing strategy of the business.

The last point identified may require some explanation. The marketing strategy of a business may have an important influence on the length of credit allowed. For example, if a business wishes to increase its market share it may decide to liberalise its credit policy in an attempt to stimulate sales. Potential customers may be attracted by the offer of a longer credit period. However, any such change in policy must take account of the likely costs and benefits arising.

To illustrate this point, consider Example 11.2.

Example 11.2

Torrance Ltd produces a new type of golf putter. The business sells the putter to wholesalers and retailers and has an annual turnover of £600,000. The following data relate to each putter produced.

	£	£
Selling price		40
Variable costs	20	
Fixed cost apportionment	6	26
Net profit		14

The business's cost of capital is estimated at 10 per cent.

Torrance Ltd wishes to expand the sales volume of this new putter, and believes that offering a longer credit period can achieve this. The business's average collection period is currently 30 days. It is considering three options in an attempt to increase sales. These are as follows:

	Option		
	1	*2*	*3*
Increase in average collection period (days)	10	20	30
Increase in sales (£)	30,000	45,000	50,000

To enable the business to decide on the best option to adopt, it must weigh the benefits of the options against their respective costs. The benefits arising will be represented by the increase in profit from the sale of additional putters. From the cost data supplied we can see that the contribution (that is, selling price (£40) less variable costs (£20)) is £20 per putter, that is, 50 per cent of the selling price. So, whatever increase there may be in sales revenue, the additional contributions will be half of that figure. The fixed costs can be ignored in our calculations, as they will remain the same whichever option is chosen.

The increase in contribution under each option will therefore be:

	Option		
	1	*2*	*3*
50% of the increase in sales revenue (£)	15,000	22,500	25,000

The increase in debtors under each option will be as follows:

	Option		
	1	*2*	*3*
	£	£	£
Projected level of debtors			
40 × £630,000/365 (Note 1)	69,041		
50 × £645,000/365		88,356	
60 × £650,000/365			106,849
Less: Current level of debtors			
30 × £600,000/365	49,315	49,315	49,315
Increase in debtors	19,726	39,041	57,534

The increase in debtors that results from each option will mean an additional finance cost to the business.

The net increase in the business's profit arising from the projected change is:

	Option		
	1	2	3
	£	£	£
Increase in contribution (see above)	15,000	22,500	25,000
Less: Increase in finance cost (Note 2)	1,973	3,904	5,753
Net increase in profits	13,027	18,596	19,247

The calculations show that Option 3 will be the most profitable one.

Notes:

1 If the annual sales total £630,000 and 40 days' credit are allowed (both of which will apply under Option 1), the average amount that will be owed to the business by its customers, at any point during the year, will be the daily sales (that is, £630,000/365) multiplied by the number of days that the customers take to pay (that is 40).

    Exactly the same logic applies to Options 2 and 3 and to the current level of debtors.

2 The increase in the finance cost for Option 1 will be the increase in debtors (£19,726 × 10 per cent). The equivalent figures for the other options are derived in a similar way.

Example 11.2 illustrates the way in which a business should assess changes in credit terms. However, if there is a risk that, by extending the length of credit, there will be an increase in bad debts, this should also be taken into account in the calculations, as should any additional collection costs that will be incurred.

Cash discounts and interest on overdue debts

A business may decide to offer a **cash discount** in an attempt to encourage prompt payment from its credit customers. The size of any discount will be an important influence on whether a customer decides to pay promptly.

From the business's viewpoint, the cost of offering discounts must be weighed against the likely benefits in the form of a reduction both in the cost of financing debtors and in the amount of bad debts.

In practice, there is always the danger that a customer may be slow to pay and yet may still take the discount offered. Where the customer is important to the business it may be difficult for the business to insist on full payment.

Surveys indicate that small businesses have a much greater proportion of overdue debts than large businesses. In the UK, the government has intervened to help deal with this problem and the law now permits small businesses to charge interest on overdue accounts. However, it is unlikely that legislation alone will make a significant improvement. Many small businesses are concerned that large customers would view charging interest as a provocative act. What is really needed to help small businesses is a change in the payment culture.

? Self-assessment question 11.1

Williams Wholesalers Ltd at present requires payment from its customers by the end of the month after the month of delivery. On average it takes them 70 days to pay. Sales amount to £4 million a year and bad debts to £20,000 a year.

It is planned to offer customers a cash discount of 2 per cent for payment within 30 days. Williams estimates that 50 per cent of customers will accept this facility but that the remaining customers, who tend to be slow payers, will not pay until 80 days after the sale. At present the business has an overdraft facility at an interest rate of 13 per cent a year. If the plan goes ahead, bad debts will be reduced to £10,000 a year and there will be savings in credit administration expenses of £6,000 a year.

Should Williams Wholesalers Ltd offer the new credit terms to customers? You should support your answer with any calculations and explanations that you consider necessary.

Collection policies

A business offering credit must ensure that amounts owing are collected as quickly as possible. An efficient collection policy requires an efficient accounting system. Invoices must be sent out promptly along with regular monthly statements. Reminders must also be dispatched promptly where necessary.

When a business is faced with customers who do not pay, there should be agreed procedures for dealing with them. However, the cost of any action to be taken against delinquent debtors must be weighed against the likely returns. For example, there is little point in taking legal action against a customer and incurring large legal expenses if there is evidence that the customer does not have the necessary resources to pay. Where possible, the cost of bad debts should be taken into account when setting prices for products or services.

➡ Management can monitor the effectiveness of collection policies in a number of ways. One method is to calculate the **average settlement period for debtors** ratio, which we dealt with in Chapter 6. This ratio, we should recall, is calculated as follows:

$$\text{Average settlement period for debtors} = \frac{\text{Trade debtors}}{\text{Credit sales}} \times 365$$

Though this ratio can be useful, it is important to remember that it produces an *average* figure for the number of days for which debts are outstanding. This average may be badly distorted by a few large customers who are also very slow or very fast payers.

➡ A more detailed and informative approach to monitoring debtors is to produce an **ageing schedule of debtors**. Debts are divided into categories according to the length of time the debt has been outstanding. An ageing schedule can be produced for managers, on a regular basis, to help them see the pattern of outstanding debts. An example of an ageing schedule is set out in Example 11.3.

Example 11.3

Ageing schedule of debtors at 31 December 2003

Customer	Days outstanding				Total
	1 to 30 days	31 to 60 days	61 to 90 days	More than 90 days	
	£	£	£	£	£
A Ltd	20,000	10,000	–	–	30,000
B Ltd	–	24,000	–	–	24,000
C Ltd	12,000	13,000	14,000	18,000	57,000
Total	32,000	47,000	14,000	18,000	111,000

This shows a business's trade debtor figure at 31 December 2003, which totals £111,000. Each customer's balance is analysed according to how long the debt has been outstanding.

Thus we can see from the schedule that A Ltd has £20,000 outstanding for 30 days or less (that is, arising from sales during December 2003) and £10,000 outstanding for between 31 and 60 days (arising from November 2003 sales). This information can be very useful for credit control purposes.

Many accounting software packages now include this ageing schedule as one of the routine reports available to managers. Such packages often have the facility to put customers on 'hold' when they reach their credit limits.

Activity 11.6

What kind of corrective action might the managers of a business decide to take if they found that debtors were paying more slowly than anticipated?

Managers might decide to do one or more of the following:

■ Offer cash discounts to encourage prompt payment.
■ Change the collection period.
■ Improve the accounting system to ensure that customers are billed more promptly, reminders are sent out promptly, and so on.
■ Change the eligibility criteria for customers who receive credit.

As a footnote to our consideration of managing debtors, Exhibit 11.4 outlines some of the excuses that long-suffering credit managers must listen to when chasing payment for outstanding debt.

Exhibit 11.4

It's in the post

Accountants' noses should be growing, if we're to believe a new survey listing the bizarre excuses given by businesses that fail to pay their debts.

'The director's been shot' and 'I'll pay you when God tells me to' are just two of the most outrageous excuses listed in a survey published by the Credit Services Association, the debt collection industry body.

The commercial sector tends to blame financial problems, and excuses such as 'you'll get paid when we do' and 'the finance director is off sick' are common. However, those in the consumer sector apparently feel no shame in citing personal relationship problems as the reason for not paying the bill.

Source: Accountancy, April 2000, p. 18

Managing cash

Why hold cash?

Most businesses will hold a certain amount of cash. The amount of cash held tends to vary considerably between businesses.

Activity 11.7

Why do you think a business may decide to hold at least some of its assets in the form of cash? (*Hint*: There are broadly three reasons.)

The three are:

1 To meet day-to-day commitments, a business requires a certain amount of cash. Payments for wages, overhead expenses, goods purchased and so on must be made at the due dates.
2 If future cash flows are uncertain for any reason, it would be prudent to hold a balance of cash. For example, a major customer that owes a large sum to the business may be in financial difficulties. Given this situation, the business can retain its capacity to meet its obligations by holding a cash balance. Similarly, if there is some uncertainty concerning future outlays, a cash balance will be required.
3 A business may decide to hold cash to put itself in a position to exploit profitable opportunities as and when they arise. For example, by holding cash, a business may be able to acquire a competitor business that suddenly becomes available at an attractive price.

How much cash should be held?

Though cash can be held for each of the reasons identified, this may not always be necessary. If a business is able to borrow quickly, the amount of cash it needs to hold can be reduced. Similarly, if the business holds assets that can easily be con-verted to cash (for example, marketable securities such as shares in Stock Exchange listed businesses, government bonds), the amount of cash held can be reduced.

The decision as to how much cash a particular business should hold is a difficult one. Different businesses will have different views on the subject.

Activity 11.8

What do you think are the major factors that influence how much cash a business will hold? See if you can think of five possible factors.

You may have thought of the following:

- *The nature of the business*. Some businesses such as utilities (for example, water, elec-tricity and gas suppliers) may have cash flows that are both predictable and reasonably certain. This will enable them to hold lower cash balances. For some businesses, cash balances may vary greatly according to the time of year. A seasonal business may accumulate cash during the high season to enable it to meet commitments during the low season.
- *The opportunity cost of holding cash*. Where there are profitable opportunities it may not be wise to hold a large cash balance.
- *The level of inflation*. Holding cash during a period of rising prices will lead to a loss of purchasing power. The higher the level of inflation, the greater will be this loss.
- *The availability of near-liquid assets*. If a business has marketable securities or stocks that may easily be liquidated, the amount of cash held may be reduced.
- *The availability of borrowing*. If a business can borrow easily (and quickly) there is less need to hold cash.
- *The cost of borrowing*. When interest rates are high, the option of borrowing becomes less attractive.
- *Economic conditions*. When the economy is in recession, businesses may prefer to hold cash so that they can be well placed to invest when the economy improves. In addition, during a recession, businesses may experience difficulties in collecting debts. They may therefore hold higher cash balances than usual in order to meet commitments.
- *Relationships with suppliers*. Too little cash may hinder the ability of the business to pay suppliers promptly. This can lead to a loss of goodwill. It may also lead to discounts being forgone.

Controlling the cash balance

Several models have been developed to help control the cash balance of the business. One such model proposes the use of upper and lower control limits for cash balances and the use of a target cash balance. The model assumes that the business will invest in marketable investments that can easily be liquidated. These

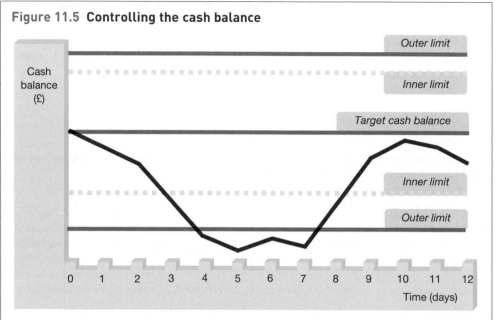

Figure 11.5 **Controlling the cash balance**

Upper and lower limits are set by management for the business's cash balance. When the balance goes beyond either the upper or lower limits, unless it is clear that the balance will return fairly quickly to within the upper or lower limit respectively, action will need to be taken. If the upper limit is breached, some cash will be used to buy some marketable securities. If the lower limit is breached, the business will need to sell some securities or borrow some cash.

investments will be purchased or sold, as necessary, in order to keep the cash balance within the control limits.

The model proposes two upper and two lower control limits (see Figure 11.5). If the business exceeds an *outer* limit, the managers must decide whether or not the cash balance is likely to return to a point within the *inner* control limits set, over the next few days. If this seems likely, then no action is required. If, on the other hand, it does not seem likely, management must change the cash position of the business by either buying or selling marketable securities.

In Figure 11.5 we can see that the lower outer control limit has been breached for four days. If a four-day period is unacceptable, managers must sell marketable securities to replenish the cash balance.

The model relies heavily on management judgement to determine where the control limits are set and the time period within which breaches of the control limits are acceptable. Past experience may be useful in helping managers decide on these issues. There are other models, however, that do not rely on management judgement and which, instead, use quantitative techniques to determine an optimal cash policy.

Cash budgets and managing cash

To manage cash effectively, it is useful for a business to prepare a cash budget. This is a very important tool for both planning and control purposes. Cash budgets were considered in Chapter 9, and so we shall not consider them again in detail. However, it is worth repeating the point that these statements enable the managers of a business to see the expected outcome of planned events on the cash balance. The cash budget will identify periods when cash surpluses and cash deficits are expected.

When a cash surplus is expected to arise, managers must decide on the best use of the surplus funds. When a cash deficit is expected, managers must make adequate provision by borrowing, liquidating assets or rescheduling cash payments/ receipts to deal with this. Cash budgets are useful in helping to control the cash held. The actual cash flows can be compared with the budgeted cash flows for the period. If there is a significant divergence between the budgeted cash flows and the actual cash flows, explanations must be sought and corrective action taken where necessary.

It would probably be helpful to look back at p. 250, Chapter 9 to refresh your memory on cash budgets.

Though cash budgets are prepared primarily for internal management purposes, prospective lenders sometimes require them when a loan to a business is being considered.

Operating cash cycle

When managing cash, it is important to be aware of the **operating cash cycle** of the business. This may be defined as the time period between the outlay of cash necessary for the purchase of stocks and the ultimate receipt of cash from the sale of the goods. In the case of a business that purchases goods on credit for subsequent resale on credit, the operating cash cycle is as shown in Figure 11.6.

Figure 11.6 shows that payment for goods acquired on credit occurs some time after the goods have been purchased, and therefore no immediate cash outflow arises from the purchase. Similarly, cash receipts from debtors will occur some time after the sale is made, and so there will be no immediate cash inflow as a result of the sale. The operating cash cycle is the time period between the payment made to the creditor for goods supplied and the cash received from the debtor.

The operating cash cycle is important because it has a significant influence on the financing requirements of the business: the longer the cash cycle, the greater the financing requirements of the business and the greater the financial risks. For this reason, a business is likely to want to reduce the operating cash cycle to the minimum possible period.

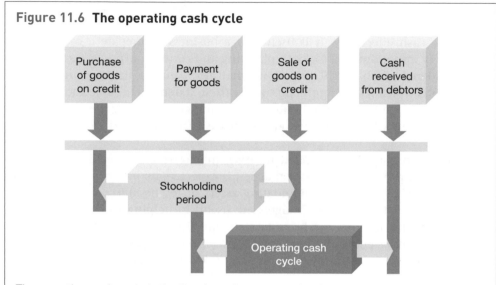

Figure 11.6 **The operating cash cycle**

The operating cash cycle is the time lapse between paying for goods and receiving the cash from the sale of those goods. The length of the operating cash cycle has a significant impact on the amount of funds that the business needs to apply to working capital.

For the type of business mentioned above, which buys and sells on credit, the operating cash cycle can be calculated from the financial statements by the use of certain ratios. The cash cycle is calculated as shown in Figure 11.7.

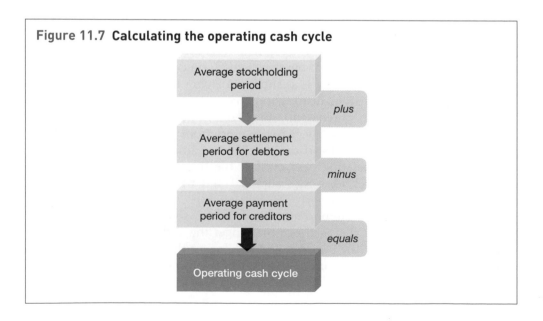

Figure 11.7 **Calculating the operating cash cycle**

Activity 11.9

The financial statements of Freezeqwik Ltd, a distributor of frozen foods, are set out below for the year ended 31 December last year.

Profit and loss account for the year ended 31 December last year

	£000	£000
Sales		820
Less Cost of sales		
Opening stock	142	
Purchases	568	
	710	
Less Closing stock	166	544
Gross profit		276
Administration expenses	(120)	
Selling and distribution expenses	(95)	
Financial expenses	(32)	(247)
Net profit		29
Corporation tax		(7)
Net profit after tax		22

Balance sheet as at 31 December last year

	£000	£000	£000
Fixed assets			
Freehold premises at valuation			180
Fixtures and fittings at written-down value			82
Motor vans at written-down value			102
			364
Current assets			
Stock		166	
Trade debtors		264	
Cash		24	
		454	
Less Creditors: amounts falling due within one year			
Trade creditors	159		
Corporation tax	7	166	288
			652
Capital and reserves			
Ordinary share capital			300
Preference share capital			200
Retained profit			152
			652

All purchases and sales are on credit.

Calculate the operating cash cycle for the business and go on to suggest how the business may seek to reduce the length of the cash cycle.

▶

Activity 11.9 continued

The operating cash cycle may be calculated as follows:

Average stockholding period: *No. of days*

$$\frac{\text{(Opening stock + Closing stock)/2}}{\text{Cost of sales}} \times 365 = \frac{(142 + 166)/2}{544} \times 365 \qquad\qquad 103$$

Average settlement period for debtors:

$$\frac{\text{Trade debtors}}{\text{Credit sales}} \times 365 = \frac{264}{820} \times 365 \qquad\qquad \underline{118}$$

$$221$$

Less
Average settlement period for creditors:

$$\frac{\text{Trade creditors}}{\text{Credit purchases}} \times 365 = \frac{159}{568} \times 365 \qquad\qquad \underline{102}$$

Operating cash cycle $\underline{119}$

The business can reduce the operating cash cycle in a number of ways. The average stockholding period seems quite long. At present, average stocks held represent more than three months' sales. Lowering the level of stocks held will reduce this. Similarly, the average settlement period for debtors seems long, at nearly four months' sales. Imposing tighter credit control, offering discounts, charging interest on overdue accounts, and so on, may reduce this. However, any policy decisions concerning stocks and debtors must take account of current trading conditions.

Extending the period of credit taken to pay suppliers could also reduce the operating cash cycle. However, for reasons that will be explained later, this option must be given careful consideration.

Cash transmission

A business will normally wish to benefit from receipts from customers at the earliest opportunity. The benefit is immediate where payment is made in cash. However, when payment is made by cheque, there is normally a delay of three to four working days before the cheque can be cleared through the banking system. The business must therefore wait for this period before it can benefit from the amount paid in. In the case of a business that receives large amounts in the form of cheques, the opportunity cost of this delay can be very significant.

To avoid this delay, a business could require payments to be made in cash. This is not usually very practical, for a number of reasons. Another option is to ask for payment to be made by standing order or by direct debit from the customer's bank account. This should ensure that the amount owing is always transferred from the bank account of the customer to the bank account of the business on the day that has been agreed.

It is also possible for funds to be transferred directly to a business's bank account. As a result of developments in computer technology, customers can pay for items by using debit cards, which results in the appropriate account being instantly debited and sellers' bank accounts being instantly credited with the required amount. This method of payment is widely used by large retail businesses, and may well extend to other types of business.

Bank overdrafts

Bank overdrafts are simply negative bank current accounts, that contain a negative amount of cash. They are a type of bank loan. We look at these in Chapter 12, p. 368 in the context of short-term bank lending. They can be a useful tool in managing the business's cash flow requirements.

Managing trade creditors

Trade credit arises from the fact that most businesses buy their goods and service requirements on credit. In effect, suppliers are lending the business money, interest free, on a short-term basis. Trade creditors are the other side of the coin from trade debtors. One business's trade creditor is another one's trade debtor, in respect of a particular transaction. Trade creditors are an important source of finance for most businesses. It has been described as a 'spontaneous' source, as it tends to increase in line with the increase in the level of activity achieved by a business. Trade credit is widely regarded as a 'free' source of finance and, therefore, a good thing for a business to use. There may be real costs associated with taking trade credit, however.

Firstly, customers who take credit may not be as well favoured as those who pay immediately. For example, when goods are in short supply, credit customers may receive lower priority when allocating the stock available. In addition, credit customers may be less favoured, in terms of delivery dates or the provision of technical support services. Sometimes, the goods or services provided may be more costly if credit is required. However, in most industries trade credit is the norm and, as a result, the above costs will not apply unless, perhaps, the customers abuse the credit facilities. A business purchasing supplies on credit may also have to incur additional administration and accounting costs in dealing with the scrutiny and payment of invoices, maintaining and updating creditors' accounts, and so on.

Where a supplier offers a discount for prompt payment, a business should give careful consideration to the possibility of paying within the discount period. An example may be useful to illustrate the cost of forgoing possible discounts.

Example 11.4

Hassan Ltd takes 70 days to pay for goods from its supplier. To encourage prompt payment, the supplier has offered the business a 2 per cent discount if payment for goods is made within 30 days.

Hassan Ltd is not sure whether it is worth taking the discount offered.

If the discount is taken, payment could be made on the last day of the discount period (that is, the 30th day). However, if the discount is not taken, payment will be made after 70 days. This means that by not taking the discount the business will receive an extra 40 days' (that is, 70 minus 30) credit. The cost of this extra credit to the business will be the 2 per cent discount forgone. If we annualise the cost of this discount forgone, we have:

$$365/40 \times 2\% = 18.3\%*$$

* This is an approximate annual rate. For the more mathematically minded, the precise rate is:

$$(((1 + 2/98)^{9.125}) - 1) \times 100\% = 20.2\%$$

We can see that the annual cost of forgoing the discount is very high, and it may be profitable for the business to pay the supplier within the discount period, even if it means that it will have to borrow to enable it to do so.

The above points are not meant to imply that taking credit is a burden to a business. There are of course real benefits that can accrue. Provided that trade credit is not abused, it can represent a form of interest-free loan. It can be a much more convenient method of paying for goods and services than paying by cash, and during a period of inflation there will be an economic gain by paying later rather than sooner for goods and services purchased. For most businesses, these benefits will exceed the costs involved.

Controlling trade creditors

To help monitor the level of trade credit taken, management can calculate the **average settlement period for creditors**. As we saw in Chapter 6, this ratio was as follows:

$$\text{Average settlement period} = \frac{\text{Trade creditors}}{\text{Credit purchases}} \times 365$$

Once again this provides an average figure, which could be misleading. A more informative approach would be to produce an ageing schedule for creditors. This would look much the same as the ageing schedule for debtors described earlier.

Summary

The main points of this chapter may be summarised as follows:

- *Working capital (WC) = stock + debtors + cash − creditors − bank overdrafts.*
  - ❑ An investment in WC cannot be avoided in practice – typically large amounts are involved.

- *Stock-in-trade.*
  - Costs of holding stock include:
    - lost interest;
    - storage cost;
    - insurance cost;
    - obsolescence.
  - Costs of not holding sufficient stock include:
    - loss of sales and customer goodwill;
    - production dislocation;
    - loss of flexibility – cannot take advantage of opportunities;
    - reorder costs – low stock implies more frequent ordering.
  - Practical points on stock management include:
    - identify optimum order size – models can help with this;
    - set stock reorder levels;
    - use budgets;
    - keep reliable stock records;
    - use accounting ratios (for example, stock turnover period ratio);
    - establish systems for security of stock and authorisation;
    - consider just-in-time (JIT) stock management.

- *Trade debtors:*
  - Five Cs of credit:
    - capital;
    - capacity;
    - collateral;
    - condition;
    - character.
  - Costs of allowing credit:
    - lost interest;
    - lost purchasing power;
    - costs of assessing customer creditworthiness;
    - administration cost;
    - bad debts;
    - cash discounts (for prompt payment).
  - Costs of denying credit:
    - loss of customer goodwill.
  - Practical points on debtor management:
    - establish a policy;
    - assess and monitor customer creditworthiness;
    - establish effective administration of debtors;
    - establish a policy on bad debts;
    - consider cash discounts;
    - use accounting ratios (for example, average settlement period for debtors ratio);
    - use ageing summaries.

- *Cash.*
  - Costs of holding cash:
    - lost interest;
    - lost purchasing power.
  - Costs of holding insufficient cash:
    - loss of supplier goodwill if unable to meet commitments on time;
    - loss of opportunities;
    - inability to claim cash discounts;
    - costs of borrowing (should an obligation need to be met at short notice).
  - Practical points on cash management:
    - establish a policy;
    - plan cash flows;
    - make judicious use of bank overdraft finance – it can be cheap and flexible;
    - use short-term cash surpluses profitably;
    - bank frequently;
    - transmit cash promptly;
    - operating cash cycle (for a retailer) = length of time from buying stock to receiving cash from debtors less creditors' payment period (in days).
  - An objective of WC management is to limit the length of the operating cash cycle, subject to any risks that this may cause.

- *Trade creditors*:
  - Costs of taking credit:
    - higher price than purchases for immediate cash settlement;
    - administrative costs;
    - restrictions imposed by seller.
  - Costs of not taking credit:
    - lost interest-free borrowing;
    - lost purchasing power;
    - inconvenience – paying at the time of purchase can be inconvenient.
  - Practical points on creditor management:
    - establish a policy;
    - exploit free credit as far as possible;
    - use accounting ratios (for example, average settlement period ratio).

→ Key terms

working capital   *p 318*
ABC system of stock control   *p 324*
economic order quantity
  (EOQ)   *p 326*
materials requirement planning
  (MRP) system   *p 328*
just-in-time (JIT) stock management
  p 328

five Cs of credit   *p 330*
cash discount   *p 333*
average settlement period for
  debtors   *p 334*
ageing schedule of debtors   *p 334*
operating cash cycle   *p 339*
average settlement period for
  creditors   *p 344*

? Review questions

Answers to these questions can be found on the students' side of the Companion Website.

11.1 Tariq is the credit manager of Heltex plc. He is concerned that the pattern of monthly sales receipts shows that credit collection is poor compared with budget. Heltex's sales director believes that Tariq is to blame for this situation, but Tariq insists that he is not. Why might Tariq not be to blame for the deterioration in the credit collection period?

11.2 How might each of the following affect the level of stocks held by a business?
- an increase in the number of production bottlenecks experienced by the business;
- a rise in the level of interest rates;
- a decision to offer customers a narrower range of products in the future;
- a switch of suppliers from an overseas business to a local business;
- a deterioration in the quality and reliability of bought-in components.

11.3 What are the reasons for holding stocks? Are these reasons different from the reasons for holding cash?

11.4 Identify the costs of holding:
(a) too little cash, and
(b) too much cash.

? Exercises

Exercises 11.4 and 11.5 are more advanced than 11.1–11.3. Those with a coloured number have an answer at the back of the book.

11.1 Hercules Wholesalers Ltd has been particularly concerned with its liquidity position in recent months. The most recent profit and loss account and balance sheet of the business are as follows:

Profit and loss account for the year ended 31 December last year

	£000	£000
Sales		452
Less Cost of sales		
Opening stock	125	
Add purchases	341	
	466	
Less Closing stock	143	323
Gross profit		129
Expenses		132
Net loss for the period		(3)

Balance sheet as at 31 December last year

	£000	£000	£000
Fixed assets			
Freehold premises at valuation			280
Fixtures and fittings at cost less depreciation			25
Motor vehicles at cost less depreciation			52
			357
Current assets			
Stock		143	
Debtors		163	
		306	
Less Creditors due within one year			
Trade creditors	145		
Bank overdraft	140	285	21
			378
Less Creditors due after more than one year			
Loans			120
			258
Capital and reserves			
Ordinary share capital			100
Retained profit			158
			258

The debtors and creditors were maintained at a constant level throughout the year.

Required:

(a) Explain why Hercules Wholesalers Ltd is concerned about its liquidity position.

(b) Explain the term *operating cash cycle* and state why this concept is important in the financial management of a business.

(c) Calculate the operating cash cycle for Hercules Wholesalers Ltd based on the information above. (Assume a 360-day year.)

(d) State what steps may be taken to improve the operating cash cycle of the business.

11.2 International Electric plc at present offers its customers 30 days' credit. Half the customers, by value, pay on time. The other half takes an average of 70 days to pay. It is considering offering a cash discount of 2 per cent to its customers for payment within 30 days.

It anticipates that half of the customers who now take an average of 70 days to pay (that is, a quarter of all customers) will pay in 30 days. The other half (the final quarter) will still take an average of 70 days to pay. The scheme will also reduce bad debts by £300,000 a year.

Annual sales of £365 million are made evenly throughout the year. At present the business has a large overdraft (£60 million) with its bank at 12 per cent a year.

Required:

(a) Calculate the approximate equivalent annual percentage cost of a discount of 2 per cent, which reduces the time taken by debtors to pay from 70 days to 30 days. (*Hint*: This part can be answered without reference to the narrative above.)

(b) Calculate debtors outstanding under both the old and new schemes.

(c) How much will the scheme cost the business in discounts?

(d) Should the business go ahead with the scheme? State what other factors, if any, should be taken into account.

(e) Outline the controls and procedures that a business should adopt to manage the level of its debtors.

11.3 The managing director of Sparkrite Ltd, a trading business, has just received summary sets of statements for last year and this year:

Sparkrite Ltd

Profit and loss accounts for years ended 30 September last year and this year

	Last year		This year	
	£000	£000	£000	£000
Sales		1,800		1,920
Less Cost of sales				
Opening stock	160		200	
Purchases	1,120		1,175	
	1,280		1,375	
Less Closing stock	200		250	
		1,080		1,125
Gross profit		720		795
Less Expenses		680		750
Net profit		40		45

Balance sheets as at 30 September last year and this year

	Last year		This year	
	£000	£000	£000	£000
Fixed assets		950		930
Current assets				
Stock	200		250	
Debtors	375		480	
Bank	4		2	
	579		732	
Less Current liabilities	195		225	
		384		507
		1,334		1,437
Financed by				
Fully paid £1 ordinary shares		825		883
Reserves		509		554
		1,334		1,437

The finance director has expressed concern at the increase in stock and debtors levels.

Required:

(a) Show, by using the data given, how you would calculate ratios that could be used to measure stock and debtor levels during last year and this year.

(b) Discuss the ways in which the management of Sparkrite Ltd could exercise control over:

(i) stock levels;

(ii) debtor levels.

11.4 Your superior, the general manager of Plastics Manufacturers Limited, has recently been talking to the chief buyer of Plastic Toys Limited, which manufactures a wide range of toys for young children. At present, Plastic Toys is considering changing its supplier of plastic granules and has offered to buy its entire requirement of 2,000 kg a month from you at the going market rate, provided that you will grant it three months' credit on its purchases. The following information is available:

1 Plastic granules sell for £10 a kg, variable costs are £7 a kg, and fixed costs £2 a kg.

2 Your own business is financially strong, and has sales of £15 million a year. For the foreseeable future it will have surplus capacity, and it is actively looking for new outlets.

3 Extracts from Plastic Toys' financial statements:

Year	1	2	3
	£000	£000	£000
Sales	800	980	640
Profit before interest and tax	100	110	(150)
Capital employed	600	650	575

Year	1	2	3
	£000	£000	£000
Current assets			
Stocks	200	220	320
Debtors	140	160	160
	340	380	480
Current liabilities			
Creditors	180	190	220
Overdraft	100	150	310
	280	340	530
Net current assets	60	40	(50)

Required:

(a) Write some short notes suggesting sources of information that you would use to assess the creditworthiness of potential customers who are unknown to you. You should critically evaluate each source of information.

(b) Describe the accounting controls that you would use to monitor the level of your business's trade debtors.

(c) Advise your general manager on the acceptability of the proposal. You should give your reasons and do any calculations you consider necessary. (*Hint*: To answer this question you must weigh the costs of administration and cash discounts against the savings in bad debts and interest charges.)

11.5 Mayo Computers Ltd has an annual turnover of £20 million before taking into account bad debts of £0.1 million. All sales made by the business are on credit, and, at present, credit terms are negotiable by the customer. On average, the settlement period for trade debtors is 60 days. The business is currently reviewing its credit policies to see whether more efficient and profitable methods could be employed. Only one proposal has so far been put forward concerning the management of trade credit.

The credit control department has proposed that customers should be given a 2½ per cent discount if they pay within 30 days. For those who do not pay within this period, a maximum of 50 days' credit should be given. The credit department believes that 60 per cent of customers will take advantage of the discount by paying at the end of the discount period, and the remainder will pay at the end of 50 days. The credit department believes that bad debts can be effectively eliminated by adopting the above policies and by employing stricter credit investigation procedures, which will cost an additional £20,000 a year. The credit department is confident that these new policies will not result in any reduction in sales.

Required:
Calculate the net annual cost (savings) to the business of abandoning its existing credit policies and adopting the proposals of the credit control department. (*Hint*: In order to answer this question you must weigh the costs of administration and cash discounts against the savings in bad debts and interest charges.)

Chapter 12

Financing a business

Introduction

In this final chapter we examine various aspects of financing a business. We begin by considering the various sources of finance available to a business. Some of these sources have already been touched upon when we discussed the structure of limited companies in Chapter 6 and the management of working capital in Chapter 11. In this chapter, we shall discuss these sources in more detail as well as discussing other sources of finance that have not been mentioned earlier. The factors to be taken into account when choosing an appropriate source of finance will also be examined.

Following our consideration of the main sources of finance, we shall go on to examine various aspects of the capital markets including the role of the Stock Exchange, the financing of smaller businesses, and the ways in which share capital may be issued.

Objectives

On completion of this chapter, you should be able to:

- **identify the main sources of finance available to a business and explain the advantages and disadvantages of each source**
- **explain the role and nature of the Stock Exchange**
- **discuss the ways in which smaller businesses may seek to raise finance**
- **outline the ways in which share capital may be issued.**

Sources of finance

When considering the various sources of finance for a business, it is useful to distinguish between *external* sources and *internal* sources of finance. Within each of these two categories, we can further distinguish between *long-term* and *short-term* sources. In the sections that immediately follow, we consider the various sources of

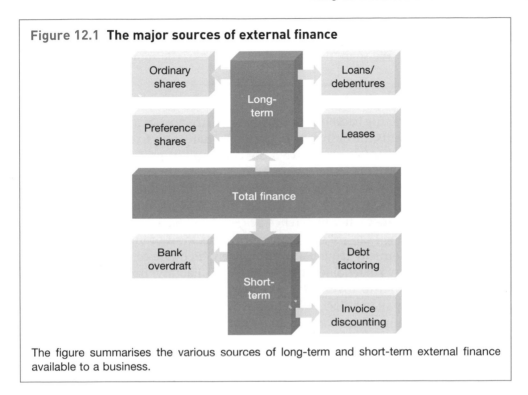

Figure 12.1 **The major sources of external finance**

The figure summarises the various sources of long-term and short-term external finance available to a business.

external finance. We then go on to consider the various sources of internal finance available.

Figure 12.1 summarises the main sources of long-term and short-term external finance. By external sources we mean sources that require the agreement of someone beyond the directors and managers of the business. Thus, finance from an issue of new shares is an external source because it requires the compliance of potential shareholders. Retained profit, on the other hand, is considered an internal source because the directors of the business have power to retain profits without the agreement of the shareholders, whose profits they are.

Long-term sources of external finance

For the purpose of this chapter, long-term sources of finance are defined as sources of finance that are not due for repayment within one year. As Figure 12.1 reveals, the major forms of long-term external finance are:

- ordinary shares;
- preference shares;
- loans;
- leases, that is, finance leases and sale-and-leaseback arrangements.

In order to decide on the form of external finance that is most appropriate for the particular needs of a business, we must be clear about the advantages and disadvantages of each. We shall, therefore, discuss each of the sources identified.

Ordinary shares

Ordinary shares form the backbone of the financial structure of a business. Ordinary share capital represents the business's risk capital. There is no fixed rate of dividend, and ordinary shareholders will receive a dividend only if profits available for distribution still remain after other investors (preference shareholders and lenders) have received their interest or dividend payments. If the business is wound up, the ordinary shareholders will receive any proceeds from asset disposals only after lenders and creditors and, often, after preference shareholders have received their entitlements. Because of the high risks associated with this form of investment, ordinary shareholders will normally require a comparatively high rate of return.

Although ordinary shareholders have limited loss liability, based on the amount that they have agreed to invest, the potential returns from their investment are unlimited. Ordinary shareholders will also have control over the business. They will be given voting rights, which will give them the power to elect the directors and to remove the directors from office.

From the business's perspective, ordinary shares can be a valuable form of financing as, at times, it is useful to be able to avoid paying a dividend.

Activity 12.1

Under what circumstances might a business find it useful to avoid paying a dividend?

Two circumstances spring to mind. An expanding business may prefer to retain funds in order to help fuel future growth. A business in difficulties may need the funds to meet its operating costs and so may find making a dividend payment a real burden.

Although a business financed by ordinary shares can avoid making cash payments to shareholders when it is not prudent to do so, the costs of ordinary shares may become higher if shareholders feel uncertain about future dividends. It is also worth pointing out that the business does not obtain any tax relief on dividends paid to shareholders, whereas interest on borrowings is tax deductible.

Preference shares

Preference shares offer investors a lower level of risk than ordinary shares. Provided there are sufficient profits available, preference shares will normally be given a fixed rate of dividend each year, and preference dividends will be paid before ordinary dividends are paid. Should the business be wound up, preference shareholders may be given priority over the claims of ordinary shareholders. (The documents of incorporation will determine the precise rights of preference shareholders in this respect.)

Activity 12.2

Would you expect the returns to preference shares to be higher or lower than those of ordinary shares?

Because of the lower level of risk associated with this form of investment, investors will be offered a lower level of return than that normally expected by ordinary shareholders.

Preference shares are no longer an important source of new finance. A major reason why this particular form of fixed-return capital has declined in popularity is that dividends paid to preference shareholders are not allowable against taxable profits, whereas interest on loan capital is an allowable expense. From the business's point of view, preference shares and loans are quite similar, so the tax deductibility of loan interest is an important issue.

Activity 12.3

Would you expect the market price of ordinary shares or preference shares to be the more volatile? Why?

The dividends of preference shares tend to be fairly stable over time, and there is usually an upper limit on the returns that can be received. As a result, the share price, which reflects the expected future returns from the share, will normally be less volatile than for ordinary shares.

Both preference shares and ordinary shares may be *redeemable*, which means that the company is allowed to buy back the shares from shareholders at some agreed future date.

Loans and debentures

Many businesses rely on loans as well as share capital to finance operations. Lenders will enter into a contract with the business in which the rate of interest, dates of interest payments and capital repayments and security for the loan are clearly stated. In the event that the interest payments or capital repayments are not made on the due dates, the lender will usually have the right, under the terms of the contract, to seize the assets on which the loan is secured and sell them in order to repay the amount outstanding. Security for a loan may take the form of a fixed charge on particular assets of the business (freehold land and premises are often favoured by lenders) or a floating charge on the whole of its assets. A floating charge will 'crystallise' and fix on particular assets in the event that the business defaults on its obligations.

Activity 12.4

What do you think is the advantage for the business of having a floating charge rather than a fixed charge on its assets?

A floating charge on assets will allow the managers greater flexibility in their day-to-day operations than a fixed charge. Assets can be traded without reference to the lenders.

One form of long-term loan is the **term loan.** This type of loan is offered by banks and other financial institutions and can be tailored to the needs of the client business. The amount of the loan, the time period of the loan, the repayment terms and the interest payable are all open to negotiation and agreement, which can be very useful. For example, where all of the funds to be borrowed are not required immediately, a business may agree with the lender that funds are drawn only as and when required. This means that interest will be paid only on amounts drawn and the business will not have to pay interest on amounts borrowed that are temporarily surplus to requirements.

Another form of long-term loan finance is the **debenture.** This is simply a loan that is evidenced by a trust deed. The debenture loan is frequently divided into units (rather like share capital), and investors are invited to purchase the number of units they require. The debenture loan may be redeemable or irredeemable. Debentures of public limited companies are often traded on the Stock Exchange, and their listed value will fluctuate according to the fortunes of the business, movements in interest rates, and so on.

Yet another form of long-term loan finance is the **eurobond.** Eurobonds are issued by businesses (and other large organisations) in various countries, and the finance is raised on an international basis. They are bearer bonds, which are often issued in US dollars but which may also be issued in other major currencies. Interest is normally paid on an annual basis. Eurobonds are part of an emerging international capital market, and they are not subject to regulations imposed by authorities in particular countries. There is a market for eurobonds that has been created by a number of financial institutions throughout the world. Here holders of eurobonds are able to sell them to would-be holders. The issue of eurobonds is usually made by placing them with large banks and other financial institutions, which may either retain them as an investment or sell them to their clients.

The extent of borrowing, by UK businesses, in currencies other than sterling has expanded massively in recent years. Businesses are often attracted to eurobonds because of the size of the international capital market. Access to a large number of international investors is likely to increase the chances of a successful issue. In addition, the lack of regulation in the eurobond market means that national restrictions regarding loan issues may be overcome.

Activity 12.5

Would you expect the returns to loan capital to be higher or lower than those of preference shares?

Investors will normally view loans as being less risky than preference shares. Lenders have priority over any claims from preference shareholders, and will usually have security for their loans. As a result of the lower level of risk associated with this form of investment, investors are usually prepared to accept a lower rate of return.

Figure 12.2 **The risk/return characteristics of long-term capital**

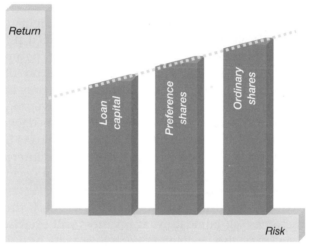

The figure shows that the higher the level of risk associated with a particular form of long-term capital, the higher will be the expected returns from investors. Ordinary shares are the most risky and have the highest expected return and, as a general rule, loan capital Is the least risky and has the lowest expected return.

Interest rates and deep discount bonds

Interest rates on loan finance may be either floating or fixed. A floating rate means that the required rate of return from lenders will rise and fall with market rates of interest. However, the market value of the lender's investment in the business is likely to remain fairly stable over time. The converse will normally be true for fixed-interest loans and debentures. The interest payments will remain unchanged with rises and falls in market rates of interest, but the value of the loan investment will fall when interest rates rise and will rise when interest rates fall.

A business may issue redeemable loan capital that offers a rate of interest below the market rate. In some cases, the loan capital may have a zero rate of interest. Such loans are issued at a discount to their redeemable value and are referred to as *deep discount bonds.* Thus loan capital may be issued at, say, £80 for every £100 of nominal value. Although lenders will receive little or no interest during the period of the loan, they will receive a gain when the loan is finally redeemed. The redemption yield, as it is referred to, is often quite high and, when calculated on an annual basis, may compare favourably with returns from other forms of loan capital with the same level of risk. Deep discount bonds may have particular appeal to businesses with short-term cash flow problems. They receive an immediate injection of cash, and there are no significant cash outflows associated with the loan until the maturity date. Deep discount bonds are likely to appeal to investors who do not have short-term cash flow needs, since they must wait for the loan to mature before receiving a significant return.

Convertible loan stocks and debentures

Convertible loan stocks or debentures give investors the right to convert a loan into ordinary shares at a given future date and at a specified price. The investor remains a lender to the business, and will receive interest on the amount of the loan until such time as the conversion takes place. The investor is not obliged to convert the loan (or debenture) to ordinary shares. This will be done only if the market price of the shares at the conversion date exceeds the agreed conversion price.

An investor may find this form of investment a useful hedge against risk. This may be particularly useful when investment in a new business is being considered. Initially the investment is in the form of a loan, and regular interest payments will be made. If the business is successful, the investor can then decide to convert the investment into ordinary shares.

The business may also find this form of financing useful. If the business is successful, the loan becomes self-liquidating, as investors will exercise their option to convert. The business may also be able to offer a lower rate of interest to investors because investors expect future benefits arising from conversion. There will be, however, some dilution of both control and earnings for existing shareholders if holders of convertible loans exercise their option to convert.

Exhibit 12.1

Man launches £350m convertible bond

Man Group is a financial institution that has issued a convertible bond (or loan). The amount raised is £350 million and will be used to pay off some of the borrowings of the business, which increased sharply following the acquisition of other financial institutions for £933 million. According to the *Financial Times*:

> Bondholders will be able to convert the debt into Man shares at £12.82 a share, which represents a 32 per cent premium over yesterday's share price. The coupon* on the bonds was set at 3.75 per cent.
> The bond issue, which matures in 2009, was 'five or six' times subscribed, according to Stanley Fink, chief executive.

* Interest rate.

Source: Financial Times, 8 November 2002, p. 24

Figure 12.3 plots the issues of capital made by UK-listed businesses in recent years. The chart reveals that loan capital and ordinary shares are the major sources of long-term external finance. Preference shares are a much less important source of new finance.

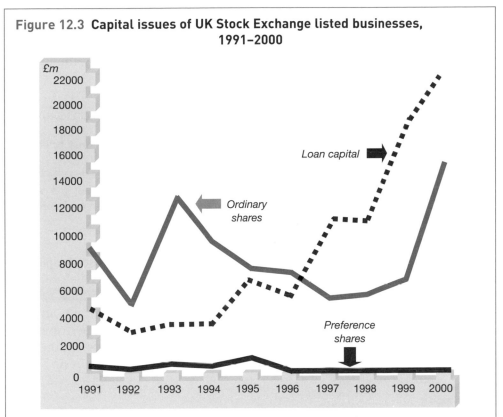

Figure 12.3 Capital issues of UK Stock Exchange listed businesses, 1991–2000

At times, the popularity of ordinary shares and that of loan capital seem to move counter to one another. When ordinary shares are popular loan capital is unpopular, and vice versa. This tends to reflect the level of interest rates and business confidence. However, in recent years, ordinary share issues and loan capital issues have both moved in the same direction. Preference shares have dwindled to virtually nothing, in terms of new issues. The chart, of course, is not the whole story. Most finance from ordinary shareholders comes from profit retentions rather than share issues. In addition, bank loans are not included.

Source: Copyright © 2001 Crown Copyright, Crown copyright material is reproduced with the permission of the Controller of HMSO

Warrants

Holders of **warrants** have the right, but not the obligation, to acquire ordinary shares in a business at a given price. In the case of both convertible loan capital and warrants, the price at which shares may be acquired is usually higher than the market price prevailing at the time of issue. The warrant will usually state the number of shares that the holder may purchase and the time limit within which the option to buy shares can be exercised. Occasionally, perpetual warrants are issued that have no set time limits. Warrants do not confer voting rights or entitle the holders to make any claims on the assets of the business.

Share warrants are often provided as a 'sweetener' to accompany the issue of loan capital or debentures. The issue of warrants in this way may enable the business to offer lower rates of interest on the loan or to negotiate less restrictive loan conditions. The issue of warrants enables the lenders to benefit from any future success of the business, provided that the option to purchase is exercised by the investor (warrant holder).

Activity 12.6

Under what circumstances will the holders of share warrants exercise their option to purchase?

Holders will exercise this option only if the market price of the shares exceeds the option price within the time limit specified. If the option price is higher than the market price, it would be cheaper for the investor to buy the shares in the market.

Share warrants may be *detachable*, which means that they can be sold separately from the loan capital.

It is probably worth mentioning the difference in status within a business between holders of convertible loan capital and holders of loans with share warrants attached if both groups decide to exercise their right to convert. In the former case, they become ordinary shareholders and are no longer lenders of the business. In the latter case, they become both ordinary shareholders and lenders in the business.

Mortgages

A **mortgage** is a form of loan that is secured on freehold property. Financial institutions such as banks, insurance businesses and pension funds are often prepared to lend to businesses on this basis. The mortgage may be over a long period (20 years or more).

Loan covenants

When drawing up a loan agreement, the lender may impose certain obligations and restrictions in order to protect the investment in the business. **Loan covenants** (as they are called) often form part of a loan agreement, and may deal with such matters as:

- *Financial statements*. The lender may require access to the financial statements of the business on a regular basis.
- *Other loans*. The lender may require the business to ask the lender's permission before taking on further loans from other sources.

■ *Dividend payments*. The lender may require dividends to be limited during the period of the loan.
■ *Liquidity*. The lender may require the business to maintain a certain level of liquidity during the period of the loan. This would typically be a requirement that the borrower business's current ratio was maintained at, or above, a specified level.

Any breach of these restrictive covenants can have serious consequences for the business. The lender may require immediate repayment of the loan in the event of a material breach.

Activity 12.7

Both preference shares and loan capital are forms of finance that require the business to provide a particular rate of return to investors. What are the factors that may be taken into account by a business when deciding between these two sources of finance?

The main factors are as follows:

■ Preference shares have a higher rate of return than loan capital. From the investor's point of view, preference shares are more risky. The amount invested cannot be secured, and the return is paid after the returns paid to lenders.
■ A business has a legal obligation to pay interest and make capital repayments on loans at the agreed dates. It will usually make every effort to meet its obligations because failure to do so can have serious consequences. (These consequences have been mentioned earlier.) Failure to pay a preference dividend, on the other hand, is less important. There is no legal obligation to pay if profits are not available for distribution. Though failure to pay a preference dividend may prove an embarrassment for the business, and may make it difficult to persuade investors to take up future preference share issues, the preference shareholders will have no redress if there are insufficient profits to pay the dividend due.
■ It was mentioned above that the taxation system in the UK permits interest on loans to be allowable against profits for taxation, whereas preference dividends are not. As a result, the cost of servicing loan capital is usually much less for a business than the cost of servicing preference shares.
■ The issue of loan capital may result in the management of a business having to accept some restrictions on its freedom of action. We saw earlier that loan agreements often contain covenants that can be onerous. However, no such restrictions can be imposed by preference shareholders.

A further point that has not been dealt with so far is that preference shares issued form part of the permanent capital base of the business. If they are redeemed, the law requires that they be replaced, either by a new issue of shares or by a transfer from reserves, in order to ensure that the business's capital base stays intact. Loan capital, however, is not viewed in law as part of the business's permanent capital base, and therefore there is no legal requirement to replace any loan capital that has been redeemed.

Finance leases and sale and leaseback arrangements

When a business needs a particular asset (for example an item of plant), instead of buying it direct from a supplier, the business may decide to arrange for another business (typically a bank) to buy it and then lease it to the first business. The business that owns the asset and leases it out is known as a 'lessor'. A **finance lease**, as such an arrangement is known, is, in essence, a form of lending. Though legal ownership of the asset rests with the financial institution (the lessor), a finance lease agreement transfers to the user (the lessee) virtually all the rewards and risks that are associated with the item being leased. The finance lease agreement covers a significant part of the life of the item being leased, and often cannot be cancelled.

Exhibit 12.2

Finance leasing at BA

Many airline companies use finance leasing as a means of acquiring new aeroplanes. The financial statements for British Airways plc (BA) for the year ended 31 March 2002 reveal that approximately 25 per cent (totalling £2,208 million) of the net book value of its fleet of aircraft had been acquired through this method.

Source: British Airways plc, Annual Report and Accounts year ended 31 March 2002

In recent years, some important benefits associated with finance leasing have disappeared. Changes in UK tax law no longer make it such a tax-efficient form of financing, and changes in accounting disclosure requirements make it no longer possible to conceal this form of 'borrowing' from investors. Nevertheless, the popularity of finance leases has continued. Other reasons must therefore exist for businesses to adopt this form of financing. These reasons are said to include the following:

- *Ease of borrowing.* Leasing may be obtained more easily than other forms of long-term finance. Lenders normally require some form of security and a profitable track record before making advances to a business. However, a lessor may be prepared to lease assets to a new business without a track record, and to use the leased assets as security for the amounts owing.
- *Cost.* Leasing agreements may be offered at reasonable cost. As the asset leased is used as security, standard lease arrangements can be applied and detailed credit checking of lessees may be unnecessary. This can reduce administrative costs for the lessor and, thereby, help in providing competitive lease rentals.
- *Flexibility.* Leasing can help provide flexibility where there are rapid changes in technology. If an option to cancel can be incorporated into the lease, the business may be able to exercise this option and invest in new technology as it becomes available. This will help the business to avoid the risk of obsolescence.
- *Cash flows.* Leasing, rather than purchasing an asset outright, means that large cash outflows can be avoided. The leasing option allows cash outflows to be smoothed out over the asset's life. In some cases, it is possible to arrange for low lease payments to be made in the early years of the asset's life, when cash inflows may be low, and for these to increase over time as the asset generates positive cash flows.

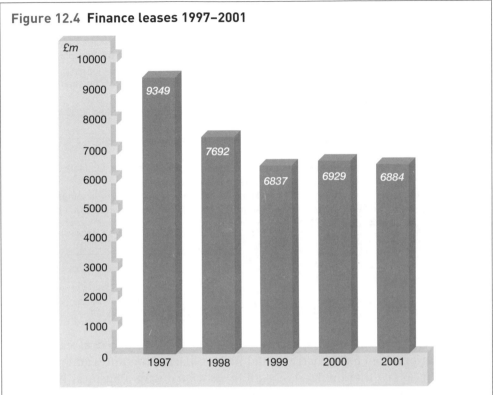

Figure 12.4 Finance leases 1997–2001

The figure shows that there has been a decline in the amount of finance leasing since 1997, but the amount of finance leasing appears to have stabilised over the most recent three years.

Source: Adapted from information kindly provided by the Finance & Leasing Association (www.fla.org.uk). Copyright © 2001 Finance & Leasing Association

A **sale and leaseback** arrangement involves a business selling an asset to a financial institution in order to raise finance. The sale is accompanied by an agreement to lease the asset back to the business to allow it to continue to use the asset. The rent payment is allowable against profits for taxation purposes. However, there are usually rent reviews at regular intervals throughout the period of the lease, and the amounts payable in future years may be difficult to predict. At the end of the lease agreement, the business must either try to renew the lease or find an alternative asset. Although the sale of the asset will result in an immediate injection of cash for the business, it will lose benefits from any future capital appreciation on the asset. Where a capital gain arises on the sale of the asset to the financial institution, a liability for taxation may also arise. Freehold property is often the asset that is the subject of such an arrangement.

A sale and leaseback agreement can be used to help a business focus on its core areas of competence. Exhibit 12.3, which is an extract from an article in the *Financial Times*, shows how a leading leisure hotels group used a sale and leaseback agreement to do this and, at the same time, return some cash to shareholders.

Exhibit 12.3

Approval for Jarvis sale and leaseback

Jarvis Hotels shareholders yesterday unanimously approved the sale of nine of the group's properties in a £150m deal that will return £85m to investors.

Under the deal, the business will continue to manage the hotels but some of the cash generated from their sale will be returned to shareholders.

John Jarvis, chairman, said there would be 'opportunities for further sale and leaseback deals when the market becomes more suitable'.

However, it is thought such deals would concern individual properties rather than a sale of several as a block.

'We are evolving into a management services business,' said Mr Jarvis. 'But if you are a business that wants a strong balance sheet, you always have to retain a core of assets.'

Peter Joseph, leisure analyst with KBC Peel Hunt, said: 'Jarvis is doing the right things. If it continues on this route it will end up as a hotel operator, not a hotel owner, which is fine – provided it has security over all of its contracts.'

Source: Financial Times, 8 November 2002, p. 28

Gearing and the long-term financing decision

In Chapter 6 we saw that gearing occurs when a business is financed, at least in part, by contributions from fixed-charge capital such as loans, debentures and preference shares. We also saw that the level of gearing associated with a business is often an important factor in assessing the risk and returns to ordinary shareholders. In the example that follows, we consider the implications of making a choice between a geared and an ungeared form of raising long-term finance.

Example 12.1

The following are the summarised financial statements of Woodhall Engineers plc:

Woodhall Engineers plc
Profit and loss account year ended 31 December

	Year 7	Year 8
	£m	£m
Turnover	47	50
Operating costs	(41)	(47)
Operating profit	6	3
Interest payable	(2)	(2)
Profit on ordinary activities before tax	4	1
Taxation on profit on ordinary activities	–	–
Profit on ordinary activities after tax	4	1
Dividends	(1)	(1)
Profit retained for the financial year	3	–

Balance sheet at 31 December

	Year 7	Year 8
	£m	£m
Fixed assets (less depreciation)	21	20
Current assets		
Stocks	10	18
Debtors	16	17
Cash at bank	3	1
	29	36
Creditors: amounts falling due within one year		
Short-term loans	(5)	(11)
Trade creditors	(10)	(10)
	(15)	(21)
Total assets less current liabilities	35	35
Less Long-term loans (secured)	15	15
	20	20
Capital and reserves		
Called-up share capital 25p ordinary shares	16	16
Profit and loss account	4	4
	20	20

The business is making plans to expand its premises. New plant will cost £8 million, and an expansion in output will increase working capital by £4 million. Over the 15 years' life of the project, incremental profits arising from the expansion will be £2 million per year before interest and tax. In addition, Year 9's profits before interest and tax from its existing activities are expected to return to Year 7 levels.

Two possible methods of financing the expansion have been discussed by Woodhall's directors. The first is the issue of £12 million 15 per cent loan capital repayable in Year 18. The second is a rights issue of 40 million 25p ordinary shares, which will give the business 30p per share after expenses.

The business has substantial tax losses, which can be offset against future profits, so taxation can be ignored in the calculations. The Year 9 dividend per share is expected to be the same as that for Year 8. The Year 9 dividend per share is expected to be the same as that for Year 8.

Prepare a forecast of Woodhall's profit and loss account (excluding turnover and operating costs) for the year ended 31 December Year 9, and of its capital and reserves, long-term loans and number of shares outstanding at that date assuming that the business issues:

1 loan capital;
2 ordinary shares.

The first part of the example requires the preparation of a forecast profit and loss account under each financing option. These profit and loss accounts will be as follows:

Forecast profit and loss account for the year ended 31 December Year 9

	1 Loan issue £m	2 Share issue £m
Profit before interest and taxation (6.0 + 2.0)	8.0	8.0
Loan interest	(3.8)	(2.0)
Profit before tax	4.2	6.0
Taxation	–	–
Profit after tax	4.2	6.0
Dividends	(1.0)	(1.6)
Retained profit for the year	3.2	4.4

The capital structure of the business under each option as at the end of Year 9 will be as follows:

	1 Loan issue £m	2 Share issue £m
Capital and reserves		
Share capital 25p ordinary shares	16.0	26.0
Share premium account*	–	2.0
Profit and loss account	7.2	8.4
	23.2	36.4
No. of shares in issue (25p shares)	64 million	104 million

* This represents the amount received from the issue of shares that is above the nominal value of the shares. The amount is calculated as follows:

$$40m \text{ shares} \times (30p - 25p) = £2m.$$

Activity 12.8

Compute Woodhall's interest cover and earnings per share for the year ended 31 December Year 9 and its gearing on that date, assuming that the business issues:

(a) loan capital;
(b) ordinary shares.

Your answer should be as follows:

	(a) Loan issue	(b) Share issue
Interest cover ratio		
$\dfrac{\text{Profit before interest and tax}}{\text{Interest payable}} =$	$\dfrac{8.0}{3.8}$	$\dfrac{8.0}{2.0}$
	= 2.1 times	4.0 times

Activity 12.8 continued

	(a) Loan issue	(b) Share issue
Earning per share		
$\dfrac{\text{Earning available to equity}}{\text{Number of ordinary shares}}$	$= \dfrac{£4.2m}{64m}$	$\dfrac{£6.0m}{104m}$
	$= 6.6p$	$5.8p$
Gearing ratio		
$\dfrac{\text{Long-term liabilities}}{\text{Share capital + Reserves + Long-term liabilities}}$	$= \dfrac{£27m}{£23.2m + £27m}$	$\dfrac{£15m}{£36.4m + £15m}$
	$= 53.8\%$	29.2%

Activity 12.9

What would your views of the proposed schemes be in each of the following circumstances?

(a) if you were a banker and you were approached for a loan;

(b) if you were an ordinary share investor in Woodhall and you were asked to sub-scribe to a rights issue.

(a) A banker may be unenthusiastic about lending money to the business. The gearing ratio of 53.8 per cent is rather high, and would leave the bank in an exposed position. The existing loan is already secured on assets held by the business, and it is not clear whether the business is in a position to offer an attractive form of security for the new loan. The interest cover ratio of 2.1 is also rather low. If the business is unable to achieve the expected returns from the new project, or if it is unable to restore profits from the remainder of its operations to Year 7 levels, this ratio would be even lower.

(b) Ordinary share investors may need some convincing that it would be worthwhile to make further investments in the business. The return on ordinary shareholders' funds in Year 7 was 20 per cent (£4m/£20m). The incremental profit from the new project is £2 million and the investment required is £12 million, which represents a return of 16.7 per cent. Thus, the returns from the project are expected to be lower than for existing operations. In making their decision, investors should discover whether the new investment is of a similar level of risk to their existing investment and how the returns from the investment compare with those available from other opportunities with similar levels of risk.

Short-term sources of finance

A short-term source of borrowing is one that is available for a short time period. The difficulty is that there is no agreed definition of what 'short-term' means. However, we shall define it as being up to one year. The major sources of short-term borrowing are as follows.

Bank overdraft

→ **Bank overdrafts** represent a very flexible form of borrowing. The size of the overdraft can (subject to bank approval) be increased or decreased according to the financing requirements of the business. It is relatively inexpensive to arrange, and interest rates are often very competitive. The rate of interest charged on an overdraft will vary, however, according to how creditworthy the customer is perceived to be by the bank. It is also fairly easy to arrange – sometimes an overdraft can be agreed by a telephone call to the bank. In view of these advantages, it is not surprising that this is an extremely popular form of short-term finance.

Banks prefer to grant overdrafts that are self-liquidating: that is, the funds applied will result in cash inflows that will extinguish the overdraft balance. The banks may ask for forecast cash flow statements from the business to see when the overdraft will be repaid and how much finance is required. The bank may also require some form of security on amounts advanced. One potential drawback with this form of finance is that it is repayable on demand. This may pose problems for a business that is illiquid. However, many businesses operate using an overdraft, and this form of borrowing, although in theory regarded as short term, can often become a long-term source of finance.

Debt factoring

→ **Debt factoring** is a service offered by a financial institution (known as a 'factor'). Many of the large factors are subsidiaries of commercial banks. Debt factoring involves the factor taking over the business's debt collection. In addition to operating normal credit control procedures, a factor may offer to undertake credit investigations and to provide protection for approved credit sales. The factor is usually prepared to make an advance to the business of a maximum of 80 per cent of approved trade debtors. The charge made for the factoring service is based on total turnover, and is often 2 to 3 per cent of turnover. Any advances made to the business by the factor will attract a rate of interest similar to the rate charged on bank overdrafts.

Many businesses find a factoring arrangement very convenient. It can result in savings in credit management and can create more certain cash flows. It can also release the time of key personnel for more profitable activities. This may be extremely important for smaller businesses that rely on the talent and skills of a few key individuals. However, there is a possibility that some will see a factoring arrangement as an indication that the business is experiencing financial difficulties. This may have an adverse effect on confidence. For this reason, some businesses try to conceal the factoring arrangement by collecting debts on behalf of the factor. When

Figure 12.5 **The factoring process**

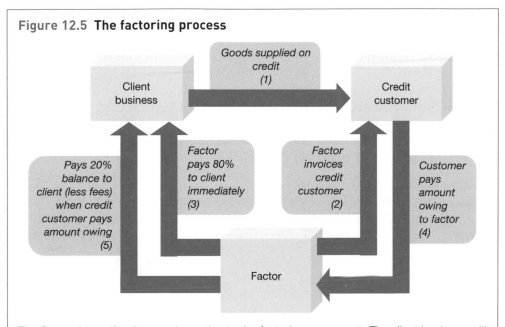

The figure shows the three main parties to the factoring agreement. The client business will sell goods on credit and the factor will take responsibility for invoicing the customer and collecting the amount owing. The factor will then pay the client business the invoice amount, less fees and interest, in two stages. The first stage represents 80 per cent of the invoice value and will be paid immediately after the goods have been delivered to the customer. The second stage will represent the balance outstanding and will usually be paid when the customer has paid the factor the amount owing.

considering a factoring agreement, the costs and likely benefits arising must be identified and carefully weighed.

Invoice discounting

Invoice discounting involves a business approaching a factor or other financial institution for a loan based on a proportion of the face value of credit sales outstanding. If the institution agrees, the amount advanced is usually 75 to 80 per cent of the value of the approved sales invoices outstanding. The business must agree to repay the advance within a relatively short period – perhaps 60 or 90 days. The responsibility for collection of the trade debts outstanding remains with the business, and repayment of the advance is not dependent on the trade debt being collected. Invoice discounting will not result in such a close relationship developing between the client and the financial institution as factoring. It may be a short-term arrangement whereas debt factoring usually involves a longer-term relationship between the customer and the financial institution.

Invoice discounting is a much more important source of funds than factoring (see Figure 12.6). There are three main reasons for this:

■ First, it is a confidential form of financing that the client's customers will know nothing about.
■ Second, the service charge for invoice discounting is generally only 0.2 to 0.3 per cent of turnover, compared with 2.0 to 3.0 per cent for factoring.
■ Finally, many businesses are unwilling to relinquish control of their customers' records. Customers are an important resource of the business, and many wish to retain control over all aspects of their relationship with their customers.

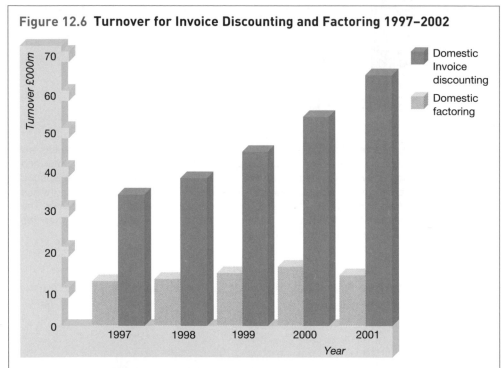

Figure 12.6 Turnover for Invoice Discounting and Factoring 1997–2002

The figure shows that, in recent years, turnover for invoice discounting has risen much more sharply than turnover from factoring. The turnover for invoice discounting for the year 2002 is more than three times the turnover for factoring.

Source: Adapted from information published by Factors & Discounters Association (www.factors.org.uk). Copyright © 2002 Factors & Discounters Association

Long-term versus short-term borrowing

Having decided that some form of borrowing is required to finance the business, managers must then decide whether it should be long-term or short-term in form. There are many issues that should be taken into account when making this decision. These include the following:

■ *Matching.* The business may attempt to match the type of borrowing with the nature of the assets held. Thus, assets that form part of the permanent operating base of the business, including fixed assets and a certain level of current assets, will be financed by long-term borrowing. Assets held for a short period, such as current assets held to meet seasonal increases in demand, will be financed by short-term borrowing (see Figure 12.7).

Figure 12.7 **Short-term and long-term financing requirements**

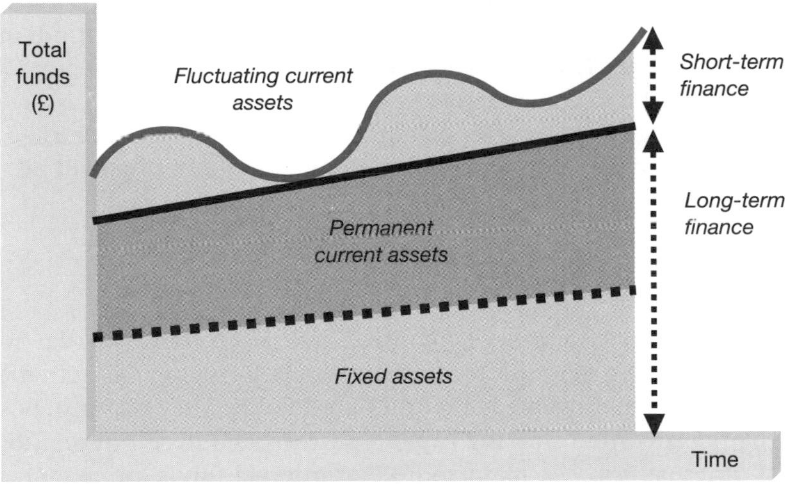

The broad consensus on financing seems to be that all of the permanent financial needs of the business should come from long-term sources. Only that part of current assets that fluctuates on a short-term, probably a seasonal, basis should be financed from short-term sources.

A business may wish to match the asset life exactly with the period of the related loan; however, this may not be possible because of the difficulty of predicting the life of many assets.

Activity 12.10

Some businesses may take up a less cautious financing position than that shown in Figure 12.7, and others may take up a more cautious one. How would the diagram differ under each of these options?

A less cautious position would mean relying on short-term finance to help fund part of the permanent capital base. A more cautious position would mean relying on long-term finance to help finance the fluctuating assets of the business.

■ *Flexibility*. Short-term borrowing may be a useful means of postponing a commitment to taking on a long-term loan. This may be seen as desirable if interest rates are high and it is forecast that they will fall in the future. Short-term borrowing does not usually incur penalties if there is early repayment of the amount outstanding, whereas some form of financial penalty may arise if long-term debt is repaid early.

■ *Refunding risk*. Short-term borrowing has to be renewed more frequently than long-term borrowing. This may create problems for the business if it is already in financial difficulties, or if there is a shortage of funds available for lending.

■ *Interest rates*. Interest payable on long-term debt is often higher than for short-term debt. (This is because lenders require a higher return where their funds are locked up for a long period.) This fact may make short-term borrowing a more attractive source of finance for a business. However, there may be other costs associated with borrowing (arrangement fees, for example) to be taken into account. The more frequently borrowings must be renewed, the higher these costs will be.

Internal sources of financing

In addition to external sources of finance, there are certain internal sources of finance that a business may use to generate funds for particular activities. These sources usually have the advantage that they are flexible. They may also be obtained quickly – particularly from working capital sources – and need not require the permission of other parties. The main sources of internal funds are described below, and are summarised in Figure 12.8.

Retained profits

Retained profits are the major source of finance for most businesses. By retaining profits within the business rather than distributing them to shareholders in the form of dividends, the funds of the business are increased.

Activity 12.11

Are retained profits a free source of finance to the business?

It is tempting to think that retained profits are a 'cost-free' source of funds for a business. However, this is not the case. If profits are reinvested rather than distributed to shareholders, this means that the shareholders cannot invest the profits made in other forms of investment. They will therefore expect a rate of return from the profits reinvested that is equivalent to what they would have received had the funds been invested in another opportunity with the same level of risk.

Figure 12.8 **Major internal sources of finance**

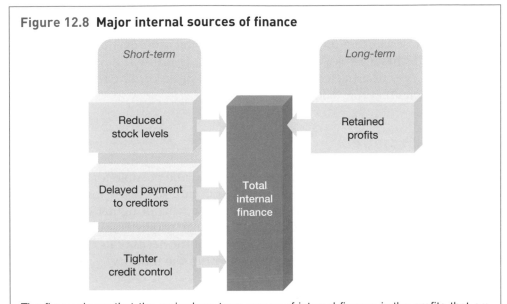

The figure shows that the major long-term source of internal finance is the profits that are retained rather than distributed to shareholders. The major short-term sources of internal finance involve reducing the level of debtors and stocks and increasing the level of creditors.

The reinvestment of profits rather than the issue of new shares can be a useful way of raising capital from ordinary share investors. There are no issue costs associated with retaining profits, and the amount raised is certain, once the profit has been made. When issuing new shares, the issue costs may be substantial, and there may be uncertainty over the success of the issue. Retaining profits will have no effect on the control of the business by existing shareholders, whereas new shares are issued to outside investors and there will be some dilution of control.

The retention of profits is something that is determined by the directors. They may find it easier simply to retain profits rather than ask investors to subscribe to a new share issue. Retained profits are already held by the business, and so it does not have to wait to receive the funds. Moreover, there is often less scrutiny when profits are being retained for reinvestment purposes than when new shares are being issued. Investors and their advisers will examine closely the reasons for any new share issue. A problem with the use of profits as a source of finance, however, is that the timing and level of profits in the future cannot always be reliably determined.

Some shareholders may prefer profits to be retained by the business, rather than be distributed in the form of dividends. By ploughing back profits, it may be expected that the business will expand, and that share values will increase as a result. In the UK, not all capital gains are liable for taxation. (For the tax year 2002/2003, an individual with capital gains totalling less than £7,700 would not be taxed on those gains.) A further advantage of capital gains over dividends is that the shareholder has a choice as to when the gain is realised. Research indicates that investors may be attracted to particular businesses according to the dividend/ retention policies that they adopt.

Tighter credit control

By exerting tighter control over trade debtors it may be possible for a business to reduce the proportion of assets held in this form and so release funds for other purposes. It is important, however, to weigh the benefits of tighter credit control against the likely costs in the form of lost customer goodwill and lost sales. To remain competitive, a business must take account of the needs of its customers and the credit policies adopted by rival businesses within the industry.

Activity 12.12

H. Rusli Ltd provides a car valet service for car-hire businesses when their cars are returned from hire. Details of the service are as follows:

	Per car	
	£	£
Car valet charge		20
Less Variable costs	14	
Fixed costs	4	18
Net profit		2

Sales are £10 million a year and are all on credit. The average credit period taken by car-hire businesses is 45 days, although the terms of credit require payment within 30 days. Bad debts are currently £100,000 a year. Debtors are financed by a bank overdraft costing 15 per cent a year.

The credit control department of H. Rusli Ltd believes it can eliminate bad debts and can reduce the average credit period to 30 days if new credit control procedures are implemented. These will cost £50,000 per year, and are likely to result in a reduction in sales of 5 per cent a year.

Should the business implement the new credit control procedures? (*Hint*: In order to answer this activity it is useful to compare the current cost of trade credit with the costs under the proposed approach.)

Activity 12.12 continued

The current annual cost of trade credit is:

	£
Bad debts	100,000
Overdraft interest [(£10m × 45/365) × 15%]	184,931
	284,931

The annual cost of trade credit under the new policy will be:

	£
Overdraft interest [((95% × 10m) × (30/365)) × 15%]	117,123
Cost of control procedures	50,000
Net cost of lost sales [((£10m/£20) × 5%) × (20 − 14*)]	150,000
	317,123

* The loss will be the contribution per unit (that is, the difference between the selling price and the variable costs).

The above figures reveal that the business will be worse off if the new policies are adopted.

Reducing stock levels

This is an internal source of funds that may prove attractive to a business. If a business has a proportion of its assets in the form of stock there is an opportunity cost, as the funds tied up cannot be used for other opportunities. (This is also true, of course, for investment in trade debtors.) By holding less stock, funds become available for other purposes. However, a business must ensure that there are sufficient stocks available to meet likely future sales demand. Failure to do so will result in lost customer goodwill and lost sales.

The nature and condition of the stock held will determine whether it is possible to exploit this form of finance. A business may be overstocked as a result of poor buying decisions in the past. This may mean that a significant proportion of stocks held are slow moving or obsolete and cannot, therefore, be reduced easily.

Delaying payment to creditors

By delaying payment to creditors, funds are retained within the business for other purposes. This may be a cheap form of finance for a business. However, there may be significant costs associated with it. For example, the business may find it difficult to buy on credit when it is a slow payer.

? Self-assessment question 12.1

Helsim Ltd is a wholesaler and distributor of electrical components. The most recent financial statements of the business revealed the following:

Profit and loss account for the year ended 31 May Year 10

	£m	£m
Sales		14.2
Opening stock	3.2	
Purchases	8.4	
	11.6	
Closing stock	(3.8)	(7.8)
Gross profit		6.4
Administration expenses	(3.0)	
Selling and distribution expenses	(2.1)	
Finance charges	(0.8)	(5.9)
Net profit before taxation		0.5
Corporation tax		(0.2)
Net profit after taxation		0.3

Balance sheet as at 31 May Year 10

	£m	£m	£m
Fixed assets			
Land and buildings			3.8
Equipment			0.9
Motor vehicles			0.5
			5.2
Current assets			
Stock		3.8	
Trade debtors		3.6	
Cash at bank		0.1	
		7.5	
Less: Creditors: amounts falling due within one year			
Trade creditors	1.8		
Bank overdraft	3.6	5.4	2.1
			7.3
Less: Creditors: amounts falling due after one year			
Debentures (secured on freehold land)			3.5
			3.8
Capital and reserves			
Ordinary £1 shares			2.0
Profit and loss account			1.8
			3.8

Self-assessment question 12.1 continued

Notes

1 Land and buildings are shown at their current market value. Equipment and motor vehicles are shown at their written-down values.
2 No dividends have been paid to ordinary shareholders for the past three years.

In recent months, trade creditors have been pressing for payment. The managing director has therefore decided to reduce the level of trade creditors to an average of 40 days outstanding. To achieve this, he has decided to approach the bank with a view to increasing the overdraft. The business is currently paying 12 per cent a year interest on the overdraft.

Required:

(a) Comment on the liquidity position of the business.
(b) Calculate the amount of finance required in order to reduce trade creditors, as shown on the balance sheet, to an average of 40 days outstanding.
(c) State, with reasons, how you consider the bank would react to the proposal to grant an additional overdraft facility.
(d) Evaluate four sources of finance (internal or external, but excluding a bank overdraft) that may be used to finance the reduction in trade creditors, and state, with reasons, which of these you consider the most appropriate.

The role of the Stock Exchange

Earlier we considered the various forms of long-term capital that are available to a business. In this section, we examine the role that the **Stock Exchange** plays in the provision of finance for businesses. The Stock Exchange acts as an important *primary* and *secondary* market in capital for businesses. As a primary market, its function is to enable businesses to raise new capital. As a secondary market, its function is to enable investors to sell their securities (that is, shares and loan capital) with ease. Thus, it provides a 'second-hand' market where shares and loan capital already in issue may be bought and sold.

In order to issue shares or loan capital through the Stock Exchange, a business must be listed. This means that it must meet fairly stringent requirements concerning size, profit history, disclosure, and so on. Some share issues on the Stock Exchange arise from the initial listing of the business. Other share issues are undertaken by businesses that are already listed and that are seeking additional finance from investors.

Advantages of a listing

The secondary market role of the Stock Exchange means that shares and other financial claims are easily transferable. Furthermore, the prices of shares and other financial claims are constantly under scrutiny by investors and skilled analysts and this helps to ensure that the prices quoted for a particular share reflects its true worth. These factors can bring real benefits to a business.

Activity 12.13

What kind of benefits might a business gain from its shares being listed?

If investors know that their shares can easily be sold for prices that reflect the true worth of the shares, they will have more confidence to invest. The business may benefit from this greater investor confidence by finding it easier to raise long-term finance and by obtaining this finance at a lower cost, as investors will view their investment as being less risky.

It is worth pointing out that investors are not obliged to use the Stock Exchange as the means of transferring shares in a listed business. However, it is usually the most convenient way of buying or selling shares.

The Stock Exchange can be a useful vehicle for a successful entrepreneur wishing to realise the value of the business that has been built up. By floating (listing) the shares on the Stock Exchange, and thereby making the shares available to the public, the entrepreneur will usually benefit from a gain in the value of the shares held and will be able to realise that gain easily, if required, by selling some shares. Exhibit 12.4 is based on an article which appeared in the *Sunday Times*.

Exhibit 12.4

Privatised stationer 'to float'

Ray Peck is an entrepreneur who runs a business that was the government's former stationery division. Newspaper reports revealed that he wished to float the business on the Stock Exchange and that stock market investors were likely to value the business at around £80m to £100m. Mr Peck, his senior managers and a financial institution bought the whole business for about £10m two years before the intention to float the business was reported. At the time, Ray Peck owned 20 per cent of the shares of the business, which means that his stake in the business would be valued somewhere between £16 million and £20 million, assuming that predictions concerning the value of the business were accurate.

Source: Sunday Times Business, 30 June 2002, p. 3

Disadvantages of a listing

A Stock Exchange listing can have certain disadvantages for a business. Strict rules are imposed on listed businesses, including requiring additional levels of financial disclosure to that already imposed by law and by the accounting profession (for example, the listing rules require that half-yearly financial reports must be published). The activities of listed businesses are closely monitored by financial analysts, financial journalists and others, and such scrutiny may not be welcome, particularly if the business is dealing with sensitive issues or is experiencing operational problems.

It is often suggested that listed businesses are under pressure to perform well over the short term. This pressure may detract from undertaking projects that will only yield benefits in the longer term. If the market becomes disenchanted with the business, and the price of its shares falls, this may make it vulnerable to a takeover bid from another business. Finally the costs of obtaining a listing are vast and this may be a real deterrent for some businesses.

Providing long-term finance for the small business

Although the Stock Exchange provides an important source of long-term finance for large businesses, it is not really suitable for small businesses. The aggregate market value of shares that are to be listed on the Stock Exchange must be at least £700,000 and, in practice, the amounts are much higher because of the high costs of listing. Thus, small businesses must look elsewhere for help in raising long-term finance. Some of the more important sources of finance that are available are considered below.

Venture capital and long-term financing

Venture capital is long-term capital provided to small and medium-sized businesses wishing to grow but which do not have ready access to stock markets because of the prohibitively large costs of obtaining a listing. The businesses of interest to the venture capitalist will have higher levels of risk than would normally be acceptable to traditional providers of finance, such as the major clearing banks. The attraction for the venture capitalist of investing in higher-risk businesses is the prospect of higher returns.

The risks associated with the business can vary in practice, but are often due to the nature of the products or the fact that it is a new business that either lacks a trading record or has new management.

Venture capitalists provide long-term capital in the form of share and loan finance for different situations including:

- *Start-up capital.* This is available to businesses that are still at the concept stage of development through to those businesses that are ready to commence trading.
- *Growth capital.* This is aimed at providing additional funding for young, expanding businesses.
- *Buy-out or buy-in capital.* This is used to fund the acquisition of a business by the existing management team or by a new management team. The two most popular kinds of management acquisition are where a large business wishes to divest itself of one of its operating units and where a family business wishes to sell out because of succession problems.

■ *Share purchase capital.* This is used to fund the purchase of shares in a business in order to buy out part of the ownership of an existing business. This may occur where a shareholder wishes to realise his investment in the business in order to retire or to pursue other opportunities.
■ *Recovery capital.* This is rescue finance, which is issued to turn a business around after a period of poor performance.

3i is the leading venture capital finance business in the UK and Europe. In Figure 12.9 below, the type of investments made by the business are shown.

The venture capitalist will often make a substantial investment in the business, and this will normally take the form of ordinary shares. In order to keep an eye on the sum invested, the venture capitalist will usually require a representative on the board of directors as a condition of the investment. The venture capitalist may not be looking for a quick return, and may well be prepared to invest in a business for

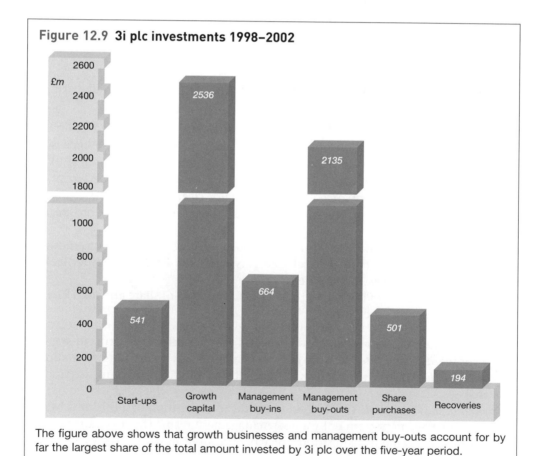

Figure 12.9 3i plc investments 1998–2002

The figure above shows that growth businesses and management buy-outs account for by far the largest share of the total amount invested by 3i plc over the five-year period.

Source: Adapted and reprinted with the kind permission of 3i Group plc, Copyright © 2002 3i Group

five years or more. The return may take the form of a capital gain on the realisation of the investment.

Business angels

Business angels are often wealthy individuals who have been successful in business. They are usually willing to invest somewhere between £10,000 and £100,000 in a start-up business or in a business that is at an early stage of development through a shareholding. Business angels fill an important gap in the market as the size and the nature of the investment that they find appealing will not often appeal to venture capitalists. In addition to providing finance, a business angel can usually offer a wealth of business experience to budding tycoons.

Business angels offer an informal source of share finance and it is not always easy for owners of small businesses to locate a suitable angel. However, a number of business angel networks has now developed to help owners of small businesses find their 'perfect partner'.

Government assistance

One of the most effective ways in which the government assists small businesses is through the Small Firms Loan Guarantee Scheme. This scheme aims to help small businesses that have viable business plans but which lack the security to obtain a loan. The scheme guarantees loans made over a 2 to 10-year period to small businesses from lending institutions for sums of £5,000 to £100,000 (increased to £250,000 for businesses that have been trading for at least two years). The government will guarantee up to 70 per cent (increased to 85 per cent for businesses that have been trading for at least two years) of the amount borrowed. In addition to other forms of financial assistance such as government grants and improving tax incentives for share investors to invest in small businesses, the government can help in providing information concerning the sources of finance available.

Share issues

A business may issue shares in a number of ways. These may involve direct appeals to investors, or the use of financial intermediaries. The most common methods of share issues for cash are as follows:

- rights issues;
- offers for sale and public issue;
- private placing.

These are discussed below.

Rights issues

The business may offer existing shareholders the right to acquire new shares, in exchange for cash. The new shares will be allocated to shareholders in proportion to their existing shareholdings. To make the issue appear attractive to shareholders, the new shares are often offered at a price significantly below the market value of the existing shares. **Rights issues** are now the most common form of share issue. It is a relatively cheap and straightforward way of issuing shares. Expenses are quite low, and procedures are simple. The fact that those offered new shares already have an investment in the business, which presumably suits their risk/return requirements, is likely to increase the chances of the issue being successful.

The law requires that shares to be issued *for cash* are to be offered first to existing shareholders. The advantage of this requirement is that control of the business by existing shareholders will not be diluted, provided that they take up the rights offer. A rights offer allows existing shareholders to acquire shares at a price below the current market price. This does not mean that entitlement to participate in a rights offer is a source of value to existing shareholders, however. Provided that shareholders either take up their rights and buy the new shares or sell the rights to someone else who will, they will be neither better nor worse off as a result of the rights issue. Calculating the value of the rights offer received by shareholders is quite straightforward, as shown in Example 12.2.

Example 12.2

Shaw Holdings plc has 20 million ordinary shares of 50p in issue. These shares are currently valued on the Stock Exchange at £1.60 per share. The directors believe that the business requires additional long-term capital, and have decided to make a one-for-four issue (that is, one new share for every four shares held) at £1.30 per share.

The first step in the valuation process is to calculate the price of a share following the rights issue. This is known as the *ex-rights price*, and is simply a weighted average of the price of shares before the issue of rights and the price of the rights shares. In the above example, we have a one-for-four rights issue. The theoretical ex-rights price is therefore calculated as follows:

	£
Price of four shares before the rights issue (4 × £1.60)	6.40
Price of taking up one rights share	1.30
	7.70
Theoretical ex-rights price	= 7.70
	5
	= £1.54

As the price of each share, in theory, should be £1.54 following the rights issue and the price of a rights share is £1.30, the value of the rights offer will be the difference between the two:

$$£1.54 - £1.30 = £0.24 \text{ per share}$$

Market forces will usually ensure that the actual and theoretical price of rights will be fairly close.

Activity 12.15

An investor with 2,000 shares in Shaw Holdings plc (see Example 12.2) has contacted you for investment advice. She is undecided whether to take up the rights issue, sell the rights, or allow the rights offer to lapse.

Calculate the effect on the net wealth of the investor of each of the options being considered.

If the investor takes up the rights issue, she will be in the following position:

	£
Value of holding after rights issue ((2000 + 500) × £1.54)	3,850
Less: Cost of buying the rights shares (500 × £1.30)	650
	3,200

If the investor sells the rights, she will be in the following position:

Value of holding after rights issue (2,000 × £1.54)	3,080
Sale of rights (500 × £0.24)	120
	3,200

If the investor lets the rights offer lapse, she will be in the following position:

Value of holding after rights issue (2,000 × £1.54)	3,080

As we can see, the first two options should leave her in the same position concerning net wealth as she was before the rights issue. Before the rights issue she had 2,000 shares worth £1.60 each or £3,200. However, she will be worse off if she allows the rights offer to lapse than under the other two options. In practice, however, the business may sell the rights offer on behalf of the investor and pass on the proceeds in order to ensure that she is not worse off as a result of the issue.

When considering a rights issue, the directors must first consider the amount of funds that needs to be raised. This will depend on the future plans and commitments of the business. The directors must then decide on the issue price of the rights shares. Normally, this decision is not critical. In Example 12.2 above, the business made a one-for-four issue with the price of the rights shares set at £1.30. However, it could have raised the same amount by making a one-for-two issue and setting the rights price at £0.65, a one-for-one issue and setting the price at £0.325, and so on. The issue price that is finally decided upon will not affect the value of the underlying assets of the business or the proportion of the underlying assets and earnings to which the shareholder is entitled. The directors must, however, ensure that the issue price is not above the current market price of the shares, or the issue will be unsuccessful.

Offer for sale and public issue

➡ An **offer for sale** involves a business, trading as a public limited company, selling a new issue of shares to a financial institution known as an issuing house. However, shares that are already in issue may also be sold to an issuing house. In this case, existing shareholders agree to sell their shares to the issuing house. The issuing house will, in turn, sell the shares purchased from either the business or its shareholders to the public. The issuing house will publish a prospectus that sets out details of the business and the type of shares to be sold and investors will be invited to apply for shares. The advantage of this type of issue, from the business's viewpoint, is that the sale proceeds of the shares are certain.

➡ A **public issue** involves the business making a direct invitation to the public to purchase its shares. Typically, this is done through a newspaper advertisement. The shares may, once again, be a new issue or those already in issue. An offer for sale and a public issue will both result in a widening of share ownership in the business.

Issues by tender

When making an issue of shares, the business or the issuing house will usually set a price for the shares. Establishing this, however, may not be an easy task, particularly where the market is volatile or where the business has unique characteristics. One
➡ way of dealing with this issue-price problem is to make a **tender issue** of shares. This involves the investors determining the price at which the shares are issued. Though the business (or issuing house) may publish a reserve price to help guide investors, it will be up to the individual investor to determine the number of shares to be purchased and the price the investor wishes to pay. Once the offers from investors have been received, a price at which all the shares can be sold will be established (known as the *striking price*). Investors who have made offers at, or above, the striking price will be issued shares at the striking price; offers received below the striking price will be rejected. Although this form of issue is adopted occasionally, it is not popular with investors, and is therefore not in widespread use.

Private placings

A **private placing** does not involve an invitation to the public to subscribe to shares. Instead the shares are 'placed' with selected investors, such as large financial institutions. This can be a quick and relatively cheap form of raising funds, because savings can be made in advertising and legal costs. However, it can result in the ownership of the business being concentrated in a few hands. Usually, unlisted businesses seeking relatively small amounts of cash will employ this form of issue.

Summary

The main points in this chapter may be summarised as follows:

- *Sources of finance*:
  - external sources of finance require the agreement of someone beyond the directors and managers of the business whereas internal sources of finance do not;
  - long-term sources of finance are not due for repayment within one year whereas short-term sources are due for repayment within one year;
  - the higher the level of risk associated with investing in a particular form of finance, the higher the level of return that will be expected by investors.

- *External sources of finance*:
  - the main external, *long-term* sources of finance are ordinary shares, preference shares, loans and leases;
  - ordinary shares are normally considered to be the most risky form of investment and, therefore, provide the highest expected returns. Loan capital is normally the least risky and provides the lowest expected returns to investors;
  - the level of gearing associated with a business is often an important factor in assessing the level of risk and returns to ordinary shareholders;
  - the main sources of external *short-term* finance are bank overdrafts, debt factoring and invoice discounting;
  - when considering the choice between long-term and short-term sources of borrowing, factors such as matching the type of borrowing with the nature of the assets held, the need for flexibility, refunding risk and interest rates should be taken into account.

- *Internal sources of finance*:
  - the major internal source of long-term finance is retained profits;
  - the main short-term sources of internal finance are tighter credit control of debtors, reducing stock levels and delaying payments to creditors.

- *Raising finance*:
  - the Stock Exchange is an important primary and secondary market in capital for large businesses. However, obtaining a Stock Exchange listing can have certain drawbacks for a business;

- ❏ venture capital is long-term capital for small or medium-size businesses that are not listed on the Stock Exchange. These businesses often have higher levels of risk but provide the venture capitalist with the prospect of higher levels of return;
- ❏ business angels are wealthy individuals who are willing to invest in businesses at an early stage of development;
- ❏ the government assists small businesses through guaranteeing loans and by providing grants, and tax incentives.

- ■ *Share issues*:
  - ❏ share issues that involve the payment of cash by investors can take the form of a rights issue, public issue, offer for sale or a private placing;
  - ❏ a rights issue is made to existing shareholders. Most share issues are of this type as the law requires that shares that are to be issued for cash must first be offered to existing shareholders;
  - ❏ a public issue involves a direct issue to the public and an offer for sale involves an indirect issue to the public;
  - ❏ a private placing is an issue of shares to selected investors.

→ Key terms

term loan *p 356*
debenture *p 356*
eurobond *p 356*
convertible loan stocks *p 358*
warrants *p 359*
mortgage *p 360*
loan covenants *p 360*
finance lease *p 362*
sale and leaseback *p 363*
bank overdrafts *p 368*

debt factoring *p 368*
invoice discounting *p 369*
Stock Exchange *p 377*
venture capital *p 379*
business angels *p 381*
rights issues *p 382*
offer for sale *p 384*
public issue *p 384*
tender issue *p 384*
private placing *p 385*

? Review questions

Answers to these questions can be found on the students' side of the Companion Website.

12.1 What are the benefits to a business of issuing share warrants?

12.2 Why might a business that has a Stock Exchange listing revert to being unlisted?

12.3 Distinguish between an offer for sale and a public issue of shares.

12.4 Distinguish between invoice discounting and factoring.

Exercises 12.4 and 12.5 are more advanced than 12.1–12.3. Those with a coloured number have an answer at the back of the book.

12.1 H. Brown (Portsmouth) Ltd produces a range of central heating systems for sale to builders' merchants. As a result of increasing demand for the business's products, the directors have decided to expand production. The cost of acquiring new plant and machinery and the increase in working capital requirements are planned to be financed by a mixture of long-term and short-term borrowing.

Required:
(a) Discuss the major factors that should be taken into account when deciding on the appropriate mix of long-term and short-term borrowing necessary to finance the expansion programme.
(b) Discuss the major factors that a lender should take into account when deciding whether to grant a long-term loan to the business.
(c) Identify three conditions that might be included in a long-term loan agreement, and state the purpose of each.

12.2 Carpets Direct plc wishes to increase the number of its retail outlets in the south of England. The board of directors has decided to finance this expansion programme by raising the funds from existing shareholders through a one-for-four rights issue. The most recent profit and loss account of the business is as follows:

Profit and loss account for the year ended 30 April

	£m
Sales	164.5
Profit before interest and taxation	12.6
Interest	(6.2)
Profit before taxation	6.4
Corporation tax	(1.9)
Profit after taxation	4.5
Ordinary dividends	(2.0)
Retained profit for the year	2.5

The share capital consists of 120 million ordinary shares with a par value of £0.50 per share. These are currently being traded on the Stock Exchange at a price earnings ratio of 22 times and the board of directors has decided to issue the new shares at a discount of 20 per cent on the current market value.

Required:
(a) Calculate the theoretical ex-rights price of an ordinary share in Carpets Direct plc.
(b) Calculate the price at which the rights in Carpet Direct plc are likely to be traded.
(c) Identify and evaluate, at the time of the rights issue, each of the options arising from the rights issue to an investor who holds 4,000 ordinary shares before the rights announcement.

12.3 Venture capital may represent an important source of finance for a business.

Required:
(a) What is meant by the term venture capital? What are the distinguishing features of this form of finance?
(b) What types of business venture may be of interest to a venture capitalist seeking to make an investment?
(c) Discuss the main factors that a venture capitalist would take into account when considering a possible investment in a business.

12.4 Gainsborough Fashions Ltd operates a small chain of fashion shops in North Wales. In recent months the business has been under pressure from its trade creditors to reduce the average credit period taken from three months to one month. As a result, the directors have approached the bank to ask for an increase in the existing overdraft for one year to be able to comply with the creditors' demands. The most recent financial statements of the business are as follows:

Balance sheet as at 31 May Year 5

	£	£	£
Fixed assets			
Fixtures and fittings at cost		90,000	
Less Accumulated depreciation		23,000	67,000
Motor vehicles at cost		34,000	
Less Accumulated depreciation		27,000	7,000
			74,000
Current assets			
Stock at cost		198,000	
Trade debtors		3,000	
		201,000	
Creditors: amounts falling due within one year			
Trade creditors	(162,000)		
Accrued expenses	(10,000)		
Bank overdraft	(7,000)		
Taxation	(5,000)		
Dividends	(10,000)	(194,000)	7,000
			81,000
Creditors: amounts falling due after one year			
12% debentures repayable in just over one year's time			(40,000)
			41,000
Capital and reserves			
£1 ordinary shares			20,000
General reserve			4,000
Retained profit			17,000
			41,000

Abbreviated profit and loss account for the year ended 31 May Year 5

	£
Sales	740,000
Net profit before interest and taxation	38,000
Interest charges	(5,000)
Net profit before taxation	33,000
Taxation	(10,000)
Net profit after taxation	23,000
Dividend proposed	(10,000)
Retained profit for the year	13,000

Notes
1 The debentures are secured by personal guarantees from the directors.
2 The current overdraft bears an interest rate of 12 per cent a year.

Required:
(a) Identify and discuss the major factors that a bank would take into account before deciding whether or not to grant an increase in the overdraft of a business.
(b) State whether, in your opinion, the bank should grant the required increase in the overdraft for Gainsborough Fashions Ltd. You should provide reasoned arguments and supporting calculations where necessary.

12.5 Telford Engineers plc, a medium-sized Midlands manufacturer of automobile components, has decided to modernise its factory by introducing a number of robots. These will cost £20 million and will reduce operating costs by £6 million per year for their estimated useful life of 10 years starting in Year 10. To finance this scheme, the business can raise £20 million either:

1 by the issue of 20 million ordinary shares at 100p; or
2 by loan capital at 14 per cent interest a year, capital repayments of £3 million a year commencing at the end of Year 11.

Extracts from Telford Engineers' financial statements appear below:

Summary of balance sheet at 31 December

	Year 6 £m	Year 7 £m	Year 8 £m	Year 9 £m
Fixed assets	48	51	65	64
Current assets	55	67	57	55
Creditors due within one year				
Creditors	(20)	(27)	(25)	(18)
Overdraft	(5)	–	(6)	(8)
	78	91	91	93
Share capital and reserves	48	61	61	63
Loans	30	30	30	30
	78	91	91	93
Number of issued 25p shares	80 million	80 million	80 million	80 million
Share price	150p	200p	100p	145p

Summary of profit and loss accounts for years ended 31 December

	Year 6	Year 7	Year 8	Year 9
	£m	£m	£m	£m
Sales	152	170	110	145
Profit before interest and taxation	28	40	7	15
Interest payable	(4)	(3)	(4)	(5)
Profit before taxation	24	37	3	10
Taxation	(12)	(16)	(0)	(4)
Profit after taxation	12	21	3	6
Dividends	(6)	(8)	(3)	(4)
Retained profit	6	13	0	2

For your answer you should assume that the corporate tax rate for Year 10 is 40 per cent, that sales and operating profit will be unchanged except for the £6 million cost saving arising from the introduction of the robots, and that Telford Engineers will pay the same dividend per share in Year 10 as in Year 9.

Required:

(a) Prepare, for each financing arrangement, Telford Engineers' profit and loss account for the year ending 31 December Year 10 and a statement of its share capital, reserves and loans on that date.

(b) Calculate Telford's earnings per share for Year 10 for both schemes.

(c) Which scheme would you advise the business to adopt? You should give your reasons and state what additional information you would require.

Glossary of key terms

ABC system of stock control   A method of applying different levels of stock control, based on the value of each category of stock. *p 324*

accounting   The process of identifying, measuring and communicating information to permit informed judgements and decisions by users of the information. *p 1*

accounting conventions   Accounting rules that have evolved over time in order to deal with practical problems rather than to reflect some theoretical ideal. *p 39*

accounting information system   The system used within a business to identify, record, analyse and report accounting information. *p 8*

accounting rate of return (ARR)   The average profit from an investment, expressed as a percentage of the average investment made. *p 285*

accounting (financial reporting) standards   Rules established by the UK accounting profession, which should be followed by preparers of the annual financial statements of companies. *p 111*

accrued expenses   Expenses that are outstanding at the end of the accounting period. *p 61*

acid test ratio   A liquidity ratio that relates the current assets (less stocks) to the current liabilities. *p 164*

activity-based costing (ABC)   A technique for more accurately relating overheads to specific production or provision of a service. It is based on acceptance of the fact that overheads do not just occur but are caused by activities, such as holding products in stores, that 'drive' the costs. *p 233*

adverse variance   A difference between planned and actual performance, usually where the difference will cause the actual profit to be lower than the budgeted one. *p 261*

ageing schedule of debtors   A report dividing debtors into categories, depending on the length of time outstanding. *p 334*

asset   A resource held by a business, that has certain characteristics. *p 24*

auditors   Professionals whose main duty is to make a report as to whether, in their opinion, the financial statements of a business do that which they are supposed to do; namely, to show a true and fair view and comply with statutory, and accounting standard, requirements. *p 112*

average settlement period for creditors   The average time taken for a business to pay its creditors. *pp 158 and 344*

average settlement period for debtors   The average time taken for debtors to pay the amounts owing. *pp 157 and 334*

average stock turnover period   An efficiency ratio that measures the average period for which stocks are held by a business. *p 157*

bad debt   Amount owed to the business that is considered to be irrecoverable. *p 78*

balance sheet   A statement of financial position that shows the assets of a business and the claims on those assets. *p 20*

bank overdraft   A flexible form of borrowing that allows an individual or business to have a negative current account balance. *p 368*

batch costing   A technique for identifying full cost, where the production of many types of goods and services, particularly goods, involves producing in a batch of identical or nearly identical units of output, but where each batch is distinctly different from other batches. *p 229*

bonus shares   Shares that have been created from the reserves of a company and which are distributed 'free' to shareholders in proportion to their existing shareholdings. *p 97*

break-even analysis   The activity of deducing the break-even point of some activity through analysing costs and revenues. *p 191*

break-even chart   A graphical representation of the costs and revenues of some activity, at various levels, which enables the break-even point to be identified. *p 192*

break-even point   A level of activity where revenue will exactly equal total cost, so there is neither profit nor loss. *p 192*

budget   A financial plan for the short term, typically one year. *p 243*

budgetary control   Using the budget as a yardstick against which the effectiveness of actual performance may be assessed. *p 274*

business angels   Investors, typically individuals, who are prepared to make investments, normally equity ones, in small businesses. Often business angels take a close interest in the running of the business(es) in which they invest. *p 381*

business entity convention   The convention that holds that, for accounting purposes, the business and its owner(s) are treated as quite separate and distinct. *p 39*

capital   The owner's claim on the assets of the business. *p 27*

capital expenditure   The outlay of funds on fixed assets. *p 127*

capital reserves   Reserves that arise from a 'capital' profit or gain rather than from normal trading activities. *p 95*

cash discount   A reduction in the amount due for goods or services sold on credit in return for prompt payment. *p 333*

cash flow statement   A statement that shows the sources and uses of cash for a period. *p 20*

claim   An obligation on the part of the business to provide cash or some other benefit to an outside party. *p 24*

common costs   Another name for indirect costs or overheads. These are costs that do not directly relate and are not measurable in respect of particular units of output, but relate to all output. *p 217*

comparability   The requirement that items that are basically the same should be treated in the same manner for measurement and reporting purposes. Lack of comparability will limit the usefulness of accounting information. *p 5*

compensating variances   The situation that exists when two variances, one adverse the other favourable, are of equal size and therefore cancel out. *p 273*

consistency convention   The accounting convention that holds that when a particular method of accounting is selected to deal with a transaction, this method should be applied consistently over time. *p 77*

contribution (per unit)   Sales revenue per unit less variable costs per unit. *p 196*

control   Compelling events to conform to plan. *p 248*

convertible loan stocks   Loan capital that can be converted into equity share capital at the option of the holders. *p 358*

cost   The amount of resources, usually measured in monetary terms, sacrificed to achieve a particular objective. *p 186*

cost behaviour   The manner in which costs alter with changes in the level of activity. *p 219*

cost centre   Some area, object, person or activity for which costs are separately collected. *p 228*

cost driver   An activity that causes costs. *p 233*

cost of sales   The cost of the goods sold during a period. Cost of sales can be derived by adding the opening stock held to the stock purchases for the period and then deducting the closing stocks held. *p 56*

cost pool   The sum of the overhead costs that are seen as being caused by the same cost driver. *p 233*

cost unit   The objective for which the cost is being deduced, usually a product or service. *p 220*

creative accounting   Adopting accounting policies to achieve a particular view of performance and position that preparers of financial reports would like users to see, rather than what is a true and fair view. *p 114*

current asset   An asset that is not held on a continuing basis. Current assets include cash itself and other assets that are expected to be converted to cash at some future point. *p 33*

current liabilities   Amounts due for repayment to outside parties within 12 months of the balance sheet date. *p 34*

current ratio   A liquidity ratio that relates the current assets of the business to the current liabilities. *p 163*

debenture   A long-term loan, usually made to a business, evidenced by a trust deed. *p 101 and 356*

debt factoring   A service offered by a financial institution (a factor) that involves the factor taking over the management of the trade debtors of the business. The factor is often prepared to make an advance to the business based on the amount of trade debtors outstanding. *p 368*

depreciation   A measure of that portion of the cost (less residual value) of a fixed asset that has been consumed during an accounting period. *p 65*

direct costs   Costs that can be identified with specific cost units, to the extent that the effect of the cost can be measured in respect of each particular unit of output. *p 216*

direct method   An approach to deducing the cash flows from trading operations, in a cash flow statement, by analysing the business's cash records. *p 132*

directors   Individuals who are elected to act as the most senior level of management of a business. *p 90*

discount factor   The rate applied to future cash flows to derive the present value of those cash flows. *p 298*

dividends   Transfers of assets made by a business to its shareholders. *p 92*

dividend payout ratio   An investment ratio that relates the dividends announced for the period to the earnings available for dividends that were generated in that period. *p 170*

dividend yield ratio   An investment ratio that expresses a business's dividend per share as a percentage of its current share price. It provides users with some measure of the dividend returns that the share generates. *p 170*

dual aspect convention   The accounting convention that holds that each transaction has two aspects, and that each aspect must be recorded in the financial statements. *p 42*

earnings per share   An investment ratio that relates the earnings generated by the business during a period, and available to shareholders, to the number of shares in issue. *p 171*

economic order quantity (EOQ)   The quantity of stocks that should be purchased in order to minimise total stock costs. *p 326*

equity   Ordinary shares and reserves of a company. *p 93*

equity dividends paid   A section of the cash flow statement that deals with the cash flows arising from ordinary share dividends paid. *p 127*

eurobond   A form of long-term bond issued in a currency that is not of the country in which the bond is issued. *p 356*

expense   A measure of the outflow of assets (or increase in liabilities) that is incurred as a result of generating revenues. *p 53*

favourable variance   A difference between planned and actual performance, usually where the difference will cause the actual profit to be higher than the budgeted one. *p 261*

finance   The raising, investment and management of funds. *p 2*

finance lease   A financial arrangement whereby the asset title remains with the owner (the lessor) but the lease agreement transfers virtually all the rewards and risks to the business (the lessee). *p 362*

financial accounting   The measuring and reporting of accounting information for external users (those users other than the managers of the business). *p 13*

financing   A section of the cash flow statement that deals with the cash flows arising from raising and repaying long-term finance. *p 127*

first in, first out (FIFO)   A method of stock valuation that assumes that the earlier stocks are to be sold first. *p 74*

five Cs of credit   A checklist of factors to be taken into account when assessing the creditworthiness of a customer. *p 330*

fixed asset   An asset held with the intention of being used to generate wealth rather than being held for resale. Fixed assets can be seen as the tools of the business, and are normally held by the business on a continuing basis. *p 32*

fixed cost   A cost that stays the same when changes occur to the volume of activity. *p 187*

flexible budget   A budget that is adjusted to reflect the actual level of output achieved. *p 257*

flexing (the budget)   Revising the budget to what it would have been had the planned level of output been different. *p 259*

full costing   Deducing the total direct and indirect (overhead) costs of pursuing some activity or objective. *p 214*

gearing   The existence of fixed payment bearing securities (for example, loans) in the capital structure of a business. *p 165*

gearing ratio   A ratio that relates the contribution of long-term lenders to the total long-term capital of the business. *p 168*

going concern convention   The accounting convention that assumes that the business will continue operations for the foreseeable future, unless the opposite is known to be true. In other words, there is no intention or need to liquidate the business. *p 41*

gross profit   The amount remaining (if positive) after trading expenses (for example, cost of sales) have been deducted from trading revenues (for example, sales). *p 55*

gross profit margin ratio   A profitability ratio relating the gross profit for the period to the sales for the period. *p 155*

historic cost convention   The accounting convention that holds that assets should be recorded at their historic (acquisition) cost. *p 41*

indirect costs (or overheads)   All costs except direct costs, that is, those that cannot be directly measured in respect of each particular unit of output. *p 216*

indirect method   An approach to deducing the cash flows from trading operations, in a cash flow statement, by analysing the business's financial statements. *p 132*

inflation   A tendency for a currency to lose value over time owing to increasing prices of goods and services. *p 295*

intangible assets   Assets that do not have a physical substance (for example, patents, goodwill and debtors). *p 26*

interest cover ratio   A gearing ratio that divides the net profit before interest and taxation by the interest payable for a period. *p 168*

internal rate of return (IRR)   The discount rate for a project that will have the effect of producing a zero NPV. *p 301*

investigating variances   The act of looking into the practical causes of budget variances, once those variances have been identified. *p 271*

invoice discounting   A loan provided by a financial institution based on a proportion of the face value of credit sales outstanding. *p 369*

job costing   A technique for identifying the full cost per unit of output, where that output is not similar to other units of output. *p 217*

just-in-time (JIT) stock management   A system of stock management that aims to have supplies delivered to production just in time for their required use. *p 328*

last in, first out (LIFO)   A method of stock valuation that assumes that the latest stocks are the first to be sold. *p 74*

liabilities   Claims of individuals and organisations, apart from the owner, that have arisen from past transactions or events such as supplying goods or lending money to the business. *p 27*

limited company   An artificial legal person that has an identity separate from that of those who own and manage it. *p 86*

limited liability   The restriction of the legal obligation of shareholders to meet all of the company's debts. *p 89*

limiting factor   Some aspect of the business (for example, lack of sales demand) that will prevent it from achieving its objectives to the maximum extent. *p 245*

loan covenants   Conditions contained within a loan agreement that are designed to protect the lenders. *p 360*

long-term liabilities   Those amounts due to other parties that are not liable for repayment within the next 12 months after the balance sheet date. *p 34*

management accounting   The measuring and reporting of accounting information for the managers of a business. *p 13*

management by exception   A system of control, based on a comparison of planned and actual performance, that allows managers to focus on areas of poor performance rather than dealing with areas where performance is satisfactory. *p 248*

management of liquid resources   A section of the cash flow statement that deals with the cash flows arising from movements in short-term liquid resources. *p 127*

margin of safety   The extent to which the planned level of output or sales lies above the break-even point. *p 196*

marginal analysis   The activity of decision making through analysing variable costs and revenues, ignoring fixed costs. *p 203*

marginal cost   The additional cost of producing one more unit. This is often the same as the variable cost. *p 202*

master budgets   A summary of the individual budgets, usually consisting of a budgeted profit and loss account, a budgeted balance sheet and a budgeted cash flow statement. *p 245*

matching convention   The accounting convention that holds that, in measuring income, expenses should be matched to revenues that they helped generate, in the same accounting period as those revenues were realised. *p 61*

materiality   The requirement that material information should be disclosed to users in financial statements. *p 6*

materials requirement planning (MRP) system   A computer-based system of stock control that schedules the timing of deliveries of bought-in parts and materials to coincide with production requirements to meet demand. *p 328*

materiality convention   The accounting convention that states that, where the amounts involved are immaterial, only what is expedient should be considered. *p 64*

money measurement convention   The accounting convention that holds that accounting should deal only with those items that are capable of being expressed in monetary terms. *p 39*

mortgage   A loan secured on property. *p 360*

net cash flow from operating activities   A section of the cash flow statement that deals with the cash flows from trading operations. *p 125*

net present value (NPV)   A method of investment appraisal based on the present value of all relevant cash flows associated with the project. *p 292*

net profit   The amount remaining (if positive) after the total expenses for a period have been deducted from total revenues. *p 55*

net profit margin ratio   A profitability ratio relating the net profit for the period to the sales for the period. *p 154*

nominal value   The face value of a share in a company. *p 92*

objectivity convention   The accounting convention that holds that, in so far as is possible, the financial statements prepared should be based on objective verifiable evidence rather than on matters of opinion. *p 44*

offer for sale   An issue of shares that involves a public limited company (or its shareholders) selling the shares to a financial institution that will, in turn, sell the shares to the public. *p 384*

operating cash cycle   The period between the outlay of cash to purchase supplies and the ultimate receipt of cash from the sale of goods. *p 339*

operating gearing   The relationship between the total fixed and the total variable costs for some activity. *p 197*

operating profit   The profit achieved during a period after all operating expenses have been deducted from revenues from operations. Financing expenses are deducted after the calculation of operating profit. *p 107*

ordinary shares Shares of a company owned by those who are due the benefits of the company's activities after all other stakeholders have been satisfied. *p 93*

overhead (or indirect cost) Any cost except a direct cost; a cost that cannot be directly measured in respect of each particular unit of output. *p 216*

overhead absorption (recovery) rate The rate at which overheads are charged to cost units (jobs), usually in a job costing system. *p 221*

payback period (PP) The time taken for the initial investment in a project to be repaid from the net cash inflows of the project. *p 289*

preference shares Shares of a company owned by those who are entitled to the first part of any dividend that the company may pay. *p 93*

prepaid expenses Expenses that have been paid in advance at the end of the accounting period. *p 64*

price/earnings ratio An investment ratio that relates the market value of a share to the earnings per share. *p 172*

private company A limited company for which the directors can restrict the ownership of its shares. *p 90*

private placing An issue of shares that involves a limited company arranging for the shares to be sold to the clients of particular issuing houses or stockbrokers, rather than to the general investing public. *p 385*

process costing A technique for deriving the full cost per unit of output, where the units of output are exactly similar or it is reasonable to treat them as being so. *p 216*

profit The increase in wealth attributable to the owners of a business that arises through business operations. *p 53*

profit and loss account A financial statement that measures and reports the profit (or loss) the business has generated during a period. It is derived by deducting from total revenues for a period, the total expenses associated with those revenues. *p 20*

profit–volume (PV) chart A graphical representation of the contributions (revenues less variable costs) of some activity, at various levels, which enables the break-even point, and the profit at various activity levels, to be identified. *p 200*

prudence convention The accounting convention that holds that financial statements should err on the side of caution. The prudence convention represents a pessimistic rather than an optimistic view of financial position. *p 42*

public company A limited company for which the directors cannot restrict the ownership of its shares. *p 90*

public issue An issue of shares that involves a public limited company making a direct invitation to the public to purchase shares in the company. *p 384*

realisation convention The accounting convention that holds that revenue should be recognised only when it has been realised. *p 60*

reducing-balance method   A method of calculating depreciation that applies a fixed percentage rate of depreciation to the written-down value of an asset in each period. *p 68*

relevance   The ability of accounting information to influence decisions. Relevance is regarded as a key characteristic of useful accounting information. *p 5*

reliability   The requirement that accounting should be free from material error or bias. Reliability is regarded as a key characteristic of useful accounting information. *p 5*

reserves   Part of the owners' claim on a limited company that has arisen from profits and gains, to the extent that these have not been distributed to the shareholders. *p 91*

residual value   The amount for which a fixed asset is sold when the business has no further use for it. *p 67*

return on capital employed (ROCE)   A profitability ratio expressing the relationship between the net profit (before interest and taxation) and the long-term capital invested in the business. *p 153*

returns on investments and servicing of finance   A section of the cash flow statement that deals with the cash flows arising from interest and dividends received and from interest paid. *p 125*

return on ordinary shareholders' funds (ROSF)   A profitability ratio that compares the amount of profit for the period available to the ordinary shareholders with their stake in the business. *p 152*

revenue   A measure of the inflow of assets (for example, cash or amounts owed to a business by debtors), or a reduction in liabilities, which arise as a result of trading operations. *p 53*

revenue reserve   Part of the owners' claim of a company that arises from realised profits and gains, including after-tax trading profits and gains from disposals of fixed assets. *p 92*

rights issues   Issues of shares for cash to existing shareholders on the basis of the number of shares already held. *pp 99 and 382*

risk   The likelihood that what is estimated to occur will not actually occur. *p 294*

risk premium   A rate of return in excess of that which would be expected from a risk-free investment, to compensate the investor for bearing risk. *p 295*

sale and leaseback   An agreement to sell an asset (usually property) to another party and simultaneously to lease the asset back in order to continue using the asset. *p 363*

sales to capital employed ratio   An efficiency ratio that relates the sales generated during a period to the capital employed. *p 159*

semi-fixed (semi-variable) cost   A cost that has an element of both fixed and variable cost. *p 190*

share   A portion of the ownership, or equity, of a company. *p 87*

share premium   Any amount above the nominal value of shares that is paid for those shares. *p 96*

stable monetary unit convention The accounting convention that holds that money, which is the unit of measurement in accounting, will not change in value over time. *p 43*

standard quantities and costs Planned quantities and costs (or revenues) for individual units of input or output. Standards are the building blocks used to produce the budget. *p 269*

stepped fixed cost A fixed cost that does not remain fixed over all levels of output but which changes in steps as a threshold level of output is reached. *p 188*

Stock Exchange A market where 'second-hand' shares may be bought and sold and new capital raised. *p 377*

straight-line method A method of accounting for depreciation that allocates the amount to be depreciated evenly over the useful life of the asset. *p 67*

tangible assets Those assets that have a physical substance (for example, plant and machinery, motor vehicles). *p 26*

taxation A section of the cash flow statement that deals with the cash flows arising from taxes paid and refunded. *p 127*

tender issue An issue of shares that involves a public limited company inviting the investing public to make offers for the shares, rather than the company setting the price itself. *p 384*

term loans Finance provided by financial institutions, like banks and insurance companies, under a contract with the borrowing business that indicates the interest rate and dates of payments of interest and repayment of the loan. They are not normally transferable from one lender to another. *p 356*

trading and profit and loss account A type of profit and loss account prepared by merchandising businesses (for example, retailers and wholesalers) that measures and reports the gross profit (loss) from trading and then deducts overhead expenses to derive the net profit (loss) for the period. *p 55*

understandability The requirement that accounting information should be capable of being understood by those for whom the information is primarily compiled. Lack of understandability will limit the usefulness of accounting information. *p 6*

variable cost A cost that varies according to the volume of activity. *p 187*

variance The financial effect, on the budgeted profit, of the particular factor under consideration being more or less than budgeted. *p 261*

venture capital Long-term capital provided by certain institutions to small and medium-size businesses to exploit relatively high-risk opportunities. *p 379*

warrants A document giving the holder the right, but not the obligation, to acquire ordinary shares in a company at an agreed price. *p 359*

weighted average cost (AVCO) A method of valuing stocks that assumes that stocks entering the business lose their separate identity and any issues of stock reflect the weighted average cost of the stocks held. *p 75*

working capital Current assets less current liabilities (creditors due within one year). *p 318*

Solutions to self-assessment questions

Chapter 2

2.1 The balance sheet you prepare should be set out as follows:

Simonson Engineering
Balance sheet as at 30 September 2003

	£	£	£
Fixed assets			
Freehold premises			72,000
Plant and machinery			25,000
Motor vehicles			15,000
Fixtures and fittings			9,000
			121,000
Current assets			
Stock-in-trade		45,000	
Trade debtors		48,000	
Cash in hand		1,500	
		94,500	
Current liabilities			
Trade creditors	(18,000)		
Bank overdraft	(26,000)		
		(44,000)	
			50,500
Total assets less current liabilities			171,500
Long-term liabilities			
Loan			(51,000)
Net assets			120,500
Capital			
Opening balance			117,500
Add Profit			18,000
			135,500
Less Drawings			15,000
			120,500

Chapter 3

3.1

TT and Co
Balance sheet as at 31 December 2003

Assets	£	Claims	£
Delivery van (12,000 – 2,500)	9,500	Capital (50,000 + 26,900)	76,900
Stock-in-trade (143,000 +			
12,000 – 74,000 – 16,000)	65,000	Trade creditors (143,000 –	
Trade debtors (152,000 –		121,000)	22,000
132,000 – 400)	19,600	Accrued expenses (630 + 620)	1,250
Cash at bank (50,000 –			
25,000 – 500 – 900 –			
300 – 12,000 – 33,500 –			
1,650 – 12,000 + 35,000 –			
9,400 + 132,000 – 121,000)	750		
Prepaid expenses (5,000 + 300)	5,300		
	100,150		100,150

Profit and loss account for the year ended 31 December 2003

	£
Sales (152,000 + 35,000)	187,000
Less Cost of stock sold	
(74,000 + 16,000)	90,000
Gross profit	97,000
Less	

Rent	20,000
Rates (500 + 900)	1,400
Wages (33,500 + 630)	34,130
Electricity (1,650 + 620)	2,270
Bad debts	400
Van depreciation ((12,000 – 2,000)/4)	2,500
Van expenses	9,400
	70,100
Net profit for the year	26,900

The balance sheet could now be rewritten in a more stylish form as follows:

TT and Co
Balance sheet as at 31 December 2003

	£	£	£
Fixed assets			
Motor van			9,500
Current assets			
Stock-in-trade	65,000		
Trade debtors	19,600		
Prepaid expenses	5,300		
Cash	750		
		90,650	
Less Current liabilities			
Trade creditors	22,000		
Accrued expenses	1,250		
		23,250	
			67,400
			76,900
Capital			
Original			50,000
Profit			26,900
			76,900

Chapter 4

4.1

Pear Limited
Balance sheet as at 30 September 2003

	£000	£000
Fixed assets		
Cost (1,570 + 30)	1,600	
Depreciation (690 + 12)	702	
		898
Current assets		
Stock	207	
Debtors (182 + 18)	200	
Cash at bank	21	
	428	
Less **Creditors: amounts due within one year**		
Trade creditors	88	
Other creditors (20 + 30 + 15 + 2)	67	
Taxation	19	
Dividend proposed	25	
Bank overdraft	105	
	304	
Net current assets		124
Less **Creditors: amount due after more than one year**		
10% debenture – repayable 2008		(300)
		722
Capital and reserves		
Shares capital		300
Share premium account		300
Retained profit at beginning of year	104	
Profit for year	18	122
		722

Profit and loss account for the year ended 30 September 2003

	£000	£000
Turnover (1,456 + 18)		1,474
Cost of sales		(768)
Gross profit		706
Less Salaries	220	
Depreciation (249 + 12)	261	
Other operating costs (131 + 2)	133	
		(614)
Operating profit		92
Interest payable (15 + 15)		(30)
Profit before taxation		62
Taxation (62 × 30%)		(19)
Profit after taxation		43
Dividend proposed		(25)
		18

Chapter 5

5.1

Cash flow statement for the year ended 31 December 2003

	£m	£m
Net cash inflows from operating activities		66
(see analysis below)		
Returns from investment and servicing of finance		
Interest received	2	
Interest paid	(4)	
Net cash outflow from returns on investment and		
servicing of finance		(2)
Taxation		
Corporation tax paid (see note 1 below)	(12)	
Net cash outflow for taxation		(12)
Capital expenditure		
Land and buildings	(22)	
Plant and machinery (see note 2 below)	(19)	
Net cash outflow for capital expenditure		(41)
		11
Equity dividends paid		
Dividends paid (see note 3 below)	(16)	
Net cash outflow for equity dividends		(16)
		(5)
Management of liquid resources		
Investment in treasury bills	(15)	
Net cash outflow for management of liquid resources		(15)
Financing		
Issue of debenture stock	20	
Net cash inflow from financing		20
Net increase in cash		0

To see how this relates to the cash of the business at the beginning and end of the year it is useful to show a reconciliation as follows:

Reconciliation of cash movements during the year ended 31 December 2003

	£m
Balance at 1 January 2003	4
Net cash inflow	–
Balance at 31 December 2003	4

Calculation of net cash inflow from operating activities

	£m	£m
Operating profit (from the profit and loss account)		62
Add Depreciation		
Land and buildings	6	
Plant and machinery	10	
		16
		78
Less Increase in debtors (26 – 16)	10	
Decrease in creditors (26 – 23)	3	13
		65
Add Decrease in stocks (25 – 24)		1
		66

Notes

1   *Taxation*

	£m
Amount owing at 1.1.2003	4
Tax charge for 2003	16
	20
Amount owing at 31.12.2003	8
Amount paid during 2003	12

2   *Fixed asset acquisitions*

	Land and buildings	*Plant and machinery*
	£m	*£m*
Position at 31 December 2002	94	53
Less 2003 depreciation	6	10
	88	43
Position at 31 December 2003	110	62
Acquisitions	22	19

3   *Dividends*

	2002	*2003*
	£m	*£m*
Total for the year (profit and loss account)	14	18
Still outstanding at the end of the year (balance sheet)	12	14
Paid during the year (interim dividend)	2	4

Thus the amount paid during 2003 was £12 million from 2002, plus £4 million for 2003, that is £16 million in total.

Chapter 6

6.1   In answering this question you may have used the following ratios:

Ali plc	*Bhaskar plc*
Current ratio $= \dfrac{853}{422.4} = 2.0$	$= \dfrac{816.5}{293.1} = 2.8$
Acid test ratio $= \dfrac{(853 - 592)}{422.4} = 0.6$	$= \dfrac{(816.5 - 403)}{293.1} = 1.4$
Gearing ratio $= \dfrac{190}{(687.6 + 190)} \times 100 = 21.6\%$	$= \dfrac{250}{(874.6 + 250)} \times 100 = 22.2\%$
Interest cover ratio $= \dfrac{(131.9 + 19.4)}{19.4} = 7.8$ times	$= \dfrac{(139.4 + 27.5)}{27.5} = 6.1$ times
Dividend payout ratio $= \dfrac{135.0}{99.9} \times 100 = 135\%$	$= \dfrac{95.0}{104.6} \times 100 = 91\%$
Price earnings ratio $= \dfrac{£6.50}{31.2p} = 20.8T$	$= \dfrac{£8.20}{41.8p} = 19.6T$

Ali plc has a much lower current ratio and acid test ratio than those of Bhaskar plc. The reasons for this may be partly due to the fact that Ali plc has a lower average settlement period for debtors. Ali plc's acid test ratio is substantially below 1.0, which may suggest a liquidity problem.

The gearing ratio of each business is quite similar. Neither business has excessive borrowing. The interest cover ratio for each business is also similar. The respective ratios indicate that both businesses have good profit coverage for their interest charges.

The dividend payout ratio for each business seems very high indeed. In the case of Ali plc, the dividends announced for the year are considerably higher than the earnings generated during the year that are available for dividend. As a result, part of the dividend was paid out of retained profits from previous years. This is an unusual occurrence. Although it is quite legitimate to do this, such action may nevertheless suggest a lack of prudence on the part of the directors.

The P/E ratio for both businesses is high, which indicates market confidence in their future prospects.

Chapter 7

7.1 (a) The break-even point if only Alpha were made would be:

Fixed costs/(Sales revenue per unit − Variable cost per unit)
= £40,000/(£30 − (15 + 6)) = 4,444 units (per annum)

(b)

Product	Alpha (per unit) £	Beta (per unit) £	Gamma (per unit) £
Selling price	30	39	20
Variable materials	(15)	(18)	(10)
Variable production costs	(6)	(10)	(5)
Contribution	9	11	5
Time on machine (hours)	2	3	1
Contribution per hour on machines	£4.50	£3.67	£5.00
Order of priority	2nd	3rd	1st

(c)

			Contributions £
Produce:	5,000 Gamma using	5,000	hours generating 25,000 (that is, 5,000 × £5)
	2,500 Alphas using	5,000	hours generating 22,500 (that is, 2,500 × £9)
		10,000	hours 47,500
			Less Fixed costs 40,000
			Profit 7,500

Leaving a demand for 500 units of Alpha and 2,000 units of Beta unsatisfied.

Chapter 8

8.1 (a) The budget may be summarised as:

	£	
Sales revenue	196,000	
Direct materials	(38,000)	
Direct labour	(32,000)	
Total overheads	(77,000)	(that is, £2,400 + 3,000 + 27,600 + 36,000 + 8,000)
Profit	49,000	

This job may be priced on the basis that both overheads and profit should be apportioned to it on the basis of direct labour cost, as follows:

	£	
Direct materials	4,000	
Direct labour	3,600	
Overheads	8,663	(that is, £77,000 × 3,600/32,000)
Profit	5,513	(that is, £49,000 × 3,600/32,000)
	21,776	

This answer assumes that variable overheads vary in proportion to direct labour cost.

Various other bases of charging overheads and profit loading the job could have been adopted. For example, material cost could have been included (with direct labour) as the basis for profit loading, or even apportioning overheads.

(b) This part of the question is, in effect, asking for comments on the validity of 'full cost plus' pricing. This approach can be useful as an indicator of the effective long-run cost of doing the job. On the other hand, it fails to take account of such factors as the state of the market and other external factors.

Chapter 9

9.1   Raw materials stock budget for the six months ending 31 December (in units):

	July units	Aug units	Sept units	Oct units	Nov units	Dec units
Opening stock (current month's production)	500	600	600	700	750	750
Purchases (balancing figure)	600	600	700	750	750	750
	1,100	1,200	1,300	1,450	1,500	1,500
Less Issued to production (from question)	500	600	600	700	750	750
Closing stock (next month's production)	600	600	700	750	750	750

Raw materials stock budget for the six months ending 31 December (in financial terms, that is, the units × £8):

	July £	Aug £	Sept £	Oct £	Nov £	Dec £
Opening stock	4,000	4,800	4,800	5,600	6,000	6,000
Purchases	4,800	4,800	5,600	6,000	6,000	6,000
	8,800	9,600	10,400	11,600	12,000	12,000
Less Issued to production	4,000	4,800	4,800	5,600	6,000	6,000
Closing stock	4,800	4,800	5,600	6,000	6,000	6,000

Creditors budget for the six months ending 31 December:

	July £	Aug £	Sept £	Oct £	Nov £	Dec £
Opening balance (current month's payment)	4,000	4,800	4,800	5,600	6,000	6,000
Purchases (from RM stock budget)	4,800	4,800	5,600	6,000	6,000	6,000
	8,800	9,600	10,400	11,600	12,000	12,000
Less Payments	4,000	4,800	4,800	5,600	6,000	6,000
Closing balance (next month's payment)	4,800	4,800	5,600	6,000	6,000	6,000

Cash budget for the six months ending 31 December:

	July £	Aug £	Sept £	Oct £	Nov £	Dec £
Inflows						
Receipts						
Debtors (40% of previous month's sales)	2,800	3,200	3,200	4,000	4,800	5,200
Cash sales (60% of current month's sales)	4,800	6,000	7,200	7,800	8,400	9,600
Total inflows	7,600	9,200	10,400	11,800	13,200	14,800
Outflows						
Payments to creditors	4,000	4,800	4,800	5,600	6,000	6,000
Direct costs	3,000	3,600	3,600	4,200	4,500	4,500
Advertising	1,000	–	–	1,500	–	–
Overheads:						
80%	1,280	1,280	1,280	1,280	1,600	1,600
20%	280	320	320	320	320	400
New plant			2,200	2,200	2,200	
Total outflows	9,560	10,000	12,200	15,100	14,620	12,500
Net inflows/(outflows)	(1,960)	(800)	(1,800)	(3,300)	(1,420)	2,300
Balance carried forward	5,540	4,740	2,940	(360)	(1,780)	520

The balances carried forward each month are deduced by subtracting the deficit (net cash outflow) for the month from (or adding the surplus for the month to) the previous month's balance.

Note how budgets are linked: in this case, the stock budget to the creditors budget and the creditors budget to the cash budget.

The following are possible means of relieving the cash shortages revealed by the budget:

❑ Make a higher proportion of sales on a cash basis.
❑ Collect the money from debtors more promptly, for example during the month following the sale.
❑ Hold lower stocks, both of raw materials and of finished stock.
❑ Increase the creditor payment period.
❑ Delay the payments for advertising.
❑ Obtain more credit for the overhead costs – at present, only 20 per cent is on credit.
❑ Delay the payments for the new plant.

9.2 (a) and (b):

Toscanini Ltd
Budget

	Original	Flexed		Actual	
Output (units)	4,000	3,500		3,500	
(production and sales)					
	£	£		£	
Sales	16,000	14,000		13,820	
Raw materials	(3,840)	(3,360)	(1,400 kg)	(3,420)	(1,425 kg)
Labour	(3,200)	(2,800)	(350 hrs)	(2,690)	(345 hrs)
Fixed overheads	(4,800)	(4,800)		(4,900)	
Operating profit	4,160	3,040		2,810	

	£	Manager accountable
Sales volume variance		
(4,160 – 3,040)	(1,120) (A)	Sales
Sales price variance		
(14,000 – 13,820)	(180) (A)	Sales
Materials price variance		
(1,425 × 2.40) – 3,420	zero	–
Materials usage variance		
[(3,500 × 0.4) – 1,425] × £2.40	(60) (A)	Production
Labour rate variance		
(345 × £8) – 2,690	70 (F)	Personnel
Labour efficiency variance		
[(3,500 × 0.10) – 345 × £8	40 (F)	Production
Fixed overhead spending		
4,800 – 4,900	(100) (A)	Various, depending on the nature of the overheads
Total net variances	(1,350) (A)	
Budgeted profit	4,160	
Less: Total net variance	1,350	
Actual profit	2,810	

(c) Feasible explanations include the following:

Sales volume	Unanticipated fall in world demand would account for 400 × £2.24 = £896 of this variance.
	The remainder is probably caused by ineffective marketing, though a lack of availability of stock to sell may be a reason.
Sales price	Ineffective selling seems the only logical reason.
Materials usage	Inefficient usage of material, perhaps because of poor performance by labour or substandard materials.
Labour rate	Less overtime worked or lower production bonuses paid as a result of lower volume of activity.
Labour efficiency	More effective working, perhaps because fewer hours were worked than planned.
Overheads	Ineffective control of overheads.

(d) Clearly not all of the sales volume variance can be attributed to poor marketing, given a 10 per cent reduction in demand.

It will probably be useful to distinguish between that part of the variance that arose from the shortfall in general demand (a planning variance) and a volume variance that is more fairly attributable to the manager concerned. Thus accountability will be more fairly imposed.

	£
Planning variance (10% × 4,000) × £2.24	896
'New' sales volume variance	
(4,000 – (10% × 4,000) – 3,500) × £2.24	224
Original sales volume variance	1,120

Chapter 10

10.1 (a) Relevant cash flows:

Year	0	1	2	3	4	5
	£000	*£000*	*£000*	*£000*	*£000*	*£000*
Sales revenue	–	80	120	144	100	64
Loss of contribution		(15)	(15)	(15)	(15)	(15)
Variable costs		(40)	(50)	(48)	(30)	(32)
Fixed costs (see Note 1)		(8)	(8)	(8)	(8)	(8)
Operating cash flows		17	47	73	47	9
Working capital	(30)					30
Capital cost	(100)					
Net relevant cash flows	(130)	17	47	73	47	39

Notes

1   Only the fixed costs that are incremental to the project (only existing because of the project) are relevant. Depreciation is irrelevant because it is not a cash flow.

2   The research and development cost is irrelevant since it has been spent irrespective of the decision on X14 production.

(b) Payback period:

Cumulative cash flows	(130)	(113)	(66)	7

Thus, the equipment will have repaid the initial investment by the end of the third year of operations.

(c) Net present value:

Discount factor	1.00	0.926	0.857	0.794	0.735	0.681
Present value	(130)	15.74	40.28	57.96	34.55	26.56
Net present value	45.09 (that is, the sum of the present values for years 0 to 5)					

Chapter 11

11.1

	£	£
Existing level of debtors (£4m × 70/365)		767,000
New level of debtors		
£2m × 80/365	(438,000)	
£2m × 30/365	(164,000)	(602,000)
Reduction in debtors		165,000
Costs and benefits of the policy		
Cost of discount (£2m × 2%)		40,000
Less Savings		
Interest payable (£165,000 × 13%)	21,450	
Administration costs	6,000	
Bad debts	10,000	37,450
Net cost of policy		2,550

The above calculations reveal that the business will be worse off by offering the discounts.

Chapter 12

12.1 (a) The liquidity position may be assessed by using the liquidity ratios discussed in an earlier chapter:

$$\text{Current ratio} = \frac{\text{Current assets}}{\text{Current liabilities}}$$
(creditors due within one year)

$$= \frac{£7.5\text{m}}{£5.4\text{m}}$$

$$= 1.4$$

$$\text{Acid test ratio} = \frac{\text{Current assets (less stock)}}{\text{Current liabilities}}$$
(creditors due within one year)

$$= \frac{£3.7\text{m}}{£5.4\text{m}}$$

$$= 0.7$$

The ratios calculated above reveal a fairly weak liquidity position. The current ratio seems quite low, and the acid test ratio seems very low. This latter ratio suggests that the business does not have sufficient liquid assets to meet its maturing obligations. It would, however, be useful to have details of the liquidity ratios of similar businesses in the same industry in order to make a more informed judgement. The bank overdraft represents 67 per cent of the short-term liabilities and 40 per cent of the total liabilities of the business. The continuing support of the bank is therefore important to the ability of the business to meet its commitments.

(b) The finance required to reduce trade creditors to an average of 40 days outstanding is calculated as follows:

	£m
Trade creditors at balance sheet date	1.80
Trade creditors outstanding based on 40 days' credit	
40/365 × £8.4 (that is, credit purchases)	(0.92)
Finance required	0.88 (say, £0.9m)

(c) The bank may not wish to provide further finance to the business. The increase in overdraft will reduce the level of trade creditors but will increase the exposure of the bank. The additional finance invested by the bank will not generate further funds, and will not therefore be self-liquidating. The question does not make it clear whether the business has sufficient security to offer the bank for the increase in overdraft facility. The profits of the business will be reduced, and the interest cover ratio, based on the profits generated to the year ended 31 May Year 10, would reduce to 1.63 times (see Note below) if the additional overdraft was granted (based on interest charged at 10 per cent a year). This is very low, and means that a relatively small decline in profits would lead to interest charges not being covered.

Note: Interest would be payable on the existing bank overdraft (£3.6m), plus the extension to cover the reduction in trade creditors (£0.9m) plus the debentures (£3.5m), that is £8.0m in total. Assuming an interest rate of 10 per cent a year, this means a yearly interest expense of about £0.8m. Before interest, the profit (for Year 10) was £1.3m (that is, 6.4 – 3.0 – 2.1). Interest cover would be 1.63 (that is, 1.3/0.8).

(d) A number of possible sources of finance might be considered. Four possible sources are as follows:

- ❑ *Issue of ordinary shares.* This option may be unattractive to investors. The return on ordinary shareholders' funds is fairly low at 7.9 per cent (that is, net profit after tax (0.3) divided by share capital and reserves (3.8)) and there is no evidence that the profitability of the business will improve. If profits remain at their current level, the effect of issuing more equity will be to further reduce the returns to ordinary shareholders.
- ❑ *Issue of loans.* This option may also prove unattractive to investors. Issuing further loans will have an effect similar to that of increasing the overdraft. The profits of the business will be reduced, and the interest cover ratio will decrease to a low level. The business's gearing ratio is already quite high at 48 per cent (that is, debentures (3.5) divided by debentures plus share capital and reserves (3.5 + 3.8)), and it is not clear what security would be available for the loan. The gearing ratio would be much higher if the overdraft were included.
- ❑ *Chase debtors.* It may be possible to improve cash flows by reducing the level of credit outstanding from debtors. At present the average settlement period is 93 days (that is, (debtors (3.6) divided by sales (14.2)) × 365), which seems quite high. A reduction in the average settlement period by approximately one-quarter would generate the funds required. However, it is not clear what effect this would have on sales.
- ❑ *Reduce stock.* This appears to be the most attractive of the four options discussed. At present the average stockholding period is 178 days (that is, (closing stock (3.8) divided by cost of sales (7.8)) × 365, based on year end stock levels), which seems to be very high. A reduction in this stockholding period by less than one-third would generate the funds required. However, if the business holds a large amount of slow-moving and obsolete stock, it may be difficult to reduce stock levels easily.

Solutions to selected exercises

Chapter 2

2.1

Profit and loss account for Day 1

	£
Sales (70 × £0.80)	56
Cost of sales (70 × £0.50)	(35)
Profit	21

Cash flow statement for Day 1

	£
Opening balance	40
Add cash from sales	56
	96
Less cash for purchases (80 × £0.50)	40
Closing balance	56

Balance sheet as at end of Day 1

	£
Cash balance	56
Stock of unsold goods (10 × £0.50)	5
Helen's business wealth	61

Profit and loss account for Day 2

	£
Sales (65 × £0.80)	52.0
Cost of sales (65 × £0.50)	(32.5)
Profit	19.5

Cash flow statement for Day 2

	£
Opening balance	56.0
Add cash from sales	52.0
	108.0
Less cash for purchases (60 × £0.50)	30.0
Closing balance	78.0

Balance sheet as at end of Day 2

	£
Cash balance	78.0
Stock of unsold goods (5 × £0.50)	2.5
Helen's business wealth	80.5

Profit and loss account for Day 3

	£
Sales (20 × £0.80 + 45 × £0.40)	34.0
Cost of sales (65 × £0.50)	(32.5)
Profit	1.5

Cash flow statement for Day 3

	£
Opening balance	78.0
Add cash from sales	34.0
	112.0
Less cash for purchases (60 × £0.50)	30.0
Closing balance	82.0

Balance sheet as at end of Day 3

	£
Cash balance	82.0
Stock of unsold goods	–
Helen's business wealth	82.0

2.4 (a)   **Balance sheet as at 30 June last year**

	£000	£000	£000
Fixed assets			
Freehold premises			320
Machinery and tools			207
Motor vehicles			38
			565
Current assets			
Stock-in-trade		153	
Debtors		185	
		338	
Less **Current liabilities**			
Creditors	86		
Bank overdraft	116	202	
			136
			701
Less **Long-term liabilities**			
Loan from bank			260
			441
Capital (missing figure)			441

(b) The balance sheet reveals a high level of investment in fixed assets. In percentage terms, we can say that more than 60 per cent of the total investment in assets has been in fixed assets. The nature of the business may require a heavy investment in fixed assets. The investment in current assets exceeds the current liabilities by a large amount (approximately 1.7 times). As a result, there are no obvious signs of a liquidity problem. However, the balance sheet reveals that the business has no cash balance and is therefore dependent on the continuing support of the bank (in the form of a bank overdraft) in order to meet obligations when they fall due. When considering the long-term financing of the business, we can see that about 37 per cent (that is, $(260/(260 + 441)) \times 100$) of the total long-term finance for the business has been supplied by loan capital and about 63 per cent (that is, $(441/(260 + 441)) \times 100$) by the owners. This level of borrowing seems quite high, but not excessive. However, we would need to know more about the ability of the business to service the loan capital (that is, make interest payments and loan repayments) before a full assessment could be made.

Chapter 3

3.1 (a) Capital does increase as a result of the owners introducing more cash into the business, but it will also increase as a result of introducing other assets (a motorcar, for example) and by the business generating revenues by trading. Similarly, capital decreases not only as a result of withdrawals of cash by owners but also by withdrawals of other assets (for example, stock for the owners' personal use) and through trading expenses being incurred. In practice, for the typical business in a typical accounting period, capital will alter much more as a result of trading activities than for any other reason.

(b) An accrued expense is not one that relates to next year. It is one that needs to be matched with the revenues of the accounting period under review, but which has yet to be met in terms of cash payment. As such, it will appear on the balance sheet as a current liability.

(c) The purpose of depreciation is not to provide for asset replacement. Rather, it is an attempt to allocate the cost of the asset (less any residual value) over its useful life. Depreciation is an attempt to provide a measure of the amount of the fixed asset that has been consumed during the period. This amount will then be charged as an expense for the period in order to derive the profit figure. Depreciation is a book entry (the outlay of cash occurs when the asset is purchased) and does not normally entail setting aside a separate amount of cash for asset replacement. Even if this were done, there would be no guarantee that sufficient funds would be available at the end of the asset's life for its replacement. Factors such as inflation and technological change may mean that the replacement cost is higher than the original cost of the asset.

(d) In the short term, it is possible for the current value of a fixed asset to exceed its original cost. However, nearly all fixed assets will wear out over time as a result of being used to generate wealth for the business. This will be the case for factory buildings. As a result, some measure of depreciation should be calculated to take account of the fact that the asset is being consumed. Some businesses revalue their freehold buildings where the current value is significantly different from the original cost. Where this occurs, the depreciation charged should be based on the revalued amount. This will normally result in higher depreciation charges than if the asset remained at its historic cost.

3.3 The upward movement in profit and downward movement in cash may be due to various reasons, which include the following:

■ the purchase of assets for cash during the period (for example, motorcars and stock), which were not all consumed during the period and therefore are not having an effect on expenses to the same extent as the effect on cash;

■ the payment of an outstanding liability (for example a loan), which will have an effect on cash but not on expenses in the profit and loss account;

■ the withdrawal of cash by the owners from the capital invested, which will not have an effect on the expenses in the profit and loss account;

■ the generation of revenues on credit, where the cash has yet to be received. This will increase the sales for the period but will not have a beneficial effect on the cash balance until a later period.

Chapter 4

4.1 (a) A reserve is part of the owners' claim of a company. The other part is share capital. Reserves arise from gains or profits accruing to the shareholders, to the extent that these have not been distributed to the shareholders or converted into share capital through a bonus issue.

(b) The nominal value of a share is its 'face' and balance sheet value. To a great extent this is a meaningless figure, since it will only by coincidence represent the worth of a share at any point in time. It is normally the value at which the original share issue was made when the company was formed.

(c) A rights issue is an issue of new shares to existing shareholders, at a discount (typically 20 per cent or more) on the current market value of the existing shares. Existing shareholders are given the 'right' to buy new shares in proportion to the number of shares that they already own. Thus, in a one-for-five rights issue, a holder of 1,000 shares would be given the right to buy 200 new shares.

4.4 Limited companies can no more set a limit on the amount of debts they will meet than can individuals. They must meet their debts up to the limit of their assets, just as we must, as individuals. In the context of the owners' claim, 'reserves' means part of the owners' claim against the assets of the company. These assets may or may not include cash. The legal ability of the company to pay dividends is not related to the amount of cash that it has.

Preference shares do not carry a guaranteed dividend. They simply guarantee that the preference shareholders have a right to the first slice of any dividend that is paid. Shares of many companies can, in effect, be bought by one investor from another through the Stock Exchange. Such a transaction has no direct effect on the company, however. These are not new shares being offered by the company, but existing shares that are being sold 'second-hand'.

The auditors are not appointed by the directors, but normally by the shareholders, to whom they report. The responsibility for preparing the annual financial statements falls on the directors, not the auditors. The auditors' responsibility is to review those financial statements and express an opinion on them, principally on whether they show a true and fair view of the company's position and performance.

Company law sets out the basic framework of company reporting; this is augmented and clarified by accounting standards, which are produced by a committee independent of the government. According to company law, company financial statements are intended to show a true and fair view.

Chapter 5

5.1 (a) An increase in the level of stock-in-trade would ultimately have an adverse effect on cash.

(b) A rights issue of ordinary shares will give rise to a positive cash flow, which will be included in the 'financing' section of the cash flow statement.

(c) A bonus issue of ordinary shares has no cash flow effect.

(d) Writing off some of the value of the stock has no cash flow effect.

(e) A disposal for cash of a large number of shares by a major shareholder has no cash flow effect, as far as the business is concerned.

(f) Depreciation does not involve cash at all. Using the indirect method of deducing cash flow from operations involves the depreciation expense in the calculation, but this is simply because we are trying to find out from the profit (after depreciation) figure what the profit before depreciation must have been.

5.3

Torrent plc
Cash flow statement for the year ended 31 December 2003

	£m	£m
Net cash inflows from operating activities		247
(see calculation below)		
Returns from investment and servicing of finance		
Interest received	14	
Interest paid	(26)	
Net cash outflow from returns on investments and servicing of finance		(12)
Taxation		
Corporation tax paid (see note below)	(41)	
Net cash outflow for taxation		(41)
Capital expenditure		
Payments to acquire tangible fixed assets	(67)	
Net cash outflow for capital expenditure		(67)
		127
Equity dividends paid		
Dividends paid (see note below)	(50)	
Net cash flow for equity dividends paid		(50)
		77
Management of liquid resources		–
Financing		
Repayments of debenture stock	(100)	
Net cash outflow from financing		(100)
Net increase (decrease) in cash		(23)

Notes

1 *Dividend* Since all of the dividend for 2003 was unpaid at the end of 2003, it seems that the business pays just one final dividend each year, some time after the year end. Thus it is the 2002 dividend that will have led to a cash outflow in 2003.

2 *Taxation*

	£m
Amount owing at 1.1.2003	23
Tax charge for 2003	36
	59
Amount owing at 31.12.2003	18
Amount paid during 2003	41

3 *Debentures* It has been assumed that the debentures were redeemed for their balance sheet value. This is not always the case, however.

4 *Shares* The share issue was effected by converting the share premium account balance and £60 million of the revaluation reserve balance to ordinary share capital. This involved no flow of cash.

Calculation of net cash inflow from operating activities

	£m	£m
Operating profit (from the profit and loss account)		182
Add Depreciation (325 + 67 − 314)*		78
		260
Less Increase in debtors (145 − 139)	6	
Decrease in creditors (54 − 41)	13	19
		241
Add Decrease in stocks (41 − 35)		6
		247

* Since there were no disposals the depreciation charges must be the difference between the start and end of the year fixed asset values, adjusted by the cost of any additions.

The following comments can be made about Torrent plc's cash flow as shown by the cash flow statement for the year ended 31 December 2003:

❑ There was a positive cash flow from operating activities.
❑ There was a net cash outflow in respect of financing.
❑ The outflow of cash to acquire additional tangible fixed assets was very comfortably covered by cash generated by operating activities, even after allowing for the net cash outflows for financing and tax. This is usually interpreted as a 'strong' cash flow situation.
❑ There was a fairly major repayment of debenture loan.
❑ Overall there was a fairly significant reduction in cash over the year, leading to a negative cash balance at the year end.

Chapter 6

6.1 The effect of each of the changes on ROCE is not always easy to predict.

(i)   An increase in the gross profit margin *may* lead to a decrease in ROCE in particular circumstances. If the increase in the margin resulted from an increase in price, which in turn led to a decrease in sales, a fall in ROCE can occur. A fall in sales can reduce the net profit (the numerator in ROCE) if the overheads of the business did not decrease correspondingly.

(ii)   A reduction in sales can reduce ROCE for the reasons mentioned above.

(iii) An increase in overhead expenses will reduce the net profit, and this in turn will result in a reduction in ROCE.

(iv)   An increase in stocks held will increase the amount of capital employed by the business (the denominator in ROCE) where long-term funds are employed to finance the stocks. This will, in turn, reduce ROCE.

(v)   Repayment of the loan at the year end will reduce the capital employed, and this will increase the ROCE, provided that the loan repayment does not affect the scale of operations.

(vi)   An increase in the time taken for debtors to pay will result in an increase in capital employed if long-term funds are employed to finance the debtors. This increase in long-term funds will in turn reduce ROCE.

6.2 The ratios reveal that the debtors collection period for Business A is 63 days, whereas for Business B the ratio is only 21 days. Business B is therefore much quicker in collecting amounts outstanding from customers. Nevertheless, there is not much difference between the two businesses in the time taken to pay trade creditors. Business A takes 50 days to pay its creditors, whereas Business B takes 45 days. It is interesting to compare the difference in the debtor and creditor collection periods for each business. As Business A allows an average of 63 days' credit to its customers, yet pays creditors within 50 days, it will require greater investment in working capital than Business B, which allows an average of only 21 days to its debtors but takes 45 days to pay its creditors.

Business A has a much higher gross profit percentage than Business B. However, the net profit percentage for the two businesses is identical. This suggests that Business A has much higher overheads compared with sales than Business B. The stock turnover period for Business A is more than twice that of Business B. This may be due to the fact that Business A maintains a wider range of goods in stock in order to meet customer requirements. The evidence suggests that Business A is the business that prides itself on personal service. The higher average settlement period is consistent with a more relaxed attitude to credit collection (thereby maintaining customer goodwill), and the high overheads are consistent with the incurring of additional costs in order to satisfy customer requirements. The high stock levels of Business A are consistent with maintaining a wide range of stock needed to satisfy a range of customer needs.

Business B has the characteristics of a more price-competitive business. The gross profit percentage is much lower than that of Business A, indicating a much lower gross profit per £1 of sales. However, since overheads are relatively low, the net profit percentage is the same as that of Business A. The low stock turnover period and average collection period for debtors are consistent with a business whose investment in current assets is at a minimum, thereby reducing costs.

Chapter 7

7.4 (a) Total time required on cutting machines = $(2,500 \times 1.0) + (3,400 \times 1.0) + (5,100 \times 0.5) = 8,150$ hours

Total time available on cutting machines = 5,000 hours, that is, a limiting factor

Total time required on assembling machines = $(2,500 \times 0.5) + (3,400 \times 1.0) + (5,100 \times 0.5) = 7,200$ hours

Total time available on assembling machines = 8,000 hours, that is, not a limiting factor

Product	A (per unit) £	B (per unit) £	C (per unit) £
Selling price	25	30	18
Direct materials	(12)	(13)	(10)
Variable production costs	(7)	(4)	(3)
Contribution	6	13	5
Time on cutting machines (hours)	1.0	1.0	0.5
Contribution per hour on cutting machines	£6	£13	£10
Order of priority	3	1	2

Therefore, produce: 3,400 Product B using 3,400 hours
3,200 Product C using 1,600 hours
5,000 hours

(b) Assuming that the business would make no savings in variable production costs by subcontracting, it would be worth paying up to the contribution per unit (£5) for Product C: that is, £5 × (5,100 − 3,200) = £9,500 in total.

Similarly, it would be worth paying up to £6 per unit for Product A or £6 × 2,500 = £15,000 in total.

7.5 (a) Contribution per hour of unskilled labour of Product X is:

$$(£30 − (£6 + £2 + £12 + £3)/(6/6) = £7$$

Given the scarcity of skilled labour, for the management to be indifferent between the products, the contribution per skilled labour hour must be the same. Thus:

For Product Y the selling price must be [£7 × (9/6)] + £9 + £4 + £25 + £7 = £55.50*
For Product Z the selling price must be [£7 × (3/6)] + £3 + £10 + £14 + £7 = £37.50*

* The contribution plus the variable costs

(b) The business could pay up to £13 an hour (that is, £6 + £7) for additional hours of skilled labour.

Chapter 8

8.1 All three of these costing techniques are means of deducing the full cost of some activity. The distinction between them lies essentially with the difference in the style of the production of the goods or services involved.

- ❑ *Job costing* is used where each unit of output or 'job' differs from others produced by the same business. Because the jobs are not identical, it is not normally acceptable to those who are likely to use the cost information to treat the jobs as if they are identical. This means that costs need to be identified, job by job. For this purpose, costs fall into two categories: direct costs and indirect costs (or overheads).

  Direct costs are those that can be measured directly in respect of the specific job, such as the amount of labour that was directly applied to the job or the amount of material that has been incorporated in it. To this must be added a share of the indirect costs. This is usually done by taking the total overheads for the period concerned and charging part of them to the job. This, in turn, is usually done according to some measure of the job's size and importance, relative to the other jobs done during the period. The number of direct labour hours worked on the job is the most commonly used measure of size and/or importance.

  The main problem with job costing tends to be the method of charging indirect costs to jobs. Indirect costs, by definition, cannot be related directly to jobs, and must, if full cost is to be deduced, be charged on a basis that is more or less arbitrary. If indirect costs accounted for a small proportion of the total, the arbitrariness of charging them would probably not matter. Indirect costs, in many cases, however, form the majority of total costs, so arbitrariness is a problem.

- ❑ *Process costing* is the approach taken where all output is of identical units. These can be treated, therefore, as having identical cost. Sometimes a process costing approach is taken even where the units of output are not strictly identical. This is because process costing is much simpler and cheaper to apply than the only other option, job costing. Provided that users of the cost information are satisfied that treating units as identical when they are not strictly so is acceptable, the additional cost and effort of job costing is not justified.

In process costing, the cost per unit of output is found by dividing total costs for the period by the total number of units produced in the period.

The main problem with process costing tends to be that at the end of any period/beginning of the next period, there will probably be partly completed units of output. An adjustment needs to be made for this work in progress if the resulting figures for cost per unit are not to be distorted.

❑ *Batch costing* is really an extension of job costing. Batch costing tends to be used where production is in batches. A batch consists of more than one, perhaps many, identical units of output. The units of output differ from one batch to the next. For example, a clothing manufacturing business may produce 500 identical jackets in one batch. This is followed by a batch of 300 identical skirts.

Each batch is costed, as one job, using a job costing approach. The full cost of each garment is then found by dividing the cost of the batch by the number of garments in the batch.

The main problem of batch costing is exactly that of job costing, of which it is an extension. This is the problem of dealing with overheads.

8.3

Offending phrase	Explanation
'Necessary to divide up the business into departments'	This can be done, but it will not always be of much benefit to do so. Only in quite restricted circumstances will it give significantly different job costs.
'Fixed costs (or overheads)'	This implies that fixed costs and overheads are the same thing. They are not really connected with one another. 'Fixed' is to do with how costs behave as the level of output is raised or lowered; 'overheads' is to do with the extent to which costs can be directly measured in respect of a particular unit of output. Though it is true that many overheads are fixed, not all are. Also, direct labour is usually a fixed cost. All of the other references to fixed and variable costs are wrong. The person should have referred to indirect and direct costs.
'Usually this is done on the basis of area'	Where overheads are apportioned to departments, they will be apportioned on some logical basis. For certain costs, for example rent, floor area may be the most logical. For others, for example machine maintenance costs, floor area would be totally inappropriate.
'When the total fixed costs for each department have been identified, this will be divided by the number of hours that were worked'	Where overheads are dealt with on a departmental basis, they may be divided by the number of direct labour hours to deduce a recovery rate. However, this is only one basis of applying overheads to jobs. For example, machine hours or some other basis may be more appropriate to the particular circumstances involved.
'It is essential that this approach is taken in order to deduce a selling price'	In practice, it is relatively unusual for the 'job cost' to be able to dictate the price at which the manufacturer can price its output. Job costing may have its uses, but setting prices is not usually one of them.

Chapter 9

9.3

	Budget				
	Original	*Flexed*		*Actual*	
Output (units)	1,000	1,100		1,100	
(production and sales)					
	£	£		£	
Sales	25,000	27,500		28,200	
Labour	(5,000)	(5,500)	(2,200 hrs)	(5,550)	(2,150 hrs)
Raw materials	(10,000)	(11,000)	(1,100 kg)	(11,630)	(1,170 kg)
Fixed overheads	(3,000)	(3,000)		(3,200)	
Operating profit	7,000	8,000		7,820	

Sales variances
Volume
£(7,000 − 8,000)   = £1,000 (F)
Price
£(27,500 − 28,200)   = £700 (F)

Direct labour variances
Efficiency
((1,100 × 2) − 2,150) × £2.50   = £125 (F)
Rate
(2,150 × £2.50) − £5,550   = £175 (A)

Direct materials variances
Usage
((1,100 × 1) − 1,170) × £10   = £700 (A)
Price
(1,170 × £10) − £11,630   = £70 (F)

Fixed overhead variances
Spending
£3,000 − £3,200   = £200 (A)
Budgeted profit = (1,000 × £7)   = £7,000

	£	£
Budgeted profit		7,000
Sales: Volume	1,000 (F)	
Price	700 (F)	1,700
Direct materials: Usage	700 (A)	
Price	70 (F)	(630)
Direct labour: Efficiency	125 (F)	
Rate	175 (A)	(50)
Fixed overheads: Expenditure		(200)
		7,820

9.4 (a) Finished goods stock budget for the three months ending 30 September (in units of production):

	July	*Aug*	*Sept*
	000 units	*000 units*	*000 units*
Opening stock (Note 1)	40	48	40
Production (Note 2)	188	232	196
	228	280	236
Less Sales (Note 3)	180	240	200
Closing stock	48	40	36

(b) Raw materials stock budget for the two months ending 31 August (in kg):

	July 000 kg	Aug 000 kg
Opening stock (Note 1)	40	58
Purchases (Note 2)	112	107
	152	165
Less Production (Note 4)	94	116
Closing stock	58	49

(c) Cash budget for the two months ending 30 September:

	Aug £	Sept £
Inflows		
Debtors: Current month (Note 5)	493,920	411,600
Preceding month (Note 6)	151,200	201,600
Total inflows	645,120	613,200
Outflows		
Payments to creditors (Note 7)	168,000	160,500
Labour and overheads (Note 4)	185,600	156,800
Fixed overheads	22,000	22,000
Total outflows	375,600	339,300
Net inflows/(outflows)	269,520	273,900
Balance c/fwd	289,520	563,420

Notes

1   The opening balance is the same as the closing balance from the previous month.
2   This is a balancing figure.
3   This figure is given in the question.
4   This figure derives from the finished stock budget.
5   This is 98 per cent of 70 per cent of the current month's sales revenue.
6   This is 28 per cent of the previous month's sales revenue.
7   This figure derives from the raw materials stock budget.

Chapter 10

10.1 (a) Annual depreciation:

$$\text{Project 1 } (£100,000 - £7,000)/3 = £31,000$$
$$\text{Project 2 } (£60,000 - £6,000)/3 = £18,000$$

Analysis of the projects

Project 1	Year 0 £000	Year 1 £000	Year 2 £000	Year 3 £000
Net profit (loss)		29	(1)	2
Depreciation		31	31	31
Capital cost	(100)			
Residual value				7
Net cash flows	(100)	60	30	40
10% discount factor	1.000	0.909	0.826	0.751
Present value	(100.00)	54.54	24.78	30.04
Net present value	9.36			

Since the NPV at 10 per cent is positive, the IRR lies above 10 per cent. Try 15 per cent:

15% discount factor	1.000	0.870	0.756	0.658
Present value	(100.000)	52.20	22.68	26.32
Net present value	1.20			

Thus, the IRR lies a little above 15 per cent, around 16 per cent.

Cumulative cash flows	(100)	(40)	(10)	30

Thus, the payback will occur after about two years, three months (assuming that the cash flows accrue evenly over the year), or three years (if we assume year end cash flows).

Project 2	Year 0 £000	Year 1 £000	Year 2 £000	Year 3 £000
Net profit (loss)		18	(2)	4
Depreciation		18	18	18
Capital cost	(60)			
Residual value				6
Net cash flows	(60)	36	16	28
10% discount factor	1.000	0.909	0.826	0.751
Present value	(60.00)	32.72	13.22	21.03
Net present value	6.97			

Clearly, the IRR lies above 10 per cent. Try 15 per cent:

15% discount factor	1.000	0.870	0.756	0.658
Present value	(60.00)	31.32	12.10	18.42
Net present value	1.84			

Thus, the IRR lies a little above 15 per cent, around 17 per cent.

Cumulative cash flows	(60)	(24)	(8)	20

Thus, the payback will occur after about two years, three months (assuming that the cash flows accrue evenly over the year), or three years (if we assume year end cash flows).

(b) Presuming that Mylo Ltd is pursuing a wealth maximisation objective, Project 1 is preferable since it has the higher NPV. The difference between the two NPVs is not very large, however. The decision may therefore be susceptible to forecast error.

(c) NPV is the preferred method of assessing investment opportunities because it fully addresses each of the following:

❏ *The timing of the cash flows.* By discounting the various cash flows associated with each project according to when they are expected to arise, the fact that cash flows do not all occur simultaneously is accommodated. Associated with this is the fact that by discounting, using the opportunity cost of finance (that is, the return that the next best alternative opportunity would generate), the net benefit after financing costs have been met is identified (as the NPV).

❑ *The whole of the relevant cash flows.* NPV includes all of the relevant cash flows, irrespective of when they are expected to occur. It treats them differently according to their date of occurrence, but they are all taken account of in the NPV, and they all have, or can have, an influence on the decision.

❑ *The objectives of the business.* NPV is the only method of appraisal in which the output of the analysis has a direct bearing on the wealth of the business. (Positive NPVs enhance wealth, negative ones reduce it.) Since most private-sector businesses seek to increase their value and wealth, NPV clearly is the best approach to use, at least out of the methods we have considered so far.

10.5 (a)

Option 1	*2001*	*2002*	*2003*	*2004*	*2005*	*2006*
	£m	*£m*	*£m*	*£m*	*£m*	*£m*
Plant and equipment	(9.0)					1.0
Sales		24.0	30.8	39.6	26.4	10.0
Variable costs		(11.2)	(19.6)	(25.2)	(16.8)	(7.0)
Fixed costs (ex. depr'n)		(0.8)	(0.8)	(0.8)	(0.8)	(0.8)
Working capital	(3.0)					3.0
Marketing costs		(2.0)	(2.0)	(2.0)	(2.0)	(2.0)
Opportunity costs		(0.1)	(0.1)	(0.1)	(0.1)	(0.1)
	(12.0)	9.9	8.3	11.5	6.7	4.1
Discount factor	1.0	0.91	0.83	0.75	0.68	0.62
Present value	(12.0)	9.0	6.9	8.6	4.6	2.5
NPV	19.6					

Option 2	*2001*	*2002*	*2003*	*2004*	*2005*	*2006*
	£m	*£m*	*£m*	*£m*	*£m*	*£m*
Royalties	–	4.4	7.7	9.9	6.6	2.8
Discount factor	1.0	0.91	0.83	0.75	0.68	0.62
Present value	–	4.0	6.4	7.4	4.5	1.7
NPV	24.0					

Option 3	*2001*	*2003*
Instalments	12.0	12.0
Discount	1.0	0.83
Present value	12.0	10.0
NPV	22.0	

(b) Before making a final decision, the following factors should be considered:

❑ The long-term competitiveness of the business may be affected by the sale of the patents.

❑ At present the business is not involved in manufacturing and marketing products. Would a change in direction be desirable?

❑ The business will probably have to buy in the skills necessary to produce the product itself. This will involve costs, and problems will be incurred. Has this been taken into account?

❑ How accurate are the forecasts made, and how valid are the assumptions on which they are based?

(c) Option 2 has the highest NPV and is, therefore, the more attractive to shareholders. However, the accuracy of the forecasts should be checked before a final decision is made.

Chapter 11

11.1 (a) The liquidity ratios of the business seem low. The current ratio is only 1.1 and the acid test ratio is 0.6. This latter ratio suggests that the business has insufficient liquid assets to pay its short-term obligations. A cash flow projection for the next period would provide a better insight to the liquidity position of the business. The bank overdraft seems high, and it would be useful to know whether the bank is pressing for a reduction and what overdraft limit has been established for the business.

(b) This term is described in the chapter.

(c) The operating cash cycle may be calculated as follows:

	No. of days
Average stockholding period	
$\dfrac{\text{(Opening stock + closing stock)/2}}{\text{Cost of sales}} \times 360 = \dfrac{((125 + 143)/2)}{323} \times 360$	149
Average settlement period for debtors	
$\dfrac{\text{Trade debtors}}{\text{Credit sales}} \times 365 = \dfrac{163}{452} \times 360$	130
Average settlement period for creditors	
$\dfrac{\text{Trade creditors}}{\text{Credit purchases}} \times 365 = \dfrac{145}{341} \times 360$	(153)
Operating cash cycle	126

(d) The business can reduce the operating cash cycle in a number of ways. The average stockholding period seems quite long. At present, average stocks held represent almost five months' sales. This period may be shortened by reducing the level of stocks held. Similarly, the average settlement period for debtors seems long, at more than four months' sales. This may be shortened by imposing tighter credit control, offering discounts, charging interest on overdue accounts, and so on. However, any policy decisions concerning stocks and debtors must take account of current trading conditions.

The operating cash cycle could also be shortened by extending the period of credit taken to pay suppliers. However, for reasons mentioned in the chapter, this option must be given careful consideration.

11.5

New proposals from credit department		
	£000	£000
Current level of investment in debtors		
(£20m × (60/365))		3,288
Proposed level of investment in debtors		
((£20m × 60%) × (30/365))	(986)	
((£20m × 40%) × (50/365))	(1,096)	(2,082)
Reduction in level of investment		1,206

The reduction in overdraft interest as a result of the reduction in the level of investment will be £1,206,000 × 14% = £169,000.

	£000	£000
Cost of cash discounts offered (£20m × 60% × 2½%)		300
Additional cost of credit administration		20
		320
Bad debt savings	(100)	
Interest charge savings (see above)	(169)	(269)
Net cost of policy each year		51

These calculations show that the business would incur additional annual costs if it implemented this proposal. It would therefore be cheaper to stay with the existing credit policy.

Chapter 12

12.1 (a) The main factors to take into account are:

- *Risk.* If a business borrows there is a risk that, at the maturity date of the loan, the business will not have the funds to repay the amount owing and will be unable to find a suitable form of replacement borrowing. With short-term loans, the maturity dates will arrive more quickly, and the type of risk outlined will occur at more frequent intervals.
- *Matching.* A business may wish to match the life of an asset with the maturity date of the borrowing. In other words, long-term assets will be purchased with long-term loan funds. A certain level of current assets that form part of the long-term asset base of the business may also be funded by long-term borrowing. Those current assets that fluctuate because of seasonality and so on will be funded by short-term borrowing. This approach to funding assets will help reduce risks for the business.
- *Cost.* Interest rates for long-term loans may be higher than for short-term loans, as investors may seek extra compensation for having their funds locked up for a long period. However, issue costs may be higher for short-term loans as there will be a need to refund at more frequent intervals.
- *Flexibility.* Short-term loans may be more flexible. It may be difficult to repay long-term loans before the maturity period.

(b) When deciding to grant a loan, the lender should consider the following factors:

- security;
- purpose of the loan;
- the ability of the borrower to repay;
- the loan period;
- the availability of funds;
- the character and integrity of the senior managers.

(c) Loan conditions may include:

- the need to obtain permission before issuing further loans, to help ensure that the existing loan is protected from competing claims on the assets of the business;

> ❏ the need to maintain a certain level of liquidity during the loan period, to help ensure that interest payments and capital repayments can be made;
> ❏ a restriction on the level of dividends and directors' pay, to help ensure that there are not excessive withdrawals that would leave lenders in a vulnerable position.

Carpets Direct plc

(a) The stages in calculating the theoretical ex-rights price of an ordinary share are as follows:

Earnings per share
Profit after taxation/no. of ordinary shares = £4.5m/120m = £0.0375

Market value per share
Earnings per share × P/E ratio = £0.075 × 22 = £0.825

For the theoretical ex-rights price:

	£
Original shares (4 @ £0.825)	3.30
Rights share (1 @ £0.66)	0.66
Value of five shares following the rights issue	3.96
Value of one share following the rights issue	£3.96
	5
Theoretical ex-rights price	= 79.2p

(b) The price at which rights are likely to be traded is derived as below:

Value of one share after rights issue	79.2p
Less Cost of a rights share	66.0p
Value of rights to shareholder	13.2p

(c) Comparing the three options open to the investor:

Option 1: Taking up rights issue

	£
Shareholding following rights issue [(4,000 + 1,000) × 79.2p]	3,960
Less Cost of rights shares (1,000 × 66p)	660
Shareholder wealth	3,300

Option 2: Selling the rights

	£
Shareholding following rights issue (4,000 × 79.2p)	3,168
Add Proceeds from sale of rights (1,000 × 13.2p)	132
Shareholder wealth	3,300

Option 3: Doing nothing
As the rights are neither purchased nor sold, the shareholder wealth following the rights issue will be:

Shareholding (4,000 × 79.2p)	3,168

We can see that the investor will have the same wealth under the first two options. However, by doing nothing the rights issue will lapse and so the investor will lose the value of the rights and will be worse off.

Index

Note: Page numbers in **bold** indicate highlighted **key terms** and their glossary definitions.